NAZI GERMANY, CANADIAN RESPONSES

Nazi Germany, Canadian Responses

Confronting Antisemitism in the Shadow of War

EDITED BY L. RUTH KLEIN

McGill-Queen's University Press
Montreal & Kingston • London • Ithaca

ISBN 978-0-7735-4017-0 (cloth)
ISBN 978-0-7735-4018-7 (paper)

Legal deposit second quarter 2012
Bibliothèque nationale du Québec

Printed in Canada on acid-free paper that is 100% ancient forest free (100% post-consumer recycled), processed chlorine free

This book has been published with a grant from the Government of Canada through the Community Historical Recognition Program of Citizenship and Immigration Canada and with funding support from the B'nai Brith Foundation.

McGill-Queen's University Press acknowledges the support of the Canada Council for the Arts for our publishing program. We also acknowledge the financial support of the Government of Canada through the Canada Book Fund for our publishing activities.

Library and Archives Canada Cataloguing in Publication

Nazi Germany, Canadian responses : confronting antisemitism in the shadow of war / edited by L. Ruth Klein.

Includes bibliographical references.
ISBN 978-0-7735-4017-0 (bound). –
ISBN 978-0-7735-4018-7 (pbk.)

1. Antisemitism – Canada – History – 20th century. 2. Jewish refugees – Government policy – Canada. 3. Holocaust, Jewish (1939–1945) – Press coverage – Canada. 4. Holocaust, Jewish (1939–1945) – Foreign public opinion, Canadian. 5. Jews – Canada – History – 20th century. I. Klein, Ruth, 1954–

DS146.C2N39 2012   305.892'407109044   C2012-901176-2

Typeset by Jay Tee Graphics Ltd. in 10.5/13 Sabon

Dedicated to those Canadians who responded to the plight of European Jewry with moral courage and generosity of spirit.

Contents

Acknowledgments

As the editor of this collection, I would like to thank all the contributing authors for the impeccable research that they have undertaken in order to explore new avenues of inquiry and analysis on an era long past. I have greatly appreciated their interest in this project, their openness to my suggestions, and their willingness to collaborate with energy and enthusiasm. Working with such eminent yet approachable academics has been a pleasure on both a professional and a personal level.

When I think back to the earliest stages of conceptualizing the content and direction of this volume, I recognize a special debt of gratitude to Professors Harold Troper and Richard Menkis. Their encouragement and friendship have been mainstays for me ever since the National Task Force on Holocaust Education, Remembrance and Research (NTF) was created in 2009 and this collection was first envisaged.

In this vein, I would like to acknowledge the core funding support of the Community Historical Recognition Program of Citizenship and Immigration Canada, which enabled the scholars featured in this book to undertake new research as part of the NTF's overall mandate. Additional funding from the B'nai Brith Foundation reflected the organization's ongoing goal of encouraging scholarship as the groundwork for contemporary advocacy on human rights issues. I would like to thank Eric Bissell, national president of B'nai Brith Canada, under whose term of office this publication was created, and CEO Frank Dimant, who has encouraged my work for over a decade and who has dedicated his career to ensuring that the injustices of history are never forgotten.

My sincere thanks go to the staff at McGill-Queen's University Press, especially Kyla Madden, the editor at the press with whom I have worked closely over the past year. Her encouragement and insights have been invaluable to me from the moment that I first brought the possibility of this book to her attention. Ryan Van Huijstee, managing editor at MQUP, graciously offered the benefit of his considerable expertise to bring the manuscript to the reality of a finished work, while the judicious eye and wise counsel of copyeditor Carlotta Lemieux greatly enhanced the final text. The careful review by indexer Lee Frew was also much appreciated.

Special thanks are due as well to two remarkable colleagues. Professor Alain Goldschläger, chair of the NTF and national director of B'nai Brith's Institute for International Affairs, is a dedicated custodian of Holocaust memoirs and testimony who has championed the goals of the NTF in both Canadian and international fora. David Matas, B'nai Brith Canada's senior legal counsel and a leading light of the organization's League for Human Rights, personifies for me the struggle for human rights and justice. By his tireless efforts to investigate crimes of the past and present, and bring perpetrators to justice, he reminds us by example that these are challenges we can never lay down.

This list of acknowledgments would not be complete without recognizing the valuable input of NTF staff members Tema Smith and Adina Klein, who have been integrally involved in ensuring that every facet of the project has been covered. My thanks also go to longtime colleagues at B'nai Brith Canada, Pearl Gladman and Anita Bromberg, who have always been supportive.

Given the painful nature of the subject matter of the book, I have greatly valued family support throughout the past months when the challenges of this volume were uppermost in my mind. My husband Dr Gerard Klein was generous in his willingness to share with me his psychological insights as we attempted, through much discussion and reflection, to fathom the depths of man's inhumanity to man and the role that indifference and apathy have played throughout history. Our children, Dov, Deborah, Moshe, and Shoshana, continue to be my inspiration as we watch them and their spouses play their part in ensuring a more hopeful future, restoring in some sense a measure of what was lost when our families were decimated in the Holocaust.

I dedicate my efforts in *Nazi Germany, Canadian Responses* to the memory of my parents: first, to my mother, Sela Schlussel Oster, a Holocaust survivor whose courage, determination, and deep compassion for the suffering of others was always an inspiration to me. Trapped in Europe despite desperate efforts to find refuge in North America, almost her entire family was murdered by the Nazis. It is an irony of history that the family she rebuilt from the ashes of Auschwitz now includes Canadian grandchildren and great-grandchildren. My father, Vivian Oster, came from a family that tried to assist refugees who managed to escape from Europe and were attempting to start life afresh in new lands. His love of history, genealogy, and community has profoundly influenced me. From my parents I learnt the power of the past – if we listen to its voices – to influence the future in a positive way, and the need to be active participants rather than passive observers in the struggle to uphold the integrity of historical truth.

L. Ruth Klein

Preface

The journey that led to the publication of this volume began in Toronto in June 2009 with a conference entitled "The *St Louis* Era: Looking Back, Moving Forward," which was co-hosted by the Government of Canada and the League for Human Rights of B'nai Brith Canada. This conference, held in partnership with the US Department of State, the French Ministry of Foreign Affairs, the US Holocaust Memorial Museum, and the Mémorial de la Shoah was the "liaison" project that led to Canada's entry as a full member of the Task Force for International Cooperation on Holocaust Education, Remembrance and Research.

The conference proceedings were designed to do more than just examine the fate of the passengers of the ill-fated voyage of the MS *St Louis* in 1939, many of whom, tragically, later perished in the Holocaust. The *St Louis* was, after all, just one boat of many bearing refugees who had taken to the seas in desperation, searching for safe haven from Hitler's Nazi regime. The goal of the conference was to look more widely at this era of prejudice and restrictive immigration policies; hence the title of the conference and the terminology used by some of the authors in this book.

Academics, educators, government officials, and human rights activists from Canada and abroad came together to take a fresh look at the perceptions and policies of the past, in some cases revisiting familiar terrain in search of new perspectives. Conference presenters set forth difficult questions and offered answers that were, of necessity, tentative. But two unmistakable conclusions emerged: first, that further research was necessary on this painful subject to encompass both the intellectual and emotional spheres of inquiry; second, that a national body should take the lead in fostering new scholarship and creating fresh educational material, with the assistance of a multi-disciplinary advisory body of experts.

The *St Louis* era conference thus marked the launch of the National Task Force on Holocaust Education, Remembrance and Research (NTF), created by the League for Human Rights with the generous funding support of the Community Historical Recognition Program (CHRP) of Citizenship and Immigration Canada and the B'nai Brith Foundation. Its mandate included the sponsorship of original historical research, such as the scholarship presented in this volume. The government funding was in itself remarkable, since it was given specifically to increase understanding of the failings of this country throughout its history in its treatment of refugees seeking sanctuary on these shores. It is, to say the least, unusual for governments to fund studies of their shortcomings.

The CHRP funding was specifically designed "to commemorate and educate Canadians about incidents which, while legal at the time, are no longer consistent with Canadian values." As such, in addition to funding for research and education on the MS *St Louis* incident, CHRP has funded projects on injustices that affected other minority communities, such as the internment of "enemy aliens" under the War Measures Act during the First and Second World Wars; the decades-long imposition of the head tax and other restrictions on immigrants from China; and the refusal to allow entry to passengers on board the *Komagata Maru* in 1914, based on the Continuous Passage Act, which was designed to curb immigration from India.

Since prejudice towards the "Other" is a common theme linking all these exclusionary moves, the NTF reflected on these harsh chapters in Canadian history in its opening project, the creation of a new educational resource for students, entitled *Welcome to Canada?* This text explores how Canadian immigration policy affected different minority groups throughout Canada's history, looking at who was welcomed and who was turned away. It is now being used by teachers across the country in a pilot project designed to enhance the study of civics and related courses.

The work of the NTF has culminated in this current volume, *Nazi Germany, Canadian Responses*, which brings together the original research of eight outstanding Canadian scholars in an in-depth study of the *St Louis* era. With this volume, these scholars collectively advance our understanding of the dynamics of inclusion and exclusion in the 1930s and 1940s, and the ways in which Canadian society became engaged in ethical debates that had at their epicentre the plight of European Jewry and the need to respond to Hitler's regime. Examining the moral and political dilemmas that Canada faced at that time, and the ways it responded or failed to respond, helps to contextualize the decisions of the day and equips us to interpret more contemporary dilemmas, as well.

Beyond this analysis, something greater emerges from the undercurrents of the authors' broader narratives: a chorus of unnamed voices, of ordinary Canadians who rose up to protest during the *St Louis* era when Jews were being vilified and victimized. Our hope is that the reader will be inspired by their example, applying the lessons of the past to the realities of today, so that future generations of Canadians will speak up and take action wherever and whenever antisemitism – or any form of bigotry, discrimination, or injustice – threatens to take root.

Alain Goldschläger
Professor, Western University
Chair, National Task Force on Holocaust Education, Remembrance and Research, B'nai Brith Canada

Introduction

L. RUTH KLEIN

We must use our scholarship to support historical truth. It is our responsibility.

Deborah Lipstadt, author of *Denying the Holocaust*

On 13 May 1939, the MS *St Louis* set sail from Germany carrying 937 passengers, primarily Jewish men, women, and children seeking refuge from Nazi persecution. It had been four years since the enactment of the race-based Nuremberg Laws that had stripped Jews of their citizenship and human rights; it was just seven months since Kristallnacht, the Night of Broken Glass, had demonstrated that the Reich was willing to initiate open violence against Jews, a precursor of much worse to come. Passengers on board the ship had left Hamburg hopeful that the landing visas they had purchased would allow them entry into Cuba, at least as a temporary crossing point into the United States. But when the ship reached Havana, the Cuban government had already invalidated these documents. The Jewish refugees, unable to meet the increasingly exorbitant amounts now being demanded for new permits, were not allowed to disembark.[1] The *St Louis* was forced to take to the seas once more, sending out increasingly desperate pleas across the Americas for a country that would accept its passengers.

One of these countries was Canada, but Canadian immigration policy was unyielding in its harsh restrictions on the entry of Jewish refugees.[2] When the *St Louis* crisis broke, Prime Minster Mackenzie King's top advisers, including Director of Immigration Frederick Blair, advised him to stand firm and, in effect, to ignore the request. So, in spite of public pleas by concerned Canadians, the official response was unmistakable: silence.

Refused permission to dock anywhere, and with food and water supplies dwindling, the *St Louis* was forced to sail back to Europe on 6 June. Only the passengers allowed to enter Britain were safe from the Holocaust to come. France, Belgium, and the Netherlands agreed – though only on a temporary basis – to accept the remaining refugees, who were at first hopeful that they were out of harm's way. Indeed, United States Holocaust Memorial Museum researchers have found that eighty-seven passengers were able to escape from Europe a second time.[3] But the rest were eventually trapped by the advancing Nazi dragnet; little more than half of them survived.

Although it was just one of several ships carrying refugees attempting to escape Nazi Europe, the *St Louis* has become a symbol of Canada's exclusionary immigration policy during these years, a period that has been called "the bleakest chapter in Canadian history." This is a view expressed in retrospect, in the light of an immense amount of evidence uncovered by historians that leaves little room for argument. Less is known, however, about contemporary perceptions in this period. How much did Canadians know at the time about the horrors unfolding in Europe in the 1930s and 1940s? Where did their information come from and how did they respond, on both public and institutional levels? And what of the prejudice and discrimination that targeted Jews in Canada itself? Did the antisemitic propaganda of this period attract Canadian adherents, and how did the Jewish community respond in return? These are just some of the questions addressed in this collection of essays, which aims to capture the tenor of society in an era when the Canadian government steadfastly refused entry to Jewish refugees seeking safe haven on these shores.

It has been thirty years since the publication of Irving Abella and Harold Troper's seminal work *None Is Too Many*, which documented the official barriers that kept Jewish refugees out of Canada even as news reports of the horrors of Hitler's regime filtered through and, arguably, forewarned of worse to come. And while many minority groups were targeted by Canada's exclusionary immigration policies at a time when the country was in the grip of a massive economic downturn, in the hierarchy of preferred and non-preferred immigrants, Jewish refugees did not even qualify for the "undesirable" classification. They were relegated to a separate "permit" class, requiring special approval by a government order-in-council. Indeed, Abella and Troper's book takes its title from a comment attributed to an anonymous Canadian official who was asked how many Jews would be allowed into Canada after the war. His reply was, "None is too many."

None Is Too Many created shock waves upon publication, won critical acclaim, and remains a landmark study in Canadian historiography. One reviewer called the book "brilliantly researched" but noted that it still left for him a key question unanswered: "Why did Canada act as it did in the 1930s? ... Why was it that the Canadian people sat on their hands and let the Jews of Europe remain to die?"[4] As the reviewer acknowledged, these are difficult questions for historians to confront, and they may ultimately be impossible to answer satisfactorily. But the research that has been done in the intervening years and the investigation that has been undertaken for this book give us a better sense of how much Canadians knew, and when, about the mounting persecution of the Jews of Europe and the atrocities that were occurring. Moreover, by turning attention to the public sphere, this research helps us to enter into the "atmosphere" of Canada in this period. People's ideas, attitudes, words, and actions – as well as what they did not say or do – were forged in part by external influences, by what they observed and discerned to be happening around them. Identifying the vital realms in which ideas and attitudes were tested, expressed, and reinforced, and information exchanged is to locate the origin of some of these influences, which moved people to think and act in one way or another. The answer to this question "why?" begins right here.

The contributors to this collection pursue this line of investigation in several realms of the public sphere – the media, international sport, literary life, the university campus, and community activism. Together, they present a picture of Canadian reactions to Nazi Germany that includes not just the indifference of officialdom or the antagonism of those openly propagating antisemitism, but a diverse range of responses from ordinary Canadians across the spectrum.

Doris Bergen opens the collection with an account of developments in Germany in the 1930s, describing the growing menace of Nazism as seen through the eyes of several Jews who managed to escape to Canada. Was this country the destination of choice for these desperate few, or did Canada's own domestic antisemitism discourage even the desperate, whose options for escape were rapidly disappearing? And what did it mean to be one of the lucky ones? As one survivor put it, "How to explain? To be a man without a country in a strange country … I was on my own. I was frantic." Bergen notes how Hitler and his propagandists welcomed acts of discrimination on Canadian soil, publicizing them in the German media in an attempt to legitimize the antisemitism that would provide the ideological foundation for Hitler's intended Final Solution – the murder of every Jewish man, woman, and child.

Richard Menkis and Harold Troper raise another significant question. Given the extensive press coverage of Germany's race-based agenda, and the groundswell of indignation from Canadians who took to the streets in protest after passage of the infamous Nuremberg Laws, what was the basis for the Canadian Olympic Committee's decision to send Canadian athletes to the "Nazi" Olympics? The authors examine the reaction of Olympic Committee observers who attended the 1935 Nuremberg Rally and witnessed its pageantry firsthand, to try to understand the reasons for its decision. The research of these scholars into the thinking of the Olympic decision makers of the day examines the divide between the Canadians who watched with grave concern Hitler's rise to power and the Nazi atrocities that swiftly followed, and those who considered that the benefits of participation in the Olympics trumped every other consideration.

The two chapters that follow analyse newspaper coverage of the period in order to understand how public opinion was informed and shaped. Amanda Grzyb begins her study of mainstream Canadian press coverage of the MS *St Louis* incident by reminding us that Canada's record for admitting Jewish refugees in the Second World War era was "the worst of all possible refugee-receiving states." With a focus on the day-by-day reporting of the fate of the passengers in English-language daily newspapers, she looks at how the plight of the European Jews was depicted in the public sphere and what responses it evoked. Combing through newspaper reports, editorials, and opinion pieces regarding incidents of antisemitism at home and abroad, including the fate of the *St Louis*, Grzyb explores how the anglophone media presented the news of the persecution of European Jews in the years leading up to the outbreak of war.

Rebecca Margolis examines another sector of the print media in her study of the coverage of the 1944 arrival in Canada of some 400 Iberian refugees aboard the SS *Serpa Pinto*, an exceptional event given the government's restrictive immigration policies. With mainstream press coverage of persecution of the Jews waning on the eve of war, the Yiddish press increasingly became the medium through which news of the fate of European Jews reached their families and the wider community. It was thus a key source of information on the concerns and responses of Canada's Jewish community during the prewar and wartime years. Margolis compares Canada's major Yiddish newspaper coverage with a sampling of the English- and French-language daily papers that covered the arrival of the *Serpa Pinto*. She includes Anglo-Jewish publications in this comparison in order to assess whether the reaction of the segment of the Jewish community that the Yiddish media reflected was any different during this time of crisis from the responses of the anglophone Jewish establishment.

Michael Brown takes us next to the university campuses, where faculty members and administrators missed one opportunity after another to speak out on the abrogation of academic freedom in Germany, let alone the anti-Jewish atrocities of the Nazi regime. Meanwhile, discrimination against Jews in Canada was entrenched in the university world, as seen in the quotas imposed on Jewish students, the restrictions on the hiring of Jewish faculty and administrative staff, and the unwillingness to assist scholars and students who sought refuge on Canadian shores. With a few notable exceptions unearthed by Brown, his study examines the ways in which leadership on campus on the moral issues of the day was largely ceded to the more vocal elements of the student press.

Norman Ravvin's essay searches wartime Canadian literary culture for a connection between European Jewry and mainstream Canada, to discern which issues were at the forefront of creative concerns. The evocative words he quotes from Earle Birney's poem "Hands" – "here is the battle steeped in silence" – could as well refer to a literary scene that, Ravvin suggests, seemed wary of referring to the war in general and to the persecution of the Jews in particular. Ravvin also considers whether Jewish authors were reticent about acknowledging and expressing their Jewishness in their work. He searches for filaments of consciousness in the literary output of the day, surveying the writing of the early stars of modern Canadian literature. Although many of these authors no longer enjoy a popular readership, Ravvin examines the extent to which their works capture some of the mood of the time and offer further insight into how Canadian culture responded to wartime events.

The foregoing chapters explore how mainstream Canadian society reacted to anti-Jewish activity, both at home and in Europe, and suggest reasons why. But what of the reaction of the Jewish community in Canada? This is the focus of the final chapter, by James Walker. Unable to persuade the government to lift restrictions on Jewish refugees by using "quiet diplomacy," the community that Walker describes looked to a variety of strategies – legislative initiatives, legal challenges, and public campaigns – in an effort to claim equality and to battle injustice and vilification, at least at home. In response to the prejudice of an era characterized by Lionel Groulx's *L'Action nationale*, the Swastika Clubs, and signs declaring "No Jews or Dogs Allowed" posted at beaches, hotels, and holiday resorts across Canada, the largely defunct Canadian Jewish Congress was revived. Walker takes us into the world of subsequent community negotiations that led to the formation of the Joint Public Relations Committee, in which B'nai Brith and the Canadian Jewish Congress joined forces to lead the charge for equality, laying the foundation for the postwar movement for racial equality for all. Building on this earlier anti-defamation work, B'nai Brith created the League for Human Rights, the entity that provided the impetus for the research undertaken for this volume.

Looking back from the vantage point of the twenty-first century at the events and attitudes of more than seven decades ago, it is challenging to recreate the mindset of the times. But the authors in this volume have taken up that challenge, digging deeper into archives, records, commentary, and testimonies that can still offer fresh insights and interpretations on the prewar and wartime years. This collection is not intended to be the definitive study of this subject or of this period. Rather, it is our hope that it will open doors to further study, not just of antisemitism but of the racism and xenophobia in Canada and elsewhere that closed the door to so many in their hour of need.

NOTES

1 Only 28 passengers were allowed to land in Havana: 4 Spaniards, 2 Cubans, and 22 Jews who held immigration visas. One Jewish passenger tried to commit suicide by slitting his wrists and jumping into the harbour; he was allowed to stay in Cuba only until he recovered.

2   Even Pope Pius xi's apostolic delegate to Canada, who had been asked in late 1938 to intercede with the Canadian government, was taken aback by its negative response (Wolf, *Pope and Devil*, 207).

3   Of the 620 who had no option but to return to continental Europe, only 365 survived (Miller and Ogilvie, *Refuge Denied*, 174).

4   Granatstein, review of *None Is Too Many*, in *American Historical Review*, June 1983.

Adolf Hitler addresses the crowds assembled during Reichsparteitag (Reich Party Day) ceremonies, with officials from the International Olympic Committee in attendance. Nuremberg, Germany, 10–16 September 1935. (United States Holocaust Memorial Museum [USHMM], courtesy of Richard Freimark William O. McWorkman)

Adolf Hitler and Joseph Goebbels sign autographs for members of the Canadian figure-skating team at the 1936 Winter Olympics. Garmisch-Partenkirchen, Germany, 6–16 February 1936. (USHMM, courtesy of National Archives and Records Administration, College Park, MD)

The popular antisemitism that Nazi state-sponsored propaganda cultivated is illustrated by this float in a village Thanksgiving Day parade, which depicts a Jew sitting at a counting table, surrounded by enormous bags of money. Altenahr, Germany, 1937. (USHMM, courtesy of Kreisverwaltung Ahrweiler, Germany)

View of the burned-out sanctuary of the Kaiser-Wilhelmstrasse synagogue that was destroyed on Kristallnacht in Ludwigshafen, Germany on 10 November 1938. (United States Holocaust Memorial Museum, courtesy of Stadtverwaltung, Stadt Ludwigshafen am Rhein).

SS guards force Jews arrested during Kristallnacht to march through the town to watch the desecration of a synagogue before being deported, while German civilians look on. Baden-Baden, Germany, 10 November 1938. (USHMM, courtesy of Lydia Chagoll)

Antisemitic sign. These signs were posted in various locations in Canada in the 1930s, such as beaches, holiday resorts, and other recreational settings. (Canadian Jewish Congress Charities Committee National Archives [CJCCCNA])

The only known photograph of the Christie Pits riot, which broke out after swastikas were unfurled at a softball game between two local teams, one of them predominantly Jewish. Toronto, 16 August 1933. (Toronto Archives, fonds 1266, *Globe and Mail* Collection, item 30791)

After Kristallnacht, the media covered Canadian proposals for a boycott of Nazi Germany as well as public protests against Hitler's persecution of German Jews. *Vancouver Sun*, 21 November 1938. (*Vancouver Sun* Archives)

Members of the Canadian National Unity Party wear swastika armbands to a meeting of the Swastika Club, which attracted proponents of fascism who advocated a "New Canada" based on Nazi ideology. Montreal, 1939. (CJCCCNA)

MS *St Louis* passenger Siegfried Chraplewski and his two young sons en route to Cuba, May 1939. Their landing papers were invalidated before they even arrived in Havana. (USHMM, courtesy of Peter Chraplewski)

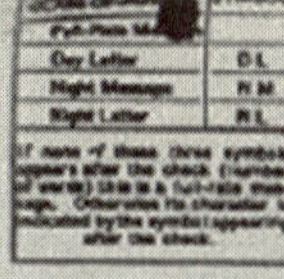

CANADIAN NATIONAL TELEGRAM

D. E. GALLOWAY, ASSISTANT VICE-PRESIDENT, TORONTO, ONT.

23857

In Connection with
WESTERN UNION
TELEGRAPH CO.
Cable Service
to all the World
Money Transferred
by Telegraph

22rz 222 132 extra

Toronto Ont 754p June 7

Right Hon W.L.McKenzie King P.C.

Premier of Canada Niagara Falls.

As a mark of gratitude to almighty God for the pleasure and gratification which has been vouchsafed the Canadian people through the visit their Gracious Majesties King George and Queen Elizabeth and as evidence of the true christian charity of the people of this most fortunate and blessed country we the undersigned as christian citizens of Canada respectfully suggest that under the powers vested in you as Premier of our country you forthwith offer to the 907 homeless exiles on board the Hamburg American ship Stlouis Sanctuary in Canada.

George M.Wrong

Elizabeth Wrong

B K Sandwell

Nellie L Rowell

Malcolm W.Wallace

May Wallace

Robert Falconer K.C. M.G.

Lady Falconer

Robert J.Renison

Bishop

Constance E Hamilton

Joseph Shaw-Wood

Ruth McLachlan Franks MD

Andrew F.Brewan

M I Brewin

(Rev) R J Irwin

F Erichsen Brown K.C.

Isabella R Erichsen Brown

The first page of a telegram sent by forty-one prominent Torontonians to Prime Minister Mackenzie King, asking him to grant refuge to the passengers aboard the MS *St Louis*, 7 June 1939. (Library and Archives Canada, William Lyon Mackenzie King fonds)

Members of the Jewish leadership outside a Canadian Armed Forces recruiting office, with a sign in Yiddish, French, and English encouraging Jews to enlist. Montreal, 1939. While their religion was originally indicated on enlistment forms and dog tags, by 1942 this had been changed to "Other Denomination" to avoid discrimination. (CJCCCNA)

NAZI GERMANY, CANADIAN RESPONSES

I

Social Death and International Isolation: Jews in Nazi Germany, 1933–1939

DORIS L. BERGEN

A joke made the rounds in Palestine in the 1930s: One Jew to another, "Did you come out of conviction or out of Germany?"

In 1933, when Adolf Hitler became chancellor of Germany, Renate Fischer was a four-year-old living in Breslau (now the Polish city of Wrocław).[1] Her father, a psychiatrist, had served as a medic in the First World War; her mother, a housewife with a beautiful voice, sang on high holidays in their synagogue. Her grandparents were well established: one side of the family owned a large toy store, the other a fruit-canning plant. Renate had no siblings. As she put it in an interview in 2005, "My mother always said Mr Hitler saw to it that I was an only child." Like most German children, she knew next to nothing about Canada, and her only associations came from fairy tales and picture books. When Renate's parents began to talk about possible immigration, her worst fear was wolves: "Four legged ones. I was petrified to think that I was going to have to live in a log cabin with ice and snow all around and the wolves in the neighborhood."[2]

Five years later, Renate Fischer and her parents found themselves in Canada, Jews fleeing Nazi Germany. They were atypical in their place of refuge: between 1933 and 1939, at most 2,000 Jews from Germany succeeded in getting permission to enter Canada and then making their way there.[3] Some of these people, like Fischer, have recorded their experiences, and these valuable sources are a reminder that the much larger number of people unable to come to Canada leave almost no trace in any records of any kind. But in one regard the Fischers were typical. Like all Jews in Germany,

they faced deprivation and crushing exclusion during the six years of
Nazi rule that preceded and prepared the devastation of the Second
World War and the Holocaust. Those years, 1933 to 1939, are the
focus of this chapter.

The situation of Jews in Germany between 1933 and 1939 can
be characterized under two headings: social death and international
isolation. "Social death," a term coined to describe the marginalization, dishonouring, and powerlessness of enslaved people,[4] is used
by the historian Marion Kaplan as a way to analyze how official
discrimination and persecution systematically cut Jews in Germany
off from the majority non-Jewish population.[5] International events
exacerbated Jewish suffering, as economic depression, ethnic and
national conflicts, fear of war, and ultimately war itself made Jews
increasingly vulnerable inside Germany yet reduced the prospect
of refuge elsewhere. By September 1939, when the Germans, followed within weeks by the Soviets, invaded Poland, Central Europe
had become a trap for Jews that left few ways out. With the German invasions of Western and Northern Europe in 1940, and South-
eastern and Eastern Europe in 1941, the remaining escape routes
slammed shut one after the other.[6]

This chapter examines the mutually reinforcing processes of social
death and international isolation in the years between the Nazi rise
to power and the onset of the Second World War. Developments
in Germany are analyzed in three chronological stages: 1933–34 –
Nazi revolution, Jewish trepidation; 1935–37 – Nazi success, ostra-
cism of Jews; and 1938–39 – Nazi expansion, Jewish desperation.
The escalating assault turned Germany into a poisonous environ-
ment for Jews and pushed half of the Jewish population out of the
country before the war even began. Canada's role in this history was
small, but attentiveness to it highlights the anguished situation of
Jews in Germany and in the Austrian and Czechoslovakian territories that came under German control in 1938 and 1939. Wolves, it
turns out, were the least of the threats that faced Renate Fischer, her
family, and their fellow Jews.

Of the approximately 60 million inhabitants of Germany in 1933,
about half a million were Jewish,[7] less than 1 percent of the population. Poland with 10 percent, and even Canada with 1.5 percent, had
proportionally more Jews than Germany.[8] German Jews, like their
counterparts elsewhere, were a diverse group. Disproportionately
present in some highly visible areas of the economy – publishing,

medicine, performing arts – they were noticeably under-represented elsewhere: in the higher ranks of the military, judiciary, and government bureaucracy, among the police, and in agriculture. Some fitted the widespread image of the acculturated German Jew, but as a group they ranged across religious and political spectrums, from Reform to Orthodox, from Zionist to German nationalist.[9] Around three-quarters of them lived in major cities – Berlin, Frankfurt am Main, Hamburg, Breslau – but others made their homes in small towns and villages, particularly in the Rhine Valley, where a Jewish presence dated back to Roman times. Jewish places of worship, most of them Orthodox synagogues, were scattered throughout southwestern Germany, where Jews raised cattle, worked in trades, and had all manner of small businesses. Like their co-religionists in the city, their lifestyle often differed little from that of the Christians around them, and most were neither wealthy nor influential.[10]

The small number of Jews in Germany stood in sharp contrast to the obsessive attention paid them by antisemites.[11] Nevertheless, those who argue for a uniquely German "eliminationist antisemitism" might note that despite the existence of anti-Jewish sentiments and practices in Germany,[12] Jews there experienced considerable success.[13] Among German Jews were Nobel Prize winners, lawyers, doctors, judges, journalists, professors, artists, film directors, and athletes. Hugo Preuss, a Jewish jurist, drafted the constitution of democratic Germany after the First World War;[14] the German Jewish industrialist Walther Rathenau was serving as foreign minister at the time of his assassination in 1922.[15] In Canada, by contrast, when Aaron Horvitz became mayor of Cornwall, a small town in Ontario, in 1943, the Jewish press announced it was the "highest elective post to be held by any Canadian Jew."[16] Abraham Klein, appointed lecturer in English poetry at McGill in 1945, was heralded as the first Jewish member of his department.[17]

1933–1934: NAZI REVOLUTION, JEWISH TREPIDATION

When Hitler took office as chancellor of Germany on 30 January 1933, his position was rather weak. He did not command a majority in the Reichstag, the German parliament; his cabinet included only two other members of the National Socialist (Nazi) Party; and non-Nazis occupied the key positions of president and vice-chancellor. Hitler's virulent antisemitism was certainly no secret[18] –

he had been screaming it in speeches and screeds since 1919 – but at this stage it was not clear how much public support he had on this score or how long his government would last. In the first two years of his rule, even very astute observers vacillated in their assessment of these issues.

Victor Klemperer, a professor of French literature in Dresden, is a case in point.[19] Klemperer, the son of a rabbi, converted to Protestant Christianity, married a gentile, served in the German army in the First World War, and identified fully with German culture. Under Nazi law, however, he counted as a Jew. In his detailed and insightful diary, one of the issues that preoccupied him was what he referred to as the *vox populi*. What did "ordinary Germans," the non-Jewish Germans around him, think of Jews? What did they make of Nazi measures? How antisemitic were they? Klemperer went back and forth on these questions, often within the same diary entry. From the outset, he understood that hatred of Jews was the centre of Hitler's world view, but until at least 1935 he held out hope that decent Germans would prevail. The supportive words and actions of individuals, including the gentile friend who, at enormous risk, accepted and hid the pages of Klemperer's diary as he smuggled them to her, encouraged the flashes of optimism that tempered his all-too-well-founded gloom.

Incidents that in hindsight appear as ominous steps on the road to destruction could seem like aberrations at the time. Margot S., born in Berlin in 1925, remembers that Hitler's rise to power immediately made the city perilous for Jews. Right away, she noted in a 1990 interview conducted in Montreal, "groups of hooligans" assaulted people at random and made it dangerous to walk the streets at night. Sometimes the ss took Jews to a beer hall to have a drink and "amuse themselves." The Jews, she recalls, "usually returned with an eye out, an ear cut off, or several broken bones." Her father, a cloth merchant born in Poland, became physically sick when he saw some Germans hack off the beard of an Orthodox Jew. According to Margot, such hostility against Jews took him and the rest of her family by surprise: they "had put a good deal of faith in their German neighbors, because Hitler was never actually elected to the Reichstag."[20] In 1935, after ss came to the door "looking for Jews," Margot's father packed up the family, and they moved to Poland. He subsequently arranged for their immigration to Uruguay and even booked a departure for late 1939, a plan scuttled by the German invasion of Poland.[21]

What Klemperer and Margot S. could not have foreseen was how power would transform Nazi antisemitism from a fringe phenomenon into a dynamic, self-fueling system. Hitler and his associates had to "educate" the German public about the purported danger that Jews posed to the "Aryan race," but as they learned in 1933, their strongest ally in this task was the power they wielded through control of the state and its organs. Power enabled implementation of antisemitic ideas that otherwise were nothing but brutal fantasies. Hitler's rule gave licence to antisemitic thugs who terrorized Jews and intimidated sympathetic non-Jews. Even worse, under Hitler's leadership the state sanctioned and in fact mandated anti-Jewish attitudes and used its courts, bureaucrats, and police to enforce them. As a result, starting in 1933, antisemitism spread rapidly, through propaganda and education but also through policies and practices that implicated ever more individuals and groups of people and gave them a vested interest in upholding a system of persecution, whether or not they shared the hatred that underpinned it.[22]

Like all forms of antisemitism, Nazi antisemitism meant hatred of Jews,[23] but it had a number of particular features that shaped policies and practices. Crucial to Hitler's world view was the notion of Jews as a security threat. This accusation was linked to the stab-in-the-back myth – the idea that Germany had lost the "Great War" in 1918 because of treachery on the homefront, led by perfidious Jews. For Hitler and others who shared this belief, eliminating Jews was necessary in order to win future wars. Also important in this regard was the Nazi emphasis on maintaining positive public opinion among the so-called Aryan elements of the population. Hitler, it must be emphasized, expected and indeed sought war. To achieve the world dominance it supposedly deserved, the "Aryan" race, he reasoned in Social Darwinist fashion, had to be in a constant state of increase. Such reproduction required land, and conquest of territory meant war. In Hitler's eyes, because the Jewish "race" was the mortal enemy of the "Aryans," any German war would be a war against "the Jews."

Another key element of Nazi antisemitism was the concept of Jews as international conspirators, puppet masters pulling the strings behind nations, organizations, and political movements of all kinds. Indeed, by Nazi logic, all of Germany's enemies were either dupes of or masks for "international Jewry." A related idea was the notion of Jews as masters of disguise, evil plotters who hid behind façades of weakness, harmlessness, and benevolence. Hence the prevalence of images of Jews as germs, parasites, rats, and bearers of disease – small, even invisible, yet deadly – and the frequent depiction of Jews as masked or otherwise concealed. Nazi propaganda used all these messages, repeating them in a monotonous way that sought to create the reality it had fabricated.[24]

Characteristic of Hitler's radical antisemitism was a religious zeal that linked fighting Jews and destroying so-called Jewish influence to a struggle against evil.[25] In *Mein Kampf*, Hitler claimed that when he attacked "the Jew" he was doing God's work. At the same time, his antisemitism built on racialist notions: "Jewishness," it assumed, was "in the blood" and could not be removed or undone through religious conversion, legal emancipation, or cultural assimilation. In fact, proponents of racial antisemitism asserted that these processes were masks designated to conceal the "Jewish threat" so that it could catch its victims off guard. Hitler also sounded a note of urgency. The clock was ticking, he and like-minded orators intoned, and it was almost too late for the "Aryan race" to save itself from the corrupting forces that had already defiled its collective bloodstream. Only rapid and violent action, they insisted, could stop "the Jew."

The antisemitism preached in Nazi speeches and tracts was rife with contradictions. Jews were said to have invented Christianity to make their enemies meek and weak, yet at the same time they were accused of killing Jesus and assaulting true Christians everywhere. Nazi antisemitism depicted Jews as at once oversexed predators and seductresses, yet weak and androgynous (effeminate men, masculine women); they were seen as both capitalists and communists, as congenitally inferior yet capable of mounting a diabolically clever conspiracy to rule the world, and as unable to conceal their true essence yet hiding everywhere. Instead of weakening the power of Nazism's particular variety of antisemitism, such contradictions strengthened it. They rendered Nazi antisemitism simultaneously amorphous and absolutely vivid and specific. And they provided an infinite number of places where a person could connect with hatred and fear of Jews, according to the individual's own anxieties and desires.

Antisemitism was central to Nazism, but it does not seem to have played a major role in bringing Hitler to power.[26] Hitler needed respectability, and before 1933 rabid antisemitism was not good form in respectable German circles. Nor did Hitler reveal action against Jews to be his top priority when he took office. Instead, his first goal was to consolidate power, which he did at the cost of major political rivals – above all, the communists. When the German Reichstag building burned in February 1933, Hitler seized the opportunity to have hundreds of communists arrested, blaming them for the fire. In response to the supposed national emergency, Germany's parliamentarians passed the Enabling Laws that dismantled what remained of their democratic system. Amid considerable fanfare, the first official concentration camp was opened at Dachau, its inmates primarily political prisoners. In the summer of 1933, Hitler achieved a major diplomatic coup when his government signed a concordat with the Vatican. That same week, he announced the Law for the Prevention of Hereditarily Diseased Offspring, which called for sterilization of people deemed to be bearers of supposed hereditary diseases, the list of which included both highly treatable and vaguely defined conditions, among them epilepsy, alcoholism, and "feeblemindedness."[27] In October 1933, as Germany stepped up its secret rearmament program, Hitler announced his country's withdrawal from the League of Nations.

Jews were by no means the only victims in this flurry of activity. The vast majority of communists arrested, beaten, and pushed or thrown out of Germany in the wake of the Reichstag fire were not Jewish. The Nazi regime also introduced measures against Jehovah's Witnesses, Freemasons, and proponents of rights for homosexuals, and the storm troopers enacted all these exclusions in the streets.[28] The prominent sexologist Magnus Hirschfeld, a gay man and a Jew, was reviled in the Nazi press, and his research institute and library were destroyed by rampaging students. Forced into exile, he died soon afterwards. In 1933 Heinrich Mann, brother of the novelist Thomas Mann and well known for his anti-militarist, anti-nationalist writings, was dismissed from his position as president of the literary section of the Prussian Academy and stripped of his German citizenship. At the infamous book burning in Berlin, Minister of Propaganda Joseph Goebbels personally consigned Mann's work to the flames, along with books by other authors deemed "un-German," among them Franz Werfel, Bertolt Brecht, Helen Keller, Ernest Hemingway, and Jack London.

Of course, Hitler still found specific ways to target Jews. In April 1933, in an effort to highlight the Jewish presence in the economy and stigmatize German Jews, the Nazi leadership proclaimed a boycott of Jewish businesses. This first public act of organized antisemitism turned out to be a failure or at least a disappointment to Hitler and Goebbels, and it was called off ahead of schedule.[29] International protest and threats to retaliate by boycotting German products and businesses worried non-Jewish Germans, and many consumers refused to be bossed around. Even some storm troopers and members of the Nazi Party violated the boycott and continued to frequent shops convenient to them. And there were other, less obvious issues. What constituted a Jewish business? If the issue was Jewish ownership, what about non-Jewish employees? What about enterprises owned jointly by Jews and non-Jews? In a complex, modern economy that included large incorporated firms with thousands of employees and stockholders, it was by no means clear who would be hurt by the boycott. Even in very small businesses, Jewish and non-Jewish interests were intertwined. Susanne Weilbach's father was a Jewish cattle farmer in the Rhine Valley. Boycotting him would also destroy the livelihood of his non-Jewish hired hand, impoverishing the man's family.[30] To Nazi leaders, the April 1933 boycott revealed how tightly Jews were woven into the fabric of German economic life and proved the need to isolate them before mounting a direct all-out attack.

In another sense, the boycott was not a failure at all. It gave hardcore Nazis an opportunity to act out their hatred of Jews.[31] A useful trial balloon, it typified what became a common pattern for Hitler: push, wait to test the public response, and then push again in the direction of least resistance.[32] In this way, Nazi authorities learned what the German people would accept and gained valuable experience for implementing subsequent measures. Moreover, by pulling back from an extreme position, they appeared flexible and concealed the radical nature of their goals.

In April 1933, the same week as the boycott, Nazi authorities introduced a law to remove Jews from the German civil service. Euphemistically labelled the Law for the Restoration of the Professional Civil Service, it was a crucial step in transforming antisemitism from an attitude that required members of the public to share Nazi ideals into a wide range of actions that did not. This measure met with much more immediate success than the boycott. Non-Jews, the regime learned, preferred anti-Jewish measures which they perceived as improving their lives over those that cost them effort. Firing Jewish civil servants, from lowly clerks to high-profile professionals, opened up positions for non-Jewish Germans, or at least held out the promise of doing so, and provided opportunities for self-serving initiatives that sometimes went beyond the law.[33] For instance, ambitious university professors targeted rivals or unpopular colleagues by denouncing them as Jewish converts to Christianity, or as being married to Jewish women, and requesting that they be expelled from their posts.[34]

Some non-Jews noticed the abuses and spoke out. In early 1934 an aristocratic Protestant leader, Wilhelm von Pechmann, announced that he was converting to Roman Catholicism in protest "against the rape of the church, against her lack of backbone, and against her silence in the face of the massive injustice and all the pain and suffering that countless 'non-Aryan' hearts and homes, Christian and Jewish, have been forced to endure, as we have swung from one extreme to another."[35] Pechmann found little support, public or private, for his outrage. And even he implied that there might be some justification for the anti-Jewish measures, with his depiction of Nazism as somehow a valid if extreme corrective to Jewish power.

In response to Nazi pressures, a wave of Jewish flight took place inside Germany as Jews in the countryside left for the cities. In this first phase of institutionalized antisemitism, rural Jews were vulnerable in particular ways.[36] In small towns and villages, everyone knew who they were. Restrictions and propaganda made it uncomfortable for non-Jews to associate with them and rewarded those who joined in the persecution. Gentiles who owed money to Jews suddenly found it easy not to repay those debts, to demand more credit or special deals, or simply to take what they wanted. Christians and Jews in friendly and loving relationships were targets of public humiliation and vicious attacks. Cities with large Jewish communities offered some safety in numbers as well as educational, religious, and social services. Also important was the proximity to the embassies and consulates necessary for those who sought to leave Germany altogether.

Indeed, during the first year of Hitler's rule, tens of thousands of people fled Germany, among them 37,000 Jews. Many did not go far: they chose destinations where they had relatives, business connections, or other prospects. For 73 percent of them, this meant elsewhere in Europe;[37] 19 percent went to Palestine,[38] and only 8 percent went overseas. Anne Frank's family from Frankfurt am Main moved to the Netherlands.[39] So did Herta Katz Wohlfarth (later Helen Waterford), a young Jewish woman who had built up a successful business distributing liquid soaps and disinfectents; accompanying her was her new husband, an accountant, who had been fired from his job as a bankruptcy officer of the courts.[40] Other German Jews went to Belgium, France, Poland, and Spain.[41] The father of George Mosse, later one of the most influential historians of the twentieth century, owned a large publishing conglomerate based in Berlin. Forced at gunpoint to sign over his assets to a fake organization for war veterans, in 1933 he departed with his family for Switzerland.[42] Still, the situation remained uncertain, and some of the emigrants returned later, believing conditions had improved, or because they were unable to find ways of supporting themselves or were unwilling to bear separation from their loved ones.[43]

Observers around the world followed developments under Nazism. *Dent's Teachers' Aid*, a Canadian booklet, spent pages exploring the "new Germany." On the whole, *Dent's* was critical. It attributed economic recovery to draconian policies, maintaining that Hitler had cut wages in half, doubled the price of commodities, and forced young men into work camps. It drew attention to Hitler's aggressive expansionism, claiming (with what turned out to be uncanny accuracy) that he planned to absorb into a "Germanic union" Norway, Sweden, Denmark, Holland, Alsace-Lorraine, Austria, Czechoslovakia, Switzerland, Yugoslavia, and Ukraine. The authors expressed less concern about Nazi antisemitism, however, and even showed some affinity with its stereotypes. Hitler "has relentlessly persecuted the Catholics and Jews," they noted, but this was only logical, they suggested, because his industrial backers were rivals with interests "controlled largely by Jews and the Catholic group."[44]

1935–1937: NAZI SUCCESS, OSTRACIZED JEWS

By mid-1934, the revolutionary phase of Nazism had ended with the internal purge known as the Night of Long Knives. Its targets included Hitler's rivals and elements within the Nazi movement that had become an embarrassment to the quest for respectability. ss men murdered Ernst Röhm, head of the storm troopers and a known homosexual; also General Kurt von Schleicher, a former chancellor, along with his wife; the Nazi ideologue Gregor Strasser; and at least eighty others.[45] Jews were not targeted in this bloodbath.

Victor Klemperer wondered whether this time Hitler had gone too far by attacking Nazi insiders rather than outsiders. Would he be overthrown or at least disciplined by less radical elements within

Germany? Or would the moral high ground he claimed by attacking Röhm in fact win him support?[46] Klemperer's pessimism was warranted. Instead of removing Hitler, German President Paul von Hindenburg, the hero of the First World War, congratulated him on restoring order. Church leaders, Catholic and Protestant, followed suit. Rather than destabilizing Hitler, the purge opened the way for the next stage of his rule – routinization of Nazi terror and stepped-up preparations for war, including increased assault on German Jews, the supposed enemy within. The boycott and civil service law had already created significant financial hardships; now a series of measures, large and small, would drive a wedge between German Jews and the rest of society and sever not only economic ties but bonds of civility, community, and family.

Manifestations of antisemitism outside Germany bolstered Hitler's position and deepened Jewish isolation. The German press gleefully reported attacks on Jews wherever they occurred and used these accounts to normalize Nazi practices and intimidate Jewish Germans and those who sympathized with them. One such case in 1935 featured Canada. A short article, picked up from a German-language newspaper in South America and reprinted across Germany, carried the headline "Jews in Canada Denied Fire Insurance!" Canadian insurance companies, it announced, considered Jews a fire hazard and refused to insure property owned or even rented by Jews. Naturally, the Jewish lobby had kicked up a fuss, the article remarked, but to no avail; even in the "mixed" society of Canada, Jews were beginning to be perceived as the threat they really were.[47] On the principle that "forewarned is forearmed," German Jews were avid readers of the Nazi press.[48] For them, this report must have confirmed the sense that the world as a whole was hostile, and Canada was no exception.

Meanwhile, other international developments played into Hitler's hands. In 1935 the eyes of the world were on Fascist Italy and its invasion of Ethiopia (Abyssinia). Mussolini's forces used all means at their disposal, including poison gas, to attack and kill tens of thousands of civilians as well as combatants.[49] For many outside observers, it was Mussolini, not Hitler, who seemed the most dangerous threat to peace.

In March 1935, in direct contravention of the Treaty of Versailles, Hitler announced full German rearmament, including conscription, creation of an air force (the Luftwaffe), expansion of the navy, and organization of all three branches of the military within the Wehr-macht. An enormous blow to the settlement drawn up after the First World War, this move boosted Hitler's prestige at home, especially among former military men and among elements of the popula-tion that had previously remained uncommitted or even skeptical. Hitler's position had already been strengthened by the outcome of the Saar plebiscite a few months earlier when, in a spectacular land-slide, voters had chosen their region to be part of Germany rather than France. These triumphs not only enhanced Hitler's standing abroad but empowered him in domestic measures and, in direct ways, isolated German Jews.

Weeks after the public announcement of the introduction of com-pulsory military service in Germany, a regulation explicitly excluded Jewish men. In hindsight, this measure may seem obvious and indeed almost a boon: what Jew would have wanted to serve in Hitler's army?[50] Viewed from the perspective of the time, however, it was a cynical betrayal. German Jews had served loyally in the previous war, paying a high price in sacrifice of life and limb that was more than commensurate with their share of the population. Nevertheless, in 1916, the German army had conducted a study to assess whether there was truth to accusations that Jews were shirking their duty. The results proved these charges to be baseless, but they were never released.[51] Antisemites seized the opportunity to insinuate that the findings had to be concealed because they were so devastating to Jews and would have produced unrest.

Similar rumors and accusations of Jewish unfitness for military service circulated in other places too, including the United States, Canada, and the Soviet Union.[52] They typified a common method used by antisemites: creation of suspicion through repetition. Jews generally responded by trying to prove their worth through publica-tion of the number and names of the war dead and other demonstra-tions of loyalty and their courage under arms.[53] In Hitler's Germany, the Jews would not even be allowed to make the case for their brav-ery. Instead, exclusion implied that Jews were dishonourable, unfit to be soldiers, and in league with the enemies that allegedly sur-rounded Germany and menaced it from within.

In late 1935, German authorities took another major step to ostracize Jews. The Nuremberg Laws, announced at the Nazi Party rally that autumn, had several parts. One, the Reich Citizenship Law, defined who legally was a Jew, who an Aryan, and who a so-called *Mischling*. The definition was based not on blood or "race," as was implied, but on the religious membership of an individual's grandparents. Three or four grandparents baptized into a Christian church made a person "Aryan"; only two put someone in the amorphous category of *Mischling*; and an individual with one or no baptized grandparents was classified as "non-Aryan." Another component, the Law for the Protection of German Blood and German Honour, introduced a series of restrictions on people defined as Jews. They could not marry or have sexual relations with people defined as "Aryans"; they could not employ in their households non-Jewish women under the age of forty-five; they could not march under the German flag; and they lost most of the rights and protections of citizenship. Exceptions were made for veterans of the front, a distinction that would later disappear.[54]

These stipulations in turn sparked a wave of investigations and prosecutions. Displays of affection or friendship could result in charges of *Rassenschande* – crimes against the race – or in public humiliation. Policemen, lawyers, and judges solicited detailed testimony from men and women accused of violating laws against sexual contact between people who found themselves deemed members of different races, even though they lived side by side, spoke the same language, and looked more or less the same. Convictions meant long sentences in prison or concentration camps, and even acquittals left reputations damaged and careers shattered.[55] Storm troopers and other thugs harassed Jews and non-Jews suspected of violating the race laws, beating them up or forcing them to stand in the street wearing sandwich boards with insulting messages.[56] Publicly displayed propaganda and children's books spread fear of Jews as a sexual threat, and even gentiles who harboured no particular ill will toward Jews discovered it was dangerous to associate with them.

Laws about sex and other concealed matters always open the door to denunciations.[57] Fred Mann, a Jewish boy in Leipzig in 1935, recalls how neighbours trumped up charges that his father had engaged in illegal sexual relations with the family's maid in the stairwell of their building. Under significant pressure, the woman nevertheless refused to substantiate the accusation, which was eventually dropped.[58] No doubt this traumatic experience was a major factor in the family's decision to leave Germany for Belgium. They eventually made their way to Canada. The Manns' situation in 1935 points to the contagious evil of the Nazi system. Not only hatred and cowardice but, in perverse ways, love and loyalty could also lead to the cutting of ties from either side. Some gentiles abandoned their Jewish spouses in order to advance their careers or save themselves trouble, but divorces were also initiated by Jews in order to spare their partners hardship or for the sake of the children.[59]

In the wake of the Nuremberg Laws the regime introduced an endless stream of restrictions and prohibitions that heaped injustices, indignities, and hardships one on top of the other and further separated Jews from their neighbours. Jews were prohibited from using public swimming pools, owning radios, telephones and typewriters, attending school, practising medicine, wearing dirndls and lederhosen, buying chocolate, shopping other than at specified times, and giving the so-called German greeting, "Heil Hitler!" Hundreds of such prohibitions tormented and stigmatized Jews by translating antisemitic ideas into everyday routines that required no effort whatsoever from most non-Jewish Germans, who only needed to obey the law and follow their self-interest.

What might seem only minor inconveniences could constitute severe blows to Jewish life and triumphs of antisemitic propaganda. For example, by forbidding Jews to purchase or receive cows' milk, Nazi authorities deprived Jewish children of tasty, comforting things, weakened their health, and reinforced the stereotype of Jews as unwholesome, dangerous, and even demonic. Meanwhile, with consumer goods scarce, the ban on milk also sent the message to non-Jewish Germans that shortages or high prices were not the result of poor planning or military spending but were somehow caused by Jewish greed. Even goods that were not forbidden could be denied to Jews. As one German Jew later recalled, when Jews entered the shop, suddenly there were no more carrots.[60] As ties between Jews and the rest of the population frayed, Jews became pariahs in their own country.

Jewish children were especially hard hit, because they had daily contact with non-Jews at school and on the way there and back. Many memoirs looking back on childhood in Nazi Germany include accounts of beatings, harassment, and other forms of violence. Georg Iggers remembers being threatened with knives and shoved down some stairs by members of the Hitler Youth in Hamburg.[61] Susanne Weilbach depicts schoolyard bullies and mean, antisemitic, or simply ambitious teachers who could do whatever they wanted to Jewish children, knowing they were backed by official policy. When her teacher banished Jewish and Romany children to a bench at the back of the room, it is not surprising that her classmates taunted her and threw stones.[62] Renate Fischer recalls a similar dynamic in her school, where a classmate once threw an inkwell at her:

> We had row monitors who were supposed to take care of people not speaking or misbehaving, and if they did talk to anybody or in any way misbehave, the name was given to the teacher. And I remember getting more ... censure for talking or misbehaving than I really should have gotten. And of course the result was that there was a stick that was used and ... I received a whipping on both my hands every time I was [*angezeigt*] ... which meant, pointed out. And that I think kind of ... discouraged me. And somehow the teachers, I don't know, they turned their backs on these things.[63]

Elderly Jews suffered the scourge of social death in particular ways. Municipal authorities often took the opportunity to save money by cutting off social benefits to Jews even though not required to do so, and the elderly were disproportionately hurt by such measures.[64] Jews seeking to leave Germany often found it impossible or prohibitively expensive to get visas for older family members, who were not valued as labour. Some people eventually left parents and grandparents behind;[65] others missed opportunities in order to keep their families together. Between 1933 and 1939, the suicide rate among older Jews in Germany skyrocketed.[66]

Renate Fischer recalls the mid-1930s as "a very difficult time" for her grandmother as her parents prepared to leave for Canada:

> Unfortunately we could not bring her with us. The Canadian government put an age limit on those whom they would permit. And of course, she was not a trained person, either a farmer or a physician, so on her own she would not be able to go. And she could not come as a member of the family, much to the everlasting sadness that my father went through. He was an only child and he was very close to his mother, and I think he suffered terribly, just the fact that she had to stay behind.[67]

Fischer's paternal grandmother was later murdered in the killing centre of Belzec;[68] her mother's mother died in 1941 in a freight car transporting German Jews to Riga to be killed.[69] Looking back, Fischer remembers that once, in the middle of the night, her mother woke them all up screaming. "This was in the 40's, the early 40's. And to this day she thinks that was the day that her mother was killed. And – probably it was."

The Christian churches in Germany played a significant role in furthering and legitimating the isolation of Jews. Nazi law required Germans in a wide range of professions, and even in volunteer positions, to prove their "Aryan blood" by establishing the religion of their forebears – and producing a record of baptism into a Roman Catholic or Protestant church was the only way to do so. Priests, pastors, and church secretaries found themselves overwhelmed with requests for documentation, and many church offices hired extra staff to handle the job. There is no evidence that all the church workers who spent long hours combing through dusty tomes and copying out names and dates of births, baptisms, and marriages were hardcore Nazis. Probably most of them were just doing a job. But their work was essential for the identification and marginalization of Jews. Meanwhile, the eagerness of Christian leaders, Roman Catholic and Protestant, to maintain good relations with the state and to capitalize on Hitler's popularity added to a dynamic that made the churches effective normalizers of Nazi antisemitism.

Some elements in the churches took a more proactive role. Calling themselves the Storm Troopers of Christ, a predominantly Protestant group known as the German Christian Movement attacked every aspect of Christianity that was related to Judaism. Members rejected parts or all of the Old Testament, revised the New Testament, and denied that Jesus was a Jew. Because the German Christians considered Jewishness to be "in the blood," they refused to accept conversion from Judaism to Christianity as valid. A sign displayed in Westphalia in 1935 stated their position with crude clarity: "Baptism may be quite useful, but it doesn't straighten any noses."[70]

For their part, German Jews proved flexible in adapting in countless ways to the rapidly changing circumstances. They created formal and informal self-help networks and expanded existing Jewish schools, hospitals, and other services.[71] With great effort and in many cases at considerable risk, they maintained and established ties to international Jewish organizations, which were often the only source of essential funding.[72] Jewish agencies provided retraining in fields that might improve people's chances of making new lives elsewhere. Under the auspices of the Organization for Rehabilitation and Training, Renate Fischer's mother studied physiotherapy. According to her daughter, the skills she developed helped "keep body and soul together" once the family arrived in Canada. When Nazi regulations forbade kosher butchering, some survivors recalled there were rabbis who allowed Jews to eat meat from regular butchers as long as it was not from a prohibited animal.[73] Jacob Wiener, a young Jewish man in Bremen, joined an organization in 1934 in which, as he put it, Jews "became more religious instead of assimilation." He told his teacher, "I want to become more Orthodox, like the Germans want to become, in quotation marks, more German."[74]

As living in Germany became increasing difficult for Jews, leaving the country posed its own difficulties. Indeed, the number of German Jews departing remained lower every year from 1934 through 1937 than it had been in the first year of Hitler's rule.[75] This was not the result of Jewish complacency. There were so many obstacles: restrictions on what could be taken out of Germany,[76] rigid quotas for the number of immigrants accepted by specific countries, and reluctance to separate families. Material, political, and emotional barriers were compounded by practical problems. Already in 1933, German Jews had lost the right to consular services outside the country, and after the 1935 Nuremberg Laws they were no longer issued German passports. Effectively stateless, they were unlikely to be accepted as immigrants or even to be granted transit visas. In Canada, where immigration was tied to the needs of the labour force and most new arrivals faced a one-year probationary period, the authorities were particularly adamant about refusing entry to stateless people. After all, people without valid passports could not be sent back to where they had come from if they turned out to be criminals, became unemployed or ill, or proved otherwise undesirable or burdensome.[77]

In hindsight, decisions made by German Jews in these middle years often appear either brilliantly prescient or fatefully misguided. But although history is written looking backward, it is lived looking forward, and it was impossible at the time to know what lay ahead. Renate Fischer remembers that in her family there was at least one "wonderful opportunity where the wrong turn was taken." In 1935 her maternal uncle returned from a trip to Palestine, excited and eager to relocate. In her words, "he saw the handwriting on the wall and he ... had a chance to buy into Egged, the bus company." But her grandmother, unwilling to leave Berlin, would not give him the money, "although it was there in spades." As a result, the uncle "did not go to Israel, had a terrible time leaving Germany, and my grandmother didn't make it at all."[78]

Seizing the right opportunity was only half the battle, as Fischer and her parents came to realize. Since Jews had no rights or protections, the German authorities could do whatever they wanted to them. "They were on our tails constantly about signing this paper and that paper. And during that period of time, many people were called to the police stations and never returned. This was a time in '36–'37, when people were called on unbelievably small details to their leaving and to their lives, they were called, and they were made to jump off buildings. And this happened indeed, to friends of ours." One day Fischer's father was summoned. "We were trembling, I think all day long, but he was one of the lucky ones. He signed whatever he needed to sign and paid whatever he needed to pay and he came back."[79] Official brutality exacted all kinds of tolls from defenceless Jews. Long after the war, Carol Ascher learned that police had tortured her grandfather in Berlin with electrodes to his penis, "just for fun."[80]

Cheaters and frauds fed on the increasing urgency with which German Jews sought ways out of Europe. Jacob Wiener and his friends in Bremen and Berlin were aware that some Latin American diplomats and others were issuing fake documents, and bribes were often required. Still, they often had no choice but to work with dubious partners to try to help Jews escape.[81] And Jews did manage to find refuge in a stunning array of places: India, South Africa, Cuba, Tashkent, the United States, Palestine, Mexico, Turkey, Spain, Portugal, Yugoslavia, Kenya, Morocco, Ireland, Shanghai, Curaçao.[82] In many cases, inquiries made and initiatives taken in these middle years were crucial in enabling departure later.

Only rarely did Canada feature in the calculations of German Jews seeking haven. According to Renate Fischer, Canada was known to be antisemitic and to admit only farmers and doctors. For her parents it was an unexpected, if welcome, last resort. Long reluctant to leave Germany, her mother had been "sure this was all going to blow over." Her father, less sanguine, "put out feelers" and received an invitation to practise medicine in "either Uruguay or Paraguay." Unable to speak Spanish, he turned down that opportunity. He also rejected Palestine. "My parents were not Zionists," Fischer recounts. "You know, in Germany there was the big schism, the blue and white and the black and white. He did not belong to the blue and white, although that changed too. I mean, he was the strongest supporter of Israel that anybody could wish for, but at the time of our move he thought he could not take the weather in Israel. That was why." But then "this wonderful telegram showed up, the one that really saved us when we were able to establish a family – a blood connection to someone who lived in Canada." A question remained, however: "Could we get into Canada? Because Canada had a very tight quota." Fischer's next words indicate that even she underestimated Canadian restrictiveness: "You might know the book, 6,000 is too many, and indeed I don't even think that they got 6,000, or allowed 6,000 in."[83]

In the middle period of Nazi rule, the interlocking of foreign and domestic policies typical of Hitler's system was starkly evident. The 1936 Olympic Games brought some public easing of measures against Jews, at least in Berlin and other places where international scrutiny might penetrate. At the same time, other target groups became even more vulnerable. As part of the "clean-up" of the city, police in Berlin arrested hundreds of homeless people, women accused of prostitution, and Romany. The first "Gypsy" prison created by the Nazis was already established in 1936, in Marzahn, on the city's outskirts. There, Romany were simply dumped in an area that included sewage lagoons. They were forbidden to leave and arrested if they did so.[84]

The Olympics captured world attention in 1936, but a much more significant event occurred that year – the German remilitarization of the Rhineland. In March, between the winter and summer Olympics, troops of the brand-new Wehrmacht advanced into an area demilitarized under the terms of the Treaty of Versailles. Hitler ordered the troops to fall back fighting if they encountered resistance from French, Belgian, and other forces in the area. They did not meet with opposition, and another piece of the Versailles settlement was shattered. For at least some German Jewish observers, this event signified that Hitler was in power to stay: he would neither be ousted by rivals within Germany nor removed by the victors of the past war.[85] The misery of Jews in Germany deepened, and consolidation of all police forces in the hands of Heinrich Himmler, Reich leader of the ss, only made matters worse.

In a 1937 meeting with leaders of the German army, navy, and air force, Hitler announced his plans for a series of wars to get "living space" for the German people. He identified Czechoslovakia as his

first target. When some military leaders showed insufficient enthusiasm for imminent war, Hitler removed them from their posts and
pushed forward with his plans. Even Renate Fischer, a young girl at
the time, could not help but notice Germany's preparations for war.
In 1936 and 1937 she vacationed at a Jewish resort in Swinemünde,
on the Baltic Sea. By then, Jews were banned from public and most
private beaches, and in Fischer's words, were "really isolated even in
where we could spend vacation time." Swinemünde, she says, was
rather frightening:

> The lodge where I stayed with my grandmother sat opposite of
> Peenemünde. And that's where the Germans were building their
> U-boats and we could see the white boats in the harbor, across
> the water. And we were well aware of the fact that in 1937, there
> were definite attempts at getting ready for a war. I still see in my
> mind's eye the very white painted ships against very gray waters.
> And rather frightening looking, they looked like sharks.[86]

Now that he was armed with a military, Hitler found ways to use
it. The new Luftwaffe had its first trials in the Spanish Civil War,
where the Germans sided with General Franco and gained infamy
for the bombing of Guernica in January 1937. In addition to flex-
ing Nazi muscle, involvement in Spain allowed Hitler to test the
resolve of the Western powers, the loyalty of the German military
leadership, and the strength of his domestic support. The results in
all three regards emboldened him. A wave of Nazi propaganda sold
involvement in the Spanish Civil War to Germans back home by
painting the defenders of the Spanish Republic as bloodthirsty athe-
ists, anarchists, communists, and Jews. This reversal of roles – presenting Jews as if they were aggressors rather than victims of Hitler's
Germany – would become a hallmark of Nazi antisemitism at war. It
eased the way for Christian leaders, Catholic and Protestant, to join
the anti-communist and anti-Jewish "crusade." The war in Spain
also deepened the marginalization of Germany's Jews by polarizing
the international situation and spreading the lie that all Jews were
Bolsheviks and all Bolsheviks were Jews. The fact that there were
practically no Jews in Spain and had not been since the expulsions of
the fifteenth century did not deter antisemites. Instead, their conspiracy mentality turned the invisibility of Jews into proof of ubiquitous,
concealed Jewish influence.

A cartoon in *L'Unité Montréal* in April 1937 captured the Canadian version of these accusations. It showed a farmer about to be guillotined beneath the hammer and sickle and the Star of David. Nearby, two caricatured figures meant to represent Jews – dark hair, suits, long noses – celebrate with glee. In Canada and Quebec, the accompanying text commented, it was "well known that all 'humanitarian,' 'popular,' or 'international' movements are covers for the 'communist plague' now devastating Russia, Spain, and Mexico."[87]

German newspapers delighted in detailing attacks on Jewish organizations and public antisemitic slurs in Maurice Duplessis's Quebec. In January 1938 headlines in Berlin and Franconia proclaimed "Racial Awakening!" and "Cleaning House!" in Canada. The accompanying story reported that Premier Duplessis had ordered police to search the offices of the Canadian Labour Circle, said to be a Jewish organization, where they had seized eight hundred communist books "written in Yiddish." This was only a first step against Jews in Quebec, the papers predicted: "Recently windows of many Jewish stores in Montreal have been shattered."[88]

1938–1939: NAZI EXPANSION, JEWISH DESPERATION

By 1938, Jews in Germany must have thought their situation could not get any worse. But it did. That year brought the massive expansion of Nazi power into Austria and Czechoslovakia, unprecedented levels of public violence against Jews, and further depths of Jewish despair. Now it was not only German Jews but Jews from Austria and, after early 1939, the newly created Protectorate of Bohemia and Moravia who lost their citizenship, jobs, livelihoods, and homes; who inundated relatives and strangers abroad with pleas for help; who crowded the embassies and consulates of Europe seeking visas; who hawked their furniture, jewellery, and whatever else they could sell to pay for bribes, exit taxes, train and ship fares, and smugglers' fees. Meanwhile, news of Nazi triumphs and of international refusals to admit refugees gave Jews in Europe ever more concrete grounds to abandon hope.

"It was a very unhappy time of my life," recalls Renate Fischer. Everything was unsettled, as mounting prohibitions and the reality of separation closed in on her family: "I was started in the Jewish school ... and all children there were Jewish. All, or most everyone was trying to leave and ... we were losing people every day ... This was a large school, and almost all the children there were being prepared, really, to leave the country. Hebrew was very big in the curriculum and I was painfully inadequate. I did not like the school. I only made two friends." Fischer's father was forced to start a new practice limited to Jewish patients. On the side, he began concocting beauty creams and lotions to sell. Both her parents took English lessons, and to make ends meet, her grandmother rented out rooms, only to Jews, of course. Garson Frankel, Silesia's largest toy store, run by the family since 1826 and named for Fischer's great-grandfather, was "Aryanized," "at the point of a gun."[89]

Among her keepsakes, Fischer's grandmother had a telegram she had received on her wedding day from relatives in Canada. Now, decades later, she revived the connection. A Canadian cousin agreed to help her son and his family, but as Fischer remembers, "not monetarily because it was in the late 30's and Canada was still reeling, as the States, I know, must have been after the depression, and really no one had much of anything." The cousin ran a small institute where he treated alcoholics. By Fischer's account, it took more than his sponsorship to get them into Canada:

> Fortunately, his daughter ... had a friend who was extremely well-to-do. He was in the manufacturing business of men's suits, and at the time just before the war, was starting to get contracts for army uniforms, and apparently had an in politically speaking. And Jack took it upon himself, and I think I'm right in saying this, that he went up to Ottawa to see whether there was some way of expediting bringing us into Canada. Well, Canada had the law, of course, that only farmers and physicians could come in, and the other law, the law stated that, if after a year's time, the person could not make it on their own in Canada, they would be sent back. So it was a trial run, so to speak. In addition to fulfilling that, the person also had to bring 3200 dollars with them, which at that point in time I guess must have been a fair amount of money. And it took many months to actually get the permission to come.[90]

Fischer was not alone in believing it took political connections to get into Canada. Jacob Wiener remembers that his father made contact with a cousin in Canada, a farmer in Yorkton, Saskatchewan. The cousin knew a Saskatchewan MP who, Wiener says, "made a special law for us to come in" and sent the necessary landing card.[91]

In Canada, Immigration was a division of the Department of Mines and Resources. Its priorities had everything to do with the need for labour and nothing to do with humanitarian relief. Nor were the people who set its policies free of prejudice. In 1938 the Canadian immigration authorities announced that entry of Jews from Europe for the year would be restricted to fifty farm families. The Nazi German press heralded this news as proof of Canadian antisemitism. "The Jew Must Go to the Farm," one headline proclaimed. "This looks to us like a deliberate prevention of Jewish immigration, a measure that is absolutely understandable," gloated the authors of the article. "There has never been a productive Jewish farming effort" and there never would be "because the Jew does not want to produce value. Now it appears that they have grasped this in Canada."[92]

In fact, contrary to widespread assumptions, there were Jews involved in agriculture, not only in Germany but elsewhere in Europe, most numerously in Subcarpathian Rus' – the borderlands in part and at times controlled and claimed by Czechoslovakia, Hungary, Poland, Slovakia, and Ukraine.[93] Those admitted to Canada as Jewish farmers in 1938 included Wilma Iggers and her family from Czechoslovakia. Her father, owner of a large, successful agricultural enterprise in western Bohemia, had organized a group of thirty-nine people to settle on farms in Ontario. He would have preferred France, but in the crisis of autumn 1938 it proved impossible. Now the Canadian immigration permits he had received for his group of farmers, among them a Swiss cattle-breeding expert, provided the only option. "We suspected," recalled Wilma Iggers, "that the Canadian immigration authorities had hoped to avoid taking in Jews. It does not seem to have occurred to them that there were Jewish farmers."[94] Concerned Canadians recognized the measure as intentionally exclusive. In September 1938, A.A. Heaps, MP for Winnipeg and one of three Jews in the House of Commons, wrote to Prime Minister Mackenzie King warning that Canada's restrictive immigration policy made the country look antisemitic.[95] He did not receive a response.

Meanwhile, details of the prohibitive Canadian position circulated within Europe, most urgently among Jews. In October 1938 a German-language newspaper in Budapest carried a story, likely based on Canadian sources, with the headline "Canada – A Rich Land with Troubles." Above all, Canada needed people for agriculture, the article observed, and it gave the address of the Canadian Immigration Office in Antwerp for anyone interested. But farmers in Canada were very poor, the article warned, and crop yields in 1937 had been disastrous. Political conditions in Canada also received a critical review: the country suffered internal divisions, the provinces were battling one another, and Premier Aberhart of Alberta was ruining his province's finances. It was unclear whether the demographic sketch provided was meant to attract or deter would-be immigrants: "Some of the Indians have been exterminated [*ausgerottet*] and the rest pushed back into the woods"; there had never been a significant immigration of "coloured people"; and most of the "Anglos" remained deeply loyal to Britain.[96]

The few Jews who managed to enter Canada through the farming loophole had widely divergent experiences. One man from a village in Poland landed on a farm near Sundance, Alberta, where at the age of forty he cleared 160 acres of land with an axe.[97] A group of Jews with considerable agricultural experience in Silesia and Czechoslovakia started the flax industry in Ontario. Brothers Henry and Walter Segalowitz, together with the Czechoslovak refugee Frank Morawetz, established two flax mills in the Ottawa area, though they did not get to Canada without obstacles, as Henry Segalowitz indicated in a 1944 interview: "I know men who had money, who had ability, and who had big positions in their homeland, who were refused admission to Canada, so I think I was lucky to get here."[98] In one Jewish household, the sixteen-year-old daughter succeeded in prying visas for the whole family from the Canadian consulate in Cologne. They ended up on a dairy farm in Ontario, a severe hardship for her parents, but she loved it.[99] Another woman's interview is marked by her repeated insistence that it was "horrendous" on the farm; her father had a nervous breakdown.[100]

Inside Germany, the many and at times conflicting stipulations about what Jews were and were not permitted to do gave the authorities carte blanche to do as they wished. Every account from Jews who managed to get out has its particularities. Almost all paid a hefty Reich flight tax of at least 25 percent of their assets,[101] but some had to add weighty bribes, and everyone lost precious possessions to greedy officials. A long and ever-changing list of valuable things, including foreign currency, could not be removed from the country at all. Fischer recalls that the authorities allowed her family to take only "old things." Her grandmother gave them her furniture because it could be certified as "old," and her father's tailor sewed labels into his suits to indicate they had been made at least ten years earlier. Two armed Nazis supervised the packing: "I remember very, very well," said Fischer, we "were in our little downstairs gardener's apartment with lots and lots of boxes on the floor, these two men with guns watching as my father packed all the books. And whenever they liked a book – and they particularly liked my children's books, they just helped themselves. And they helped themselves to some of my father's stamps too, and there wasn't a thing we could do about it."[102]

In March 1938, Hitler took a major gamble to annex Austria. Wehrmacht units streamed across the border, unopposed by Austrian or international forces and greeted by euphoric crowds. Although ill prepared – German tanks reportedly had to stop en route to refuel at commercial gas stations – the *Anschluss* was a tremendous success for the Nazi regime. It was also the final blow to the system created by the Treaty of Versailles, which explicitly forbade a union of Germany and Austria. This time, Jews bore the full brunt of German aggression. Measures that had been introduced over the course of five years in Germany were swept in overnight in Austria with the eager help and often on the initiative of local gentiles. Vienna, 10 percent of whose residents were Jewish, erupted in pogroms. Mobs robbed, plundered, and assaulted Jews and their property, and staged public humiliations.[103] Thugs forced Jews to clean public toilets with their hands, scrub streets with toothbrushes, sing and dance as onlookers jeered. In some cases the targets were prominent people – public figures, employers, professors, and neighbours of those who abused them – though Jews of all kinds were hit. In a city plagued by housing shortages, Jews' homes were often the first thing stolen from them.[104]

The *Anschluss* added almost 200,000 people to the ranks of Jews desperate to escape Nazi rule. Overnight it rendered Austrian Jews stateless. On the other side of what had been the border, Victor Klemperer was terrified by the confluence of Nazi triumph, international indifference, and brutal antisemitism. "The last few weeks have been the most wretched of our life so far," he wrote in his diary on 20 March 1938. "The immense act of violence of the annexation of Austria, the immense increase in power both internally and externally, the defenceless trembling fear of England, France, etc. We shall not live to see the end of the Third Reich ... *Der Stürmer* [a Nazi newspaper] has dug up its usual ritual murder; I would truly not be surprised if next I were to find the body of a child in the garden."[105]

Under pressure to address the looming refugee crisis, American officials called an international conference at Evian in France for July 1938.[106] It brought no relief; no nation, certainly not Canada, wanted to take in the German and Austrian Jews. Only the Dominican Republic agreed to admit a substantial number of refugees, but in the circumstances, only about seven hundred people were ever able to take up the offer.[107] For Hitler, the outcome of Evian confirmed the absolute isolation of his Jewish victims and proved that he could act against them with impunity. Meanwhile, the widespread belief that Jews were omnipotent international conspirators remained unshaken by the demonstrated fact that Jewish Germans and Austrians found no government anywhere willing to come to their aid.

Emboldened, Hitler took another step toward war. This time his focus was the Sudetenland, a border region of Czechoslovakia with a significant ethnic German population. Urged on by Germany, local Nazis accused the Czech government of violating their minority rights.[108] Representatives of the European powers agreed to meet in Munich in the autumn of 1938 to address the crisis. The result has become known as "appeasement": British, French, and Italian leaders agreed that Czechoslovakia should cede the contested area to Germany, expecting that this would satisfy Hitler's expansionist aims. Of course, this was not the case.

Since the debacle of the Second World War, the policy of appeasement has become a symbol of the weakness, cowardice, and failure of will of the Western powers. But it is important to keep in mind that Hitler also viewed the settlement agreed upon at Munich as a mistake. Indeed, he soon came to believe that he had been cheated out of war in 1938 at a moment when Germany held the advantage over a weak Czechoslovakia and unprepared Britain and France.[109] Once he decided on war against Poland in 1939, he made sure the same thing would not happen. This time there would be no negotiations that might lead to compromise, nor would pusillanimous voices at home be allowed to raise doubts about the prospect of German success. In the wake of the Munich Conference,

Hitler purged the German military leadership, removing those who had been insufficiently enthusiastic about his plans. Police arrested a group of Protestant pastors who had read a prayer for peace from the pulpit during the Sudetenland crisis, and the propaganda industry unleashed a massive campaign to prime the population for war. Increased attacks on Jews and efforts to expel them from the country were part of these preparations.

This offensive culminated in the Kristallnacht pogrom of 9–10 November 1938. A month earlier the German government had expelled 14,000 Jews who resided in Germany but held Polish citizenship. Among them were the parents and sister of Herschel Grynszpan, a seventeen-year-old student living in Paris. Grynszpan read about the situation in French newspapers and learned details of his family's ordeal in a postcard from his sister. Days later, he went to the German Embassy and shot an official. For the Nazi leadership, this incident provided the excuse for a violent assault against Jews. All over Germany, which now included Austria and the Sudetenland, storm troopers and local helpers torched synagogues and violated ritual objects; they smashed the windows of businesses owned by Jews, vandalized and stole Jewish property, and attacked Jewish homes, forcing their way in, robbing, beating, raping, and destroying. Local Nazi Party leaders received their orders by telephone down the chain of command from Berlin. In some cases they misunderstood instructions, in others they seized the opportunity to settle old scores. At least one hundred Jews were killed during Kristallnacht, and many died afterward as a result of injuries and trauma.[110]

Jews of all ages, no matter where they were, felt the scourge of Kristallnacht. "That was the worst thing in the world," remembers Jacob Wiener, whose mother was shot and killed in Bremen during the pogrom.[111] In Hanover, ten-year-old Gerhard Weinberg was devastated by the destruction of the city's beautiful synagogue.[112] In the Rhine Valley, Susanne Weilbach's schoolteacher permitted children to watch through the window as men they knew, perhaps their own fathers, taunted and beat their Jewish neighbours. Her father was among those arrested, and he returned a broken man.[113] Horace Philipp, ten years old in 1938 and living in Schneidemühl (today known as Piła in Poland), remembers the terror of domestic wreckage: "We were sent out to the yard – came back and saw the pieces of furniture damaged, dishes, china pulled out of cupboards and smashed." His father, a master tailor, had a cousin in Canada who provided an affidavit for the family, and four months later they arrived in Montreal.[114]

In November 1938 Renate Fischer was already in Canada, but the pogrom affected her too: "We probably learned about it through the radio, and of course knew at once that if synagogues were the targets, ours, both in Ratibor and in Breslau were undoubtedly part of the picture, and indeed they were." Her parents, she recalls, were "just speechless with the news that was coming in. I still see us sitting around the radio, the whole family, and really despairing."[115]

During and immediately after the pogrom, German police arrested thirty thousand Jewish men and sent them to concentration camps: Dachau, Sachsenhausen, Buchenwald. There they were held hostage while their wives and families scrambled to gather funds and arrange to leave the country. Over the next months, thousands of Jewish women tried to get their men released, selling homes, businesses, jewellery, and possessions of all kinds for whatever price they could get; waiting at consulates and embassies in the hope of obtaining visas, and using every charm, connection, and resource they could muster.

Family members outside Germany also tried to help. Gerhard Maass, from Hamburg, arrived in Canada on 3 November 1938, the twenty-year-old employee of a Swedish firm. Rather than feeling relief to be safely across the Atlantic, he was traumatized by the news from Germany – so frightened that he could neither work nor think. He had come to Canada with no idea of what it was like, what he would need, or how long he would stay. The enormous container of furniture, including a grand piano, that his family managed to send him via Sweden became a heavy burden rather than the intended help. During Kristallnacht his father was arrested and sent to a concentration camp, and although his brother and cousins told him all about it in letters, he could do nothing. He took consolation in his brother's assurance that this was only a Nazi scare tactic; it would be "technically impossible," he reasoned, to arrest all the Jews in Hamburg. He did not realize, Maass says, that "such things could be preparation for worse things to come."[116]

Hundreds of Jewish men died in the camps, and many of those who were let out were unrecognizable to their families – physically debilitated and emotionally crushed. The authorities at the camps made them swear upon release never to speak of what they had suffered. Although silenced, these men acted on the terrible lessons they had learned as prisoners. Many who had previously been reluctant to leave Germany were now frantic to get out. It is no coincidence that the Kindertransport, which brought ten thousand unaccompanied Jewish children from Central Europe to England, took off after Kristallnacht. In hindsight, the biggest hurdle appears to have been persuading the British authorities to admit refugee children,[117] but of course Jewish parents had to be willing to send their children off into the unknown.

Anecdotal evidence and timing suggest that fathers who suffered Nazi incarceration were instrumental in making this wrenching decision. After Max S., a tailor in Berlin, was released from Dachau, he and his wife Golda arranged to put their two oldest sons, thirteen-year-old Heinz and nine-year-old Benno, on a train to Holland with nothing but tickets, a suitcase, and ten marks each. They hoped the boys would make contact with Jewish refugee aid organizations.[118] Indeed, the two boys escaped into Holland and from there joined a Kindertransport to England. Benno later settled in Canada. His parents and younger brother, who remained in Berlin, were murdered in Auschwitz. Another Jewish father from Cologne arranged for his teenaged daughter to go alone to Belgium. In mid-1939 he managed to get her and the rest of the family into Canada, but they entered as gentiles, not as Jews. As the daughter recalled in an interview, her father "was very busy with whoever he was dealing" and paid "a high price to get papers to get to Canada." The "original passport had Hebrew/Jew in it but that got taken out."[119]

Kristallnacht is usually regarded as the beginning of the end, the first blow of the Holocaust. Seen in context, however, it was a continuation and escalation of the interlocking processes of social death and isolation of Jews in Germany since 1933. Hitler's regime benefited in numerous ways from the putatively spontaneous but coordinated attack on Jews, Jewish property, and sites of Jewish worship and communal life. Impatient Nazis satisfied their thirst for violent action. German gentiles, initially uncomfortable with the crude tactics of their government, found that paying rock-bottom prices for property from Jews who were eager to get out of the country fostered a new loyalty to the Nazi system. Goebbels further sweetened the deal by making Jews pay for the material damage from the pogrom so that insurance prices for non-Jews would not rise. Meanwhile, the open attack served to stigmatize Jews as

dangerous outsiders. Still, people in Germany grumbled about public disorder, and international observers decried the violence. Why
were Hitler and Goebbels, generally so keen to maintain a positive
image at home and abroad, willing to take this public relations risk?
A key reason was their desire to force Jews out of Germany before
launching into war.[120] By Nazi logic, every Jew gone meant one less
traitor who would stab Germany in the back.

This line of reasoning exposes the bottomless pit and self-fulfilling
logic of Nazi antisemitism. The more than 200,000 Jews who fled
Germany between 1933 and 1939 settled where they could – elsewhere on the European continent or in Britain and its dominions, in
the United States, Palestine, China, the Caribbean, India, or Africa.
From these new homes, Nazi conspiracy theorists claimed, Jews
would plot against Germany and lead an international effort to
destroy the "Aryan race." By making it impossible for Jews to live in
Germany but simultaneously increasing their numbers abroad, Nazi
Germans fed their own paranoia about international enemies and
hardened their emerging conviction that what was needed was total
annihilation of the Jewish threat.

Even before Hitler's war began, it was an assault on the Jews. "Europe cannot find peace until the Jewish question has been solved,"
Hitler told the Reichstag on 30 January 1939, less than three months
after thugs had torched synagogues and pillaged the homes and businesses of Jews all over the enlarged Germany. The war, Hitler had
already decided, would begin that year. "In the course of my life I
have very often been a prophet," he proclaimed, "and have usually
been ridiculed for it." Now things were different, he said: "Today I
will once more be a prophet: if the international Jewish financiers
in and outside Europe should succeed in plunging the nations once
more into a world war, then the result will not be the bolshevizing of
the earth, and thus the victory of Jewry, but the annihilation of the
Jewish race in Europe!"[121] Later, Goebbels and others often quoted
this "prophecy," which they consistently misdated to coincide with
the German invasion of Poland on 1 September 1939. This mistake
revealed a sleight-of-hand, an attempt to cast Hitler's words as self-
defence, a response to attack, rather than a declaration of murder-
ous intent.

In March 1939, with the world distracted by Franco's recent victory in Spain, Hitler ordered the dismantling of what remained of
Czechoslovakia. The creation of a satellite state in Slovakia and
incorporation of Bohemia and Moravia into German rule as a so-

called protectorate added to the number of would-be refugees and increased the pressure on possible destinations.[122] It did not, however, cause doors for Jews to open in Canada[123] or, for that matter, anywhere else. Less than 10 percent of Jews from the territory of Czechoslovakia – some 26,000 people – managed to escape the Nazi trap through emigration.

Anyone who has ever been tempted to ask, "Why didn't the Jews leave?" will gain valuable insights from the memoir of Anka Voticky, a Czech Jew born in 1913.[124] She and members of her family showed enormous ingenuity and expended considerable time and money to devise plans for escape – to the United States, England, Palestine, Italy, and Yugoslavia. All came to naught until in 1940 they succeeded in reaching Shanghai, the only city in the world that permitted refugees to enter and take up residence without a visa.[125] Voticky and others in her circle of acquaintance sought and found havens on every continent, but even their creative and frenzied efforts, with very few exceptions, bypassed Canada. For Jews from Czech lands, among them Emil Beamt – a young man whose letters to his family chronicle his desperate search for an exit – Canada, if it featured in their plans at all, was ruled out, as a site of disappointment and rejection in those crucial months after March 1939, and closed tight once the war began.[126] After September 1939, people from German territories were deemed enemy aliens. Even Polish Jews, if they could somehow get out of Europe, had a better chance of getting into Canada than "Germans."[127]

In May 1939 the *St Louis*, a German transatlantic liner, set sail from Hamburg to Havana. On board were almost one thousand passengers, the overwhelming majority Jewish and all but one of them refugees.[128] When the ship arrived, Cuban authorities refused to allow the passengers to disembark. Some of their visas had been issued, against the orders of the Cuban government, by a diplomat who had enriched himself in the process, and there was vociferous opposition within Cuba to allowing in more refugees. For days the ship remained offshore while representatives of the passengers tried to negotiate with the Cubans or find another destination. Finally the *St Louis* left Havana. Sailing up the coast of Florida and then northward, its captain radioed to officials all along the way in the United States and Canada, but no one would permit the ship to dock.

After weeks at sea, the ship returned to Europe. Its protracted route bought Jewish organizations time to arrange refuge for all of the passengers – in Britain, France, Belgium, and the Netherlands.

Of the *St Louis* passengers who ended up in Britain, all but one, who died in an air raid, survived the war. However, nearly half of those who returned to the Continent were killed in the Holocaust. Susanne Weilbach, her parents, and grandfather were among the refugees who made it to England. Like Fred Mann, Benno S., and Anka Voticky, she came to Canada only after the war had ended.

By the time German forces invaded Poland on 1 September 1939,[129] over half of the Jews of Germany had fled. Instead of waning as Jews departed, antisemitism inside Hitler's Reich continued to intensify. Many non-Jewish Germans who had acquired homes, businesses, jobs, or promotions thanks to the expropriation or emigration of Jewish Germans discovered compelling reasons to hate Jews or at least to support policies against them. The widespread perception of Jews as fabulously wealthy meant that even gentiles who had not yet profited from the persecution and expulsion expected to do so and worried that criticism of the regime could cost them their share of the spoils. Given these circumstances, debates about how antisemitic "ordinary Germans" were somewhat miss the point. The Nazis in power offered powerful incentives for people to behave like antisemites even if they did not share that world view.

War raised the stakes of Nazi antisemitism in every possible way. Most obvious, it multiplied almost tenfold the number of Jews under German rule. It also meant that those Jews who had made it to Canada were totally cut off from their families. They had to try to find ways to communicate, because sending letters directly was forbidden. In the fall of 1939, the RCMP paid a visit to Gerry Maass in the Jewish General Hospital in Montreal after he almost lost his foot in an accident at work. If he tried to send another letter to Germany, they warned him, he would be deported. Years later, Maass struggles to describe his state of mind at the time: "How to explain? To be a man without a country in a strange country ... I was on my own. I was frantic."[130]

Renate Fischer found her world "totally consumed with the war":

My father used to keep a map on the wall and punch pins into where the Germans were ... how the forces were progressing, both into the east zone towards Russia, as well as through France and into Holland. And we would listen to news every night, of course, and as many times during the day as there were news on ... It was the most trying of times because my father was trying to tell people in Canada what was happening and nobody listened. My father brought out clippings from newspapers, German newspapers ... He hid them in the linings of the suitcases, to show the powers that be on this side of the ocean what was happening because nobody was listening and nobody wanted to believe what was going on.[131]

Of the Jews left behind in Germany after 1939, only a few thousand survived the war. Almost all of them, like Victor Klemperer, were adults married to non-Jews.[132] Amid the persecution and international upheaval that engulfed Jews under German rule in the prewar years, Canada was not much help.[133] Nevertheless, for those Jews from Germany, Austria, and Czechoslovakia who managed to get there, it made the difference between life and death.

Still, reaching Canada offered no miraculous happy ending. When Renate Fischer and her parents arrived in July 1938, they encountered new challenges and found that pain from the past had come with them:

> I should mention to you that the day that we did in fact land in Montreal, I woke up and could not move. I had total paralysis of both my legs and my father had to carry me off the boat. This happened twice in my life. This was the first time, and the second time it happened was as a student in 1948. I was on an international student service seminar and I had the opportunity to go back to Germany and the same thing happened. I woke up paralyzed from my waist down. The paralysis did not last very long. My father carried me off the boat. The relatives were there to meet us. And in a day the paralysis was gone. I think they call this a hysterical paralysis, which it undoubtedly was. I was terribly frightened.[134]

In the circumstances, Fischer's family fared about as well as could be expected. Her mother, an adverturesome spirit, threw herself into the new life. Her father, initially unable to find work, fell into depression. He tried to join the army and the medical corps but was turned down as a non-citizen. All his efforts to get the grandmothers out of Germany failed. Finally he found a position as an intern in a hospital in Saint John, New Brunswick, where he spent the war years separated from his wife and daughter in Montreal, a difficult situation, as

Fischer recalls: "He went through a horrible period of time in which his life was made miserable by the powers that be because they considered him an enemy alien whom they suspected of being a spy. The Mounties came to visit him one day and he said, take the cameras, because they were afraid that he was photographing installations on the seacoast of New Brunswick ... And it was not an easy time in Canada. It was not."[135] After the war, Fischer's parents adopted a Jewish refugee, a boy from Poland, and later brought the two surviving members of his family to Canada. In this and other ways they pushed back against the powerlessness, isolation, and loss they had endured.

The years 1933 to 1939 were of fateful significance for the Jews of Germany, Austria, and Czechoslovakia. After Hitler came to power in 1933, he led Germany on a course toward war, a war that would mean the conquest and occupation of almost all of Europe, the murder of millions of Jews, and the destruction of Jewish communities from Amsterdam to Vilna, Kiev, Warsaw, Salonika, and Budapest. By the time the Second World War began in 1939, it was extremely difficult for the targets of Nazi attack to escape Europe, and the fall of France in 1940 and German invasion of the Soviet Union a year later made exit all but impossible. But flight from Hitler's Reich was an option for at least some Jews in Central Europe during the six "peacetime" years of Nazi rule in Germany, and around 300,000 German, Austrian, and Czech Jews seized the opportunities they found to flee. Their economic, legal, and social marginalization within Germany (and after 1938 and 1939 in annexed Austria and German-controlled Czechoslovakia) pushed them out at the same time as it robbed them of the resources and contacts they needed in order to leave and start new lives. Meanwhile, Hitler's foreign policy, world events, and widespread antisemitism combined to isolate Jews, as pariahs within Germany and as unwanted, stateless refugees elsewhere.

Canada was a minor yet typical part of the hostile world that surrounded Jews in the prewar Nazi years. According to contemporary and postwar accounts, it rarely featured in the calculations of those seeking haven. Cold, distant, and known to have a restrictive immigration policy, Canada was a site of rejection for all but 2,000 of the European Jews who pursued it as a destination before the war began in September 1939. Those Jews who did manage to get in brought with them a desperate urge to know what was happening to the relatives and friends they had left behind. Through their physical presence and their efforts to communicate, they embodied the many ways in which Canada, though far from the sites of the Holocaust, was nevertheless part of this history.

NOTES

1 On the history of Jews in Breslau, see van Rahden, *Jews and Other Germans: Civil Society, Religious Diversity, and Urban Politics in Breslau, 1860–1925.*

2 Interview with Renate Fischer Chernoff, 23 June 2005, sound recording and transcript in United States Holocaust Memorial Museum archives (hereafter USHMM), RG–50.106*0166, pp. 1–7, 28. For the sake of clarity, in some of the passages quoted I have made small adjustments to the transcript – for example, removing words that appear twice. These edits do not alter the meaning. Many thanks to Vincent Slatt, Reference Library at the USHMM, for drawing my attention to the interview with Renate Fischer Chernoff and many of the other items used in this chapter.

3 It is impossible to know exactly how many Jews from Germany and German-annexed and -controlled territories entered Canada between 1933 and 1939. According to a contemporary source, by late 1945 there were 3,500 Jewish refugees in Canada, but this number included people "brought to Canada by the Canadian Jewish Congress from Spain, Portugal and Tangiers, those who came through Japan and refugees who were released in Canada after they had been interned in Great Britain as technically 'enemy aliens' after Dunkirk." See news release, Press Office of the Canadian Jewish Congress, November 1945, in USHMM, LMO365 (Testaments to the Holocaust, series 2, Wiener Library thematic press cuttings), reel 151, file 195. Abella and Troper estimate that a total of 4,000 Jews from all over Europe entered Canada between 1933 and 1939 (Abella and Troper, "'The Line Must Be Drawn Somewhere': Canada and Jewish Refugees, 1933–9," 181). A valuable overview and contextualization is Dwork and van Pelt, *Flight from the Reich: Refugee Jews, 1933–1946.*

4 The insight stems from Patterson, *Slavery and Social Death.*

5 Kaplan, *Between Dignity and Despair: Jewish Life in Nazi Germany*, esp. 5, 235–9.

6 The notion of Jewish entrapment is a theme in Aronson, *Hitler, the Allies, and the Jews.*

7 S. Friedländer, *Nazi Germany and the Jews, 1933–1945*, 4. Friedländer gives 525,000 as the number of Jews in Germany in 1933.

8   Rome, "Canadian Jewish Activities in '43," in *Jewish Press*, New Year's
     Edition [1944], USHMM, LM0365, reel 151, file 195. Rome gives the figure
     of 156,726 Jews in Canada in 1931, which he computes to be 1.5 percent
     of the population. By 1943 the number of Jews had increased to 176,130,
     but as a share of the population it had fallen to 1.47 percent.

9   On the significance of Zionism within Germany on the eve of Nazism,
     see Berkowitz, *Western Jewry and the Zionist Project, 1914–1933*. For a
     look at one acculturated family, see the memoir by Peter Gay, *My German
     Question: Growing Up in Nazi Berlin*. On German Jewish cultural, eco-
     nomic, and organizational life under Nazi rule, see Benz, *Die Juden in
     Deutschland 1933–1945. Leben unter nationalsozialistischer Herrschaft*.
     A useful overview is Ruth Gay, *The Jews of Germany: A Historical
     Portrait*.

10   For a look at one rural German Jewish family, see Weilbach, *Singing from
     the Darktime: A Childhood Memoir in Poetry and Prose*.

11   On antisemitism as part of German intellectual history, see the classic
     work by George L. Mosse, *Germans and Jews: The Right, the Left, and
     the Search for a "Third Force" in Pre-Nazi Germany*.

12   The notion of a uniquely German eliminationist antisemitism is developed
     in Goldhagen, *Hitler's Willing Executioners*.

13   But see analysis in Bering, *The Stigma of Names: Antisemitism in German
     Daily Life, 1812–1933*.

14   On Preuss, see Jacobson and Schlink, *Weimar: A Jurisprudence of Crisis*,
     esp. 110–27.

15   For more on Rathenau, see Fink, "The Murder of Walther Rathenau."

16   Clipping from *Canadian Jewish Chronicle*, byline Jewish Telegraphic
     Agency, 31 December 1943, in USHMM, LM0365, reel 151, file 195.

17   Press release of the Canadian Jewish Congress, September 1945, clipping
     in USHMM, LM0365, reel 151, file 195.

18   On Hitler's world view, see essays in Weinberg, *Germany, Hitler, and
     World War II*.

19   Klemperer, *I Will Bear Witness: A Diary of the Nazi Years, 1933–1941*.

20   "Margot S., July 1990," in Lindeman, *Shards of Memory: Narratives of
     Holocaust Survival*, 150.

21   Ibid., 151.

22   Popular support for Nazism is analyzed in Fritzsche, *Life and Death in the
     Third Reich*.

23   Lindemann and Levy, *Antisemitism: A History*.

24   Aspects of Nazi antisemitic propaganda are analyzed in Herf, *The Jewish
     Enemy: Nazi Propaganda during World War II and the Holocaust*; also

in Berkowitz, *The Crime of My Very Existence: Nazism and the Myth of Jewish Criminality*.

25 Friedländer accordingly labels Hitler's antisemitism "redemptive antisemitism" (S. Friedländer, "Redemptive Antisemitism in Its Epoch," 75–114).

26 See Kershaw, *Hitler*, vol. 1: *1889–1936*. The importance of grassroots organizing to the spread of Nazism is highlighted in Allen, *The Nazi Seizure of Power*.

27 On development of the so-called Euthanasia Program, see H. Friedlander, *The Origins of Nazi Genocide*.

28 For a discussion of various target groups, see Gellately and Stoltzfus, *Social Outsiders in Nazi Germany*.

29 Aly, *Hitler's Beneficiaries: Plunder, Racial War, and the Nazi Welfare State*. Also relevant here, although critical of Aly, is Tooze, *The Wages of Destruction: The Making and Breaking of the Nazi Economy*.

30 Weilbach, *Singing from the Darktime*.

31 On the dynamics of the boycott in one major city, see Bajohr, *"Aryanisation" in Hamburg: The Economic Exclusion of the Jews and the Confiscation of Their Property in Nazi Germany*, 28–34.

32 On the Nazi use of trial balloons, see Bergen, *The Holocaust: A Concise History*, esp. 52–68.

33 Gellately, *Backing Hitler: Consent and Coercion in Nazi Germany*.

34 Ericksen, *Complicity in the Killing? German Churches, German Universities, and the Holocaust*.

35 Letter from D. Wilhelm Freiherr von Pechmann to Reich Bishop Ludwig Müller, Munich, 2 April 1934, in Wilhelm Niemoeller Collection, Landeskirchenarchiv Bielefeld, Germany.

36 Local dynamics and the intimacy of rural communities could also work in favour of Jews. For discussion of Nazism in the countryside, see Stephenson, *Hitler's Home Front: Württemberg under the Nazis*.

37 S. Friedländer, *Nazi Germany*, vol. 1: *Years of Persecution*, 64.

38 Nicosia, *Zionism and Anti-Semitism in Nazi Germany*.

39 Anne Frank's matter-of-fact description hinted that the family's move had its complications. In an entry from 20 June 1942 she provided this sketch: "I lived in Frankfurt until I was four. Because we're Jewish, my father immigrated to Holland in 1933, when he became the Managing Director of the Dutch Optekta Company, which manufactures products used in making jam. My mother, Edith Holländer Frank, went with him to Holland in September, while Margot and I were sent to Aachen to stay with our grandmother. Margot went to Holland in December, and I followed in February" (Frank, *The Diary of a Young Girl*, 7).

40   Waterford, *Commitment to the Dead: One Woman's Journey toward Understanding*, 8–16.

41   Among the Jews from Germany who left for Spain in 1933 were Max and Toni Ringel and their children. Born in Galicia, the Ringels had moved to Germany before the First World War. When the Civil War broke out in Spain, the family was dispersed, with some members ending up in hiding in Amsterdam, others in England and the United States. Toni Ringel used her diary to try to bridge the painful separation from her children (Garbarini, *Numbered Days: Diaries in the Holocaust*, 105–7).

42   Mosse, *Confronting History: A Memoir*, 44.

43   For example, the family of David Rubin, who was born in Warsaw in 1922, moved to Vancouver in 1933 but returned to Poland in 1938. His mother had left her entire family behind and missed them terribly; his father, a Royalist and admirer of the British navy, could not imagine that Germany would ever prevail over Britain. David Rubin, interviewed in Australia in 1997, Shoah Foundation no. 35317, accessed at USHMM.

44   *Dent's Teachers' Aid* 4, no. 1 (September 1935): 4–12, in USHMM, LMO365, reel 20, file 33.

45   Evans, *The Third Reich in Power, 1933–1939*, 85.

46   In his diary entry for 14 July 1934, regarding the Röhm Putsch, Klemperer wrote: "And how nauseating. In the reports at the beginning of July the pederast group was pushed into the foreground. As if only they had 'mutinied,' as if Hitler were a moral cleanser ... But of course Fräulein von Rüdiger & Co. will now believe with a vengeance in their heaven-sent pure Führer" (Klemperer, *I Will Bear Witness*, 75).

47   Clipping, *Westdeutscher Beobachter*, Aachen, 1 August 1935, headline "Jüdische Rasse feuergefährlich!" in USHMM, LMO365, reel 20, file 33, "Canada – August 1935 – March 1939." All translations from German are my own unless otherwise specified.

48   On the press in Nazi Germany, its role in anti-Jewish measures, and Jewish readership, see Pegelow Kaplan, *The Language of Nazi Genocide: Linguistic Violence and the Struggle of Germans of Jewish Ancestry*.

49   Sbacchi, *Legacy of Bitterness: Ethiopia and Fascist Italy, 1935–1941*.

50   Contrary to the impression created by Rigg in *Hitler's Jewish Soldiers*, there were no Jews serving in the Wehrmacht, though men with some Jewish ancestry, who did not count under Nazi racial laws as Jews, did serve.

51   Angress, "The German Army's 'Judenzählung' of 1916 – Genesis – Consequences – Significance."

52   On Canada, see Rome, "Canadian Jewish Activities in '43," *Jewish Press*, New Year's edition [1944]; clipping in USHMM, LMO365, reel 151, file

195. Rome refers to the "libel that Jews are not enlisting in numbers that accord with their population." He reports almost 11,000 Jews in the services; Jews made up 3 percent of the membership of some branches, he indicates, though their portion of the total population was only 1.5 percent. On the United States, see Bendersky, *The "Jewish Threat": Anti-Semitic Politics of the U.S. Army*. On the Soviet Union, see Altshuler, "Jewish Warfare and the Participation of Jews in Combat in the Soviet Union as Reflected in Soviet and Western Historiography," and Budnitsky, "The 'Jewish Battalions' in the Red Army."

53 An example is the article "Juden in der kanadischen Armee" [Jews in the Canadian Army], *Israelitisches Wochenblatt für die Schweiz* 39 (27 September 1940), including the following statement: "Jews are present in the different divisions of the Canadian Army in very significant numbers. Although exact statistics are not available from the Canadian government, one sees Jewish soldiers everywhere. Some Jewish families have two or three soldiers. Among the Jewish soldiers of Canada are also young Jews from the United States, who volunteer for military service in Canada." In late 1944, sources in Canada reported a figure of more than 15,000 Jewish men and women in the Canadian armed forces; over 300 were reported to have fallen, and 41 had been awarded decorations or honours ("Jews in Services Receive Messages," Montreal *Gazette*, October 1944). By late 1945 the figures were updated to 701 Canadian Jewish casualties and 122 decorated: "Update on War: Jewish Contribution," news release, September 1945, Press Office of the Canadian Jewish Congress – United Jewish Refugee and War Relief Agencies and War Efforts Committee of the Canadian Jewish Congress. All three clippings are in USHMM, LMO365, reel 151, file 195.

54 Documents on the Nuremberg Laws in Noakes and Pridham, *Nazism 1919–1945*, 3:530–41.

55 Szobar, "Telling Sexual Secrets in the Nazi Courts of Law: Race Defilement in Germany, 1933 to 1945."

56 See accounts in Engelmann, *Inside Hitler's Germany*.

57 On the wider phenomenon, see Fitzpatrick and Gellately, *Accusatory Practices: Denunciation in Modern European History, 1789–1989*.

58 Mann, *A Drastic Turn of Destiny*, 22.

59 On the widely varying outcomes of marriages between German Jews and Christians under the pressures of Nazism, see Stoltzfus, *Resistance of the Heart: Intermarriage and the Rosenstrasse Protest in Nazi Germany*, and Kueter, *My Tainted Blood*.

60 Ascher, *Afterimages: A Family Memoir*, 35.

61 Iggers and Iggers, *Two Lives in Uncertain Times: Facing the Challenges of the Twentieth Century as Scholars and Citizens*, 28. Georg Iggers was ten at the time, so the incident occurred in 1937 or late 1936.

62 Weilbach, *Singing from the Darktime*.

63 Fischer Chernoff transcript, 63, USHMM.

64 Gruner, "The German Council of Municipalities (Deutscher Gemeindetag) and the Coordination of Anti-Jewish Local Politics in the Nazi State."

65 One German Jewish family's correspondence across the continents is presented in Boehling and Larkey, *Life and Loss in the Shadow of the Holocaust: A Jewish Family's Untold Story*.

66 Goeschel, *Suicide in Nazi Germany*.

67 Fischer Chernoff transcript, 52, USHMM.

68 On Belzec, see Hilberg, *The Destruction of the European Jews*.

69 On transports of German and Austrian Jews to Riga, see Schneider, *Journey into Terrror: Story of the Riga Ghetto*.

70 Quoted in Bergen, "Storm Troopers of Christ: The German Christian Movement and the Ecclesiastical Final Solution," 40. On the German Christian movement, see also Bergen, *Twisted Cross: The German Christian Movement in the Third Reich*, and Heschel, *The Aryan Jesus: Christian Theologians and the Bible in Nazi Germany*.

71 See the important work of Beate Meyer, "Der Traum von einer autonomen jüdischen Verwaltung – Die Reichsvereinigung der Juden in Deutschland, Auswanderer und Zurückbleibende in den Jahren 1938/39 bis 1941," and "Between Self-Assertion and Forced Collaboration: The Reich Association of Jews in Germany, 1939–1945."

72 Heim, "Reaktionen internationaler jüdischer Hilfsorganisationen auf die Situation der deutschen Juden."

73 Iggers and Iggers, *Two Lives*, 26; see also Weilbach, *Singing from the Darktime*.

74 Jacob Wiener interview, 8 February 1996, transcript, USHMM, oral history interviews, RG–50.030 0425, p. 7. For more information, see Jacob Wiener, born 1917, Bremen, interviewed 1998, Shoah Foundation no. 21349, accessed at USHMM. Wiener came to Canada with four members of his family in May 1939.

75 S. Friedländer, *Nazi Germany*, vol. 1: *Years of Persecution*, 64, gives the numbers of German Jews leaving as 23,000 (1934); 21,000 (1935); 25,000 (1936); and 23,000 (1937).

76 For details on the financial restrictions and penalties for Jews seeking to leave Germany in this period, see Dean, *Robbing the Jews: The Confiscation of Jewish Property in the Holocaust, 1933–1945*, 54–83.

77 For elucidation on this point, see van Pelt, "Without a Right of Return a Refusal of Arrival: An Examination of the Architecture of a Paper Wall."

78 Fischer Chernoff transcript, 73, USHMM.

79 Ibid., 83.

80 Ascher, *Afterimages*, 35.

81 Wiener transcript, 4–6, USHMM.

82 For scholarly discussions and personal accounts of German Jewish refugees in France, England, Palestine, the Netherlands, Canada, Shanghai, and Brazil, and of women refugees' involvement in various occupations and professions, see Quack, *Between Sorrow and Strength: Women Refugees of the Nazi Period*.

83 Fischer Chernoff transcript, 39, USHMM. The reference, of course, is to Abella and Troper's *None Is Too Many: Canada and the Jews of Europe, 1933–1948*.

84 For a rare personal account of Marzahn and more, see O. Rosenberg, *A Gypsy in Auschwitz*.

85 Georg Iggers says that until remilitarization of the Rhineland in 1936, his parents in Hamburg had assumed that the Nazi regime would not last (Iggers and Iggers, *Two Lives*, 34).

86 Fischer Chernoff transcript, 35–6, USHMM.

87 Clipping from *L'Unité Montréal*, 22 April 1937, USHMM, LMO365, reel 20, file 33. My translation from the French.

88 Clippings, "Aufräumen in Kanada," *Berliner Börsen-Zeitung*, 8 January 1938, and "Erwachen in Kanada," *Frankische Tageszeitung*, 10 January 1938, USHMM, LMO365, reel 20, file 33.

89 Fischer Chernoff transcript, 43, USHMM.

90 Ibid., 46.

91 Wiener interview, Shoah Foundation no. 21349, segment 71, accessed at USHMM.

92 Clipping from *Amstetten Anzeiger*, 23 June 1938, "Jude muß auf den Acker," USHMM, LMO365, reel 20, file 33. Note the derogatory use of the singular "the Jew," rather than the plural "Jews" in the headline.

93 Jelinek, *The Carpathian Diaspora: The Jews of Subcarpathian Rus' and Mukachevo, 1848–1948*, esp. 37–42.

94 W.A. Iggers, "Refugee Women from Czechoslovakia in Canada: An Eyewitness Report," 121. See also Iggers and Iggers, *Two Lives*, esp. 1–22.

95 A.A. Heaps, MP for Winnipeg North, to Mackenzie King, September 1938, in Draper and Troper, *Canada*, 45–6.

96 Clipping, "Kanada – ein reiches Land das Sorgen hat," *Ost-Kurier*, Budapest, 19 October 1938, USHMM, LMO365, reel 20, file 33.

97   Bronia Wyle interview, 15 October 1995, Shoah Foundation no. 51887, accessed at USHMM.

98   Clipping, "Jewish Refugees Bring New Industry to Eastern Ontario – New Flax Mills Enrich Farmers in Ottawa Area," *Congress Bulletin*, January 1944, USHMM, LMO365, reel 151, file 195.

99   Ilse Grosberg-Cohen, born Feibelmann, 1923, Cologne, interviewed May 1997, Shoah Foundation no. 28770, accessed at USHMM.

100 Ilse Seetner, born 1925, Cologne; interviewed February 1998 in Toronto, Shoah Foundation no. 38300, accessed at USHMM.

101 In more than 90 percent of cases, the Reich flight tax was applied against Jews (Dean, *Robbing the Jews*, 55).

102 Fischer Chernoff transcript, 102, USHMM.

103 Bukey, *Hitler's Austria: Popular Sentiment in the Nazi Era, 1938–1945*.

104 Botz, "Non-Jews and Jews in Austria before, during, and after the Holocaust," 272. For more, see Botz, *Nationalsozialismus in Wien*; and Safrian and Witek, *Und keiner war dabei. Dokumente des alltäglichen Antisemitismus in Wien 1938*.

105 Klemperer, *I Will Bear Witness*, 251–2.

106 A broad perspective is provided by Marrus, *The Unwanted: European Refugees in the Twentieth Century*.

107 For the outcome, see Marion A. Kaplan, *Dominican Haven: The Jewish Refugee Settlement of Sosua, 1940–1945*.

108 Bryant, *Prague in Black: Nazi Rule and Czech Nationalism*.

109 Weinberg, *Germany, Hitler, and World War II*, 118.

110 The best treatment is Steinweis, *Kristallnacht 1938*.

111 Wiener interview, Shoah Foundation no. 21349, segment 43, USHMM.

112 Weinberg, *Kristallnacht 1938 as Experienced Then and Understood Now*, 1–2.

113 Weilbach, *Singing from the Darktime*.

114 Horace Philipp, born Dec. 1928, interviewed in 1998, Shoah Foundation no. 47376, accessed at USHMM.

115 Fischer Chernoff transcript, 76, USHMM.

116 Gerry (Gerhard) Maass, born 1918, Hamburg, interviewed May 1998, Montreal, Shoah Foundation no. 40498, accessed at USHMM.

117 For context, see London, *Whitehall and the Jews, 1933–1948: British Immigration Policy, Jewish Refugees, and the Holocaust*.

118 Goldstein, Hamilton, and Share, *Ten Marks and a Train Ticket: Benno's Escape to Freedom*. Benno's surname does not appear in the book.

119 Ilse Seetner interview, Shoah Foundation no. 38300, USHMM.

120 Weinberg, *Kristallnacht 1938*.

121 Noakes and Pridham, *Nazism*, 3:441.

122 Wilkes, *Letters from the Lost: A Memoir of Discovery*.

123 An excellent exploration is K. Iggers, "Through the Trap Door: Czechoslovak Jewish Immigration to Canada, 1938–1945."

124 Voticky, *Knocking on Every Door*.

125 An estimated 18,000 Jews, most of them from Germany and Austria, found refuge in Shanghai – more than in Canada and all the other dominions combined. For personal accounts, see Falbaum, *Shanghai Remembered: Stories from Jews Who Escaped to Shanghai from Nazi Europe*.

126 Emil and Erich Beamt Papers, USHMM, RG–03.006*01. By October 1939, Emil Beamt had acquired at least some of the necessary papers to enter Canada, but the outbreak of war nullified that possibility.

127 For one family's odyssey from Poland to Canada on the eve of the Second World War, see Bluman, *I Have My Mother's Eyes: A Holocaust Memoir across Generations*.

128 Miller and Ogilvie, *Refuge Denied: The St. Louis Passengers and the Holocaust*. See also Vincent, "The Voyages of the *St. Louis* Revisited."

129 Weinberg, *A World at Arms: A Global History of World War II*.

130 Maass interview, Shoah Foundation no. 40498, USHMM.

131 Fischer Chernoff transcript, 72, USHMM.

132 On Jews in the capital city after November 1938, see Meyer, Simon, and Schutz, *Jews in Nazi Berlin: From Kristallnacht to Liberation*.

133 The classic treatment is Abella and Troper, *None Is Too Many*.

134 Fischer Chernoff transcript, 62–3, USHMM.

135 Ibid., 67.

2

Racial Laws vs. Olympic Aspirations in the Anglo-Canadian Press of Fall 1935

RICHARD MENKIS AND HAROLD TROPER

Two years ago I believed sadistic anti-Semitism to be a temporary Nazi policy, practiced by Nazis not yet fully under central party discipline. I fear I was wrong.

Vernon McKenzie, Toronto *Globe*, 21 September 1935

The twenty-first of November 1935 must have been a "slow news day." Among the few newsworthy events that press wire services could come up with was the takeoff of the first transpacific commercial flight of Pan American Airways' now legendary China Clipper – from San Francisco to Honolulu, Midway Island, Wake Island, Guam, and finally to Manila in the Philippines. The event was hailed as opening a new era in international aviation. Far less media attention, even in Canada, was accorded the Canadian Olympic Committee (COC) decision to accept Nazi Germany's invitation to participate in the upcoming 1936 winter and summer Olympic Games. A motion to accept the German invitation was passed unanimously and without debate. Instead of debate, the COC, then a subcommittee of the Amateur Athletic Union of Canada (AAUC) and meeting in Halifax in conjunction with the annual meetings of the AAUC, simply rubber-stamped a motion of the AAUC Executive Committee that Canada follow Great Britain's lead. Since Great Britain had accepted the German invitation, Canada should do likewise. The COC agreed. The matter was settled. Canada would send teams to both the winter and summer 1936 Olympic Games in Nazi Germany.[1]

The delegates to the Halifax meetings demonstrated a unanimity of purpose rarely duplicated on other issues. For example, delegates were not nearly so amenable to a recommendation of the AAUC Executive Committee that delegates approve a loosening of stringent prohibitions against the mixed participation of professional and amateur athletes at AAUC-sanctioned sporting events. A motion on the subject sparked an acrimonious three-hour debate that ended with delegates rejecting the motion. A lengthy *Winnipeg Free Press* article devoted to this and several other contentious issues occupying delegates at the Halifax meetings noted, "There was no discussion about whether or not Canada would participate in the Olympics. The resolution committee said the Union had given careful consideration to communication on the subject and its recommendation that 'Canada follow the action of Great Britain' passed without question."[2]

IN THE SHADOW OF NUREMBERG

In retrospect, it should come as no surprise that the COC unanimously approved Canadian participation in the games. The purpose of the AAUC, the COC's governing body, was to arrange for Canadian athletes (in select sports) to compete at the highest levels. AAUC and COC officials, drawn from the Anglo-Canadian elite, believed that well-ordered sports would lead to national self-improvement. But as historian Bruce Kidd has shown, the Olympics also became displays of national pride, of nation building. When Canada's 1924 Summer Olympic athletes returned with a mere four medals, none of them gold, nobody rejoiced that Canadian youth had had an educational experience. Nor did anybody really think that Canada should spread its resources, as had previously been the case, to support mediocre performance. Medals fed national pride, and Canada was hungry.[3]

For the COC to reject an invitation to participate in the Olympic Games would have been like a mother rejecting her child. COC members enjoyed basking in the reflected glory of the Canadian Olympic team's sporting achievements and no doubt looked forward to hobnobbing with the social and economic elite who dominated the international Olympic community. And if members of the COC wanted to go to the games, so did Canada's Olympic-quality athletes. Any Canadian boycott of the Olympics would certainly disappoint all those athletes, the cream of Canadian youth, who had trained for so long and were already participating in Olympic trial events being held across Canada. And what of the disappointment that the Canadian public might feel? The COC regarded Canadian Olympic participation as an exercise in nation building. As much as Canadian participation offered athletes an opportunity to demonstrate sporting prowess, it also offered Canadians an opportunity to demonstrate pride in country. And rejecting the German invitation would most certainly insult the 1936 Olympic host, Germany, and set back any hopes Canada had for expanded trade with Germany.

And what would compel the COC to reject the German invitation? The displeasure of some Canadians disgruntled with the direction of Germany's current domestic politics and policies? But why should Canadian participation in the games be held hostage to politics? Shouldn't the Olympic Games stand above politics? Rejection of the German invitation would be a political act, an act that Canadian Olympic supporters declared would disgrace the very ideals of fairness and sportsmanship for which the Olympic Games stood. If anything, the Olympics should be held up as the antithesis of politics – an opportunity for the world's youth, irrespective of political or other differences, to gather as one and compete in sport and for the sake of sport, untainted by politics. And since Great Britain and the other British dominions intended to participate in the Olympics in Nazi Germany, it seemed obvious, at least to the COC, that Canada should stand shoulder to shoulder with its Empire partners and take part in the German Olympic Games. To do so was not to endorse Nazism. It was to support sport and uphold the Olympic ideal.

Others disagreed. Together with the Canadian left, the organized Canadian Jewish community, as represented by the Canadian Jewish Congress, rejected the notion that Nazi Germany was a deserving host for the 1936 Olympics and decried Canadian participation in the games.[4] In advance of the COC's final decision to participate in the Nazi Olympics, the Canadian Jewish Congress, following the lead of Jewish communities in Britain and the United States, organized a boycott campaign, which it hoped would convince the COC to reject the German invitation. As far as the campaign organizers were concerned, any Canadian participation in the games held in Nazi Germany would be an affront to human dignity and to the ideals of openness and fair play for which the Olympic Games stood; certainly, the repeated and bellicose Nazi violations of the Treaty of

Versailles, signed at the end of the First World War, and the Nazi record of state-sanctioned racism and antisemitism disqualified Germany from hosting the games. For the COC even to consider sending Canadian athletes to Nazi Germany after the Reichstag's passage of the odious Nuremberg Laws, which gave legal sanction to the Nazi campaign to forcefully exclude Jews from participating in German society, only made matters worse. Supporters of the boycott campaign doubled their efforts. Of course, Canadian Jews understood that the Nuremberg Laws were not the genesis of Nazi attacks on German Jews. Nazi demonization of Jews – individual and collective – had begun even before Hitler assumed power in Germany in 1933. But the passage of the Nuremberg Laws in September 1935, only five months before the opening of the Olympic Winter Games and less than two months before the COC was set to vote on Canadian participation in the Olympics, added urgency to the Jewish boycott campaign. A Canadian boycott might not derail the Olympics, but Canadian Jews hoped it would convince the Nazis that the world was watching and there would be a price to pay for their continuing abuse of German Jews.

While the organized Jewish community in Canada pressed for an Olympic boycott, the Nazis pressed on with their campaign of state-mandated antisemitism, though that campaign was not without problems. The Nuremberg Laws that so enraged boycott proponents were envisioned by Hitler as a major step toward resolving these problems. He had announced the laws at the most celebratory of annual Nazi events, the yearly Nuremberg Nazi Party Congress, better know as the Nuremberg Rally. Historian Karl Schleunes notes that the multiday rally, first held in 1927, six years before the Nazis assumed power in Germany, was "calculated to renew the [Nazi] spirit and enthusiasm of the movement through a meticulously planned pageantry, unmatched in the twentieth century."[5] The 1935 Nuremberg Rally was no exception. Like its predecessors, it was designated a special theme. The 1935 theme was "Freedom," which in Nazi double-think was interpreted to mean the freedom to serve Hitler and a rearmed fatherland, afforded by the 1935 implementation of compulsory military service – an act in blatant violation of the Treaty of Versailles, which had severely restricted German rearmament. With choreographed passion, the 1935 rally exalted the German martial spirit even as it proclaimed Hitler to be the heroic saviour of the German nation – a man anointed by divine providence to lead his people, reborn out of the humiliation of defeat in the First World War, toward the triumphant destiny that awaited them.

All this made for spectacle. Historian Klaus Fischer notes that these annual Nuremberg rallies "evolved in time into gigantic rituals of mass intoxication, featuring blood rituals, funereal orations, marches, torchlight parades, and sacred chants of victory ("Sieg Heil") or to the führer (Heil Hitler)."[6] In 1935, two years after the Nazis assumed power, the rally began with thousands of uniformed Nazi stalwarts standing rigidly in military formation and swearing an oath of loyalty to the Nazi Party and its leader. After several prominent Nazi leaders addressed the gathering, Hitler took the podium. In cult-like fashion the crowd erupted in an explosion of "Heil Hitler" salutes.

The Nuremberg rallies, with all their fiery theatre and raw appeal to the emotions, seldom proved an occasion for formal policy announcements, let alone discussion of important policy initiatives. This was not their purpose. But the 1935 rally was an exception. As the thumping salute to Hitler died down, he began his address to the party faithful. They listened, then cheered as he announced a major new legislative initiative, the Nuremberg Laws – which, together with complementary edicts, Hitler promised would deny Jews any and all protections of the German state and would give legal sanction to the total excision of Jews from German society. Why did Hitler feel these laws were necessary? The Nazi campaign against German Jews had begun years earlier. Weren't the draconian measures already taken against German Jews sufficient? No. The Nazi antisemitic campaign had several snags. No matter how many restrictive regulations had already been proclaimed or how iron-fisted their application, the effort to restrict Jewish interaction with non-Jews – and in the process eliminate, root and branch, any and all Jewish influence on German society – had been impeded by the lack of a clear and workable definition of who was and was not a Jew. Without knowing for sure who was a Jew, it was difficult if not impossible to ensure that all Jews and their corrupting impact on German society could be identified and true Germans sheltered from Jewish contact. Not all Jews had Jewish-sounding names, hooked noses and ear locks, or gathered in synagogues. Not all Jews even acknowledged their Jewishness. Clearly, a legal definition was needed. And for that matter, it was necessary to decide what was to be done about closet Jews – Jews who, Nazis alleged, passed as Germans so that they could worm their way into German society, sometimes even marrying true Germans. These dissemblers needed to be identified and exposed.[7]

Recognizing there was a problem was not the same as solving it. And when it came to solving the problem of who was a Jew, there were a number of considerations to be taken into account. For example, did someone have to "behave" as a Jew or "look" like a Jew or somehow self-identify as a Jew to be a Jew? Or was being a Jew simply a fact of biology, a matter of lineage? And if being a Jew was a biological inheritance, what was to be done about non-Jews who converted to Judaism or non-Jews who married Jews, and all those born of mixed ancestry, partial Jews? Were they Jews or not? And if they were not Jews, were they Germans or were they some kind of racial hybrid? If so, were they subject to the same constraints as full-blooded Jews? And for that matter, was there some genetic tipping point after which someone of Jewish ancestry could be nothing else but a Jew? What percentage of Jewish blood had to pump through an individual's veins before he or she had to be legally designated a full Jew and therefore subject to all state sanctions on Jews?

Resolving these thorny questions was a key goal of the Nuremberg Laws and their accompanying edicts, which promised to set down legally binding racial markers separating Jew from German and, in so doing, pave the way for the delegitimization and legal denaturalization of those defined as Jews, rendering them stateless in the country of their birth and thereby beyond the protection of the law. But the Nuremberg Laws did more than this. They also facilitated the orderly looting of Jewish assets by the state, a matter of some urgency to the German Treasury. In the months preceding the 1935 rally, Hitler and his finance minister had faced a series of setbacks to the German economy. Among other things, Germany's economic renewal had been faltering as a result of growing public anxiety at the ability of the state's authorities to maintain order. Odd as it may seem in retrospect, much of this disorder was laid at the feet of Nazi Party enthusiasts who felt free to engage in indiscriminate and often violent antisemitic actions across German, often abetted by local police and Nazi officials.

It was not that antisemitic actions posed any kind of moral problem. Far from it. It was the disorderly and random nature of anti-Jewish violence, sometimes inflicted on non-Jews mistaken for Jews, that was problematic. It eroded the sense of order and stability essential to economic stability. It even made foreign money markets skittish about investing money in a Germany that tolerated if not incited violence on the streets. Also problematic was the wanton destruction of Jewish property or forced closure or disruption of Jewish-owned and Jewish-operated enterprises that were essential to local, regional, and even national job security and economic growth. If the crushing of Jewish economic power and the removal of Jews from positions of influence in civil society was the Nazis' intent, violence that undermined the national economic interest or disrupted the orderly transfer of Jewish assets and enterprise to the Nazi state was not. Jewish wealth needed to be transferred to the state, not smashed or looted by the mob. Thus, if few questioned the Nazi credo that Jews had to be isolated from contact with the mainstream and Jewish assets assumed by the state, economic self-interest dictated that this had to be done in the most orderly and efficient fashion. And it required, not just control of the mob but, as noted, specific and exact determination of who was or was not a Jew so as to enable an orderly process for identifying and separating Jews from their wealth.

Hitler also had another reason for putting a lid, at least temporarily, on the more public and egregious assaults on Jews and others considered enemies of the state. As historian Ian Kershaw notes, the Führer was concerned that spontaneous, wanton, and excessively violent antisemitic outbursts might cause Western governments to question their participation in an Olympic Games intended to be a showcase of Nazi power and prestige. "With one eye on the approaching Olympics and the other on the foreign and economic situation, the regime needed a period of calm. In August 1935, Hitler and Deputy Führer [Rudolph] Hess had expressly banned 'individual actions' against Jews."[8] The temporary hiatus in public antisemitic activity did not go unnoticed by foreign visitors. Vernon McKenzie, dean of the Faculty of Journalism at the University of Washington and a former Torontonian and editor of *Maclean's* magazine, observed first hand that "during 1934 and 1935 anti-Jewish stickers, signs, and placards increased in number trnd in bitterness. But in 1936, especially around the time of the Olympic Games, they dwindled."[9] This whitewashing of the visible signs of antisemitism lasted only until the Olympic Games ended, and certainly did not change the ongoing Nazi campaign that was turning German Jews into a pariah people.

Moreover, if Hitler ordered an intermission in "individual actions" against Jews, this was not the same as halting "state actions" against Jews. With the Nuremberg Laws, Hitler intended it to become the responsibility of the German state, not the mob, to ensure that Germans were protected from the Jewish scourge; and as suggested, the state took steps to pinpoint which Jewish assets it should confiscate. To these ends, passage of the Nuremberg Laws had to be a very public act and the content of the laws widely publicized.

Hitler, as absolute ruler of Germany, could have decreed all that was in the Nuremberg Laws quietly, behind closed doors. But instead of using stealth, he announced the impending passage of these laws – laws that would denationalize German Jews and, in effect, turn them into foreigners, unwelcome aliens in the land of their birth – in his address at the Nuremberg Rally. True to his word, the next day the Reichstag, meeting not in Berlin but in Nuremberg for the first time since 1534, enacted the laws without debate and certainly without dissent. The first law, the Law for the Protection of German Blood and German Honour, specifically prohibited marriages and extra-marital relations between Germans and "Jews." The second law, the Reich Citizenship Law, stripped all Jews of their German citizenship and, since they were no longer citizens, also stripped away any legal protections they may have previously claimed as German citizens. Of paramount importance, the Reich Citizenship Law and its subsequent edicts legally defined exactly who was and who was not a Jew. As a point of reference, the law defined a "German" as a person with four grandparents with "German or kindred blood." As opposed to Germans, Jews were defined as those with three or four grandparents who were not baptized into a Christian church or those with an attachment to Judaism. A person with one or two Jewish grandparents and no known attachment to Judaism was a *Mischling* – of "mixed blood" – not Jewish but not German either. Lineage was destiny.

The laws and their supplementary edicts quickly reshaped life in Germany. Falling on the wrong side of the German-Jewish divide could prove devastating. Fear gripped those who suspected that a Jewish skeleton might be rattling in the family closet. Others made a premium of letting it be known that their family tree was *juden-*

rein. This was no small matter. Might not a soon to be father-in-law have reason to be concerned about the family lineage of the young man his daughter wanted to marry? What was the best way to protect one's family and assets from the threat of Jewish taint? Perhaps it would be best to hire one of a growing number of genealogical researchers who were suddenly doing a thriving business digging into individual family histories for any sign of Jewish contamination.[10] If the Nuremberg Laws dictated caution with regard to individual wedding and business plans, at the national level they choked off almost all interaction between Jews with non-Jews and threatened severe punishment to those who dared ignore the law.

With the Jew legally defined, it was possible to enforce much more fully and effectively, the many regulations already restricting Jewish access to the public square. Known Jews and newly designated Jews were banished from public employ as lawyers, doctors, teachers, and journalists. The same was true of other Jewish professionals. Jews were also prohibited treatment in state hospitals and, after the age of fourteen, denied a place in state-funded schools. Public parks, libraries, and beaches were closed to them. Sexual contact between Jews and Germans was criminalized. To guard against lascivious Jewish behaviour, the law also forbade Jews from employing non-Jewish female domestics under the age of forty-five. The list of legal prohibitions, restrictions, and prohibitions went on and on. Names of Jewish war casualties were to be expunged from official monuments and memorials. Jews were prohibited from winning prizes in the national lottery. German passports issued to Jews were stamped with a large "J," and Jews were given to understand that they were welcome to use these passports to leave Germany – but not to return. And important to Nazi economic planning, Jewish property was cleared for state expropriation, or Aryanization, as it was officially called.

The implications of the Nuremberg Laws may not have been clear to all those at the 1935 Nuremberg Rally who applauded Hitler's promise of decisive legislative action against Jews, but none could mistake his intent. Among the dignitaries who sat in the Nuremberg stands and heard Hitler's announcement of the new laws was a prominent American member of the International Olympic Committee, Charles H. Sherrill. While visiting Germany on Olympic business, Sherrill had been invited by Hitler to be his guest at the November event. What Sherrill thought of Hitler's lengthy harangue against

Jews and his announcement of the Nuremberg Laws is unknown. What is known is that he was impressed, as he was meant to be, by what he saw – the flawless organization of the rally, the enthusiastic crowds, the stirring parades and the triumphalist celebration of *Volksgemeinschaft*, a vision of a nation united by mythic bonds of racial purity.

Perhaps Sherrill was there at the close of the first day's official events and watched as the thousands of Nazi stalwarts spilled out of the rally grounds to command the larger city. Locked arm-in-arm, they marched through the streets of Nuremberg to the cheers of enthusiastic onlookers and eventually regrouped in the torch-lit town square, where they were again received by Hitler. There, the assembled crowd was entertained by a public performance of Richard Wagner's opera *Die Meistersinger von Nürnberg*, which depicts legendary tales of heroic Aryan triumphs over menacing enemies. If the Nazis could put on a show like this for the party faithful, Sherrill may well have imagined the kind of show the world could expect when the 1936 Olympic Games opened – the Winter Games, scheduled to open only a few months later, and the Summer Games just six month after them. In his autobiography, Sherrill recalled with pleasure his time with Hitler at Nuremberg: "I was Hitler's personal guest for four days in mid-September 1935 ... It was beautiful! You could almost hear the [Nazi] units click, as each fitted into place, exactly on time." Sherrill left Nuremberg convinced the coming Olympics would be an event to remember. He was right.[11]

But what of the Olympic Games? How was it that Nazi Germany – a blatantly racist state, already in abrogation of the Treaty of Versailles and threatening to its neighbours – should be hosting the Olympic Games? Looking back, it is easy to forget that the Olympics were not originally awarded to Nazi Germany. In 1931, several years before the Nazis seized power in Germany, the International Olympic Committee had awarded the German Weimar Republic the 1936 Olympic Games. The gesture was celebrated by Weimar officials as a sign that Germany, defeated in the First World War, burdened with debt, and struggling to maintain a shaky and centrist democratic government, was nevertheless being welcomed back into the family of nations. But theirs was a short-lived celebration. A little more than two years later, with planning for the Olympic Games still very much in the infant stage, the Weimar Republic was gone. So were democracy and any German affection for the value of internationalism. Hitler was in power. Political repression, militarism, and racial determinism quickly became the order of the day.

Given the obvious disconnect between the much-vaunted Olympic dedication to international athletic excellence and peaceful competition unfettered by political and religious division or racial discrimination, on one side, and the overtly racist and aggressively militaristic priorities of the Nazi regime, on the other, some questioned whether Nazi Germany was an appropriate venue for the games. Would the Nazis even want the games? Perhaps not. During the 1920s the Nazis, still years from power, had voiced contempt for supporters of the Olympics, whom they contemptuously dismissed as rootless cosmopolitans and naïve internationalists who encouraged sporting competition in which "inferior" and "degenerate" races – Jews, Gypsies, Slavs, and Blacks – not only were invited to participate as equals but were honoured with medals. One Nazi spokesman dismissed the entire Olympic movement as "an enhancement of Bolshevism's war against the White People."[12] Hitler, too, disparaged the Olympic ideal. Shortly after the 1932 Olympic Games ended in Los Angeles, and only a year before the Nazis assumed power in Germany, Hitler denounced the Olympic Games as "a plot of Freemasons and Jews."[13]

What, then, made Hitler change his mind? Instead of demanding the International Olympic Committee pack its bags and find another venue, why did he embrace the idea of Germany hosting the Olympics? Hitler was convinced by prominent members of the German Olympic Committee, supported by his propaganda minister, Joseph Goebbels, that hosting the games would give Nazi Germany, the new Germany, a unique opportunity to impress the world with German organizational skills, industrial vitality, and, above all, Aryan racial superiority; and there would be hundreds of journalists from all over the world on hand to chronicle the event. Convinced, Hitler not only affirmed Germany's willingness to host the spectacle of the games, but he also assumed a hands-on role in ensuring that they would be worthy of his Third Reich. He took an active role in approving the architectural plans for the Summer Games' site in Berlin and monitored other aspects of the games' planning. Having only a year earlier dismissed the Olympics as a tool of the Jews, Hitler was now invested in assuring that the Olympic Games in Germany, both winter and summer, would stand as a worthy testament to the greatness that was the new Germany.[14]

If Hitler changed his mind on the Olympics, he did not change his mind on the necessity of ridding the new Germany of any and all Jewish and other non-Aryan influences and shredding the Treaty of Versailles. Even as Germany prepared to host the world in sport, Hitler moved to further his racist and aggressively militant agenda. In so doing, the Nazis made a mockery of the Olympic creed as articulated by the founder of the modern Olympics, Pierre de Coubertin, and repeated during every Olympic opening ceremony: "The most important thing in the Olympic Games is not to win but to take part, just as the most important thing in life is not the triumph, but the struggle. The essential thing is not to have conquered but to have fought well." To Hitler, the Olympic creed was laughable – empty words, hollowed out of meaning. To win, to conquer, to stand triumphant were Hitler's life imperatives. As a result, he and his Olympic officials demonstrated nothing but contempt for the International Olympic Committee's oft-repeated commitment to a depoliticized and discrimination-free Olympics.

As the Olympics drew near, only the most self-deluded Olympic observers would deny the obvious: the Nazis intended that the games would advance their nation-building priorities, including racism. Nobody could claim surprise that German Jews, stripped of their German citizenship by the Nuremberg Laws, were ruled ineligible for membership on the German Olympic team. In fact, Hitler's agreement to host the games ran parallel with an upswing in state antisemitic decrees and violence. As a concession to the sensitivities of foreign athletes and visitors who might take offence at too overt a display of Nazi antisemitism, Hitler ordered a fig-leaf cover-up of the more eye-offending antisemitism, including anti-Jewish posters, highway signs, and even the publication of demeaning Jewish caricatures in the German press. But the Nuremberg Laws were in place and being applied in the very shadow of the upcoming Winter and Summer Games.

Germany was equally brazen in abrogating the Treaty of Versailles. Rearmament and the introduction of compulsory military service, specifically prohibited by the treaty, were instituted even as the Olympic facilities were being readied. Germany also took an increasingly menacing tone in its dealings with neighbouring states: Austria, France, Czechoslovakia, and Poland. None of this seemed to generate much international stir or disturb the International Olympic Committee. The committee preferred to turn a blind eye to what Germany was doing, even when this involved the application of racist and antisemitic criteria in selection of the German Olympic team in obvious contravention of the Olympic creed.

What of Canada? The COC spared itself the need to address the rights and wrongs of Germany hosting the Olympic Games simply by choosing to follow Great Britain's lead in attending the games. But this begs an important question. Did the COC act out of benign ignorance of the events unfolding in Nazi Germany or was its decision to follow the British lead just a convenient ploy, saving it the need to factor what was happening in Germany into its decision to approve sending Canadian athletes to Nazi Germany? It is impossible to know with any certainty what any particular individual member of the COC knew about events unfolding in Germany. It is equally impossible to know how much any one individual cared about what was happening there. However, it is possible to know something of the information flow available to COC members on what was happening in Germany, especially that reported by the mainstream Canadian press during the two years leading up to the COC's 21 November 1935 approval of Canadian participation in the Nazi Olympics.

THE CANADIAN RESPONSE

When the Nazis came to power in early 1933, the Anglo-Canadian press took immediate notice of the new Germany. There was little or no consensus on the significance or severity of Hitler's unfolding policies. Two newspapers, in particular, raised immediate alarm at the direction of events in Nazi Germany. At the *Winnipeg Free Press*, the editor-in-chief, John W. Dafoe, applied his bedrock liberal political perspectives on domestic matters to international affairs. In March 1933, shortly after Hitler was named chancellor of Germany, Dafoe's reporters and editorialists began railing against the Nazis' suppression of free speech in Germany, and Dafoe expressed himself very clearly on the regime's antisemitism. In a caustic editorial in late March 1933, written with obvious disdain, Dafoe argued, "There is no mania quite so revealing as that of Jew baiting ... The nation that indulges in it 'places' and 'dates' itself far beyond the power of the most skilful casuists to enter apology or defence."[15] In the summer and fall of 1933, the *Free Press* also reported with alarm on the Nazification of German universities and the compromising of the

German justice system, both of which involved the wholesale expulsion of Jews.[16]

The *Toronto Star* shared many of the same anti-Nazi positions as the *Free Press*. After the First World War, the owner of the *Star*, Joseph E. Atkinson, turned his paper into a voice of progressive reform. Soon it was the most read newspaper in Canada, and its more conservative rivals frequently denounced the paper as communist. Certainly not communist, the *Star* generally supported the federal Liberal Party, but it could turn on the Liberals when it felt they were backsliding on progressive issues.[17] The *Star* was equally outspoken on international affairs and maintained its own small stable of foreign-based journalists. Atkinson's correspondents in Europe, most notably Pierre van Paassen, Coralie van Paassen, and Matthew Halton, all wrote detailed and harrowing reports of the ongoing Nazification of German society. Like the *Winnipeg Free Press*, within months of Hitler's seizure of power, the *Star* offered its readers disturbing front-page coverage of the regime's economic, cultural, and physical assault on Germany's minorities, especially the Jews.[18]

The more conservative Canadian newspapers also carried extensive German coverage, but much of it was far less negative in tone. In the summer of 1933, the Toronto *Globe* and the Montreal *Gazette* published a number of articles by Erland Echlin, who was said to have "admired Hitler's record of achievement since his assumption of power at the end of January [1933]" and portrayed Hitler as commanding the total support, if not adulation, of Germans of all ages. Echlin dismissed the negative reports on Nazi Germany appearing in the *Free Press* and the *Star*, including reports of Nazi antisemitism, as being inaccurate and wildly anti-German. The truth, he claimed, was that these reports of antisemitism in Germany were "like the rumours of Mark Twain's death, an exaggeration." After an exclusive interview with Hitler, Echlin described the Führer as "moderate" and "kindly" and as a man who "stands for peace."[19] Like the *Globe* and the *Gazette*, the Toronto *Evening Telegram* also took the *Toronto Star* to task for supposedly sensationalist journalism, even as the *Evening Telegram* frequently lauded Hitler as a great anti-Bolshevist leader.[20]

The mainstream Canadian daily press may have been politically partisan, but it was rarely monochromatic and never painted Hitler and the Nazis either entirely white or black. On one occasion, the

Toronto Star even ran a story that assigned part of the blame for Nazi antisemitism to the behaviour of the Jews.[21] And the *Evening Telegram*, the same paper that had reacted scornfully to the *Star*'s descriptions of the horrific brutality of the Nazi regime, included in its issue of 29 July a careful refutation of the more outlandish Nazi propaganda, including German claims that denied that Jews were being mistreated.[22] Many other newspapers also sent out mixed messages on Germany. In Vancouver, the *Sun* and the *Province* oscillated between mocking Hitler as a political clown and expressing horror at his untrammelled power. These two newspapers also condemned Nazi antisemitism, but their coverage generally lacked specifics, and concern for antisemitism often took second place to concern for the brutal Nazi repression of other political enemies.[23] Thus, while English Canadian papers accorded events in Nazi Germany considerable column space during the year or so after the Nazis assumed power in 1933, the various newspapers were not above filtering news coverage through the prism of their own politics when it suited them. Depending on what newspaper one chose to read, a person could be left with a more or less positive impression of the Nazi regime.

THE SEARCH FOR ALLIES

If, in the wake of Hitler's 1933 accession to power, Canadian newspapers differed from one another in their assessment of Hitler and the Nazi regime, a clearer press consensus had formed by the summer of 1935. It was increasingly clear that the Nazi state was a racist state, and this became even more apparent after passage of the Nuremberg Laws in the fall.

For some Canadian press observers of the Third Reich, the first few weeks of September 1935 actually promised hope that Nazi racism might be toned down, despite anti-Jewish riots during the spring and summer. Both the *Toronto Star* and the *Globe*, previously at odds over events unfolding in Germany, reported rumours of internecine fighting within Nazi Party ranks over state racial policy. Hjalmar Schacht, president of the Reichbank and Germany's minister of economics, was said to be concerned about the effect the persecution of the Jews was having on the country's economy and was making his voice heard. On 5 September the *Toronto Star* reported that Schacht had announced a new bond issue and even intended to allow several foreign Jewish banks to be involved.[24] On

11 September an editorial in the *Star* referred to growing tensions between high-ranking Nazi Jew-baiters and Schacht over attacks on Jews. The editorial noted that Schacht did not know "how much longer he can hold things together if Nazi extremists continue to give offence to international financiers."[25] The editorial pointed out that Hitler, rather than taking sides, had "a pat on the back for both antagonistic elements of the Nazi party." According to the *Star*, Hitler would do well to follow the path laid out by Schacht: "Were Dr Schacht to resign – a development that looms up as an early possibility – Hitler would be at his wits' end to save Germany from economic collapse." In an article of 14 September, the *Globe* claimed Schacht seemed to be making some headway in convincing Propaganda Minister Josef Goebbels – an outspoken advocate of harsh measures against the Jews – to ease up on anti-Jewish actions. In what the *Globe* took as a sign that Goebbels was backing off from his confrontation with Schacht, Goebbels had invited Schacht to be interviewed in Goebbels's newspaper, *Der Angriff*.[26]

If the Canadian Press made much of rumoured disagreements over antisemitism, in truth there was no fundamental Nazi disagreement about the necessity of antisemitism, and in no way was Schacht a counterpoint to Nazi Jew-baiters. He was not opposed to the persecution of Jews or even its intensification; he just wanted the persecution to be less chaotic and more in keeping with the state's economic priorities. Misreading Schacht's intent, some in the press reported a flicker of hope, expecting that Schacht's concern for economic development would result in a lid being put on the persecution of Jews. After a month, the *Calgary Herald* poured cold water on this flicker of hope. In a short editorial that drew on the American periodical *Business Week*, the *Herald* pointed out that in his tug-of-war with Schacht, Goebbels had prevailed, "and it explains the recent defeats of business in Germany."[27] Six weeks later, an editorial in the *Globe* insisted that the struggle between Schacht and Goebbels continued but did not affect other Nazi Party leaders or the party rank and file, who were determined to press on with the campaign. Jews would continue to be forced out of businesses and Jewish workers forced out onto the street. Schacht could go on squabbling with Goebbels about antisemitism all he wanted, but the hardliners were winning out.[28]

Canadian newspaper readers had ample opportunity to read about the antisemitic screeds of Goebbels and other Nazi hardliners.

The *Toronto Star* and *Calgary Herald* reported in detail Goebbels's rabidly antisemitic speech at the 1935 Nuremberg Rally, in which he railed against the dangers of Jewish-controlled Soviet communism.[29] On 18 October, Coralie van Paassen reported to *Star* readers that Goebbels publicly justified anti-Jewish violence in Berlin as a reasoned response to recalcitrant Jews, who were defiant of the German state and needed to be forcefully put in their place.[30] Adding weight to the notion that Nazi leaders were unrestrained in their antisemitism, there were press reports of the activities of Julius Streicher, editor of the notoriously antisemitic Nazi Party newspaper *Der Stürmer* and himself a scurrilous antisemite. On 5 October the *Toronto Star* reported on a speech Streicher had delivered in Berlin, in which he claimed that insidious Jewish interests were responsible for the Italian-Ethiopian conflict that had just begun: "The Jews are out to make money from every massacre between nations."[31] The most detailed – albeit somewhat rambling – account of Streicher's antisemitism comes from the *Globe* reporter Vernon McKenzie. Writing on 21 September, McKenzie explained that some Nazi supporters he knew personally had confided that they found Streicher unsavory but conceded that his antisemitism resonated well with many across Germany. McKenzie pointed out that *Der Stürmer*, "which thrives almost entirely upon racial hatred," remained one of the most widely circulated newspapers in Nazi Germany. And if Streicher's antisemitic rantings made for sensationalist news copy outside Germany, they were widely accepted inside Germany and were fully endorsed by Hitler.[32]

Through the summer and into the fall of 1935, the Canadian press was more and more coming to understand that the greatest challenge for German Jews was not the inflammatory and scurrilous antisemitism of *Der Stürmer* or even Goebbels's encouragement of antisemitic thuggery. It was antisemitism turned to state policy and action. As noted, at the Nuremberg Rally of 1935 Hitler had promised laws that would institutionalize Nazi racism and quarantine Germans from contact with Jews, and the very next day, 15 September, the Reich Citizenship Law and the Law for the Protection of German Blood and German Honour had been introduced in the Reichstag, voted on, and become law. Within hours Canadian papers, picking up on Associated Press reports, began to publish stories of how the Nuremberg Laws would reshape Germany. The *Calgary Herald* had a front-page headline stating, "Nazis Bar Jews from Citizenship,"[33] and the Toronto *Globe*'s front page announced, "Nazis Outlaw Jews and Lash Lithuanians."[34]

But not all Canadian newspapers made antisemitism their lead story. Echoing the American press,[35] some of them focused more on Nazi symbolism than on Nazi antisemitism. In addition to passing the Nuremberg Laws, the Reichstag had passed a law officially designating the Nazi Party flag, the swastika flag, as the national flag of Germany. The *Winnipeg Free Press* ran a front-page article under the banner "Declare Swastika as Flag." The article discussed, in order of importance, first the flag change and then, in second place, the new anti-Jewish legislation. Despite being somewhat buried in the article, the antisemitic thrust of the new legislation was made clear. Readers were informed that German Jews were now excluded from citizenship in the new Germany. As such, they were rendered stateless in the country of their birth. And as a step toward total separation of German from Jew, the Nazis forbade sexual relations between Jews and non-Jews as a threat to "blood and honour" and a punishable offence.[36]

Canadian newspapers again focused on the Jewish loss of citizenship in mid-November. In order to implement the Reich Citizenship Law more thoroughly and leave no lingering doubt about who is and is not a Jew and therefore who is and is not a citizen of Nazi Germany, the press reported on 14 November a supplementary decree that Germany had issued outlining the fine points to be applied in determining a person's Jewish bloodline. Drawing on Associated Press reports, on 15 November the *Calgary Herald* ran a front-page headline, "Jews in Germany Lose All Political Rights by Government Decree,"[37] and a day later the Toronto *Globe* published a second-page story under the headline "German Jews Lose Franchise."[38] A few days later, a toughly worded editorial in the *Globe* took the German ambassador to the United States to task. The ambassador, Hans Luther, had declared that there was "no persecution of any kind in Germany." The *Globe* editorial countered with specific details of the Nuremberg Laws, noting that the effect of the decrees was "to segregate a million German-born inhabitants, deny them the right of citizenship and place them socially in a class with criminals and imbeciles." The severity of these laws was so plain for all to see, the editorial concluded, that it "might have resolved a seeming paradox if Dr. Luther could have been persuaded to give ... an ambassadorial definition of what Nazi Germany calls persecution."[39]

English Canadian newspapers not only reported on the removal of German citizenship from German Jews but also told of the legally sanctioned humiliation and public mistreatment of Jews and other minorities in Germany. The *Toronto Star* published a series articles, many of them special reports to the *Star* written by Coralie van Paassen, exploring how difficult day-to-day life had become for Jews in Germany. On 28 September the *Star* reported on the ongoing harassment of Jewish-owned business establishments and reproduced images of the two "tickets" that all Jewish-owned businesses were required to post for public view. One berated those Aryans who still frequented Jewish-owned businesses and accused them of being traitors to Germany. The other proclaimed the Jew a "bloodsucking enemy."[40] On 12 October the *Star* also ran the story of a German-produced ballet that was playing in London but not in Berlin because the pianist-composer was a Jew, "with whom the company refused to part."[41] More dramatically, that same day van Paassen reported that *Die jüdische Rundschau*, the last independent Jewish newspaper in Germany, had been suspended.[42] On 5 November, van Paassen pointed out that the number of regulations and decrees restricting Jewish life in Germany was so great that "the anti-Jewish laws in various parts of the Reich could fill a book."[43] She went on to describe one town's municipal ordinances that, among other things, prohibited Jews from entering the town museum, restricted Jews from hiking in the nearby Bavarian mountains, and even prohibited Jewish butchers from shipping cattle for slaughter in the same trucks used to transport cattle for slaughter by non-Jews.[44]

Other newspapers may not have offered readers the same depth of detailed as the *Star*, but they did include stories of the crippling restrictions imposed on Jews in Germany. On 1 October the *Calgary Herald* picked up on an Associated Press story dealing with the forceful removal of the last Jewish notaries from their offices – those who had previously been allowed to remain in practice because of their war service. That same article underscored the degree to which the Jews, defined as the enemy of the German people, were held responsible for all of Germany's woes – no matter how absurd the accusation. The article noted that the Jews were collectively to blame for a collapse in the Berlin subway in which several workers had died.[45] On 25 September, the *Globe* published a front-page story, extended to the next page, under the headline "Jew-Baiting Is Popular with Hitlerite," written by Vernon McKenzie. McKenzie wrote a series of articles from Berlin as the *Globe*'s "European correspondent." In one article he looked to the future of antisemitism in Germany: "Striking indications have been observed during the past two months to show that the Nazi hatred and harassing of Jews is not going to abate." Indeed, it was going to get worse, McKenzie warned, noting that signs of antisemitism in the public square, already widespread, were increasing, "not only in number, but in bitterness." In the face of these facts, McKenzie was saddened that there were still people in Canada who fooled themselves into believing that Nazi antisemitism was not deep-seated in German society. According to him, anyone who still adhered to this view in the fall of 1935 was engaging in wilful blindness. But he admitted that he too had previously underestimated the depth of antisemitism in Germany: "Two years ago I believed sadistic anti-Semitism to be a temporary Nazi policy, practiced by Nazis not yet fully under central party discipline. I fear that I was wrong."[46]

In 1933, when the Nazis took power in Germany, Canadian journalists like McKenzie, as well as the larger Canadian public, may be forgiven for thinking that Nazi antisemitism, while pernicious, was secondary to the Nazis' state-building agenda. By the fall of 1935, with the Nuremberg Laws in place and being aggressively implemented, even the most conservative of Canadian newspapers had come around to acknowledging that McKenzie was correct: antisemitism permeated Nazism and the German state.

THE VOICE OF THE PRESS

The depth and significance of Nazi antisemitism was hardly news to Germany watchers in the Canadian Jewish community. And given the grim news from Germany, many Canadian Jews were convinced that Germany had disqualified itself of the right to host the Olympics. Shortly after Rabbi Maurice Eisendrath returned to Toronto from his visit to Nazi Germany in the summer of 1935, he wrote an urgent letter to the general secretary of the Canadian Jewish Congress (CJC), H.M. Caiserman. "One of the main messages with which I have come back from my unexpected but necessary visit to Germany," wrote Eisendrath, "is the absolute necessity of moving heaven and earth to keep Canada and America out of the Olympics. This is far more crucial than most of us on this side can even imagine."[47]

Caiserman needed little prodding. Like Eisendrath, he feared that Hitler was going to turn the Olympic Games – with the world media in attendance – into a propaganda windfall for Nazi Germany by discreetly masking the ugliness of state-initiated racism and persecution, and portraying the new Germany as a benevolent and peace-loving member of the family of nations. To prevent this, Eisendrath and Caiserman agreed that they needed to convince the Amateur Athletic Union of Canada and its Canadian Olympic Committee, scheduled to meet in Halifax in late November, to vote for a boycott of the games.

Eisendrath and Caiserman, already working furiously on the boycott campaign, redoubled their efforts after the Nazi enactment of the Nuremberg Laws. Advocates of the boycott were especially eager to win the support of the Canadian amateur sporting establishment and that of Canadian politicians and other key sports movers and shakers. They also hoped that their message would resonate with the Canadian press. In an early circular, labelled "Urgent" and "Confidential," which was sent to CJC boycott supporters across Canada, it was suggested that a prime target for the pro-boycott message should be the "Sports editor of the newspaper in your community." Bringing sports editors onside with the boycott message promised a positive outcome: "NOTE – If an opinion of the Sports Editors were found to favour withdrawal, a poll would be taken by the Canadian Press or La Presse Centrale Canadienne, and this poll, favouring [Olympic] withdrawal, would be published in every newspaper in Canada." [48]

It was also judged essential that the boycott campaign should not appear to be a parochial Jewish issue. To win support among non-Jews, it would be best if the campaign appeared to have wide non-Jewish support already. Accordingly, the CJC created a shell organization, the Unity and Goodwill Association, with a non-Jew, George Langsner, as its president. Much of the CJC's pro-boycott activities were funnelled through the Unity and Goodwill Association, including the publication of a series of pro-boycott newsletters and press releases.

In an effort to reach key sports columnists, the CJC enlisted the aid of Colin A. Gravenor, the sympathetic Montreal editor of several Canadian sports publications. He provided insight into the Canadian sports establishment and supplied the names of prominent sportswriters across the country. [49] Eisendrath, suspecting that sports columnists were a different breed from news columnists – less concerned with social and political issues and perhaps even indifferent to the editorial position of the newspaper for which they worked – contacted and met with a number of Toronto sportswriters, among them the influential Lou Marsh of the *Toronto Star*.[50] Boycott advocates did the same elsewhere in Canada, and in the lead-up to the Halifax meeting and the critical COC vote on whether Canada would formally accept the German invitation to attend the Olympics, the CJC used the Unity and Goodwill Association to barrage sports editors across the country with pro-boycott material.[51] The material included excerpted speeches by American proponents of a boycott and various editorials – especially from non-Jewish publications – in opposition to holding the Olympics in Germany. The pitch was hardly subtle. Under the association's name on the newsletter masthead was the impassioned plea, "In the name of Truth, we implore you to give proper publicity to the following."

Sportswriters felt besieged by the onslaught of material. On 8 November, Andy Lytle of the *Toronto Star* described his desk as "well littered with literature, pro and con on the German Olympic Games question."[52] On 14 November, Hal Straight of the *Vancouver Sun*, who had previously written about the boycott, complained that the avalanche of material he was receiving about the Olympics showed no sign of letting up: "This bureau continues to be swamped with Olympic games propaganda. Jewish organizations, and Catholic, too, sent page after page of the stuff which draws Herr Hitler over the coals. One set of stuff is always titled 'In the name of truth, we implore you to give proper publicity to the following.'"[53] But boycott advocates did not have a monopoly in reaching out to the press for support. There were those, including German diplomatic officials and Nazi supporters in Canada, who were vitally concerned to ensure that Canada attend the Olympics. In late October, Ralph Wilson of the *Calgary Herald* informed his readers that "Germany Olympics Games officials are turning out more publicity on the 1936 athletic classic than any country in the history of the event ... Pamphlets pour in from the London, Ontario, distributing offices of the German Olympic Committee in formidable bundles."[54]

With all this pressure, pro and con, what did the newspapers have to say about the issue of the Olympics and the boycott campaign? More news stories in the Canadian press dealt with the debate taking place in the United States over whether or not it should attend the Olympic Games, and the corollary issue of the Nazi treatment

of minority and particularly Jewish athletes in Germany. The attention accorded the American debate is understandable. Not only was
the American debate well covered by the wire services to which Canadian newspapers subscribed, but it was understood that any Canadian boycott, while newsworthy, would not greatly disrupt the
games, whereas an American Olympic boycott would not only crip-
ple the Olympics but would be seen as a sharp rebuff of Nazi Germany. And the American boycott debate was turning out to be a
cliffhanger. On one side was Judge Jeremiah T. Mahoney, president
of the influential Amateur Athletic Union, (AAU), who lent his personal support to an American boycott and in the fall of 1935 made
it clear that he was going to push for a boycott of the Nazi Olympics
when the AAU met to vote on the issue in December 1935. Leading
the anti-boycott campaign in the United States were Avery Brundage,
president of the American Olympic Committee, and Charles Sherrill,
one of the three American members of the International Olympic
Committee, who was Hitler's guest at the 1935 Nuremberg Rally.
They were supported in their efforts by the German Olympic Committee, which knew that an American boycott would spell disaster
for the Olympics and undermine the propaganda bonanza the Nazis
expected to flow from the games.

One of the key arguments raised in favour of a boycott was that
the Nazis, in violation of the Olympic rules, were systematically
excluding German Jews and others defined as non-Aryans from
the German Olympic team.[55] The issue of sports racism was well
covered in the Canadian press. On 24 October the Toronto *Globe*
and the *Winnipeg Free Press*[56] published stories on Nazi prejudice
against Jewish and "Gypsy" athletes in Germany. Two days earlier,
both papers (and the *Calgary Herald*)[57] had quoted the head of the
German Olympic Committee as having discounted reports of prejudice against Jewish and Catholic athletes. If no Jews were appointed
to the German Olympic team, he had argued, it was because none
qualified for the team. Both the Toronto and Winnipeg newspapers ran a forceful Associated Press story challenging the German claim. The articles told of German Jewish athletes being denied
access to training facilities, such as sports fields and pools, and the
state-mandated dismantling of Jewish athletic clubs in Germany.
According to these newspapers, much as the Nazis might deny that
there were any qualified Jewish athletes in Germany, there were in
fact some, including the members of a highly competitive 400-metre

relay team and record-holding Martel Jacob, a female javelin champion. The newspapers also reported Mahoney's impatience with what he regarded as the unconvincing arguments being made by American Olympic supporters for why the United States should participate in the Nazi Olympics, including a claim that an American boycott of the Olympics could inflame American antisemitism.[58]

Canadian newspapers also gave extensive coverage of the counter-offensives by those favouring American Olympic participation. In the fall of 1935, the press reported on Sherrill's visit to Nazi Germany when, again claiming there was no systematic discrimination in picking athletes for the German Olympic team, he had quietly won the Nazis' agreement to allow token participation on the German team by minority athletes in order to still American criticism. No sooner did the Nazis announce that both the Jewish high-jumper Gretel Bergmann and the "half-Jewish" fencing champion Helene Mayer were being invited to join the German team than Sherrill declared that this was proof positive that the Germans were living up to their Olympic obligation to hold an Olympic Games free from prejudice: "Whether or not they [Bergmann and Mayer] accept the invitation doesn't matter. Germany has done her part by inviting them in good faith. This ought to answer any charges of discrimination." As to the larger issues of racism in Germany, Sherrill dismissed it all as a German domestic matter, not unlike the treatment of Blacks in the United States: "It does not concern me one bit the way that the Jews in Germany are treated any more than the lynching of negroes in the south of our country."[59] Over the next few days, Canadian newspapers reported that not only had Nazi Germany issued invitations to the two female athletes but that Helene Mayer had accepted.

Sherrill, who hoped that the Nazis' promise to allow two athletes of mixed Jewish lineage to join the German Olympic team would still criticism of racism in Nazi sport, was disappointed. American boycott advocates, including many American Jews, were not quieted. Sherrill was reportedly angered by the continuing stream of protest. On 1 November the *Calgary Herald*, the *Winnipeg Free Press*, and the Toronto *Globe* all reported that Sherrill, who claimed he had intervened on behalf of Jewish interests in securing the two places for Jewish athletes on the German Olympic team, declared that he was going to withdraw from "those friendly efforts in the future." He was, he said, disappointed that his generous efforts should be met by so ungracious a Jewish response. But, he assured the press, none of the abuse heaped on him by Jews "can succeed in making me anti-Jewish."[60]

If Canadian press coverage of the American boycott debate often overshadowed the Canadian debate, opponents of Canadian Olympic participation may have been partly responsible. In an effort to build support for its cause, the Unity and Goodwill Association filled its newsletter with American pro-boycott material. One can understand why. Not only was the clash between Mahoney and Brundage front-page news in both the United States and Canada, but the arguments both men raised in advocating their respective positions echoed the arguments on Canadian attendance at the games. But unlike the American debate, which attracted wide above-the-fold American press coverage, coverage of the Canadian debate was largely relegated to the sports pages and letters to the editor.

Whatever the press coverage, for Canadian boycott proponents the key issue was crystal clear. Hitler's regime was so stained by its racism, antisemitism, aggressive militarism, and bare-knuckled brutality that it had forfeited any right to host the Olympic Games. On 9 October, Casriel Katz wrote to the *Calgary Herald* protesting, "Since the Nazis are persecuting the Jews, the Catholics and Protestants who do not accept Hitler's platform, the holding of the games there would be a mockery of the objectives of this quadrennial international institution of fair play."[61] On 13 November a *Toronto Star* editorial by "An Observer" also underscored the unrelenting brutality of the Nazi regime. The writer focused on Hitler's systematic destruction of German trade unions, his determination to drive "men of courage and liberal thought" out of German universities, his persecution of Jews and Christians, and his determination to "shut up in concentration camps all whom he feared." In the face of all the evidence of Nazi evil, the "Observer" was shocked by the audacity of Hitler and the German Olympic Committee's call to "summon the youth of the world" to compete in Olympic sport.[62] In addition to pointing out the racial prejudice of the regime, in a 12 October edition of the *Winnipeg Free Press*, Fred Kazor decried Hitler's militarism, stating that his beating of war drums made a mockery of Pierre de Coubertin's dream that the modern Olympic Games would serve to promote peace and toleration: "It is well known that all sport in Germany is under military control. The war preparations in

Germany and the Nazis' war plan are common talk. Can we allow such a ruler to be the patron of such a wonderful peace ideal?"[63]

Letters to the editor in favour of the boycott claimed that despite denials by the German Olympic Committee, Jewish athletes in Germany were being treated unfairly. Casriel Katz, writing to the *Calgary Herald*, observed that "the known facts are that to compete one must belong to certain athletic clubs approved by Nazis. In this manner non-Aryans – Jews – are not accepted in such organizations and Catholics and Protestants who refuse to subscribe to the Nazi doctrines are excluded from membership."[64] In a 26 October letter to the editor of the *Winnipeg Free Press*, Fred Watson also heaped scorn on the promises of the German Olympic Committee that visiting non-Aryans athletes at the games would be treated fairly: "Hitler's Aryan clause states that no Jew can become a member or participate in the activities of Nazi sports organizations, (which are the only legal sports organizations in Germany today)."[65]

Supporters of the boycott also argued that Hitler should be denied the prestige that would come from hosting the Olympic Games. Casriel Katz dismissed the entire Nazi Olympics as no more than a propaganda ploy by Hitler to bolster his regime's domestic popularity: "It is now known conclusively that the Nazis are planning to use the Olympic games as a means of making the people of Germany believe that the world is approving the Nazi dictatorship." A boycott, Katz argued, might wake up the German people: "If the games are not held in Berlin, then the fact will be forcefully brought to the attention of the German people that the moral conscience of the world is aroused and cries against injustices and persecutions and brands the Nazi platform as despicable and intolerant."[66] The *Toronto Star*'s "Observer" offered a similar view. He claimed that the German people were being duped by Hitler into believing that by sending athletes to the Olympic Games in Germany the world was endorsing the Nazi regime. By boycotting the Olympics, Canada would help prevent the Nazis from continuing this deception: "The docile Germans expect to see the world responding to the Führer's summons and falling over itself to place its stamp of approval on Nazi barbarities." The "Observer" hoped that the Western democracies would deny Hitler the world stage he so craved. [67]

The CJC and other Olympic boycott activists hoped that these arguments would bring the sports establishment, including the sports columnists, onside with the boycott campaign, and they did score some limited success. On 1 November, Hal Straight of the *Vancouver Sun* wrote that he had been closely monitoring the American debate over Olympic participation and had originally been neutral about the issue "because big sport affairs nowadays have a habit of stirring up controversy for publicity reasons." But he said that during the previous few months he had come to realize that Hitler's animosity to the Jews was not a passing phenomenon and that Jewish athletes were not being treated equally in Germany: "Personally, now, I think it is a serious affair myself." He saw it as the latest in a long line of historical injustices inflicted on Jews and argued that any countries that had accepted Jews needed to respect their rights. In the offbeat style that seemed to be favoured by sports columnists, Straight called for a boycott: "So in conclusion of this subject ... I suggest all the flags be put together, made into a nice bright blanket and wrapped around Herr Hitler's head and thus boycotting his athletic plans and waiting for the Olympic games until another year. Nobody has the right to interfere with such a beautiful tradition as the Olympics."[68]

Two weeks and many propaganda leaflets later, Straight restated his views (buttressed by material from Unity and Goodwill Association newsletters). But apparently he had given up hope that the "Old Boys" of the coc would vote against accepting the German invitation. Consequently, he no longer called on the coc to vote in favour of the boycott. Instead, he argued for a campaign to discourage Canadians from contributing to any fundraising designed to cover the cost of sending Canadian athletes to Germany. If enough propaganda was circulated, he argued, "by the time athletic organizations go panhandling for money the public will be lukewarm and won't dig very deep ... The result will be most likely a small entry at the games which would no doubt bother Herr Hitler. I hope so."[69]

Press supporters of Canadian Olympic participation were no less determined. On 30 October, Ralph Wilson of the *Calgary Herald*, drawing on pro-Olympic literature he had received from the German Olympic Committee, pronounced Canadian attendance at the games not just a *fait accompli* but a good thing for Canada and for sport.[70] Meanwhile in Toronto, Eisendrath failed in his bid to convince the dean of Canadian sports journalists, Lou Marsh, editor of the sports pages of the *Toronto Star*, of the moral and ethical necessity for an Olympic boycott. After a rather heated exchange with Marsh (which, reportedly, ended on friendly terms), Eisendrath summarized Marsh's isolationist view, which he conceded was widespread in the sporting fraternity: "The sporting editor [Marsh], and the sport world as a whole, takes the position that the whole matter [of Nazi antisemitism] is an internal matter that concerns Germany and not ourselves."[71]

Andy Lytle, also of the *Toronto Star*, shared Marsh's enthusiasm for Canadian participation. According to Lytle, German mistreatment of visiting Jewish Olympic athletes was of little or no concern to Canada. There were very few competitive Jewish athletes in Canada, so why worry about them? he asked. And even if a Canadian Jew did qualify for the Canadian team, Lytle had been assured by a COC spokesperson that any German prejudice against a Jewish athlete from Canada would result in the whole Canadian team withdrawing. All other issues raised by boycott advocates were dismissed by Lytle as incidents of "class hatred" between German and Jew which, like Marsh, he rejected as irrelevant to the Canadian Olympic team's participation. The purpose of the Olympic Games was sporting competition, and nobody should be allowed to use the games to advance narrow and parochial interests.

Lytle also suggested that the aggressive advocacy tactics of Canadian boycott supporters were doing harm to their cause. If COC officials held themselves aloof from the ongoing propaganda war, which Lytle assessed to be the wisest course, he viewed with disdain the importation into Canada of the kind of mud slinging and name calling he described as common in the American Olympic debate. Canadian Olympic officials, he said, felt unjustly attacked by boycott proponents for being pro-Nazi, unpatriotic, and lacking in the quality of brotherly love. This, Lytle declared to be repugnant. Moreover, it would backfire: "The gorge rises against such underhand methods. If it has any particular effect now or later, it will simply be that the official neck will bow more strongly in the direction of participation by a full Canadian team at Berlin. *I have that information as directly as it is possible to obtain it.*"[72]

It is impossible to know exactly whom Lytle knew, although it is likely that he had personal access to one or more members of the COC, which was indeed trying to appear publicly "aloof" from the boycott debate, though privately maintaining a vital stake in seeing that the pro-boycott campaign fail. What we do know for certain is that Canadian boycott advocates hoped against hope that they could persuade the COC that Nazi racial persecutions and violations of the Treaty of Versailles in the fall of 1935 – all of which were well covered in the Canadian press – disqualified Germany from hosting the 1936 Olympic Games. But their case was compromised by a counter-campaign by those who favoured Canadian participation, aided by the German government and its supporters. Declaring that the Nazi Games would be in keeping with the Olympic spirit, the games' supporters raised doubts about the motives of those who claimed otherwise. According to Olympic supporters, it was the boycott advocates – not the Nazis – who were subverting sport for political gain. Sport and politics, they insisted, were separate spheres and should remain separate; those, like the organized Jewish community, who urged a boycott demonstrated neither interest in the Olympic Games nor appreciation for the Canadian athletes who had trained so hard and so long to represent Canada in Germany. Boycott supporters, they argued, cared only about scoring points in their tiresome political dispute with Germany, and if this meant sacrificing Canadian Olympic hopes, then that was a price they were apparently willing to pay. Not so the COC.

In spite of all evidence that the Nazis were wilfully corrupting the Olympic ideal and that behind their carefully constructed Olympic façade they were moving ahead with their racist and militaristic agendas, the members of the Canadian Olympic Committee and the larger Amateur Athletic Union of Canada, with deeply vested interests in Canadian participation in the Olympic Games, unanimously endorsed Canadian Olympic participation. And as a review of the Canadian press from the day makes clear, they did so not out of ignorance of the events in Nazi Germany, especially during the fall of 1935, but in full knowledge of what was going on.

NOTES

1   *Mail and Empire* (Toronto), 22 November 1935.

2   *Winnipeg Free Press*, 22 November 1935, 17.

3   Kidd, *The Struggle for Canadian Sport*, 67–8.

4   D. Rosenberg, "The Canadian Jewish Congress and the 1936 Berlin Olympic Boycott Movement," 133–45. For a discussion of the left's anti-Olympic campaign, see Kidd, "Canadian Opposition to the 1936 Olympics in Germany."

5 Schleunes, *The Twisted Road to Auschwitz: Nazi Policy toward German Jews, 1933–1939*, 121.

6 Fischer, *Nazi Germany: A New History*, 208.

7 For a full airing of issues related to Nazi race science and its practical application, see Ehrenreich, *The Nazi Ancestral Proof: Genealogy, Racial Science, and the Final Solution*.

8 Kershaw, *Hitler, the Germans, and the Final Solution*, 161

9 McKenzie, *Through Turbulent Years*, 58.

10 Hilberg, *The Destruction of the European Jews*, 43–53; Graml, *Antisemitism in the Third Reich*, 116–25.

11 Sherrill, as quoted in Large, *Nazi Games: The Olympics of 1936*, 85. See also Wenn, "A Tale of Two Diplomats: George S. Messersmith and Charles H. Sherrill on Proposed American Participation in the 1936 Olympics," 37.

12 Krüger, "Germany: The Propaganda Machine," 17.

13 Large, *Nazi Games*, 49.

14 Hart-Davis, *Hitler's Games: The 1936 Olympics*, 46–58; Krüger, "Germany: The Propaganda Machine," 17–43.

15 Donnelly, *Dafoe of the Free Press*, 140–6; Dafoe's editorial is cited on 146.

16 Young, "Hitler's Early Critics: Canadian Resistance at the *Winnipeg Free Press*." On the editor John W. Dafoe, see also Cook, *The Politics of John W. Dafoe and the Free Press*, and Donnelly, *Dafone of the Free Press*.

17 Harkness, *J.E. Atkinson of the Star*.

18 Levitt and Shaffir, *The Riot at Christie Pits*, 51–75.

19 Mount, *Canada's Enemies: Spies and Spying in the Peaceable Kingdom*, 56–7; the passage quoted in the press is from 57.

20 Levitt and Shaffir, *The Riot at Christie Pits*, 228–49.

21 Ibid., 229.

22 Ibid., 250–1.

23 Studniberg, "One Shudders to Think What Might Happen': Vancouver Newspapers and the First Twelve Months of the Third Reich."

24 *Toronto Daily Star*, 5 September 1935, 42.

25 Ibid., 14 September 1935, 6.

26 *Globe* (Toronto), 11 September 1935, 2.

27 *Calgary Daily Herald*, 4 October 1935, 4.

28 *Globe*, 19 November 1935, 4.

29 *Toronto Daily Star*, 13 September 1935, section 2, 1; *Calgary Daily Herald*, 14 September, 1.

30 *Toronto Daily Star*, 18 October 1935, 1 and 29.

31 Ibid., 5 October 1935, 16.

32 *Globe*, 21 September 1935, 1.

33 *Calgary Daily Herald*, 16 September 1935, 1.

34 *Globe*, 16 September 1935, 1.

35 Lipstadt, *Beyond Belief: The American Press and the Coming of the Holocaust*, 58–9.

36 *Winnipeg Free Press*, 16 September 1935, 1.

37 *Calgary Daily Herald*, 15 November 1935, 1.

38 *Globe*, 16 November 13, 2.

39 *Globe*, 19 November 1935, 4.

40 *Toronto Daily Star*, 28 September 1935, 35.

41 Ibid., 12 October 1935, 12.

42 Ibid., 23 October 1935, 21.

43 The anti-Jewish laws did, in fact, fill a book. See Walk, *Das Sonderrecht für die Juden im NS-Staat.*

44 *Toronto Daily Star*, 5 November 1935, 13 and 37.

45 *Calgary Daily Herald*, 1 October 1935, 4.

46 *Globe*, 21 September 1935, 1 and 2.

47 Rabbi Maurice N. Eisendrath to H.M. Caiserman, 19 September 1935, Canadian Jewish Congress Charities Committee National Archives (CJCCCNA), CJC collection, series ZA 1935, box 2, file 16.

48 Undated, but from internal evidence from September or October 1935, CJCCCNA CJC collection, series ZA 1935, box 2, file 16.

49 Caiserman to Eisendrath, 27 October 1935, Caiserman to Finkelstein (president, Western Division of CJC), 14 November 1935, CJCCCNA CJC collection, series ZA 1935, box 2, file 16.

50 Eisendrath to Caiserman, 31 October 1935, P. Stuchen (executive director, Central Division, CJC) to Caiserman, 15 November 1935, CJCCCNA, CJC collection, series ZA 1935, box 4, file 22.

51 Caiserman to mass meeting of the Conference of Labour Oragnizations, 8 November 1935, CJCCCNA CJC collection, series ZA 1935, box 2, file 1.

52 *Toronto Daily Star*, 8 November 1935, 13.

53 *Vancouver Sun*, 14 November 1935, 23.

54 *Calgary Daily Herald*, 30 October 1935, 6. Ellipses in original.

55 Large, *Nazi Games*, 69–109.

56 *Globe*, 24 October 1935, 6, and *Winnipeg Free Press*, 24 October 1935, 14.

57 *Globe*, 22 October 1935, 6; *Winnipeg Free Press*, 22 October 1935, 17; *Calgary Daily Herald*, 22 October 1935, 6.

58 *Toronto Daily Star*, 26 October 1935, 10.

59 *Calgary Daily Herald*, 22 October 1935, 6.

60 Ibid., 1 November 1935, 8; *Winnipeg Free Press*, 1 November 1935, 22; *Globe*, 1 November 1935, 6.
61 *Calgary Daily Herald*, 9 October 1935, 4.
62 *Toronto Daily Star*, 13 November 1935, 6.
63 *Winnipeg Free Press*, 12 October 1935, 33.
64 *Calgary Daily Herald*, 9 October 1935, 4.
65 *Winnipeg Free Press*, 26 October 1935, 31.
66 *Calgary Daily Herald*, 9 October 1935, 4.
67 *Toronto Daily Star*, 13 November 1935, 6.
68 *Vancouver Sun*, 1 November 1935, 23.
69 Ibid., 14 November 1935, 29.
70 *Calgary Daily Herald*, 30 October 1935, 6.
71 Eisendrath to Caiserman, 31 October 1935, CJCCCNA, CJC collection, series ZA 1935, box 4, file 42.
72 *Toronto Daily Star*, 8 November 1935, 13.

3

From Kristallnacht to the MS *St Louis* Tragedy: Canadian Press Coverage of Nazi Persecution of the Jews and the Jewish Refugee Crisis, September 1938 to August 1939

AMANDA GRZYB

Silence is not possible when people are being treated like animals, being deliberately deprived of homes, of means of subsistence and the right to pursue a normal life unmolested ... In view of the official silence of this country when Canada's democratic ideals called for a vigorous protest, it is well that the voice of the people rose in mass volume.

Globe and Mail editorial, 22 November 1938[1]

We often characterize the late 1930s as a time when more liberal immigration policies might have changed the course of history for the European Jews. Every democratic nation bore some responsibility for the dismal response to the refugee crisis of 1933–39, but Irving Abella and Harold Troper suggest that Canada's record for admitting Jewish refugees was the "the worst of all possible refugee-receiving states,"[2] a dubious distinction in a global climate of restricted immigration quotas, bureaucratic barriers, and widespread antisemitism.[3] While Prime Minister William Lyon Mackenzie King and the Canadian government maintained an official silence after the Kristallnacht pogroms and negotiated Canada's response to the refugee crisis behind closed doors, how did the plight of the European Jews resonate in the public sphere? What did the average Canadian know about the Nazi persecution of the Jews and the spread of antisemitic violence across Europe? What did the newspapers say about Canada as a potential haven for Jewish refugees? And how was antisemitism – both at home and abroad – addressed by newspaper editorials and opinion pieces?

I begin to address these questions by analyzing the representation of Jewish persecution in the English Canadian press from 1 September 1938 to 31 August 1939, the year before the German Reich and the Slovak Republic invaded Poland and instigated the Second World War. Month after month leading up to the war, the *Globe and Mail* published articles and opinion pieces – some very brief and some quite detailed – about the spread of antisemitic ordinances and pogroms across the German Reich (comprised of Germany, Austria, Sudetenland, and the Protectorate of Bohemia and Moravia)[4] and in the Slovak Republic, Italy, Poland, Hungary, Czechoslovakia, Japan, Romania, and Lithuania. The *Globe and Mail* also ran dozens of articles about Jewish refugees and made prophetic references to Hitler's desire to annihilate the Jewish population.

I focus in particular on three significant moments in the coverage – Kristallnacht in November 1938, the MS *St Louis* incident in May–June 1939, and antisemitism in Quebec in August 1939 – and compare the *Globe*'s treatment of these events with concurrent coverage in six other Canadian newspapers. I identify the narrative threads and editorial positions that dominated the coverage and reflected or influenced public opinion about Jewish persecution. I conclude that the English Canadian press – like other newspapers around the world – gave significant coverage to the plight of the Jews, especially in the weeks after Kristallnacht. The *Globe* took a sympathetic view of the Jewish suffering, denounced antisemitism at home and abroad, and repeatedly called on the Canadian government to break its silence, condemn the persecution of the Jews, and open Canada's doors to Jewish refugees.

At the same time, I suggest that a combination of factors – event-driven coverage, a dramatic peak in the number of articles in November 1938, inadequate follow-up on the antisemitic ordinances introduced across Europe, and unfortunate ebbs in the coverage from March to May and July to August 1939 – eventually took Jewish persecution from a national priority to the back pages of the papers. A month before the war began, the English Canadian press was more preoccupied with antisemitic incidents in Quebec than with the continued persecution of the Jewish population across the Atlantic. As interest waned in the summer of 1939, Canadian newspapers – like the rest of the international community – turned their attention to the war and left European Jews to face an inconceivable torrent of destruction.

My methodology was as follows. I examined a full year of coverage – from 1 September 1938 to 31 August 1939 – in Canada's national, agenda-setting daily newspaper, the *Globe and Mail*, using the ProQuest Pages of the Past digitized newspaper archive. I found 408 relevant articles using the Boolean search term jew*, which retrieved every article that mentioned the word "Jew," "Jews," "Jewess," or "Jewish" in its headline or content. I retained all the articles that addressed the persecution of the European Jews, the Jewish refugee crisis, and global antisemitism (including antisemitic incidents in Canada). In some cases, these issues were the primary subject of the article, and in some cases they were mentioned only briefly as a secondary concern. I also retained articles that were primarily about "the Jewish community" or "the Jews" (for example, a series of letters to the editor in the *Globe* about "Jews and Communism"[5] and "Jewish contributions to the Great War")[6] because they would likely have influenced the general discourse about contemporaneous Jewish issues and could have promoted or challenged antisemitic stereotypes. I manually excluded articles that dealt exclusively with the British Mandate for Palestine, including Arab-Jewish conflict and advocacy for and against the establishment of a Jewish state. I did, however, retain articles that *directly* addressed the immigration of imperilled European Jews to Palestine.

I tabulated the number of articles that ran each month and then subdivided those groups into four categories: (1) news articles of significant length (more than one-paragraph) in which the persecution of the Jews was the primary subject; (2) brief one-paragraph news items about the persecution of the Jews or new articles of significant length in which the persecution of the Jews was a secondary subject; (3) editorials and opinion pieces about the "the Jews" and the persecution of the Jews; and (4) letters to the editor that addressed "the Jews" and the persecution of the Jews. Next, I performed a qualitative content analysis of these texts. I identified the ebbs and flows in the *Globe*'s coverage of Jewish persecution, the discernable tone in the objective news pieces, the primary and secondary sources that defined the content of the articles, the views expressed in editorial and opinion pieces, and the dominant narratives that both reflected and influenced public opinion.

Once I had established the major historical nodes in the *Globe's* coverage, I conducted targeted archival microfilm research for six additional newspapers – the *London Free Press*, the Montreal *Gazette*, the *Ottawa Citizen*, the *Toronto Daily Star*, the *Vancouver Sun*, and the *Winnipeg Free Press* – during three critical episodes: the Kristallnacht pogroms in Germany in November 1938; the MS *St Louis* incident in May and June 1939, when the Jewish refugees on board the ship were refused entry by Canada and other countries; and reports of antisemitic incidents in Ste-Agathe-des-Monts, Quebec, in August 1939. By examining national and regional stories about the same critical events, I was able to fill out the nuances of the newspaper coverage across the country and obtain additional details about instances of local antisemitism and about the local anti-Nazi rallies organized across the country on 20 November 1938.

PREWAR COVERAGE: US AND CANADIAN PERSPECTIVES

In *The Holocaust in American Life*, Peter Novick suggests that the "prewar Nazi actions against the Jews, from early discriminatory measures to the enactment of the Nuremberg Laws in 1935 and culminating in Kristallnacht in 1938, were widely reported in the American press."[7] Jewish persecution was, Novick claims, a part of the "public consciousness."[8] However, despite the extensive reports and front-page coverage of the Kristallnacht pogroms, America's paper of record, the *New York Times*, did not always give sufficient context to its reports. Laurel Leff claims that the *Times*'s "editorials maintained throughout the 1930s that the refugee crisis was not particularly a Jewish problem."[9] Both Novick and Leff suggest that while Americans knew about Jewish suffering "in a general way,"[10] once the war began, the Holocaust assumed a place of "marginality ... in the American mind."[11] For Deborah Lipstadt, this marginality was generated, in part, by the inability of the American press to grasp why the Nazis repeatedly allowed antisemitic violence to strain its relationship with the international community. She writes, "[H]ad the American press and other Western observers understood the central role of antisemitism in Nazi ideology, they would have been less perplexed by the violence, which seemed to run counter to Germany's intention to win investing nations' confidence in the Reich."[12]

The Canadian press also reported extensively on the prewar plight of the Jews. During the year preceding the Nazi invasion of Poland, the *Globe and Mail* ran 408 articles and opinion pieces about the persecution of the European Jews, the Jewish refugee crisis, and anti-semitism at home and abroad. Unlike the *New York Times* – where the Jewish publishers hesitated to single out Jewish victims[13] – Can-adian newspapers took strong editorial positions opposing the wide-spread abuse of the Jews. Abella and Troper write: "The activities of the pro-refugee committees, combined with a general unease among some Canadians over their government's policy [to keep the door closed to Jewish refugees], brought forth from Canadian newspapers an almost unanimous denunciation of the 'pusillanimous' behavior of the King administration. Since Kristallnacht most of the press – including even the odd paper in Quebec – had urged the govern-ment to be more generous toward the Jewish refugees." If, indeed, the English-language newspapers reflected feelings of outrage in the Canadian public sphere, the exceptionally extensive coverage also influenced public opinion, widely broadcasting the content of public talks, events, and rallies and inspiring impassioned letters to the editor.

It is important to recognize, however, that while the English Can-adian press was relatively unified in its condemnation of Nazi vio-lence against the Jews and many Canadians took a stand to oppose Jewish persecution, the country was far from united. Antisemitism continued to proliferate in Canadian culture, particularly in Quebec. Franklin Bialystok writes: "In the interwar period and increasingly in the 1930s, antisemitism had become a constant in Canadian soci-ety. It was not confined to any one region, nor was it promoted by one dominant movement. Antisemitism was found in every region and manifested itself in several forms ... Jews were discriminated against in education, employment, and housing, and were prevented from sponsoring their families and townspeople in Europe because of stringent immigration restrictions."[14] Indeed, the extensive press coverage of Jewish persecution is even more noteworthy in light of widespread discrimination against Jews in Canada in the 1930s.

In September 1938 the *Globe and Mail* ran eighteen items that addressed the spread of Jewish persecution across Europe and the

Table 1
Globe and Mail Articles about Jewish Persecution and the Refugee Crisis, September 1938 to August 1939

Month	News: primary	News: secondary	Editorial or opinion	Letters	Total
Sep 1938	7	7	2	2	18
Oct 1938	8	14	1	1	24
Nov 1938	69	8	12	4	93
Dec 1938	35	14	8	4	61
Jan 1939	23	13	4	4	44
Feb 1939	15	25	6	6	52
Mar 1939	6	12	2	5	25
Apr 1939	1	7	2	7	17
May 1939	4	4	1	1	10
June 1939	20	15	3	0	38
July 1939	4	4	2	0	10
Aug 1939	9	1	3	3	16
	(6 Canada)		(2 Canada)	(2 Canada)	(10 Canada)
TOTAL	201	124	46	37	408

growing refugee crisis, and in October the number rose to twenty-four. The number spiked dramatically to ninety-three items in November following Kristallnacht, the state-sponsored pogroms committed against Jews in Germany and Austria after the shooting in France on 7 November of a German official, Ernst vom Rath, by a young Polish Jew. The number of articles declined over the next six months – sixty-one in December, forty-four in January, fifty-two in February, twenty-five in March, seventeen in April, and ten in May – until the MS *St Louis* incident in 1939 generated episodic coverage and reignited Canadian interest in the refugee crisis, resulting in a small spike of thirty-eight articles in June. Two months before the beginning of the war, in July and August 1939, the *Globe* published only ten and sixteen articles, respectively. A majority of the coverage in August dealt with antisemitic drives in Quebec; with domestic stories excluded, there were only six articles in the entire month that dealt with the persecution of the European Jews.

What do these numbers tell us? First, even though the number of articles ebbed and flowed, the *Globe and Mail* focused a remarkable amount of attention on Jewish persecution in the year before the war began. Almost one-quarter of the relevant articles were published in

the aftermath of Kristallnacht, with another modest surge during
the MS *St Louis* incident in June 1939. The stories were reactive and
event-driven, and most of the reports about pogroms or antisemitic
ordinances were descriptive, not overly analytical. While certain episodes, such as the trial of vom Rath's assassin, Herschel Grynszpan,
or the ill-fated voyage of the *St Louis*, were reported in a serial style,
most of the articles were not explicitly linked together. Instead, the
reportage had a cumulative effect, producing an overarching narrative understanding that Jews were increasingly imperilled across
Europe and that racial doctrine and antisemitic ordinances were
spreading from country to country (not all of them annexed by or
allied with the German Reich).

In very general terms, the national and regional newspaper coverage oscillated between reports about European antisemitism (in the
form of both pogroms and discriminatory ordinances) and reports
about the international Jewish refugee crisis. More specifically,
four long-range themes emerged from all seven newspapers in the
study: (1) antisemitic laws, ordinances, segregation, and other forms
of institutionalized discrimination in the German Reich and other
European countries; (2) antisemitic pogroms, which peaked during
Kristallnacht in November 1938, and the Canadian rallies protesting
this violence; (3) the Jewish refugee crisis, which culminated in the
coverage of the MS *St Louis* tragedy in June 1939; and (4) Canadian
antisemitism, which included periodic incidents throughout the year
and received sustained coverage in August 1939 during discriminatory drives in Ste-Agathe-des-Monts, Quebec.

Canadian newspapers obtained the majority of their stories about
Jewish persecution in Europe from newswire services such as Associated Press (AP), Canadian Press (CP), and Havas. The main sources
or primary definers for these articles were often official documents
or proclamations, state leaders or their spokespeople (e.g., Hitler,
Mussolini, Goebbels, Mackenzie King, Roosevelt, and Chamberlain),
and authoritative summaries of previously published stories in foreign newspapers. There were also articles that offered sympathetic
commentary on Jewish "character," Jewish persecution, and the Jewish refugee crisis vis-à-vis summaries of dozens of public statements,
talks, and sermons by religious figures, community leaders, politicians, and scholars.

While most of the articles relayed a sense of mass Jewish suffering,
the individual victims themselves were rarely quoted as sources.

Indeed, the articles typically referred to "the Jews" as a monolithic national/ethnic/religious group. For example, in November 1939 the *Globe* wrote of "9000 Polish Jews"[15] deported from Germany and of "German Jews, most of them in seclusion and an estimated 40,000 under arrest," who awaited "their ultimate fate."[16] On 14 November the *Vancouver Sun* described "a new flood of German Jews seeking safety" in France.[17] The same month, the Montreal *Gazette* published a story that warned, "unless the democracies evacuate German Jews at once and at their own expense, the 'non-Aryans' will be starved into crime, then exterminated with 'fire and sword.'"[18] While Canadians certainly had a sense of the large-scale persecution of Polish Jews and German Jews – and even the foreboding possibility of Jewish extermination – there was very little to connect the reader to singular narratives that would give a relatable, individual face to mass suffering. The only exceptions were the periodic reports of suicide in which a Jewish victim might be named and individualized. Even when the coverage was daily or almost daily – as it was between November 1938 and February 1939 – the articles had the inadvertent effect of objectifying the European Jews, of describing mass violence so pervasive and so prolific that it had the potential to overwhelm Canadian readers with a sense of hopelessness or inevitability.

Of the seven newspapers I examined, the *Globe* had a particularly strong record of editorials and opinion pieces about Jewish persecution in 1938 and 1939. They deplored the mistreatment of the Jews, called for Canadian intervention in the ongoing refugee crisis, and, in some cases, exerted pressure on the Canadian government to increase immigration quotas. However, dramatic ebbs and flows in news and editorial coverage, from the remarkable peak in November 1938 to the lows in May, July, and August 1939, suggested that interest in Jewish persecution was waning by the summer. There was a general preoccupation with impending war, which the Canadian press predicted month after month. While we might speculate that the international community developed a sense of "compassion fatigue"[19] from reading the same unresolved narratives of Jewish suffering again and again, or that repeated incidents may have either "normalized" the persecution or desensitized the reader to its gravity, there was also evidently some optimism in the winter of 1939 that the Nazis were willing to "ransom" the German Jews and allow them to emigrate in a mass "exodus" to Africa or South America.[20]

The overarching narrative from September 1938 to August 1939 contradicted some of the simultaneous predictions about Jewish annihilation, suggesting perhaps that the Kristallnacht pogroms had been the worst of the violence.

PRELUDE TO KRISTALLNACHT

In the fall of 1938 there was a moderate amount of coverage in the *Globe and Mail* addressing Jewish persecution, including eighteen articles in September and twenty-four in October. These stories generally fitted into four categories: (1) the continued persecution of the Jews by the Nazis, particularly in the newly annexed areas of Austria and Sudetenland; (2) antisemitism in other European countries, including Czechoslovakia, Hungary, and Poland; (3) the implementation of a new antisemitic race doctrine in Italy; and (4) the problem of Jewish refugees. While each of these categories bore roughly the same number of articles – many of them quite brief – the limited front-page coverage focused primarily on Italian antisemitism and the ongoing Jewish refugee crisis.

The month of September began with a long opinion piece by *Globe and Mail* columnist J.V. McAree, who reminded his readers about the extent of state-sponsored Jewish persecution by the Nazis and made dire predictions for the future of the Jews. The article, "Planned Atrocities Aimed at Jews," recounted a report in the *Nation* by former US ambassador to Nazi Germany, William E. Dodd. McAree quoted Dodd at length:

> Says Mr. Dodd: "Unless one has been an eyewitness of the atrocities inflicted upon the Jewish population of Germany and Austria, it is almost impossible to imagine the extent and violence of Nazi persecution. An entire race is being broken by methodical torture, perpetrated not by isolated individuals but by the State itself. Never in modern times has a sovereign power bent itself so savagely on the extinction of its own inhabitants or so deliberately transgressed every tradition of culture and humanity."[21]

McAree cited Dodd's clear assertion – two months before Kristallnacht – that the violence against German and Austrian Jews was systematic and state sponsored. He identified antisemitic propaganda as the core of Nazi rule, and he closed his column with a chilling – and seemingly prophetic – warning about the scale of Hitler's threats: "The plain intention of the German Reich is to drive the Jews out. Probably they would leave in a body if they could take their property with them, but this they are forbidden to do. What is called the 'cold program' will get them in the end. Hitler is on record as promising that no Jews will survive in Germany by 1950."[22] While Peter Novick claims that the use of terms such as "extinction," "extermination," and "annihilation" before 1942 "was not prescience but hyperbole,"[23] it is difficult to dismiss Dodd's first-hand observations about the nature of Jewish persecution in the German Reich and McAree's reference to Hitler's own words.

The *Globe*'s lead editorial on 10 September, "No Peace with Hitler," mentioned Jewish persecution but ultimately undermined McAree's emphasis on the Jews as special victims of the Reich. The editorial began by recounting the horrors endured by the Jews: "What era in history has any more dreadful chapters than those Hitler has written in the persecution of the Jews."[24] However, for the *Globe* editors, the mistreatment of the Jews was merely the starting point for Nazi violence. They continued, in the following paragraphs, to note – correctly – that the inmates of the Nazi concentration camps were not imprisoned exclusively on grounds of racial or religious identity: "Though beginning with the Jews, Nazi depravity has by no means stopped there. The concentration camps are non-racial in their frightfulness."[25] Novick suggests that this interpretation was common prior to Kristallnacht: "No one doubted the Jews were high on the list of actual and potential victims of Nazism, but it was a long list, and Jews, by some measures, were not at the top ... [U]ntil late 1938 there were few Jews, as Jews, among those imprisoned, tortured, and murdered in the camps. The victims were overwhelmingly Communists, socialists, trade unionists, and other political opponents of the Hitler regime."[26] Thus, in early September 1938, McAree's dire warning about Hitler's plan to eradicate the Jews was tempered by an editorial that sought to universalize the Nazis' victims.

Likewise, the *Globe*'s spotty news coverage of Jewish persecution by the Nazis in the two months prior to Kristallnacht did nothing to support the urgency of McAree's message. In the entire month of September, the *Globe* ran only two very brief, one-paragraph news articles about Nazi treatment of the Jews: "Reich Defines Circumstances Voiding Will" on 9 September[27] and "German, Austrian

Exiles Say Things Bad in Germany" on 24 September;[28] two letters to the editor, on 20 September[29] and 29 September,[30] mentioning the plight of German Jews; and a summary, on 26 September, of a Rosh Hashanah *Derasha* condemning the Nazis, which was delivered at a Toronto synagogue.[31] In October there were only four articles that detailed Nazi persecution of the Jews, all in annexed territories: a one-paragraph front-page article, "Anti-Semitic Signs Spring Up on Heels of Nazi Occupation" on 4 October,[32] which cited anti-semitic signs in Sudeten after German annexation; and three very brief mentions of antisemitic incidents in Austria: a celebration of "Jew free" status in Mattersdorf on 11 October,[33] crowds denouncing Austrian Cardinal Innitzer by shouting "Innitzer to Dachau! The Jews friend in Dachau!" on 14 October,[34] and "a new wave of anti-Semitism against the some 220,000 Jews who still remain in Vienna," which included smashed windows in "twenty buildings – synagogues, private dwellings, and some stores operated by Jews" on 17 October.[35]

While the *Globe*'s stories about Nazi abuses of the Jews were brief and limited in September and October, there was significant coverage of the ominous spread of Jewish persecution across other parts of Europe. Taken alone, a single article might have suggested an isolated incident, a momentary outburst of antisemitic violence. Taken together, the stories painted a pernicious portrait of systematic, bureaucratized antisemitism outside the German Reich that further limited the number of possible safe havens for Europe's Jews. Indeed, some of the countries enacting new antisemitic laws, such as Poland and Hungary, were themselves threatened by the Nazis. On 5 September the *Globe* ran a front-page article about military conscription in Hungary that included a reference to the government's new plan for "anti-Semitic measures to check Jewish influence."[36] While the *Globe* did not directly follow up on the implications of these new "measures," it did run a one-paragraph front-page story, "Several Hundred Jews Reported Held in Hungary," on 12 October, which referenced the internment of seven hundred Jews in a concentration camp at Nagy-Kanizsa [sic].[37] On 14 September there was a brief mention that "many shop windows of Jewish merchants were smashed in Sudetenland towns" during clashes between Czechs and Sudetens in Czechoslovakia prior to German annexation.[38] A small one-paragraph article on 19 September reported on the Polish government's desire to remove thousands of "would-be emigrants," mostly Jews, from the country.[39]

While the references to Hungary, Czechoslovakia, and Poland suggested widespread antisemitism in countries that were not yet allied with or occupied by the German Reich, the *Globe* focused most of its September-October coverage on antisemitic measures in Italy. In July 1938 the Mussolini government procured and published the "Manifesto of the Racist Scientists," and in the following months instituted a number of Nazi-like antisemitic laws that limited Jewish participation in Italian public life. The leading story on 2 September, "10,000 Jews are Ordered to Quit Italy," reported that the Italian government had revoked the citizenship of all Jews who had settled in Italy since the Great War[40] and ordered them to leave the country within six months.[41] During the next month, the *Globe* published a report on 3 September about the expulsion of Jews from Italian universities[42] and an article on 8 September detailing the removal of Jewish politicians, lawyers, and military officers, and the view of Pope Pius XI "that the anti-Semitic doctrine 'concerns a great and serious error which reaches the steps of the altar, touching the Catholic doctrine.'"[43] This was followed by a one-paragraph front-page article on 22 September reporting confirmation from the Italian Broadcast System that "no music by Jewish composers would be broadcast."[44] The following month, the *Globe* published an article on 7 October about British-Italian relations that included mention of the ban of textbooks written by Jewish authors and "measures to 'limit participation of Jews in the national life in proportion to their numerical representations'";[45] a one-sentence report on 8 October that referenced "sweeping decrees limiting activities of Jews and forbidding mixed marriages";[46] an editorial on 15 October lambasting the Italian government's decree that its citizens must not laugh at Jewish comedians;[47] and one sentence on 18 October reporting the ban of Jewish stockbrokers from the Rome Exchange.[48]

During the first week of November, before the initial reports about the shooting of Ernst vom Rath, coverage of Jewish persecution appeared to be on the decline. There were only two relevant articles that week, both on the front page: an article on 1 November about 13,000 Polish refugees deported by the German Reich[49] and a very brief mention in a 3 November article that referred to "panicky" Jews who feared Hungarian antisemitism when Czechoslovakian land was ceded to Hungary.[50] There was nothing to suggest the Nazi pogroms and the resulting surge of international newspaper coverage that would soon follow.

NIGHT OF BROKEN GLASS

On 27–28 October, two weeks before the assassination that purportedly sparked Kristallnacht, the Gestapo had deported thousands of Polish Jews from Germany to the Polish border, where they were denied entrance. On 1 November the *Globe* reported that there were "some 9,000 Polish Jews huddled together in temporary quarters tonight on the German side of the Polish frontier anxiously awaiting results of negotiations in Warsaw tomorrow between the two nations."[51] As discussed in chapter 1, among the refugees was the family of Herschel Grynszpan, a 17-year-old Polish Jew living in Paris, who, incensed at his family's plight, shot German Embassy official Ernst vom Rath, sparking the Kristallnacht riots.

The international response to Kristallnacht was striking. Saul Friedlander cites "scathing" comments in the media, noting Goebbels's observation that "the foreign press [was] very bad."[52] Deborah Lipstadt claims that there were "almost 1000"[53] editorials in the US press condemning the violence. Indeed, nearly one-quarter of the *Globe and Mail*'s articles about Jewish persecution and the refugee crisis between September 1938 and August 1939 were published during the month of November. Other Canadian newspapers – the *London Free Press*, the Montreal *Gazette*, the *Ottawa Citizen*, the *Toronto Daily Star*, the *Vancouver Sun*, and the *Winnipeg Free Press* – also carried extensive front-page coverage, often using the same newswire services as the *Globe*. In total, the *Globe* published ninety-three relevant articles in November 1938, including sixty-nine primary stories, eight secondary stories, twelve opinion and editorial pieces, and four letters to the editor.

The plight of the European Jews was on the front page of the *Globe* for twenty days straight between 9 and 29 November, and every issue of the paper included multiple articles describing antisemitic violence, the international political response to the Nazis, and demonstrations of public outrage. Canadian coverage peaked on 21–22 November, immediately after Canadians held rallies across the country protesting the Nazis' persecution of the Jews. With a combined total of eighteen articles, there was more *Globe* coverage

Table 2
Articles in the *Globe and Mail* Addressing Jewish Persecution during
and after Kristallnacht, 8–30 November

Day	Total number of articles	Front-page articles
8 November	1	1
9 November	5	0
10 November	3	1
11 November	2	1
12 November	6	3
14 November	7	2
15 November	6	3
16 November	3	3
17 November	4	3
18 November	8	3
19 November	7	2
21 November	9	4
22 November	9	3
23 November	7	5
24 November	4	2
25 November	7	3
26 November	2	1
28 November	4	1
29 November	2	2
30 November	2	0

about the plight of European Jews in those two days than in July and August 1939 combined.

On 9 November the *Globe* reported that the shooting of vom Rath was "answered in the German press ... with blazing wrath and a unanimous demand for retaliation against both German and foreign Jews in the Reich."[54] The article also mentioned the first signs of physical violence against Jewish property: the destruction of a synagogue and smashed shop windows in Kassel. Ironically, the *Globe*'s editorial on the same day addressed antisemitic window smashing not in Germany but in Brantford, Ontario. In "Stupid Racial Persecution," the editors wrote, "A front window in a house occupied by a Jewish family was smashed on Saturday night. Before the house was tenanted someone entered and daubed paint on the walls and windows, one message being 'Jew, you can't stay here.' This is a deliberate and reprehensible persecution."[55] The piece ended with a condemnation of the act: "This country, at least, should be free of racial persecution."[56] A second editorial, on 9 November, mentioned the Jews in the context of Armistice Day: "Let us also remember the Jews and other minorities who have suffered in order that there might be no war."[57]

By 11 November, the *Globe* reported "vengeance on Jewish shops, offices, and synagogues" across the German Reich and cited Joseph Goebbels's description of the violence as "justified and understandable anger by the German people."[58] Although the Nazis maintained that the violence was spontaneous, Sir Martin Gilbert cites an entry in Goebbels's diary that confirms how the Nazis sponsored and facilitated the violence:

> On the evening of November 9, [Hitler] was told that vom Rath was dead. Hitler's Minister of Propaganda, Dr. Goebbels, who was with him in Munich, told him that violence against Jews had already broken out in several German cities. Goebbels recorded Hitler's response in his diary: "He decides: demonstrations should be allowed to continue. The police should be withdrawn. For once the Jews should get the feel of popular anger." Goebbels added: "I immediately give the necessary instructions to the police and the Party. Then I briefly speak in that vein to the Party leadership. Story applause. All are instantly at the phones. Now people will act."[59]

The editors of the *Globe* were not convinced by Goebbels's denial of responsibility, and on 11 November they published the following statement in their "Notes and Comments" section of the editorial page: "Propaganda Minister Goebbels 'strictly requested' that the mob attacks on German Jews should cease. We do not know what 'strictly requested' means in German; but obviously it falls somewhat short of a command."[60] Likewise, the *Toronto Daily Star* published a similar note in its "Note and Comment" section on 11 November: "The highest authorities in Germany permitted, if they did not organize, the wrecking of Jewish stores in Berlin yesterday. Not a mob but a group of men acting under directions committed shameful acts of vandalism while the police looked on. A country in which such occurrences are possible cannot be regarded as really civilized."[61] In an editorial on 14 November, the *Globe*'s editors again expressed their opinion that the pogroms were planned and state-sponsored: "Far from spontaneous [the attacks] can now be seen as an attempt to manufacture an excuse and prepare the public mind for the 'complete liquidation of the Jews.'"[62] An editorial in the

Toronto Daily Star ran the same day, citing the desperate Jewish victims of state-organized violence: "Members of the Nazi ruling class drove about in trucks under their leaders attacking every Jew they could find and destroying commercial houses and sacred edifices owned by the Jews, while the agents of law and order looked on. Such tragic scenes were witnessed that hundreds of Jews were driven to commit suicide."[63]

Day after day, the Canadian press documented new levels of Jewish persecution by the Reich. On 11 November, *Globe* correspondent Otto D. Tolischus reported, "[I]t is assumed that Jews who have now lost most of their possessions and livelihood will be thrown either into the streets or put in ghettos and concentration camps, or impressed into labor brigades and put to work for the Third Reich."[64] On 12 November the *Globe* described trainloads of Jews who were sent to Buchenwald.[65] On 14 November it reported that Jews were "forced to pay a $400,000,000 fine" for vom Rath's assassination,[66] that Jewish stores were being "passed to non-Jewish owners,"[67] and that the "The Jewish Old People's Home" in Munich had been closed.[68] On 15 November the *Globe* reported that Jewish students were being expelled.[69] And on 18 November it reported that Jews were barred from hotels[70] and that the Nazis had seized Jewish art.[71] Discussions in the press about the refugee crisis also took on new urgency in light of reports about pogroms and new antisemitic laws in the German Reich. In the *Globe* alone there were almost thirty articles between 10 and 29 November addressing the refugee crisis.

How did Canada react to Kristallnacht and the antisemitic measures imposed by the Nazis in its aftermath? There were three potential outlets for Canadians to participate in a collective condemnation of the violence: official government statements, advocacy by the press, and public rallies and demonstrations. While both Roosevelt and Chamberlain publicly denounced the pogroms on behalf of Americans and Britons, the Canadian government made no such official statement.[72] In a particularly scathing editorial on 18 November, the *Globe* chastised "the complacency of Canada's government" and Mackenzie King's silence.[73] The editors concluded:

If we know anything of the vigor and directness of Canadian people they are becoming bitterly tired of the laissez-faire attitude towards things that matter. Must we await declaration of

war with arms before recognizing that human ideals are in a
life-and-death struggle with forces seeking to ruin civilization?
Defend the Jews of Central Europe in their terrible plight or not,
we cannot afford to let the spirit of righteousness lie dormant
while barbarity marches in triumph. We can at least assert our
principles. We can keep the mark of human forbearance alive
by proclaiming the creed we believe. We can and should match
every ruthless act of Nazism with an official avowal that it is a
blot on world sanity, a desecration of human justice, a step further into the jungle of wild beasts.[74]

Interestingly, the editorial criticized the Canadian government for
its silence about the persecution of the Jews during Kristallnacht
but also used the Jewish victims as an example of the Nazis' overarching attack on "righteousness" and "human justice." For the
Globe editors, responding to Kristallnacht was not so much about
defending the Jews *as Jews* – as special victims of Nazi antisemitic
violence – but defending civilization against "barbarity."

In November the *Globe* published seven editorials and five opinion
pieces referencing Kristallnacht, the refugee crisis, and the shameful
silence of the Canadian government. The other newspapers in this
study, particularly the *Toronto Daily Star*, also condemned the violence in editorial commentary. Many of these editorials drew parallels between the Jews and other victims and potential victims of
Nazi attacks. On 12 November, for example, the *Globe* published an
editorial, "More Nazi Horrors," which stated, "[T]omorrow it may
well be another race, given the opportunity, which falls under the
displeasure of mobilized axe and torch ... [H]ow safe can any nation
or race be while Nazism lives?"[75] And on 15 November another
Globe editorial claimed, "[I]t is not a question of interests. It is a
matter of being able to live one's own conscience after having con-
doned atrocities. It makes no difference whether they be against Jews
or Gentiles, Protestants or Catholics. Such practices are the negation
of the elemental decencies in our conception of human affairs."[76]

In a generous reading, we might interpret the tendency of the
Canadian press to universalize the victims as an anti-racist gesture
that asked Canadians to see themselves in the Nazis' crosshairs, to
be outraged by the Nazi violence for the simple reason that it was
morally wrong, regardless of the identity of the targeted group. On
the other hand, such characterizations had the potential to down-

play the special role of antisemitism in Nazi ideology and to obscure the warning signs of an impending genocide or "race murder." The notion that there were multiple targets of Nazi violence was often in direct tension with warnings about the potential for mass violence against the German Jews. Still, in the same 15 November editorial which claimed that victim identity "makes no difference," the *Globe* editors acknowledged the ominous possibilities of continued Jewish persecution in the German Reich: "The 'liquidation of the Jews is the most brutal in an unbroken sequence of reminders that the Hitler program cannot be compromised. When he promised the elimination of the Jews he meant just that."[77] On 16 November the *Toronto Daily Star* made a similar editorial juxtaposition. In "A Frenzy of Persecution," the *Star*'s editors began by identifying broad-reaching persecution: "The Nazi madmen who are controlling the affairs of Greater Germany are warring upon Roman Catholicism and evangelical Protestantism as well as upon the helpless Jewish minority."[78] Yet later on in the editorial, the *Star* editors warned of future Jewish annihilation: "The Hitler regime appears to be determined to exterminate the Jews of Germany."[79]

In the midst of the official silence of the Canadian government and the remarkable coverage by the Canadian press, how did the Canadian people respond? While antisemitism was still common in Canada – a fact that would be absolutely clear, for example, during domestic antisemitic incidents in Quebec in August 1939 – there was significant public outrage after Kristallnacht. Some Canadians rose up in protest against the Nazis, organizing local rallies across the country on 20 November. These protests were a tremendous example of how the Canadian public sphere – the people and the press – exerted a collective political will and put pressure on elected representatives to speak out against Jewish persecution. In an editorial about the protest of 20,000 Torontonians at Maple Leaf Gardens, the *Globe* editors wrote: "The remarkable gathering in this city on Sunday last to protest against Nazi persecution of the Jewish race and express sympathy for the victims was the natural expression of a democracy. Jews and gentiles knew no racial barriers. It was the brotherhood of man asserting itself."[80]

Regional newspapers also reported on local meetings to protest Nazi barbarity. The *London Free Press* ran a long and detailed article about a "mass meeting at the Grand Theatre" in London, where participants unanimously passed a resolution that expressed "deepest sympathy" with the Jews and "resolve[d] to stand in readiness to support, through any well accredited channels, any general relief that may be decided upon."[81] The *Winnipeg Free Press* reported that "following scathing denunciation by prominent speakers of Hitler's persecution of the Jews in Germany, a representative throng of citizens who filled the Winnipeg Auditorium Sunday afternoon, unanimously passed a resolution calling on the Dominion government to take ... appropriate action."[82] In Montreal, the *Gazette* reported that 4,500 people attended a meeting that "assail[ed] the pogrom,"[83] and an editorial cited the "righteous protest ... gathering force throughout the civilized world."[84] The *Vancouver Sun* reported that 2,000 people attended a meeting in Vancouver, where there was "bitter condemnation of Germany's treatment of the Jewish minority, requests for a government boycott of German and Fascist-made goods, and offers of assistance for Jewish refugees."[85] And the *Ottawa Citizen* ran a Canadian Press article citing Canadians across the country who had "packed auditoriums and theaters ... to join in protests against the maltreatment of Jews in Germany and to ask that the Dominion government take steps to aid Jewish refugees."[86]

The Nazis were not silent in the face of such overt outrage. On 12 November the *Globe* reported the Nazis' first attack on the international media: "The National Socialist regime ... moved today to silence all criticism abroad. It warned the foreign press that any 'lies and exaggerations' would not be ineffective, but that Jews in Germany might have to pay for them."[87] On 20 November – the same day that Canadians rallied across the country to protest the Nazi's treatment of the Jews – the Nazi newspaper *Völkischer Beobachter* published an editorial attacking Canada's treatment of its First Nations people. The following day the *Globe* reported the details of the Nazi charges as one of its lead stories. The article, "Hitler Paper Sees 'Atrocities' Among Canadian Indians," quoted a translated excerpt from the Nazi editorial:

Now in Canada we see unleashed against Germany a campaign of hatred which has no equal in baseness ... But why should Canadians look abroad? If Canadian journalists want to see real atrocities they need only go to the Indian reservations of their own country. There they will find out what inhuman treatment really means, see how the old native Indian population was destroyed by starvation and liquor. In these circumstances, Canadians should cease mixing in the affairs of other countries of which they know nothing about.[88]

It was not uncommon for the Nazis to point to racist laws and institutionalized inequities abroad, particularly in response to criticism of Nazi antisemitism. For example, in addition to indicting Canada for the conditions on its First Nations reservations, a 19 November letter to the *Toronto Daily Star* reveals that *Völkischer Beobachter* had accused the British "of committing inhumanities in the Transvaal."[89] The following month, the Nazis cited the Jim Crow segregation laws in the United States as a precedent for forcing local and foreign Jews to ride in separate railway cars throughout the Reich. On 28 December 1938 the *Globe*'s lead story, "Nazis Demand 'Jim Crow' Law for Jews," quoted the *Schwarze Korps* as saying that segregated rail travel in the Reich "follows the documented democratic example for the world's freest country, where even Presidents denounce the devilish invention of race-consciousness, does not permit state citizens with equal rights but of darker hue to sit, much less sleep, next to a white person."[90]

The *Globe* framed the Nazi charges against Canadian treatment of "Indians" as a "savage attack" and "a lie," but the prominence of the article's placement – which ran ahead of stories about the 20 November anti-Nazi rally in Toronto, the Canadian Corps' anti-immigration stance, and fearful Jewish refugees bound for Australia – demonstrated that charges about abuses of First Nations people struck a nerve with the *Globe*'s editors. And rather than allowing the Nazis' charges to fade from memory, the *Globe* ran several follow-up articles and letters, including a series of on-the-street interviews with Canadians, in a piece on 22 November called "Inquiring Reporter Asks: Do you think that Indians are receiving fair treatment in Canada?"[91] The Nazi attack on Canada's treatment of First Nations people is interesting for at least two reasons. First, it uncomfortably calls into question the potential hypocrisy of nationwide rallies protesting the Nazis' treatment of the Jews against the backdrop of Canada's Indian residential school system and other abuses of the First Nations people. Second, it clearly demonstrates the power of the Canadian public sphere in November 1938. Mackenzie King and the Canadian government may have maintained an official silence about Jewish persecution, but the voices of the Canadian press and

Table 3
Globe and Mail Coverage, December 1938 – May 1939

Month	Dec	Jan	Feb	Mar	Apr	May	Total
Refugees	19	16	15	8	6	6	70
International response	9	3	1	0	0	0	13
Public advocacy	7	0	1	0	0	1	9
Nazi antisemitism	9	4	8	1	1	0	23
European antisemitism	8	3	4	6	0	1	22
Canadian antisemitism	2	3	3	0	0	0	8

the Canadian people had a significant impact on international relations; in this case, the Canadian newspapers did not just reflect public opinion but helped to shape it to the extent that Nazi Germany
was compelled to respond directly to editorial criticism.

THE GROWING REFUGEE CRISIS AND THE MS *ST LOUIS*

The *Globe* carried significantly prominent coverage of Jewish persecution in December, January, and February, followed by a sharp
decline in March, April, and May. While the Nazis did not again
perpetrate the very public concentrated physical destruction that
the world witnessed during Kristallnacht, the Canadian press continued to report periodic antisemitic incidents in the German Reich,
in other European countries, and occasionally in Canada. In December and January there were also several reports detailing the international response to the German Reich by the United States,[92] the
United Kingdom,[93] France,[94] the Pope,[95] and India.[96] Public demonstrations and advocacy on behalf of Jewish victims was a frequent
topic in December 1938, but rarely after that point. Almost half of
the coverage between December and May concerned the plight of
Jewish refugees, a concern that peaked during the MS *St Louis* incident in June 1939.

As the exceptional press coverage of Kristallnacht had shown,
Jews in the German Reich were in danger, and commentators made
disturbing predictions about the "extermination" of the Jewish
population. In the aftermath of the November pogroms, the public
discourse emphasized the political and bureaucratic barriers to getting the Jews out of Nazi territory and into safe havens. Coverage in
the *Globe* provided Canadian readers with contradictory messages.
On the one hand, there were relatively hopeful reports about a Nazi

agreement to "ransom" the Jews and organize a mass Jewish "exodus" from the Reich. On the other hand, there were reports about Canada's refusal to raise the Jewish immigration quota, of desperate suicides, and of ships filled with Jewish refugees turned away from international ports. After six months of articles about Jewish refugees, the story of those stranded on the MS *St Louis* in late May and June 1939 was not an anomaly; it was a symbol of the very crisis.

On 9 December 1938 the *Globe* published a map showing the Nazis' plans for a Jewish ghetto in central Berlin, a move that would further "restrict ... Jews under [the] Nazi regime."[97] On 19 December the *Globe*'s lead story was of a new Nazi plan to "blackmail" the international community by exploiting Jewish emigration in return for "more trade and more foreign currency,"[98] and the following day the *Globe* ran an editorial expressing outrage over the plan to exploit Jewish suffering for economic gain:

> Brutal as [the ransom plans] are, they are so much of a place with the Nazi genius for cruelty that they will occasion no surprise. If more coldblooded than even the legalized robbery of Jewish property, they are a "natural" end to the purge. Decent men would free the animal before bargaining on the pelt. The Nazis instead use torture to exploit the sympathizers. To ordinary God-fearing people there are no standards by which to judge such savagery. The only conclusion must be that nazism is a reversal of everything on which social progress depends. In the development of the creed the masters have discarded even the instinctive code of human conduct. Power mad, the whole system has been built on hate. The primitive passions which are in all people have been cultivated, as its motivating force ... The Jews have been singled out, branded, prepared for the purge.[99]

Despite protests, the possibility of a plan for a Jewish "ransom" and "mass exodus" held sway for several months and seemed to offer hope that the Nazis might be persuaded to help facilitate the emigration of Jews from the German Reich. While the international community sympathized with the refugees, the British and American governments wanted the Nazis to loosen restrictions on Jewish assets so that the persecuted Jews would not become charges of the state. On 10 January the *Globe* reported continued negotiations between the Reich and the Allies to "solve the problem of

Jewish emigration from Germany and the transfer of at least part of the Jewish capital in Germany to help finance the refugees."[100] The *Globe*'s coverage of the Jewish exodus continued through the winter, with a report on 20 January of Nazi concessions to "ease" ransom demands,[101] a report on 3 February that international officials were "optimistic that a Jewish exodus plan was advancing,"[102] a report on 14 February that the Evian intergovernmental committee had arranged financing for the "orderly emigration of refugees from the Reich,"[103] and an article on 10 March entitled "Hope Is Seen for Refugees," which suggested that the "outlook was brighter" for "an orderly exodus of oppressed Jewish minorities from Germany."[104]

Despite the repeated suggestions by the international press that a mass exodus was on the horizon and that the general outlook for the Jews was improving, there also were stories that cautioned against an overly optimistic view. On 31 January the *Globe* reported that the Canadian government steadfastly refused to adopt a more liberal immigration policy and would not open its doors to the German Jews,[105] and on 27 February the *Globe* reported that attempts to settle the Arab-Jewish conflict – which it suggested might lead to concessions for Jewish immigration – were failing in the British Mandate for Palestine.[106] At the same time, Jews in the German Reich were growing increasingly desperate amidst continued hardships and Nazi threats of annihilation. On 1 December the *Globe* reported "a wave of Jewish suicides"[107] across Germany. Two months later it cited dozens of suicides in Nazi-occupied Prague: "Hospitals reported eighty Jewish suicides had been brought to them. A man and woman on a park bench behind the Bohemian Museum shot themselves. Another couple jumped from their apartment window."[108]

On 26 January a front-page story in the *Globe* reported on an antisemitic rally in Berlin at which Julius Streicher called Kristallnacht "just a little test."[109] The *Globe* quoted Streicher's menacing threats at length: "'I proclaim before you,' said Streicher, 'that solution of the Jewish question has only begun. I say further that whether it will be solved is written in eternity. And if there still be one single Jew free on this earth and able to conduct himself according to his inborn instincts, the Jewish question would not be solved.'"[110] On 1 February the *Globe* repeated Streicher's threat in the "Notes and Comments" editorial section: "Hitler says that the European peace can come only after the Jewish question is settled. Streicher, the leading German anti-Semite, has said that the Jewish question will not be settled as long as a Jew remains alive."[111] By April and May 1939, reports about Jewish persecution and the refugee crisis had dropped off significantly in the *Globe*. In June the coverage jumped back up to thirty-eight articles, of which sixteen addressed the MS *St Louis* incident that had captivated the entire world's attention.

The *New York Times* carried the first North American story about the *St Louis* on 28 May 1939, reporting that Jewish refugees aboard the ship had been refused entry to Cuba the previous day. The article explained that there was a growing sentiment in Cuba against Jewish refugees, who numbered about 5,000 in Havana. On 30 May, in a fit of desperation, one of the *St Louis* passengers, Max Loewe, slashed his wrists and jumped into the ocean.[112] Loewe survived, but news of the suicide attempt pushed the story onto the front pages of newspapers around the world the following day. Loewe's desperate act and the subsequent threats of mass suicide by other passengers on the ship partly account for why the story resonated so strongly in the public sphere. The *St Louis* was the ultimate symbol of the Jewish refugee crisis.

Like most newspapers, the *Globe* first covered the *St Louis* incident on 31 May, mentioning Loewe's suicide attempt in the second paragraph: "One refugee, Max Loewe, 48-year old Hamburg lawyer, slashed his wrists and leaped into the sea today when informed he would not be allowed to land."[113] After the initial article, the dramatic story of the *St Louis* refugees appeared on the front page of the *Globe* every day for the first week of June. On 1 June the *Globe* reported fears that the refugees would "enter a death pact" or that there would be "open mutiny" if the ship left the port.[114] On 2 June the captain defied orders to leave Havana,[115] and on 3 June there was an offer – later rescinded – for the refugees to land at Dominica.[116] On 4 June the liner was reportedly cruising "leisurely through Caribbean waters" while "powerful strings were being pulled in Miami and elsewhere" in the United States.[117] On 6 June the *Globe* reported that Cuba had offered the *St Louis* refugees a "temporary stay" if "they agreed to live in a concentration camp established on the isle."[118] However, the next day a brief article reported that the "Cuban government a second time refused to grant a haven to 907 refugee German Jews" and that the *St Louis* was "headed back to Germany."[119]

On 8 June the *Globe* columnist Judith Robinson described a telegram delivered to Mackenzie King with the signatures of forty-one

Canadian Christian leaders, who admonished the prime minister for not offering sanctuary to the *St Louis* refugees. Robinson quoted Matthew 25:40, suggesting that Christians must help "the least of these." The following day the *Globe* ran an article summarizing the remarks of Bishop Renison, one of the forty-one signatories to the telegram, who spoke publicly about Canada's moral failure: "Canada, a spacious land of resources where people could afford to be helpful as well as happy, had just condemned nearly 1,000 refugee Jews to return 'with death and suicide in their hearts' to a cruel Europe that expelled them."[120] While the *St Louis* story appeared to have a relatively happy ending when the *Globe* reported on 14 June that Britain, France, Belgium, and Holland would provide havens for the refugees, the final *Globe* article on 19 June reported that an "anti-Semitic outburst" had greeted the Jews as they arrived in Antwerp.[121]

However compelling, the MS *St Louis* story was far from unique. Before, during, and after the *St Louis* passengers were denied entry to Cuba, the international press published dozens of stories about other ships that were filled with desperate Jewish refugees. For example, on 27 February the *Globe* published a story about sixty-eight Jewish refugees who were held at port in Buenos Aires on the Italian liner *Conte Grande* after being rejected by Uruguay.[122] The following day, the *Globe* ran a front-page story about 185 Austrian Jews stranded on the German steamship *Koenigstein*, which was headed for Venezuela after being turned away from British Guiana.[123] On 1 March the *Globe* reported that the *Conte Grande* would be sent back to Europe just as another German ship, the *General San Martin*, was arriving in Buenos Aires with twenty-eight Jewish refugees, who also had been unable to land in Uruguay. The article described the suicidal desperation of the Jews on the *Conte Grande*: "spiritless and tearful, assembled in the ship salon under heavy guard as the ship sailed. Argentine guards said several had declared they would rather die than return to Germany."[124]

Between 28 May and 14 June, as the international press was providing serial coverage of the *St Louis*, the *Globe and Mail* and the *New York Times* also published one-off reports of refugee vessels languishing in other harbours around the world: Jewish refugees on the *Orduna* were refused entry to Cuba; 100 Jewish refugees aboard the French liner *Flandre* were refused entry to Cuba and Mexico; 78 Jewish refugees on the *Monte Olivia* were refused entry to Chile, Paraguay, and Argentina;[125] 200 Jewish refugees aboard the SS *Ornico* were removed from the ship in Cuxhaven before the liner continued on to Cuba;[126] 906 Jewish refugees were seized by the British aboard a cattle boat attempting to land illegally in Palestine;[127] 500 Jewish refugees departed from Romania on the steamship *Mamara* hoping to land in Palestine or somewhere on the African coast;[128] 552 Jewish refugees on the Greek steamship *Aghios*, were prevented from leaving port;[129] and 1,300 Jewish refugees were stranded in riverboats on the Danube River in Romania, awaiting permission to continue on to Shanghai.[130]

Clearly, we must consider the symbolic story of the MS *St Louis* in the context of the wider Jewish refugee crisis, a problem that had preoccupied the *Globe* for most of the previous year. At the end of June, the *Globe*'s editors gestured to the great weight of the global refugee crisis:

What is true of the Spanish refugees is equally true of literally millions of Central Europeans. We doubt that those in the French camps are any worse off than the 50,000 Polish Jews huddled in concentration camps on the German frontier. Could any suffering be worse than the anguish of the tens of thousands of Czechs interned in labour camps, or hiding out, living by the hope escape will come before the Nazis? There are as many, perhaps more, Austrians tortured by every breath they draw. They will die in torture unless ransomed out. There are still upward of 600,000 German Jews and other non-Aryans for whom escape is the only ambition left in life. In Belgium, in France, in England, thousands more Spaniards, Austrians, Germans, and Czechs are being supported in camps and in private homes until friendly nations find a home for them. Is the need of one of these groups more worthy than another? Collectively they create a giant problem to which we in Canada, along with the other still-civilized nations, should give thought.[131]

CANADIAN ANTISEMITISM ON THE EVE OF WAR

With the exception of the serial reports about the *St Louis* refugees in June, Canadian press coverage of Jewish persecution had steadily declined since Kristallnacht, signalling perhaps a degree of complacency in the public sphere. In July 1939 the *Globe and Mail* published only ten articles about the plight of the European Jews, and in August the number dropped to six. Regional Canadian newspapers published even fewer. On the eve of the war, the Canadian press was far more preoccupied with antisemitic incidents in Quebec than with the growing peril of the Jews across the Atlantic.

On 6 July the *Globe* reported that Lord Dufferin, under-secretary of the colonies, had addressed criticism about Britain's restrictions on Jewish immigration by suggesting, with rather twisted logic, that "an influx of Jews would increase anti-Semitism" in the United Kingdom.[132] Additional *Globe* articles suggested that the German Reich was still committed to Jewish emigration, including a 7 July report that the Nazis had eliminated existing Jewish organizations and replaced them with the Reich's Union of Jews in Germany to help facilitate the departure of German Jews.[133] On 8 July the *Globe* followed up with a more detailed report, describing six Jews selected by the Gestapo to lead the "Jewish exodus" from Germany.

A prototype for the Jewish "self-management" which the Nazis would later organize in the Polish ghettos (the *Judenrat*), the Union of Jews was responsible for the welfare of all Jews in the German Reich. According to the *Globe*, "Less than one-quarter of the Jewish population will now be required, besides paying to the government the highest taxes possible under German law, to feed, clothe, and educate the overwhelming majority of Jews in Germany who have no income."[134] The *Globe* did not mention the Union of Jews again before the war, but the limited coverage in early July suggests a clear contradiction: the Nazis appeared to be encouraging emigration yet refusing to fund it, and at the same they were setting up conditions that would make life impossible for the Jews who remained in the Reich. The *Globe* called the Reich's lack of financial support the "Joker in the deck" of the new decree and ended the article by citing an ominous "hope" that "the Reich, however harsh its ordinances may be, [would] not let [the Jews] starve."[135]

The continued desperation of the European Jews was clear when the *Vancouver Sun* reported, on 4 August, yet another suicide by a Jewish refugee, this time in Chicago: "Mrs. Adele Langer, 43, [Jewish] refugee from Czechoslovakia, fearing she would have to return there and live under Nazi rule, clutched her two small sons in her arms late last night and plunged with them from a 13th floor hotel window to the sidewalk of Michigan Boulevard. All were killed instantly."[136] Yet despite the growing peril of the European Jews and the refusal of the international community to alter immigration restrictions sufficiently, Canadian newspapers cut their coverage of the crisis down to a trickle. Instead, they focused on domestic anti-semitism in Quebec, where Christians were attempting to drive Jews out of vacation resorts.

Over the previous year, the *Globe* had carried periodic stories about nationalist, anti-immigrant, "Jew-baiting," and antisemitic organizations in Canada. It had also reported several instances of antisemitic activity, including an incident on 12 February in which Jewish store windows in Toronto had been painted with Swastikas.[137] It was in Quebec, however, that Canadian antisemitism was most prevalent. According to Jacques Langlais and David Rome, antisemitism "swept over prewar Quebec" like a wave:[138]

> [Antisemitism] permeated the entire collective life of French Quebec to varying degrees, leaving its mark on the economy, trade unions, culture, social affairs, politics, and, naturally, on education and religion. The press of the period, from large dailies such as *Le Devoir* and *L'Action catholique* to a plethora of nationalist reviews (*Vivre, Les Cahiers noirs, Indépendance, La Nation, Le Patriote, L'Oeil, Le Franc Parleur, L'Action nationale*) expressed mistrust, hostility, and even hatred towards Jews.[139]

In the summer of 1939, antisemitism was palpable in Ste-Agathe-des Monts, a small resort town in the Laurentian Mountains. On 1 August the *Globe* ran a front-page story, "Quebec Resort Anti-Jew Drive Near Violence," detailing growing antisemitism in the region.[140] On the same day, the Montreal *Gazette* reported that a "drive to oust the Jews from the Laurentian Mountains district came out in the open [in Ste-Agathe]. Placards posted in the town Saturday bade Jews 'scram while the going is good.'"[141] On 2 August the *Globe* reported that a Catholic priest, Father J.B. Charland, was "fanning the flames of anti-Semitism" in Ste-Agathe with a self-proclaimed "education campaign."[142] By 4 August, resorts and hotels were reportedly refusing to lodge Jews,[143] and a bridge leading to a Jewish-owned hotel in Ste-Agathe was set on fire.[144] On 5 August the *Globe* reported suspected fascist connections in Ste-Agathe and cited Jewish groups that had requested intervention from Ottawa: "Organized Jewry yesterday urged Prime Minister Mackenzie King to sponsor Federal legislation outlawing anti-Semitism 'before it becomes uncontrollable.'"[145]

As news of domestic antisemitism preoccupied the Canadian press, the coverage of Jewish persecution in Europe almost entirely disappeared. On 11 August the *Globe* published one of the few articles that month addressing the plight of European Jews, reporting that only 800 Jewish refugees had been admitted to Canada between January and June 1939.[146] As this chapter demonstrates, in that same six-month period, Canadian newspapers had published hundreds of articles reporting the dire conditions of European Jews, editorials had called for the Canadian government to lift immigration quotas and open Canada's doors to the Jewish refugees, and the Canadian people had come together at rallies and talks around the country to voice their outrage about the Nazis' treatment of the Jews. But Jewish persecution – the most important news story in Canada in the month of November 1938 – had now faded into the background. My sustained analysis of one year of coverage of Jewish persecution shows that the exceptional coverage of November 1938 ebbed to a trickle by the summer of 1939. This change is significant for two primary reasons: first, it demonstrates that there was both unprecedented newspaper coverage and deep public concern about Jewish persecution and the refugee crisis in late 1938 and early 1939; second, it suggests that this concern had all but disappeared by the summer of 1939. The Canadian public and the Canadian press had grown complacent, either hopeful that Kristallnacht had been the worst of the violence, or overwhelmed by a sense that Jewish suffering was somehow unsolvable, inevitable, eternal.

As the world turned its attention to the impending hostilities, the *Globe and Mail*'s final word on Jewish persecution before the war began was printed on 28 August 1939. The story, however, came in a different package. It was not another report – like the hundreds before it – that detailed antisemitic ordinances, violent pogroms, limited immigration quotas, suicides, or desperate refugees. This time, it was a poem by Robert Nathan, which aptly described the abandonment of the European Jews by the international community and the coming carnage of a world war that was then only hours away:

ON THE JEWISH EXILE
Ay, send them out, the dark ones, into the desert,
If there is desert enough in all the world
To hold these lonely few, these trembling goats
Who take for burden all the sins of the flesh
Into the wilderness,

> Blow Bugles, Pomp.
> Build armies, march with beautiful banners flying,
> Young men and old with shouts and hands flung upward,
> Under the birds of death
> Make a place for graves;
> A field for bones, a meadow for all the people.
> No need of flowers or grass or marble tombs;
> For all will die, under the falling fire.
> Who lives by sword shall perish, too, by the sword.
> Alas for Rome,
> The days of her life are numbered.
> Only the goats in the wilderness will survive this
> Burning of cities, this war, this crying of children.
> Only the kids in the desert will see the morning.
> And slowly making their way back over the mountains
> Feed again in peace in the shattered cities,
> Browse again in the weeds of the ruined gardens.[147]

NOTES

1 "Canadian People Protest," *Globe and Mail*, 22 November 1938, 6.

2 Abella and Troper, *None Is Too Many: Canada and the Jews of Europe, 1933–1948*, xxii. According to Abella and Troper, Canada took in fewer than 5,000 Jewish refugees between 1933 and 1945, compared with the United States, which took in 200,000.

3 There is significant scholarly debate about the role of the United States, Canada, and Britain in the Final Solution. Some scholars – such as David Wyman and Deborah Lipstadt – claim that the Allied governments were "complicit" in the Nazi genocide, while others – such as Peter Novick, Martin Gilbert, and Lucy Dawidowicz – do not think the available options for rescue would have had a significant impact. See Novick, *The Holocaust in American Life*, 47–59. Likewise, there is debate about the reasons behind Canada's restrictive immigration policies. In *None Is Too Many*, Abella and Troper suggest that the decision to limit the intake of Jewish refugees was a crudely political decision on the part of the Mackenzie King government, while Robert Jan van Pelt urges us to consider the role of bureaucracy and international relations in addition to Canadian antisemitism. See van Pelt, "Without a Right of Return a Refusal of Arrival: An Examination of the Architecture of a Paper Wall."

4   Austria was annexed to the German Reich on 12 March 1938. Sudeten-
    land – part of Czechoslovakia – was annexed to the German Reich on
    10 October 1938. Bohemia and Moravia – also part of Czechoslovakia –
    became a protectorate of the German Reich on 15 March 1939.

5   The *Globe and Mail* ran letters to the editor debating the relationship
    between Jews and communism on 5 and 11 January, 3 February, 10, 15,
    and 21 April, and 4 May 1939.

6   The *Globe and Mail* ran letters to the editor debating the role of Jews in
    the Great War on 8 and 29 March, 17, 20, and 25 April 1939.

7   Novick, *The Holocaust in American Life*, 20–1.

8   Ibid.

9   Leff, *Buried by the Times: The Holocaust and America's Most Important
    Newspaper*, 33.

10 Novick, *The Holocaust in American Life*, 19.

11 Ibid., 20.

12 Lipstadt, *Beyond Belief: The American Press and the Coming of the Holo-
    caust, 1933–1945*, 40–1.

13 Leff writes: "If its Jewish ownership meant the *Times* recognized what
    was happening to European Jews, it also made the newspaper more hesi-
    tant to highlight it ... The *Times* publisher ... was philosophically opposed
    to emphasizing the unique plight of the Jews in occupied Europe, a con-
    viction that at least partially explains the *Times*' tendency to place stories
    about Jews inside the paper, and to universalize their plight in editorials
    and front-page stories" (*Buried by the Times*, 13).

14 Bialystok, *Delayed Impact: The Holocaust and the Canadian Jewish Com-
    munity*, 19.

15 "9000 Polish Jews Still Await Fate," *Globe and Mail*, 1 November, 1938,
    1.

16 "Jews Fear New Reign of Terror," *Globe and Mail*, 17 November 1938, 1.

17 "Jewish Exodus to France," *Vancouver Sun*, 14 November 1938, 10.

18 "Extermination of Jews Bared as Hitler Goal," *Gazette* (Montreal), 23
    November 1938, 1.

19 Moeller, *Compassion Fatigue: How the Media Sell Disease, War, and
    Death*.

20 Otto D. Tolischus, "Hear 'Ransom' Demand Eased," *Globe and Mail*, 20
    January 1939.

21 J.V. McAree, "Planned Atrocities Aimed at Jews," *Globe and Mail*, 1 Sep-
    tember 1938, 6.

22 Ibid.

23 Novick, *The Holocaust in American Life*, 23–4.

24 "No Peace with Hitler," *Globe and Mail*, 10 September 1938, 6.

25 Ibid.

26 Novick, *The Holocaust in American Life*, 13.

27 "Reich Defines Circumstances Voiding Wills," *Globe and Mail*, 9 September 1938, 7.

28 "German, Austrian Exiles Say Things Bad in Germany," *Globe and Mail*, 24 September 1938, 4.

29 Stewart C. Easton, "Letter: Germany the Old and the New," *Globe and Mail*, 20 September 1938, 6.

30 T.J. Mellor, "Letter: A Simple Plan," *Globe and Mail*, 29 September 1938, 6.

31 "Hitler's Role Said a Return to Barbarism," *Globe and Mail*, 29 September 1938, 11.

32 "Anti-Semitic Signs Spring Up on Heels of Nazi Occupation," *Globe and Mail*, 4 October 1938, 1.

33 "Austrian Town Cheers Departure of Last Jew," *Globe and Mail*, 11 October 1938, 1.

34 "Hitler Aide Flays Church Politicians (continued from page 1)," *Globe and Mail*, 14 October 1938, 9.

35 "Hitler Asserts Church Hoards Great Riches," *Globe and Mail*, 17 October 1938, 13.

36 "Conscription Decreed for Hungarians; Arms Speeded," *Globe and Mail*, 5 September 1938, 1.

37 "Several Hundred Jews Reported Held in Hungary," *Globe and Mail*, 12 October 1938, 1.

38 "Czechs Defy Ultimatum," *Globe and Mail*, 14 September 1938, 2.

39 "Poles Seek Jews Removal," *Globe and Mail*, 19 September 1938, 9.

40 The First World War.

41 "10,000 Jews are Ordered to Quit Italy," *Globe and Mail*, 2 September 1938, 1.

42 "Jews Barred from Italian Universities," *Globe and Mail*, 3 September 1938, 2.

43 "Vatican-Italian Discord Renewed over Fascist Race Doctrine," *Globe and Mail*, 8 September, 1938, 2.

44 "Jewish Composers' Music Banned on Italian Radio," *Globe and Mail*, 22 September, 1938, 1.

45 "Italy Cool to British Overtures," *Globe and Mail*, 7 October 1938, 1.

46 "International Situation at a Glance," *Globe and Mail*, 8 October 1938, 1.

47 "It Is to Laugh," *Globe and Mail*, 15 October 1938, 6.

48 "Rome Bans Jewish Brokers," *Globe and Mail*, 18 October 1939, 19.

49 "9000 Polish Jews Still Await Fate," *Globe and Mail*, 1 November 1938, 1.

50 "Hungary Given 860,000 People," *Globe and Mail*, 3 November 1938, 1–2.

51 "9000 Polish Jews Still Await Fate," *Globe and Mail*, 1 November 1938, 1.

52 S. Friedländer, *Nazi Germany and the Jews*, vol. 1: *The Years of Persecution, 1933–1939*.

53 Lipstadt, *Beyond Belief*, 99.

54 Otto D. Tolischus, "Germans Rage over Shooting," *Globe and Mail*, 9 November 1938, 3.

55 "Stupid Racial Persecution," *Globe and Mail*, 9 November 1938, 6.

56 Ibid.

57 "Shall We Remember Them?" *Globe and Mail*, 9 November 1938, 1.

58 Otto D. Tolischus, "Reich Swept by Anti-Jew Terrorism," the *Globe and Mail*, 11 November 1938, 1.

59 Gilbert, *Kristallnacht: Prelude to Destruction*.

60 "Notes and Comments," *Globe and Mail*, 11 November 1938, 6.

61 "Note and Comment," *Toronto Daily Star*, 11 November 1938, 6.

62 "Nazi Savagery Goes the Limit," *Globe and Mail*, 14 November 1938, 6.

63 "Hitler's Germany," *Toronto Daily Star*, 14 November 1938, 4.

64 Otto D. Tolischus, "Reich Swept by Anti-Jew Terrorism," *Globe and Mail*, 11 November 1938, 1.

65 "Move 1,000 Jews to Prison Camps," *Globe and Mail*, 12 November 1938, 1.

66 "Jews Fined One-Eighth of Wealth," *Globe and Mail*, 14 November, 1938, 1.

67 "Jewish Stores Pass to Aryans," *Globe and Mail*, 14 November 1938, 4.

68 "Jewish Home Closed," *Globe and Mail*, 14 November 1938, 9.

69 "Nazis Crafting More Decrees to Stifle Jews," *Globe and Mail*, 15 November 1938, 1.

70 "Nazis Put New Bans on Jews," *Globe and Mail*, 18 November 1938, 1.

71 "Nazis Seize Art Treasures," *Globe and Mail*, 18 November 1938, 1.

72 Abella and Troper, *None Is Too Many*, 38–42.

73 "Canada's Silent Voice," *Globe and Mail*, 18 November 1938, 6.

74 Ibid.

75 "More Nazi Horrors," *Globe and Mail*, 12 November 1938, 6.

76 "Nazi Purge Blow to Peace Deals," *Globe and Mail*, 15 November 1938.

77 Ibid., 6.

78 "A Frenzy of Persecution," *Toronto Daily Star*, 16 November 1938, 4.

79 Ibid.

80 "Canada's Silent Voice," *Globe and Mail*, 18 November 1938, 6.

81 "London Protests Cruelty to Jews," *London Free Press*, 21 November 1938, 3.

82 "Indignation: Aid to Persecuted Jews Urged at Mass Meeting," *Winnipeg Free Press*, 21 November 1938, 1.

83 "Leading Citizens Assail Pogrom before 4,500 at a Meeting Here," *Gazette*, 21 November, 1938, 1.

84 "The Refugee Problem," *Gazette*, 22 November 1938, 7.

85 "Canadian Home for German Jew Refugees Demanded," *Vancouver Sun*, 21 November 1938, 2.

86 "Big Canadian Meetings Urge Aid to Refugees," *Ottawa Citizen*, 21 November 1938, 15.

87 "Reich Condones Anti-Jewish Terrors," *Globe and Mail*, 12 November 1938, 1.

88 M.K. Whiteleather, "Hitler Paper Sees 'Atrocities' among Canadian Indians, *Globe and Mail*, 21 November 1938, 1.

89 J. Green, "British 'Atrocities,'" *Toronto Daily Star*, 19 November 1938, 5.

90 Otto D. Tolischus, "Nazis Demand 'Jim Crow' Law for Jews," *Globe and Mail*, 28 December 1938, 1.

91 "Inquiring Reporter Asks," *Globe and Mail*, 22 November 1938, 17.

92 Otto D. Tolischus, "Roosevelt Rips Schacht Plan, Germans Fear," *Globe and Mail*, 6 January 1939, 1.

93 "Drive on Jews Gives Germany New Problems," *Globe and Mail*, 26 December 1938, 2.

94 "Jewish French Ministers Absent from Pact Dinner," *Globe and Mail*, 7 December 1938, 1.

95 "Pope Deplores Fascist Blows at Concordat," *Globe and Mail*, 26 December 1938, 1.

96 "India Willing to Aid Britain against Nazis," *Globe and Mail*, 12 December 1938, 1.

97 "How Berlin Will Restrict Its Jews under Nazi Regime," *Globe and Mail*, 9 December 1938, 7.

98 P.J. Philip, "'Blackmail' Seen in Nazi Plan for Jews," *Globe and Mail*, 19 December 1938, 1.

99 "Now Exploiting Torture," *Globe and Mail*, 20 December 1938, 6.

100 "May Restrict Jewish Exodus to Young Folk," *Globe and Mail*, 10 January 1939, 1.

101 "Hear 'Ransom' Demand Eased," *Globe and Mail*, 20 January 1939, 9.

102 "Jewish Exodus Plan Advanced," *Globe and Mail*, 3 February 1939, 9.

103   Ferdinand Kuhn, "Jewish Exodus Plan Hailed," *Globe and Mail*, 14 Feb-
        ruary 1939, 1.

104   "Hope Is Seen for Refugees," *Globe and Mail*, 10 March 1939, 28.

105   "Canada Will Not Adopt Open Door to Refugees, Premier King Intim-
        ates," *Globe and Mail*, 31 January 1939, 1.

106   Robert P. Post, "Britain to End Mandate over Palestine," *Globe and Mail*,
        27 February 1939, 1.

107   "Jews Suiciding through Reich," *Globe and Mail*, 1 December 1938, 8.

108   "Concentration Camp Opened Near Prague," *Globe and Mail*, 18 March
        1939, 9.

109   "Trial of Jews 'Only Begun,'" *Globe and Mail*, 26 January 1939, 1.

110   Ibid.

111   "Notes and Comments," *Globe and Mail*, 1 February 1939, 6.

112   Thomas and Witts, *Voyage of the Damned*.

113   "Cuba Rejects German Jews," *Globe and Mail*, 31 May 1939, 1.

114   "Fears Jews Will Enter Death Pact," *Globe and Mail*, 1 June 1939, 1.

115   "Refugee Liner Ignores Order to Leave Cuba," *Globe and Mail*, 2 June
        1939, 1.

116   "Dominica Offers Haven to Refugees Barred at Havana," *Globe and Mail*,
        3 June 1939, 1.

117   "Liner Carries Refugee Jews into Caribbean," *Globe and Mail*, 5 June
        1939, 1.

118   "Offer Respite to Wandering Jews on Liner," *Globe and Mail*, 6 June
        1939, 1.

119   "The World at a Glance," *Globe and Mail*, 7 June 1939, 1. This report
        speaks of 907 refugees, though there were originally 937 passengers on
        board. Of the original passengers, one died en route to Cuba and was bur-
        ied at sea. The passenger who slit his wrists and jumped ship while the *St
        Louis* was in Havana harbour was rescued by Cuban policemen, taken
        to hospital, recovered, and was then sent to live with family members in
        England; he is counted neither among the 28 who disembarked in Cuba
        nor among the 287 who found refuge in England; 224 were accepted by
        France, 214 by Belgium, and 181 by the Netherlands. One passenger was
        a European businessman, not a refugee; he is not included in number sent
        to France, Belgium, Holland, or England.

120   "Canada Condemns Jews to Suicide, Says Renison," *Globe and Mail*, 9
        June 1939, 4.

121   "Anti-Semitic Outbursts Meet Refugees' Arrival in Antwerp," *Globe and
        Mail*, 19 June 1939, 1.

122   "Refugees Held Aboard Liner," *Globe and Mail*, 27 February 1938, 9.

123 "Jews Leave British Guiana," *Globe and Mail*, 28 February 1939, 1.

124 "Wandering Jews Refused Refuge, Return to Reich," *Globe and Mail*, 1 March 1939, 1.

125 "Fears Jews Will Enter Death Pact," *Globe and Mail*, 1 June 1939, 1.

126 "Refugee Liner Ignores Order to Leave Cuba," *Globe and Mail*, 2 June 1939, 1.

127 "British Seize Cattle Boat with 906 Jews," *Globe and Mail*, 2 June 1939, 1.

128 "Other Refugees Adrift," *Globe and Mail*, 14 June 1939, 10.

129 Ibid.

130 Ibid.

131 "Only One Refugee Solution," *Globe and Mail*, 24 June 1938, 6.

132 "Fears Trouble If Many Jews Are Admitted," *Globe and Mail*, 6 July 1939, 3.

133 "Germany Lists Jews in One Organization," *Globe and Mail*, 7 July 1939, 13.

134 "Gestapo Picks Six Jews to Lead Exodus," *Globe and Mail*, 8 July 1939, 1.

135 Ibid., 3.

136 Fran Leary, "Kills Self, 2 Sons, to Escape Nazis," *Vancouver Sun*, 4 August 1939, 2.

137 "Jewish Store Windows Painted with Swastikas," *Globe and Mail*, 13 February 1939, 2.

138 Langlais and Rome, *Jews and French Quebecers: Two Hundred Years of Shared History*, 96.

139 Ibid.

140 "Quebec Resort Anti-Jew Drive Near Violence," *Globe and Mail*, 1 August 1939, 1.

141 "Anti-Jewish Drive Shocks Bercovitch," *Gazette*, 1 August 1939, 1.

142 "Jostled Off Street by Jews, Claim at Laurentian Resort," *Globe and Mail*, 2 August 1939, 1.

143 "Jews Forced from Resort by Campaign," *Globe and Mail*, 4 August 1939, 1.

144 "Bridge Leading to Jews' Hotel Is Set on Fire," *Gazette*, 4 August 1939, 1.

145 "Anti-Semitism Curb Is Sought from Ottawa," *Globe and Mail*, 5 August 1939, 1.

146 "English Lead Immigration from Europe," *Globe and Mail*, 11 August 1939, 3.

147 Robert Nathan, "On the Jewish Exile," *Globe and Mail*, 28 August 1938, 13.

4

A Review of the Yiddish Media: Responses of the Jewish Immigrant Community in Canada

REBECCA MARGOLIS

The music of freedom ... I felt the freedom of Canada.
A Jewish refugee, quoted in Keneder adler, 12 April 1944[1]

INTRODUCTION

From the turn of the twentieth century through the First World War, Canada's relatively open immigration policy brought waves of Eastern European Jews to the country, a majority of them Yiddish speakers. After the war, Canadian immigration laws were tightened, and in 1931 Order-in-Council PC 695 was passed, prohibiting virtually all immigration. It remained stringently in force until after the Second World War. As discussed in Abella and Troper's *None Is Too Many* as well in other studies, restrictive Canadian immigration policies and their strict implementation shut the country's doors to all but a few thousand individuals, with the few Jews who did gain entry into Canada between 1933 and 1948 largely doing so as a result of extensive lobbying on their behalf by supporters in Canada.[2] With the gates to Canada shut and danger looming over European Jewry, how and where did Canadian Jews get their news about the fate of Jews trapped in Nazi Europe? What information did they have access to and what did they do with it? Did they make the transition from "information" (the facts) to "knowledge" (internalized information as "a basis for reaction and action") suggested by Yehuda Bauer in his study *American Jewry and the Holocaust*?[3]

This chapter offers a glimpse into the Canadian Yiddish press during the Second World War by examining a key moment in the country's history: the 1944 arrival of some 400 Iberian refugees in Canada, which marked an exception to the Canadian government's approach to that point. This event has been examined in depth in Patrick Reed's thesis "A Foothold in the Whirlpool." However, Reed discusses the response of the English-language press to the arrival of the refugees, whereas this study looks at coverage of the event in Canada's major Yiddish newspapers – Montreal's *Keneder adler/Jewish Daily Eagle*, Winnipeg's *Yidishe vort/Israelite Press*, and Toronto's *Yidisher zhurnal/Daily Hebrew Journal* – comparing this coverage with a sampling of the country's English- and French-language daily newspapers as well as its Anglo-Jewish publications. And rather than detailing the coverage of events in the Yiddish press that did not appear in non-Yiddish publications, the study examines coverage of one rare event involving European Jewry that received a comparatively large amount of mainstream press coverage in Canada. The study posits that the Yiddish press offers a very different perspective on the history of Canadian Jewish life during the Holocaust in comparison with the existing historiography. The latter focuses on the political weakness of the Canadian Jewish community in helping its European brethren during and immediately following the Nazi era, whereas the Yiddish press presents a Jewish community determining a variety of responses to the unfolding realities of Nazi Europe.

THE YIDDISH PRESS AND THE HOLOCAUST

Within Holocaust scholarship, the mainstream press's marginalization of the Jewish genocide during the Second World War has been axiomatic. According to studies on the American or European press such as Laurel Leff's *Buried By the Times*, Deborah Lipstadt's *Beyond Belief*, and the essays in Robert Moses Shapiro's edited volume *Why Didn't the Press Shout?*, the popular press consistently failed in its coverage by downplaying or ignoring the Jews in its reporting of Nazi atrocities.[4] Studies indicate that the mainstream press in the wartime years differed from the prewar period in that the escalating peril facing the Jews in Nazi Europe received little attention. Scholars have suggested intertwining factors to explain how and to what extent the persecution and subsequent annihilation of Europe's Jews were covered: a prioritizing of the war effort; a lack of reliable information and a reluctance to believe incoming reports about increasing Nazi atrocities; and pervasive antisemitism.

Research on the Canadian media has drawn similar conclusions.[5] David Goutor's "The Canadian Media and the 'Discovery' of the Holocaust, 1944–1945" and Norman Erwin's "Making Sense of Mass Murder" posit that large-circulation English-language newspaper coverage of the liberation of the Nazi death camps failed to identify the Jewishness of the vast majority of those targeted for systematic annihilation; the focus in these reports remained on the evil of the Nazi perpetrators rather than the identity of the victims. More recently, scholars have begun to question the pervasive notion that the mainstream press did not address the Nazi Holocaust as it was unfolding. Ainsley Fuller's study "The *Winnipeg Free Press*, the *Globe and Mail*, and the Jewish Refugee Crisis, 1933–1939" suggests that the coverage in Canadian newspapers in the years leading up to the Second World War ranged from sympathetic to hostile with regard to Jewish immigration. Ulrich Frisse's study of the *Toronto Daily Star* during 1933–45 argues that the persecution and destruction of European Jewry was a "recurrent and overall continuous theme that allowed Canadians to understand the true nature of the destruction process."[6] The stance of the *Star* was "pro-Jewish," and it offered regular coverage of topics of interest to the Canadian Jewish community.[7] At the same time, this coverage was inconsistent. It was contingent on access to reliable sources – missing in 1941 and 1942 – which led to a lack of coverage of the mass killings by the Einsatzgruppen. Further, coverage of Nazi atrocities against the Jews appeared alongside atrocities committed against other groups and without a guiding editorial policy: "No comprehensive conclusion can be drawn in regards to the news selection process on Holocaust-related items at the *Star*'s Toronto office," with editors facing time constraints in choosing which stories would appear in their newspapers and where they would be placed.[8]

While more regular and extensive coverage on the fate of Europe's Jews appeared in the English-language Jewish press, the topic did not occupy central stage. Factors behind this include the desire of North American Jews to highlight their patriotic participation in the battle against Hitler and minimize their difference; the promotion of ideological responses to the catastrophe, such as Zionism; and the assumption that a Jewish readership would have access to the information through other channels.

Even with new, more nuanced readings of the North American press coverage of the Nazi Holocaust, the picture of what appeared in print about the Jews in Nazi Europe during the Second World War remains woefully incomplete. Outside the frame of existing scholarship lies the Jewish community's own Yiddish-language press – in particular, its daily newspapers, which reached hundreds of thousands of readers across North America during the period under discussion – where the destruction of Jewish life in Nazi Europe known as *der khurbn* ("the destruction") was front and centre, prominently placed on the front page as well as integrated throughout. Deborah Lipstadt's brief but cogent essay on the contemporaneous coverage of the Holocaust in New York's largest Yiddish daily, the *Forverts* (The Forward) asserts:

> [A] great deal of news about the persecution and annihilation of European Jewry was available to newspaper readers in America during the years of the Third Reich, but much of it may have been missed by readers of English-language papers, buried as it was on inside pages ... This was not the case for the reader of the *Forverts*. Its pages were filled with news about what was happening to Jews in Germany and then, as the Third Reich spread its grasp, throughout Europe. For the English-language press, what was happening to the Jews was a sidebar, a story that was ancillary to the main news – namely the progress of the war. In contrast, for the editor of the *Forverts* and for the paper's readers, what was happening to the Jews was of primary importance ... It was *the* story, not one among many.[9]

Lipstadt's analysis, which represents one of the few discussions of the topic, is corroborated by the recollections of scholar and journalist Marvin Kalb's introductory chapter of *Why Didn't the Press Shout?*: "I remember, during the war, that my father would read the Yiddish-language newspaper, the *Forward*, and he would share the gruesome news from Europe about the Nazi slaughter of the Jews. We knew about the slaughter. We knew, and many other Jews knew."[10] Yet Yiddish newspapers have not been closely investigated to determine what they knew, when they knew it, and in what ways that knowledge translated into thought, discussion, expression, and action. As Hasia Diner points out in *We Remember with Reverence and Hope*, a study of American responses to the Holocaust in the post-War years, "A monumental but crucial research project awaits the scholar who would study the daily Yiddish press of the postwar years and uncover patterns of engagements with the 'hurban' [Holocaust]."[11] The same can certainly be said for the years of Holocaust. Unlike the inconsistent coverage of the Jewish experience in the Nazi Holocaust provided by English- and French-language newspapers, the Yiddish press consistently covered this story and from a variety of angles. Rather than focusing on the limitations of the mainstream press in reporting the Holocaust, the government's knowledge and inaction, or the Jewish community's political weakness, a study of the Yiddish press offers a window onto Jewish communities' contemporaneous and variegated understanding of and responses to the events as they were unfolding.

In the Canadian context, the country's major Yiddish dailies offer a rich and hitherto understudied picture of a community generating diverse mechanisms to address the mounting crisis as well as its aftermath. Franklin Bialystok's *Delayed Impact* alludes to the wealth of material contained in the Yiddish press: "Local organizations made strides within their respective communities ... These various activities were reported in a plethora of Yiddish and English-language Jewish newspapers and periodicals." However, he does not elaborate on these activities, focusing rather on a local community that was "fragmented and ineffectual."[12] This focus on the impotence of Canada's organized Jewish community in the realm of public policy obscures the sense of agency that did express itself in the Yiddish community. Canadian Jews organized public protests and campaigns as well as a range of other activities. However, because many of these events were community-based and their coverage relegated to the Yiddish press, and because of the unprecedented scope of the catastrophe, they have not received their due in the historiography of the Holocaust and Canadian Jewish life.

In short, the vitality of the Yiddish community during the war years has been subsumed by the enormity of the Holocaust itself. As Anita Norich has revealed, during the Holocaust period American Yiddish culture experienced a renewed vibrancy, whose omission in discourse about the era has distorted a wider understanding of American Jewish culture.[13] In the Canadian context, the different mechanisms developed by the Jewish community to cope with the mounting European crisis have been overshadowed in much of the existing historiography by the refusal of various Canadian bodies to intervene on behalf of Jewish refugees. In contrast, an examination of Canada's Yiddish newspapers reveals a plethora of ways in which the Jewish community responded to the mounting onslaught against European Jewry as it escalated. These newspapers were widely read by Jews across the country as a primary source of local, national, and international news, and of current events, community life, cultural activity, and the arts. They remain a vital yet virtually untapped source on the Canadian Jewish experience in the first half of the twentieth century, especially during the pivotal years of the Holocaust.

By 1931, Canadian Jewry numbered over 155,000 individuals, a vast majority of them immigrants from Eastern Europe whose first language was Yiddish and who maintained strong ties to the Old Country. In comparison with the neighbouring United States, where the mass immigration of Yiddish-speaking Jews spanned the 1880s through the tightening of immigration laws in the 1920s, Canada's did not get underway until the turn of the twentieth century. This meant that even in the 1930s, with Jewish immigration basically cut off, the country's Jews were largely first- and second-generation immigrants from Eastern Europe whose mother tongue was Yiddish. Canada's major Jewish population centres of Montreal, Toronto, and Winnipeg housed networks of religious, political, mutual aid, and philanthropic organizations as well as libraries, schools, and newspapers spanning the religious and political spectrum, many of which operated in the Yiddish language into the 1940s.

After multiple attempts, enduring newspapers to serve Canada's Yiddish community were founded in each of the country's major Jewish centres by the eve of the First World War. The *Keneder adler/ Jewish Daily Eagle*, established in 1907 as the country's first lasting Yiddish newspaper by Montreal businessman Hirsch Wolofsky, aimed to represent all parts of the community, from leftist secular to ultra-Orthodox. It offered a wide variety of content and featured virtually all of the country's Yiddish writers as contributors. The only non-English- or French-language daily in the province of Quebec, it also spoke for Canada's Jews as a whole as the country's largest Yiddish newspaper.[14] *Dos yidishe vort/Israelite Press*, founded in Winnipeg in 1910 (originally under the title *Der keneder yid* [The

Canadian Jew] and then *Der yid* [The Jew]) was strongly leftist and Zionist in orientation, but like the *Keneder adler* it represented the more religiously observant parts of the community as well. The newspaper acted not only as the primary organ for Winnipeg's Jews, but served Canada's Prairie and western Jewish populations as a whole.[15] During the period under discussion, it appeared twice a week (Tuesdays and Fridays). Toronto's *Yidisher Zhurnal/Daily Hebrew Journal* was founded in 1911 as a weekly and subsequently appeared as a daily. It likewise served as a forum for the diverse elements of the city's Yiddish population, including its prominent left wing. These newspapers included pages in English for their more linguistically acculturated readers. The three publications often shared resources by occasionally publishing the same articles, with content generally first appearing in the *Keneder adler*.

By the late 1930s, with Canada virtually closed to new arrivals, the Jewish population was undergoing steady linguistic acculturation, and English was rapidly becoming the dominant language of the community. In the 1931 census, 96 percent of Canadian Jews declared Yiddish as their mother tongue; however, only 4 percent declared themselves unable to speak English. By 1941, the percentage claiming Yiddish as a mother tongue was 76 percent, and in 1951 – even with a post–Holocaust influx of Yiddish-speaking refugees – it had dropped to 50 percent.[16] However, Yiddish maintained an important role as a Jewish vernacular as well as a language of politics and culture. Although a 1938 study indicated that English had become the Montreal Jewish community's preferred language for periodicals,[17] the Canadian Yiddish newspapers as well as the New York City dailies remained a principal source of news on European Jewry for the local community, in particular during the turbulent 1930s and 1940s.

During the years of the Third Reich, Canadian Jewry did not rely on the country's English-language Jewish newspapers for news on Europe's Jews. The *Canadian Jewish Chronicle*, which was also published by Wolofsky and shared office space with the *Keneder adler*, appealed to Canada's more established and anglicized Jewish community. It published extensively on the fate of European Jewry, especially after 1942, when the systematic extermination of Jews under Nazi-controlled and -occupied lands was set into place. As Max Beer points out, the *Canadian Jewish Chronicle* published its reports on the annihilation of European Jewry some six months before a handful of reports appeared in Canada's non-Jewish newspapers, and the *Chronicle* made far more explicit reference to the Jewish identity of the victims.[18]

As discussed below, this earlier and more complete coverage reflects the particular orientation of that newspaper's editor and a large proportion of its readership, who were first- or second-generation immigrants from Eastern Europe and for whom the fate of European Jewry was of great personal interest. However, at the same time, the newspaper continued to offer much content of a general cultural and social bent, with the underlying assumption that its readers were looking to the daily *Keneder adler* for in-depth news of an international scope. Winnipeg's weekly, the *Jewish Post*, published regularly on the Jews of Europe, but in less depth than its bi-weekly and larger Yiddish-language counterpart. Meanwhile, according to a study by David Levy, Canada's other major Anglo-Jewish weekly, the *Canadian Jewish Review*, rarely mentioned the specific plight of Europe's Jews or the engagement of Canadian Jewry with their situation; Levy posits that fear of an anti-Jewish backlash, combined with a desire to prove their Canadianness led the newspaper's editors to downplay Nazi atrocities toward the Jews during the war years.[19]

By contrast, the Canadian Yiddish press published news on the fate of Europe's Jews under the Nazis that did not appear in other sources.[20] The publications also acted as clearinghouses for information as well as fora for political, cultural, literary, spiritual, emotional, and personal responses in editorials, essays, and poetry by the community's cultural figures. The various articles offered extensive and contemporaneous detail about Europe's Jews under the Nazis: mass shootings and gassings, the establishment of ghettos, concentration and death camps, and the resulting death of millions of Jews. While mainstream English- and French-language publications focused on Canada's role in the war effort, the Yiddish press catered to a readership with close personal connections to European Jewry. The readers and writers for this press were themselves immigrants or children of immigrants with family and friends in Europe, and news of Nazi atrocities against the Jews affected them personally and represented a primary concern. Deborah Lipstadt's observations on the New York daily *Forverts* could just as well apply to Canada's Yiddish newspapers:

[I]n contrast with mainstream reporters, many of whom were sceptical about the stories of genocide, the editors and writers of this newspaper had no problem believing what they were hearing from Europe. The news was coming from sources they trusted implicitly and explicitly. Moreover, the victims were their *landsleit*, people from their hometowns, and, in too many cases, their families. For the *Forverts*, the tragedy of the death of their fellow Jews, who were their readers' parents, siblings, children, relatives, and friends, was overwhelming.[21]

Canada's Yiddish papers published news from a variety of American as well as European sources, including underground reports from the Soviet Union and firsthand accounts from Jews across Europe who had managed to evade death. Because they were published in Yiddish, the newspapers were not subject to the same degree of scrutiny under wartime censorship as English- or French-language publications. While skepticism about the accuracy of reports of Nazi atrocities was one underlying factor that limited their publication in the mainstream press, the producers and readers of the Yiddish press were far less likely to question the veracity of the accounts they received; given their own experiences of persecution in Europe, Canada's Jews did not doubt what they were told. Further, those accounts all too often corroborated the harrowing news sent by family members, many of whom they subsequently lost contact with. In short, readers of the Yiddish press were extremely well informed about news, both nationally and internationally, with daily headlines simultaneously keeping them up to date on the Great Depression, the world war and Canada's war efforts, and the fate of Europe's Jews under the Nazis.

A close examination of a sample month, September 1944, in Canada's eastern and westernmost major Yiddish newspapers spotlights fundamental differences between the Yiddish and non-Yiddish press in Canada. This month included several news stories that would be pivotal to the history of Canada and the Holocaust, including the aftermath of Polish liberation, a meeting of the UNRRA (United Nations Relief Rehabilitation Administration) held in Montreal, and local efforts on behalf of European Jewry. When these stories did appear in the mainstream press, they were allotted minimal attention, and the Jewish angle was omitted altogether. In contrast, the extensive and multifaceted coverage of events in Europe in the Yiddish newspapers warrants two conclusions about its many readers spanning the Canadian Jewish community: they knew and they acted. This sample month reveals a Canadian Jewish community with wide access to information that generated a variety of responses to a crisis of unprecedented scale.

Montreal's *Keneder adler* included daily coverage of the Holocaust from a variety of angles. Essays by local poet J.I. Segal called for renewed unity and vitality in the face of Nazi atrocities (1, 5 September). A report by a correspondent from Lublin offered an eyewitness account of the recently liberated Majdanek death camp and the atrocities perpetrated against countless Jews. His appeals to world Jewry for aid prompted the Canadian Jewish Congress to establish a community-wide campaign to tackle the situation of these Jews (1, 3 September). The newspaper went on to offer detailed first-hand accounts of the death camps in Poland, with a focus on the Jewish victims (4, 6, 12, 17 September). In addition, ongoing emergency campaigns sought to collect funds and clothing to send to the remnants of Polish Jewry. Thus, while studies such as *None Is Too Many* detail the extensive but largely unsuccessful efforts of the local community to lobby the Canadian government to open the country's borders to Jewish refugees during the 1930s and 1940s, a study of the Yiddish press reveals many other mechanisms employed by the Jewish community in its efforts to aid its European brethren, such as fundraising campaigns, protests, and other forms of lobbying.

For example, the *Keneder adler* offered extensive coverage of the UNRRA meeting that was held locally and detailed the pivotal role of the Jewish lobby in assuring support to European displaced persons, most of whom were Jews. In contrast, the mainstream press offered minimal reports that did not discuss the wide-ranging activities of the Jewish lobby. Most tellingly, the Anglo-Jewish *Canadian Jewish Chronicle*'s single brief summary of the UNRRA meeting for its non-Yiddish readers opened by stating, "Unless they are also readers of the Yiddish daily press, Canadian Jews might easily have missed the significance of an important achievement in Jewish life which took place in our Montreal and which, in part at least, was due to the activities of our own Canadian institutions."[22] It was thus understood within the community that the major source of information on Jewish life during this period was the Yiddish press.

Winnipeg's bi-weekly *Yidishe vort* for September 1944 contained similar stories. Coverage of Lublin stated that the few remaining

Jews in the city were liberated from the concentration camps there, where approximately one million Jews had been killed; another article on the same page detailed attempts to find relatives of the Jews found alive in the city (5 September). The forthcoming UNRRA meeting was described (12 September), and an English-language column bemoaned the uselessness of past conferences and expressed hope that the UNRRA conference would be more effective at assisting Jewish refugees (22 September). An editorial urgently called on Canadian Jewry to assist survivors (*shares-hapleyte*, "remnants") in the newly liberated areas of Poland and reminded readers that they would have been in the same position had they not left Europe (8 September); another called on Jews to use both their money and their influence on behalf of the survivors (15 September). Three reports from the Canadian Jewish Congress detailed efforts to reunify families (12 September) and called for a coordinated aid campaign for survivors (15 September), in response to the appeal from Toronto organizations (22 September). Again, the Yiddish newspaper offered wide and in-depth coverage of events that received minimal attention in the non-Yiddish press.

Despite this wealth of information, scholars have only just begun to examine the ways in which Canada's Yiddish press engaged with the Holocaust. Daniel Stone's study, "Coverage of the Holocaust in Winnipeg's Jewish and Polish Press," provides a comparison of the city's Yiddish, Anglo-Jewish, and Polish newspaper coverage.[23] Max Beer's thesis "What Else Could We Have Done?" touches on ways in which both the *Canadian Jewish Chronicle* and the *Keneder adler* reported the persecution and annihilation of European Jewry. Many other scholars have entirely overlooked this rich source of documentation on what Canadians were reading and writing about Nazi Europe in the Yiddish press. For example, Lewis Levendel's *A Century of the Canadian Jewish Press, 1880s–1980s*, offers an overview of the Yiddish press, but his chapter on the years surrounding the Holocaust focuses on the Anglo-Jewish press and points to the failure of the ongoing efforts of Canada's Jewish newspapers to publicize the genocide. A large part of this omission stems from linguistic issues, in particular the lack of access to Yiddish-language sources by interested scholars who do not read the language. The result has been an inaccurate perception that Canadians were not informed of what was taking place in Nazi Europe and that when the Jewish community did act, it did so ineffectually.

THE IBERIAN REFUGEES

In April, May, and October 1944, three groups of Iberian refugees, known collectively as the "*Serpa Pinto* refugees," arrived in Canada from Lisbon, an overwhelming majority of them Jews or Christians married to Jews. All had escaped Nazi persecution by making their way from various points across Europe to politically neutral Portugal, where they were supported by international Jewish agencies and awaited the opportunity for emigration. By coincidence, each voyage of the ss *Serpa Pinto* that transported refugees from Lisbon to Canada landed on a major Jewish holiday. The first ship landed on 6 April, the eve of Passover, and brought 280 refugees, 276 of them Jewish, to Canada. It docked in Philadelphia amidst mobs of security officers to maintain secrecy; the arrivals were swarmed by newspaper reporters. The refugees boarded a sealed train to Montreal to avoid the possibility of passengers claiming status in the United States. They were met at the Bonaventure Station by a large group of Jewish and Christian representatives from various community and refugee organizations and were brought to the Talmud Torah Jewish school for refreshments. Members of the group then travelled on to homes in Montreal or to their final destination in Toronto. The second boatload, which landed on 25 May during the festival of Shavuot, carried 74 passengers bound for Canada, most of them refugees. Despite its neutral flag and safe conduct, a German u-boat intercepted the vessel en route, and the passengers spent nine hours floating in lifeboats until they were able to reboard the ship. A third boatload landed on 1 October, during the holiday of Sukkot, with 45 refugees on board. The land portion of their trip was delayed for religious reasons after their arrival in Philadelphia because the passengers refused to travel by train on the Sabbath or on the festival of Sukkot.

These three groups of refugees marked a notable exception to the long-standing practice whereby only individual Jews or family units were allowed into the country under special orders-in-council, while various efforts to bring in Jewish groups, including orphans, ultimately failed due to bureaucratic red tape. The various strategies of the organized Jewish community, in particular through the Canadian Jewish Congress (cjc), had been unsuccessful in moving Prime Minister Mackenzie King and his cabinet to change its policies or to get his bureaucrats, notably Frederick Blair, director of the Immigration

Branch of the Department of Mines and Resources (where immigration was housed), to interpret the existing policies less stringently. In fact, Blair often went beyond the letter of the law in his implementation of Canadian immigration policy.

The impetus for the Iberian refugee scheme, which marked the first time a sizable group of Jewish refugees was granted asylum since the outbreak of the war, came from the Canadian government. In November 1943, Thomas Crerar, minister of the Department of Mines and Resources, made an announcement in the House of Commons that Canada would admit refugees, including Jews, from neutral Portugal, where many had been stranded for several years. While the initial allotment was for 200 families, Canada's agent in Lisbon, Odilon Cormier, applied the restrictions of Canada's Immigration Branch – health standards, racial quotas, the requirement for complete family units only (father, mother, and children under age eighteen), the inadmissibility of refugees from non-Allied countries, and the requirement for documentation such as identity and travel papers – so strictly that far fewer than the permitted 200 Iberian families actually arrived in Canada.[24]

Moreover, the Canadian government had opted for a venture with few risks attached, in particular in the arena of public opinion. The humanitarian gesture was finite and temporary: the group was to be admitted to Canada for the duration of the war only – offered temporary asylum rather than immigrant status. There was almost no financial cost to the government, since the costs of transportation to Canada and the refugees' upkeep while in the country were absorbed by various non-governmental agencies. Much of the logistical work on behalf of the refugees was handled by the CJC, with its president Samuel Bronfman, executive director Saul Hayes, and general secretary H.M. Caiserman at the helm. Transportation was funded by the American Joint Distribution Committee and the HICEM,[25] and the costs of reception, settlement, and care were paid by an affiliate of the CJC, the United Jewish Refuge and War Relief Agencies. Further assistance was provided by the United Jewish Refugee and War Relief Agencies and the Jewish Immigrant Aid Society in association with the Canadian National Committee on Refugees,[26] the National Council of Jewish Women, and various free loan institutions.[27] Local CJC representatives met the refugees on the ship, helped them with paperwork, and travelled with them to Montreal or on to Toronto.

Reception committees in both cities extended welcome, housing, and legal assistance.

Patrick Reed suggests that the refugee scheme "was motivated by William Lyon Mackenzie King's politics of limited gestures" in an administration that was marked by ambivalence regarding the refugee question and remained noncommittal in order to maintain national unity. He posits that the Iberian refugee movement was historically significant as one of a very few Canadian refugee initiatives in the important nation-building period between the Statute of Westminster (1931) – the British Act of Parliament granting legal and political independence to Commonwealth countries – and the end of the Second World War. However, in practice, it amounted to what Reed terms "an act of calculated kindness, an attempt to afford [Canada] political time and space"[28] in a public gesture of limited scope rather than the opening of the floodgates to Jewish refugees, as was feared by so many Canadians. Thus, the Canadian government closed its Lisbon office several days after the third ship landed.

MEDIA COVERAGE

Canada's mainstream English- and French-language newspapers in Montreal, Toronto, and Winnipeg covered the story of the Iberian refugees with a number of them giving the story multi-day as well as front-page coverage of a generally positive nature. David Rome, press officer of the CJC, remarked in his report in the 1944–45 *American Jewish Year Book*, "The press of the Dominion welcomed the newcomers, commended the government for admitting them, and urged that many more be permitted to enter the country."[29] According to Patrick Reed's analysis, mainstream English-language media coverage of the first sizable entry of refugees into Canada was "widespread and generally favourable." He explains a focus on the tiny Christian contingent in the refugee group: "In a predominantly Christian country, empathy for the fundamentally familiar was, not surprisingly, more newsworthy than aid to the hitherto exotic stranger." Emphasis was on the "education and refinement" of the refugees, with the CJC apparently content to downplay the Jewish specificity of the group. The refugees were depicted as "guests" and "honourary Canadian compatriots." In sum: "Conforming the story to the Canadian context, media representations of the Iberian refugees were sympathetic yet asymmetrical. Generally focusing on arrival rather than Europe, on Christians rather than Jews, on war angles rather than refugee issues, on present rather than past failure, press coverage implicitly engendered a quite narrow perception of a much larger problem."[30]

The largest group of the Iberian refugees – the first group, which arrived in April 1944 – received the widest coverage in the mainstream English- and French-language newspapers, as well as in the Yiddish press. How did the Yiddish and non-Yiddish coverage compare? This issue is discussed below by examining the newspapers published in the major cities that housed a Yiddish newspaper – Montreal, Toronto, and Winnipeg. The newspapers include major English- and French-language as well as Anglo-Jewish and Yiddish publications, as follows: the *Canadian Jewish Chronicle* (Montreal), *Canadian Jewish Review* (Montreal/Toronto), *Montreal Daily Star*, *Le Devoir* (Montreal), *Gazette* (Montreal), *Globe and Mail* (Toronto), *Jewish Post* (Winnipeg), *Kenader adler/Jewish Daily Eagle* (Montreal), *La Presse* (Montreal), *Toronto Daily Star*, *Winnipeg Tribune*, *Winnipeg Free Press*, *Yidisher zhurnal/Hebrew Journal* (Toronto), and *Yidishe vort/Israelite Press* (Winnipeg).[31]

The non-Jewish English- and French-language newspapers in Montreal and Toronto each allotted at least one article to the event, ranging from numerous headlining articles with photographs to a single small article. As a rule, the reports focused on the human-interest angle of the story, in particular the experiences of the refugees once they had arrived in Canada. Some of the newspapers, notably Canada's largest circulation daily at that time, the *Toronto Daily Star*, included extensive photo spreads of the ship and snapshots of smiling refugees as well as brief portraits.[32] This is less surprising for the *Star*, which, as Ulrich Frisse argues, advocated for human rights and against injustice and frequently spoke out against the Nazi regime.[33] However, the content of the reports in the *Star* and other mainstream newspapers was qualitatively different from that of the Yiddish press. The reports generally paid far more attention to the media frenzy than to the experiences of the refugees before their arrival in Canada. For example, an article in the *Gazette* stated, "The refugees had harrowing stories to tell of their persecution by Hitlerian authorities and their wanderings ... But they were not permitted to tell their stories. Seldom has so much security guard been thrown about a transfer of steamship passengers." From leaving the ship to being sealed in trains, "they were surrounded by enough police to provide a guard for each refugee."[34]

Much space was devoted to the difficult journey that many of the refugees had made over the Pyrenees Mountains from Spain, with relatively few allusions to the hazards they had escaped. A reporter from *La Presse* remarked, "Les courses et randonnés à travers du mont Royal apporteront autrement de joie et de repos à ces forçats de l'alpinisme pyrénéen!" (Runs and hikes over Mount Royal will otherwise bring joy and relaxation to these hardcore fans of Pyrenean mountain climbing).[35] This characterization of the refugees' flight through the Pyrenees casts the Jews' escape from the Nazis as a sporting escapade rather than an escape from persecution and death. At best, it reflects a lack of understanding of the conditions that Jews endured to escape the Nazis. The systematic persecution and annihilation of Europe's Jews under the Nazis, which would have been beyond the ken of most Canadian readers, was generally omitted from these stories. According to a front-page article in the *Gazette*, "With one exception, they showed little evidence of the hardships most had suffered." The exception provided was a woman whose feet froze while crossing the Pyrenees.[36] The experiences of the refugees in Europe were presented in very mild terms that reflected a perception of the Nazi concentration camps as internment camps rather than places where systematic brutality and mass murder took place: "Concentration camps, insults, bribery and a hazardous trek over the Pyrenees Mountains, followed by more concentration camps and passport difficulties in Portugal marked the struggle for freedom."[37]

The lack of wider context was exacerbated by the circumstances under which the refugees arrived. Reporters complained about tight security and the organizers' orders to the refugees not to speak with reporters as a precautionary measure to protect their families still in Europe, which made it virtually impossible to interact with the new arrivals.[38] A front-page article in the *Gazette* was indignant at the lack of access to the refugees and the ban on picture taking, despite the fact that photographs were being freely sold in the streets: "The refugees had harrowing stories to tell of their persecution by Hitlerian authorities and their wanderings ... But they were not permitted to tell their stories."[39] Montreal's largest French-language daily, *La Presse*, made a more concerted effort to speak with the new arrivals by sending reporters to the breakfast reception hosted at the local

Talmud Torah school. They were among the first individuals to chat with the refugees, a number of whom spoke French.[40] Exceptionally, an article in the *Montreal Daily Star* alluded to the tribulations the refugees had suffered before their arrival: "Tragic Odyssey Over: Refugees from Hitler's Europe Find Haven on Canadian Soil."[41]

The mainstream press presented the story in terms familiar to the average Canadian reader of the time: a Christian who may well have been uncomfortable with, or hostile to, the idea of mass Jewish immigration to Canada, especially during wartime. Coverage of the Iberian refugees spotlighted the few Christian members of the group, to whom Canadian readers could best relate. A long article with photographs that appeared in the *Gazette* several days after the refugees' arrival focused on a Roman Catholic doctor in the group, while a separate headline, "Four Christian families among 138 persons to be guests of Montrealers," featured short anecdotes about the members of these families, "related to the Jewish race in some manner," as Christian converts or as Christians married to Jews. *La Presse* observed that among the group "se trouvent seulement deux catholiques et un protestant" (are found only two Catholics and one Protestant)[42] and subsequently published a large article under the headline "Familles catholiques: Munderer et Mandl."[43] When specific mention was made of the Jewish heritage of the refugees, it tended to be in relation to the upcoming holiday of Passover, a word that would likely have been familiar to the newspapers' readers. A headline in the *Gazette* read, "Local Jews to Welcome Refugees into Homes for Passover Service,"[44] while a front-page article in the *Globe and Mail* read, "Refugee Jews Expected Here before Passover."[45]

The mainstream media reflected the Canadian public's ambivalence about Jewish immigration to Canada. All of the English- and French-language newspapers that covered the story made it clear that the refugees had been permitted entry into Canada legally – no special exceptions had been made – and were to remain for the duration of the war only. This was unambiguously stated in the Montreal *Gazette* as well as in the *Montreal Daily Star*'s front-page article, which also indicated that various agencies were looking after the refugees.[46] The French-language press was likewise explicit about the temporary arrangement and stated that the refugees would not become public charges.[47] The refugees' gratitude to Canada, the local support they received, and their potential contribution to the country were also stressed in articles such as the *Globe and Mail*'s

"Haven in Canada Thrills Refugees."[48] In this vein, the *Gazette* mentioned the skilled workers in the group and cited a younger member's statement: "[W]e wish to thank Canada for its generosity and we hope that we may become of real service to your people."[49]

Only one newspaper, Montreal's French-language daily, *Le Devoir* – Quebec's leading nationalist newspaper during this period[50] – adopted a decidedly negative tone. The day after a very short announcement stating that a group of refugees was en route to Montreal,[51] *Le Devoir* published a longer article that presented the new arrivals in a less than flattering light. The author offered questionable information – he had been given to understand by a Toronto representative that "plusieurs de ces Juifs sont catholiques" (several of these Jews are Catholic) – and depicted the refugees as deliberately manipulating the media attention they were receiving. When journalists "tentatively" attempted to exchange a few words with the refugees, "Nous n'avons pas entendu autres choses que les réponses fort evasives, en excellent français d'ailleurs. Tous nous ont répété les boniments que nous avons lu dans les journaux de la veille" (We have heard nothing but extremely evasive responses, in admittedly excellent French. Everyone repeated to us the same spiel we'd read in yesterday's newspapers). Further, amidst a horde of photographers, reporters, and even filmmakers, "il était amusant de remarquer que si les réfugiés se faisaient un devoir de d'être peu loquaces, ils manifestaient d'autre part un goût prononcé pour le spectacle photographique" (it was amusing to note that while the refugees were making a point of doing very little talking, they showed a marked penchant for the photo op).[52]

Farther west, in Winnipeg, coverage of the event in the English-language press was more constrained. This can be explained by the fact that although the Yiddish press later reported plans for some of the refugees to travel on to that city,[53] Winnipeg did not absorb any of the Iberian refugees in the first and largest group. The *Winnipeg Tribune*, the city's second-largest English-language newspaper, offered no coverage. The *Winnipeg Free Press*, the city's largest paper, included two related news items, both of which appeared before the arrival of the refugees and focused on the wider political dimensions of the story. The first discussed the imminent arrival of a group of "war refugees" from Spain and Portugal who were on their way to Canada, with a focus on political leaders' views on Canada's role in assisting refugees – namely, that with the deterioration of relationships between the world's major powers, it was time for smaller countries to become involved in external affairs. While the article did not state the Jewish identity of the refugees, this was implied by its discussion of the question of Jewish immigration to Palestine.[54] A subsequent, smaller article discussed a motion by a Winnipeg Jewish community leader, M.A. Gray, that the legislature recommend to the federal government an extension of sanctuary to "victims of Nazi terror," in particular those stranded in Portugal.[55] This broad interest in the refugee question can be explained by the highly multi-ethnic character of the city, which was home to Swedish, Ukrainian, Croatian, German, Polish, Icelandic, and Norwegian weekly newspapers. With a history of editorial freedom and prominent coverage of international news, the *Winnipeg Free Press* tended to offer relatively wider and more sympathetic coverage of the plight of European Jewry than Canada's other mainstream newspapers.

The Anglo-Jewish press offered varied responses to the situation. The story received no coverage in the *Canadian Jewish Review*. The post-Passover issue[56] of the *Jewish Post* published a brief news item about the arrival of the refugees[57] as well as an announcement of an upcoming "Refugee Mass Meeting" in Winnipeg to fundraise for the support of these and future refugees.[58] The subsequent issue contained a follow-up article stating that Canada was considering admitting more refugees, the number to be determined based on health inspections and transportation arrangements.[59] The *Canadian Jewish Chronicle* devoted two lengthy stories to the event in its post-Passover issue. The first, a front-page editorial titled "Welcome to the Refugees," was authored by the editor of the newspaper, poet and writer A.M. Klein, who also was speechwriter for CJC national president Samuel Bronfman. Klein remarked on the symbolic timing of the Passover landing and characterized the refugees as a remnant of those Jews remaining in Europe. Much of the editorial was devoted to expressing gratitude to Canada for admitting the refugees and to effusive praise of the Canadian government's role in offering refuge to European Jewry. Klein's attitude suggests the response of a population that found itself vulnerable during the wartime crisis, when any assistance at all was considered miraculous and a suitably grateful response was seen as prudent:

> To the Dominion government, which made possible the arrival of these victims of Hitlerism, this journal, as all of Canadian Jewry,

expresses its special debt of gratitude. The granting of asylum to the victims of religious and political persecution is of the great tradition of British justice and fair play. It is not a thing of to-day; from time immemorial, this hospitality towards the harried and hunted has contributed one of the noblest characteristics of the democratic legislator. It is, indeed, the typical realization of man's humanity to man. In opening the doors of Canada to these refugees, the Canadian Government has achieved many purposes with a single gesture. It has, after all, saved the lives of human beings. It has illustrated again the broad tolerance and the far- . sighted vision of the late Sir Wilfrid Laurier, its spiritual mentor. And it has provided an example which other countries could do well to follow. Nor has this latest act of the Dominion Government constituted a new departure in its policy. Canadian Jewry has not forgotten the fact that immediately prior to the outbreak of war, the Government admitted into the country refugees who, with the help of the Committee on Refugees, later the nucleus for the United Jewish Refugee and War Relief Societies, are now completely orientated into the economic and social fabric of the land. With gratitude, too, it recalls the prompt and generous response of the Prime Minister, replying to a letter of Mr. Samuel Bronfman, president of the United Jewish Refugee and War Relief Societies, offering asylum to one thousand persons in France, a response which was unfortunately frustrated by the German occupation of that unhappy land.[60]

The editorial ended with mention of the various refugee agencies involved in "the great mission of mercy." A second article in the *Canadian Jewish Chronicle* offered a human-interest approach to the story. It described the refugees' "solemn eyes" and "gaunt faces," despite their being neat in appearance and well dressed, and stated that some wanted to tell their stories while others preferred not to talk about their experiences.[61]

Canada's Yiddish newspapers offered far more frequent and greater in-depth coverage of the event, and from an insider perspective. The newspapers' contributors forged relationships with the refugees themselves, not solely as reporters but also as members of their adoptive communities. Many of the newspapers' writers and readers were personally involved in the venture via fundraising, meeting the new arrivals at the train station and welcoming them, or serving as host families. The focus of the articles was less on the legal aspects of the refugees' arrival than on their experiences. The newcomers also served as a source of rare first-hand news about the fate of their home communities in Europe and as representatives of European Jewry in ruins. This resonated deeply with Canadian Jews who had lost contact with loved ones from those places and who feared the worst. The significance of the refugees' arrival was heightened by news of the wholesale destruction of Polish Jewry that appeared in every issue of the Yiddish newspapers during this period. After years of virtually no Jewish newcomers entering Canada, the refugees' arrival was deemed nothing short of miraculous. Despite interruptions in newspaper production on account of the Jewish holidays that coincided with the arrival of the refugees, the story received sustained and consistent attention.

The most extensive coverage of the Iberian refugees appeared in the *Keneder adler*. This is hardly surprising, given the newspaper's position in Canada's primary Jewish immigrant centre, which was also the headquarters of many Jewish organizations, notably the cjc. Many of those involved with the *Keneder adler* as editors and writers were also community activists who had a stake in the venture. For example, *Keneder adler*'s publisher Hirsch Wolofsky was among those who rallied for the admittance of Jewish refugees to Canada and who personally greeted the Iberian refugee arrivals.[62] H.M. Caiserman, a regular contributor to the *Keneder adler*, was also one of those who welcomed the refugees; he was able to provide the newspaper with detailed information about the refugees' arrival because of his involvement with one of the venture's core organizing bodies in his capacity as general secretary of the cjc.

The Yiddish newspapers reported extensively on the arrival of the refugees, starting with numerous brief announcements, reports, and editorials ten days before the refugees' landing. The first article appeared in Winnipeg's *Yidishe vort* in a short news item from Lisbon. It stated that close to three hundred Jewish refugees from all over Europe would be arriving on the ss *Serpa Pinto* and would remain in Canada for the duration of the war; and that the cjc had promised the government that the refugees would not be a burden on the general population.[63] Numerous articles and editorials followed, detailing the circumstances that had led to the refugees' entry into Canada and discussing logistical issues and the special significance of the venture.[64] For example, longtime *Keneder adler* staff writer

Israel Medresh offered a lengthy report on the imminent arrival of the Jewish refugees, comparing the situation with the Exodus from Egypt and associating it with the holiday of Passover that coincided with their landing in Canada.[65] An editorial in the *Yidisher zhurnal/ Daily Hebrew Journal* called for the community to "welcome our wandering brethren with open hearts."[66]

Caiserman's welcoming speech, *"Brukhim haboim"* (Welcome), which was published in the *Keneder adler* to mark the arrival of the refugees, was reprinted in both the Toronto and Winnipeg papers.[67] Caiserman characterized the venture as the culmination of long-standing efforts to lobby the Canadian government, and made concrete appeals to his readers for logistical assistance: reception, finding homes for the newcomers, promoting their independence, in particular by helping the refugees find work with Jewish factory owners, and providing guidance to help the newcomers integrate into Canadian life. Caiserman also listed the challenges facing the newcomers, with the media and public opinion set against immigration and the refugees slated to be sent back to Europe at the war's end. The article concluded with a message of hope: "We welcome our 300 brothers and sisters to our home. Let your arrival mark the beginning of larger groups to share the free air of our Dominion. May your arrival mark an end of the torment that you have under gone and may each of you find your economic and spiritual fortune as a part of the organized Canadian Jewish community."

Several days after Caiserman's speech appeared in the *Keneder adler*, the newspaper published the full text of Samuel Bronfman's welcoming address in his capacity as CJC national president. Bronfman's speech praised the efforts made by his organization on behalf of European Jewry to raise awareness of its plight as well as to advocate for Jewish refugees to be admitted to Canada. It also spoke of the joy of the local community in welcoming the refugees. It conveyed a sense of hope about the potential for rescuing other Jews from the perils of Hitler's Europe. The new arrivals, Bronfman con- cluded, "will help to build our future."[68] While the speech glossed over the overall ineffectiveness of the CJC in getting the restrictions on Jewish immigration relaxed, it reflected a renewed optimism within the community.

A shared feature of the reports in the Yiddish press following the arrival of the Iberian refugees was the amount of detail pro- vided about the past and current experiences of the members of

the group. Detailed reports about the arrival of the refugee contingent in Toronto that appeared in the *Yidisher zhurnal/Daily Hebrew
Journal* also included information about logistical arrangements for
the refugees in that city.[69] In the *Keneder adler*, a special report by
Medresh on the welcome reception held at the Talmud Torah school
described a number of the refugees and their stories, giving detailed
accounts of their escape from mass slaughter. Medresh's writing
includes seemingly mundane anecdotes that point to a far more
intimate connection to the story than the mainstream press would
have experienced. For example, a young boy repeatedly asked in
French, "Mommy, where are we?" until he was finally told, in Yiddish, "*mir zaynen bay di gute onkels* (we are with the good uncles)."
Medresh's report indicates that these individuals were a part of his
and his readers' community rather than just a news story.[70]

A lengthy report by staff writer Mordkhe Ginzburg offered his
impressions of meeting with the refugees after their arrival in Montreal. The article presented an image of the new arrivals as part of
living history, with their mix of languages and cultures characterized as a mirror of *goles* (the Jewish diaspora) itself. Ginzburg wrote
explicitly about the experiences of the refugees, both physical and
psychological. All had narrowly escaped a cruel death, some of them
appearing confused and resigned, and others expressing a wish that
they had remained to fight as heroes in the Warsaw Ghetto. Many
had survived concentration camps, where they had experienced terrible brutality and witnessed the murder of countless individuals.
They had seen their families split up and were permanently scarred.
As the first sizable group of refugees from Nazi Europe to arrive in
Canada, they presented "the first, horrifying true image of the current war." Ginzburg also detailed the "electrifying" atmosphere at
the reception when one of the refugees declared his city of origin
and located a Montreal resident from the same place: "*A ki-e-v-e-r?!
mayn landsman* (Someone from Kiev?! My countryman)." The article expressed hope that this "chapter of rescue history" would mark
the beginning of many to come.[71] Winnipeg's *Yidishe vort/Israel-
ite Press* presented a more sobering account of the arrivals, with a
front-page article focused on one member of the group who had sustained crippling mutilation to her feet in a Nazi concentration camp;
its editorial expressed a sentiment of "too little, too late," along with
its welcome of the newcomers.[72]

A particular characteristic of the Yiddish press was that it appealed
to the refugees as a channel through which to gain first-hand

information on Jewish Europe – information to which reporters and readers would not otherwise have had access. Medresh's lengthy article "Vos yidishe pleytim dertseyln vegn dem itstign tragishn lebn fun yidn in mayrev eyrope" (What the Jewish refugees recount about the current tragic life of Jews in Western Europe) offered first-hand accounts based on his conversations with some of the refugees who had recently resided in those countries. The views they expressed ranged from optimism to pessimism. Some interviewees anticipated positive changes in France and Spain which they felt would surely come with the inevitable defeat of the Nazis; with allies of the Jews among the French resistance and with priests hiding Jews, they expressed hope for the Jews of Europe. One interviewee expected a full defeat of the Nazis but added that "the Jews in Western Europe have lost the war," since virtually nothing remained of French, Belgian, and Dutch Jewries. The article discussed in depth what Medresh characterized as the most harrowing aspect of the story under the heading "The Tragedy of Jewish Children": he reported that many French families had taken in Jewish children whose parents had gone missing and that *yidishe "tatelekh" un "mamelekh"* – little Jewish "fathers" and "mothers" – were left to care for their siblings. Medresh's interviewees promised their brethren left behind in Europe that they would appeal to Canada's "good Christians" on their behalf. Under the heading "The Music of Freedom," the article concluded by describing one refugee's first visit to a synagogue in six years: "I felt the freedom of Canada."[73]

In sum, the coverage of the Iberian refugee story in the Yiddish press was sustained and multifaceted. It included the information provided by the mainstream English- and French-language newspapers as well as by the Anglo-Jewish press, with added layers of detail and nuance. The reports in the Yiddish newspapers allowed readers not only to identify with the refugees but to become personally involved in the venture by responding to appeals for assistance in areas such as housing. The articles humanized the story by expressing a wide range of emotional responses, from euphoria and optimism at the arrival of a sizable group of refugees, to sadness and despair at the unimaginable scope of the loss.

CONCLUSION

The treatment of the Iberian refugee story in the Canadian press reflects wider perceptions of the country's various communities during the Second World War. The mainstream press, which was largely the purview of Canada's two charter groups – English Protestant and French Catholic – had long been ambivalent toward Jewish immigration. The English press treated the episode as a news or human-interest but not specifically Jewish story. The coverage was superficial in nature, focusing only on the readily available information and expressing ambivalence about the question of the Jewish newcomers remaining in Canada. The French press offered the same sort of coverage, with one newspaper even expressing open mistrust of the Jewish refugees. Although the mainstream press had published brief reports in the winter of 1942 about the Nazi plan for the extermination of European Jewry, this systematic annihilation was not linked to the story of the Iberian refugees. The Anglo-Jewish press varied in its responses: the *Canadian Jewish Review* did not treat the story at all, the *Jewish Post* published several informative articles and calls for assistance, and the *Canadian Jewish Chronicle* emphasized the positive role of the Canadian government. These varying approaches can be understood as part of a broader tendency among English-language Jewish newspapers to negotiate a dual role: to convey support for local and world Jewry and at the same time to express undivided loyalty to Canada during wartime.

The Yiddish press offered broad coverage of the story in the form of news, editorials, and opinion pieces, with primary loyalty to the Jewish community in both Canada and abroad. The newspapers mirrored their consumer base and chronicled events that directly affected their readers. Consumers of the Yiddish press, by virtue of reading ethnic newspapers, reinforced their identification with their European roots and the realities facing European Jewry, even as they made their homes in Canada. These readers, as well as the writers of the Yiddish press, shared a common European immigrant background, with strong ties to the Old Country. The Iberian refugees offered a striking reminder of what the readers might have experienced had they not immigrated to Canada. Further, the Yiddish community forged personal connections with the Iberian refugees as supporters, members of welcoming committees, and purveyors of long-term assistance. Initial contact was extended as the newcomers were billeted in the homes of local Jews. These relationships give a perspective on the integration of the Jewish refugees into the mainstream Jewish community during wartime that offers a very different picture from the findings of Franklin Bialystok, who focuses on the linguistic and cultural gaps between Holocaust survivors who came to Canada in the postwar period and the established Jewish community.[74] This current review of the Yiddish press indicates that the gap between resident Jewish Canadian and refugee was far narrower within the Yiddish community, where members shared a language and wider cultural connections.

While the news stories about the Iberian refugees in the mainstream press concentrated on the refugees' arrival, coverage in the Yiddish press was ongoing. This was no mere story alongside many other wartime stories; for the Yiddish community, this was *the* story. It marked the culmination of long-lasting efforts to open Canada's gates to Jewish refugees and offered hope for the rescue of other Jews from Nazi Europe. The case of the Iberian refugees also involved members of their own communities who had personal ties to their places of origin. Readers of the Yiddish press, most of them first-generation immigrants from Europe who had experienced some form of persecution before their arrival, could all too easily imagine themselves in the situation of the Iberian refugees or of those not lucky enough to have escaped.

The Yiddish newspapers indicate that this community was gripped by the imperative to be proactive and vocal during this time of crisis rather than relying on the more muted and diffident approach of the English-language Jewish establishment. With few if any readers from outside the Jewish community, the Yiddish press was able to publish more extensively on the fate of European Jewry, with less concern about being accused of split loyalties in the Canadian war effort or of contravening Canada's wartime regulations governing information. The readers and writers of the Yiddish press had a deeply vested emotional interest in the story of Jews under Nazi-controlled or -occupied Europe. This was much more than the narrative of "them" within a broader international calamity; it was "us," our story through which all other events – whether the war or local anti-semitism – were viewed.

NOTES

1   All translations from the Yiddish and French are the author's.
2   See also Zimmerman, "'Narrow-minded people': Canadian Universities and the Academic Refugee Crises, 1933–1941."

3   Bauer, *American Jewry and the Holocaust: The American Jewish Joint Distribution Committee, 1939–1945*, 264.

4   Studies of the American press include Booth Jr. and Gordon, "The Holocaust: General Jewish and Christian Media Perspectives"; Camp, "Religion and Horror: The American Religious Press Views Nazi Death Camps and Holocaust Survivors"; Drake, "Manipulating the News: The U.S. Press and the Holocaust, 1933–1945"; Leff, "When the Facts Didn't Speak for Themselves: The Holocaust in the *New York Times*, 1939–1945"; Ross, *So It Was True: The American Protestant Press and the Nazi Persecution of the Jews*; and Wadia, "*The New York Times* Covers the Holocaust: All the News That's Fit to Print?" Studies of the United Kingdom press include Mosley, "'Frightful crimes': British Press Responses to the Holocaust 1944–45"; Sharf, *The British Press and Jews under Nazi Rule*; and Thilo, *Das Deutschlandbild der Irish Times, 1933–1945*.

5   Beer, "What Else Could We Have Done? The Montreal Jewish Community, the Canadian Jewish Congress, the Jewish Press and the Holocaust"; Erwin, "Making Sense of Mass Murder: Toronto's Media Coverage of the Liberation of the Concentration Camps and Trials of War Criminals, 1944–1946"; Fuller, "The *Winnipeg Free Press*, the *Globe and Mail*, and the Jewish Refugee Crisis, 1933–1939"; Goutor, "The Canadian Media and the 'Discovery' of the Holocaust, 1944–1945"; and Levy, "The Canadian Jewish Review: An In-Depth Look on Its Coverage of the Holocaust."

6   Frisse, "The 'Bystanders' Perspective': The 'Toronto Daily Star' and Its Coverage of the Persecution of the Jews and the Holocaust in Canada, 1933–1945."

7   Ibid., 240.

8   Ibid., 229–31.

9   Lipstadt, "The Holocaust," 170.

10 Shapiro, *Why Didn't the Press Shout? American and International Journalism during the Holocaust*, 3.

11 Diner, *We Remember with Reverence and Love: American Jews and the Myth of Silence after the Holocaust, 1945–1962*, 413fn114. See also Diner, "Post-World-War-II American Jewry and the Confrontation with Catastrophe."

12 Bialystok, *Delayed Impact: The Holocaust and the Canadian Jewish Community*, 23, 55–6.

13 Norich, *Discovering Exile: Yiddish and Jewish American Culture during the Holocaust*.

14 See Margolis, "The Yiddish Press in Montreal, 1905–1950."

15 See Jones, "Primary Source Analysis: Der Kanader Yid."

16 Statistics taken from L. Rosenberg, *Jew: A Social and Economic Study of the Jews in Canada in the 1930s*, 255–7, and Rosenberg, "Jewish Population Characteristics," 3.

17 Tulchinsky, *Branching Out: The Transformation of the Canadian Jewish Community*, 23.

18 Beer, "What Else Could We Have Done?" 81–5.

19 Levy, "The *Canadian Jewish Review*."

20 Goutor, "The Canadian Media and the 'Discovery' of the Holocaust, 1944–1945."

21 Lipstadt, "The Holocaust," 173.

22 *Canadian Jewish Chronicle*, 6 October 1944, 2.

23 Stone, "Coverage of the Holocaust in Winnipeg's Jewish and Polish Press."

24 Abella and Troper. *None Is Too Many*, 164–8.

25 Established in 1927 to facilitate European Jewish emigration, HICEM is an acronym for the three organizations it merged: HIAS (Hebrew Immigrant Aid Society, New York), ICA (Jewish Colonization Association, Paris), and Emigdirect (Berlin).

26 The Canadian National Committee on Refugees and Victims of Political Persecution (CNCR) was founded in response to Kristallnacht and worked with the Canadian Jewish Congress Refugee Committee.

27 Rome, "Canada," 198.

28 Reed, "A Foothold in the Whirlpool: Canada's Iberian Refugee Movement," 117.

29 Rome, "Canada," 199.

30 Reed, "A Foothold in the Whirlpool," 92–9.

31 A listing of the newspapers is included in the bibliography at the end of this paper.

32 "Greeting their new …" *Toronto Daily Star*, 8 April 1944, 19; "Jewish Refugees Welcomed in City," *Gazette* (Montreal), 10 April 1944, 11, 17; "133 réfugiés juifs arrivent à Montréal," *La Presse*, 10 April 1944, 11, 21; "Reach Their Brave New World," *Toronto Daily Star*, 10 April 1944, 3.

33 Frisse, "The 'Bystanders' Perspective."

34 "272 Refugees en route Here," *Gazette*, 8 April 1944, 1.

35 "133 réfugiés juifs arrivent à Montréal," *La Presse*, 10 April 1944, 11, 21.

36 "272 Refugees en route Here," *Gazette*, 8 April 1944, 1.

37 "Jewish Refugees Welcomed in City," *Gazette*, 10 April 1944, 11, 17.

38 "Refugiés arrivés à Montréal," *La Presse*, 11 April 1944, 19.

39 "272 Refugees en route Here," *Gazette*, 8 April 1944, 1.

40 "133 réfugiés juifs arrivent à Montréal," *La Presse*, 10 April 1944, 11, 21.

41 "Tragic Odyssey Over: Refugees from Hitler's Europe Find Haven on Canadian Soil." *Montreal Daily Star*, 8 April 1944, 1.

42 "Réfugiés arrivés à Montréal," *La Presse*, 8 April 1944, 19.

43 "133 réfugiés juifs arrivent à Montréal," *La Presse*, 10 April 1944, 11, 21.

44 "Local Jews to Welcome Refugees into Homes for Passover Service," *Gazette*, 7 April 1944, 11.

45 C.R. Blackburn, "Refugee Jews Expected Here before Passover," *Globe and Mail*, 7 April 1944, 13.

46 "Local Jews to Welcome Refugees into Homes for Passover Service," *Gazette*, 7 April 1944, 11; "Tragic Odyssey Over: Refugees from Hitler's Europe Find Haven on Canadian Soil," *Montreal Daily Star*, 8 April 1944, 1.

47 *La Presse*, 8 April 1944, 19.

48 "Haven in Canada Thrills Refugees," *Globe and Mail*, 10 April 1944, 7.

49 "Jewish Refugees Welcomed in City," *Gazette*, 10 April 1944, 11, 17.

50 There is debate about the extent to which the newspaper espoused antisemitism during the Nazi era. See Anctil, *Le Devoir, les Juifs et l'immigration*, and Delisle, *Le traître et le Juif: Lionel Groulx, Le Devoir, et le délire du nationalisme d'extrême droite dans la province du Québec, 1929–1939*.

51 "Réfugiés en route vers le Canada," *Le Devoir*, 8 April 1944, 3

52 "Des réfugiés juifs arrivent à Montréal," *Le Devoir*, 11 April 1944, 3.

53 "Pflikhlinge familyes far vinipeg kumen on shpeter," *Dos yidishe vort/Israelite Press*, 9 June 1944, 1.

54 "House Debates Refugee Issue," *Winnipeg Free Press*, 31 March 1944, 1.

55 "Refugee Sanctuary Move Is Approved," *Winnipeg Free Press*, 5 April 1944, 1.

56 These Jewish newspapers did not publish during the Passover holiday.

57 "276 Refugees Arrive in Canada," *Jewish Post*, 13 April 1944, 1.

58 "Refugee Mass Meeting Sunday," *Jewish Post*, 13 April 1944, 1.

59 "More Refugees to Be Admitted," *Jewish Post*, 20 April 1944, 1.

60 "Welcome to the Refugees," *Canadian Jewish Chronicle*, 13 April 1944, 1.

61 "Refugees Find Freedom and Welcome in Canada," *Canadian Jewish Chronicle*, 13 April 1944, 10.

62 Israel Medresh, "Grupe pflikhlinge krigt hartsige oyfnam fun higer yidisher bafelkerung," *Keneder adler*, 10 April 1944, 1, 6.

63 "Pflikhtlinge oyfn veg keyn kanade," *Dos yidishe vort/Israelite Press*, 28 March, 1.

64 "256 pflikhlinge in veg keyn kanade, dertseylt Crerar," *Yidisher zhurnal/Daily Hebrew Journal*, 31 March 1944, 1; "Makht plats far a yidishn pflikhling," *Yidisher zhurnal/Daily Hebrew Journal*, 3 April 1944, 4;

"Sealed Train to Bring Jewish Refugee Group to Toronto," *Yidisher zhurnal/Daily Hebrew Journal*, 3 April 1944, 6 (English page); "Jewish Refugee Group Will Arrive Here April 7," *Yidisher zhurnal/Daily Hebrew Journal*, 5 April 1944, 6 (English page); "Pflikhtling familyes veren do ervartet di vokh," *Keneder adler*, 6 April 1944, 1; "A reporter" (Israel Medresh), "Morgn kumt keyn kanade di ershte grupe yidish pleytim fun shpanye un portugal," *Keneder adler*, 6 April 1944, 5.

65 "A reporter" (Israel Medresh), "Morgn kumt keyn kanade di ershte grupe yidish pleytim fun shpanye un portugal," *Keneder adler*, 6 April 1944, 5.

66 "Lomir mit ofene hertser oyfnemen undzere vanderende brider," *Yidisher zhurnal/Daily Hebrew Journal*, 7 April 1944, 4.

67 H.M. Caiserman, "Brukhim haboim," *Keneder adler*, 7 April 1944, 5, 7. Reprinted in *Yidisher zhurnal/Daily Hebrew Journal*, 7 April 1944, 5, 7, and in *Dos yidishe vort/Israelite Press*, 11 April 1944, 2.

68 Samuel Bronfman, "Prezident fun dem kanader yidishn kongres bagrist ongekumene pleytim," *Keneder adler*, 11 April 1944, 2.

69 "47 mishpokhes bashteyn in tsaytvaylige heymen," *Yidisher zhurnal/Daily Hebrew Journal*, 10 April 1944, 1; "Jewish Refugees Warmly Received in Toronto," *Yidisher zhurnal/Daily Hebrew Journal*, 10 April 1944, 6.

70 Israel Medresh, "Grupe pflikhlinge krigt hartsige oyfnam fun higer yidisher bafelkerung," *Keneder adler*, 10 April 1944, 1, 6.

71 M. Ginzburg, "Endlikh tsvishn mentshn ...," *Keneder adler*, 11 April 1944, 4, 3.

72 "70 protsent fun di ongekumene pflikhlingen zaynen yidn," *Dos yidishe vort/Israelite Press*, 11 April 1944, 1; "Undzere geratevete brider," *Dos yidishe vort/Israelite Press*, 11 April 1944, 2.

73 Israel Medresh, "Vos yidishe pleytim dertseyln vegn dem itstign tragishn lebn fun yidn in mayrev eyrope," *Keneder Adler*, 12 April 1944, 4.

74 See Bialystok, *Delayed Impact* and "'Greener' and 'Gayle': Relations between Holocaust Survivors and Canadian Jews."

5

On Campus in the Thirties: Antipathy, Support, and Indifference

MICHAEL BROWN

I frankly confess that I have more sympathy for the students ... driven out of McGill because they lack financial resources to see them through ... I believe many students in Germany have suffered persecution. I would throw no cold water on efforts to help them ... but were I able to contribute more than I do now, I should give my support here.

Sir Arthur Currie, principal of McGill, 1933

To academics on Canadian campuses in 1930, the coming decade looked to be depressed and depressing. Funds were increasingly limited. Public hysteria over communism made speaking on political issues or topics of the day risky. The place of professors was considered to be the classroom only, and they were generally expected to be detached. In any case, professors and university administrators seemed to carry little weight with the general public.

For Canadian Jews, the decade ahead looked ominous. The effects of the Great Depression were felt most by people on low incomes, especially those with high aspirations. The racism of Canadian individuals and institutions was palpable and worsening, exacerbated by the economic difficulties of the time. In Europe, for those with foresight, the rise of Nazism portended catastrophe. Traditionally, education had offered Jews a way to a brighter future. At Canadian universities in the thirties, however, quotas for Jewish students were being implemented, and it was almost impossible for Jews to join the faculty ranks. For Canada and its Jews, the future looked bleak as the decade opened.

In discussing antisemitism on Canadian campuses in the 1930s and the behaviour of students, administrators, and faculty members, one must begin with the context or, more appropriately, contexts. Among these are general feelings about Jews and other minorities; Canadian isolationism and pacifism; declining enthusiasm for the Empire in certain sectors of the population; socialism and communism, as well as heightened fear of both; notions about academics' freedom of speech; the degree to which professors were considered influential or not by Jews and by society at large; the Great Depression and its effects on universities; and differences among the regions of Canada, especially between French and English Canada.

The specific developments and events to be considered against these backdrops are several. They include the openness of universities to Jewish students and faculty members; the participation of students, faculty members, and administrators in protests on and off campus against antisemitic activities, especially in Germany; participation in academic conferences in Germany and in exchange programs with that country, and the popularity of studies and extra-curricular activities related to German language and culture; and openness to refugee students and scholars. In evaluating these phenomena, it is useful to compare Canadian campuses to those in the United States in order to gain perspective.

It should be said at the outset that, for a number of reasons, this chapter cannot treat in depth all of these issues. Time, funding and space constraints, and the ready availability of archives and student publications have led to the primary focus being largely on two universities – Montreal's McGill University and the University of Toronto. These were arguably the premier academic institutions of English Canada at that time, which made them in some respects bellwethers, although regarding the issue at hand, they were not necessarily representative even of English-language Canadian universities. Still, their academic standing, their location in the only two large Jewish communities in Canada, and the fact that McGill was a private university while the University of Toronto relied heavily on provincial funding justify the inclusion of both and suggest inferences about English Canadian campuses in general.

The post-secondary institutions of French Canada are, for the most part, not covered here, partly because the context and issues were somewhat different. There will, however, be some mention of

Abbé Lionel Groulx, the pre-eminent French Canadian academic of the time – at least the most famous and the most influential – and of the Université de Montréal, the premier post-secondary institution in French Canada, where Groulx taught. The views of the historian/priest on the nature of French Canada are instructive and helpful in understanding some of the differences between French Canadian and English Canadian universities. A broader detailed investigation may, of course, offer correctives to this study. One final caveat: privacy laws in Quebec and Ontario have made it impossible to examine many files that might have been useful for this study.

AGAINST A BACKDROP OF PREJUDICE

Much has been written about Canadian attitudes and policy regarding Jews, most especially in the interwar and Second World War years. The path-breaking work of Irving Abella and Harold Troper, *None Is Too Many: Canada and the Jews of Europe, 1933–1948*, details the unwillingness of the Canadian government to allow more than a token number of refugees from Nazi Europe to enter the country, including professors and students, despite awareness that Jews' lives were in jeopardy and despite Canada's vast empty spaces and considerable wealth. That stance was a continuation of a policy essentially set out by the end of the First World War, a policy which classified Jews, along with people of colour, as particularly "non-preferred" immigrants. It was a policy that reflected popular attitudes, reinforced by the financial difficulties experienced by most Canadian individuals and institutions during the Great Depression.

Attitudes towards Jews in the larger Canadian society that influenced the atmosphere on campus are sketched out in a number of works. Among these, Gerald Tulchinsky's *Branching Out: The Transformation of the Canadian Jewish Community* provides a great deal of information about Canadian antisemitism in the interwar years. In *"Race," Rights, and the Law in the Supreme Court of Canada*, James W.St.G. Walker presents a convincing indictment of Canadian law and society for their manifest racism during the entire first half of the twentieth century. Alan Davies's edited volume, *Antisemitism in Canada: History and Interpretation*, is a very useful interpretive work, and Alan Mendelson's recent *Exiles from Nowhere: The Jews and the Canadian Elite* relates historical vignettes that illustrate the

antisemitism of many members of Canada's social, business, political, and intellectual elites. Especially germane to this study is Paul
Axelrod's *Making a Middle Class: Student Life in English Canada
during the Thirties*. As might be expected, attitudes of students, faculty members, and administrators in the universities often mirrored
those of the general public or, at the very least, were influenced
by them.

A 1933 exchange of letters between Sir Arthur Currie and Walter
Molson can serve as an illuminating example of the penetration of
popular notions about Jews into the universities and the social elite
of Canada. Currie, the principal of McGill University (the university
president was called the "principal" at McGill), had been the highly
successful commander of the Canadian Expeditionary Force in the
last years of the First World War, and he retained a heroic image that
was largely untarnished by the revelation that he had used $11,000
of regimental funds to pay his private debts. Molson was a scion
of one of Montreal's "first [Anglo] families" and a member of the
McGill board of governors.

Molson wrote to Currie about the law firm of Myerson and Sigler.
The two obviously Jewish graduates of the McGill Faculty of Law
were representing a Jewish farmer whose horse had been disabled
and chickens killed as a result of the poor condition of a road passing Molson's country estate, the maintenance of which was Molson's
responsibility. Molson thought the lawyers' temerity in demanding
damages of ten dollars would "cause [Currie] to smile." The beer
magnate "recalled to mind our several conversations on McGill's
mission in educating various elements of our population." Currie
responded with a similar story about an accident with his car. The
other driver was represented by a "firm of lawyers (newly gradu-
ated Jews from our Law School)." These "young Jews" suggested
that Currie "contribute some 10% [of the insurance settlement] to
them for the part they had played" in settling the case. He added that
Molson and his friends would be pleased to know "that the Jews
have deserted our Law School." According to Currie, only one of the
thirty-nine students in the entering law class of 1933–34 was Jewish, other Jews having chosen the Université de Montréal because,
Currie claimed, it was less demanding.[1]

More telling and more insidious is an unsigned copy of a letter
undoubtedly from Dean Ira MacKay of the Faculty of Arts and Sciences at McGill to Principal Currie, dated 21 July 1933. In discussing

the possibility of bringing refugee Jewish scholars from Germany to McGill, the writer asserted the "simple obvious truth ... that the Jewish people are of no use to us in this country. Almost all of them," he said, "adopt ... merchandising, money lending, medicine and law, and we have already far too many of our own people engaged in these occupations ... As a race of men," he went on to say, Jews "do not fit in with a high civilization."[2]

In French Canada, prevailing attitudes to Jews tended to be even more negative. This was the case regarding everyone who was not of French descent and Roman Catholic, but Jews were a special problem because of their religion and "race." This author's *Jew or Juif? Jews, French Canadians, and Anglo-Canadians, 1759–1914*, discusses the period before the First World War. In *The Traitor and the Jew: Anti-Semitism and the Delirium of Extremist Right-Wing Nationalism in French Canada from 1929–1939*, Esther Delisle offers a damning portrait of French Canadian attitudes towards Jews in the 1930s. In a number of books and articles, Pierre Anctil suggests a more benign view, although he tends to differ less on the facts than on their interpretation.

In the thirties at the Université de Montréal, Abbé Groulx, a Catholic priest who was the guru of the French Canadian nationalist movement, expressed admiration for DeValera, Mussolini, Salazar, and Dolfuss, and, by inference, Hitler, and longed for the emergence of a similar charismatic strongman for French Canada. (He was also an admirer of the French fascist Charles Maurras and of the high-handed Quebec premier, Maurice Duplessis but he did not see the latter as the hoped-for leader.) In the fifties, he still held Marshal Pétain, the puppet head of Vichy France, in high esteem.[3] Groulx "insisted on the purity and homogeneity of the French and Catholic 'race' that had founded New France."[4] He was the inspiration behind many of the most influential institutions of the resurgent French Canadian nationalism of the period between the turn of the century and 1940, including the Association catholique de la jeunesse canadienne, the journal *L'Action nationale*, which he edited, and the "Achat chez nous!" campaign to boycott Jewish merchants. He tended to see Jews as "Judaeo-Bolshevists," and from his bully pulpit at the Université de Montréal, he regularly denounced "Jewish materialism, communism, and capitalism."[5] From 1933 on, when Germany's Jews hoped to find sanctuary in Canada and other countries, Groulx's rhetoric increasingly harped upon the communist-

Jewish equation, playing into the anxiety regarding communism of numerous French and English Canadians and their hesitations regarding Jews. "Many reputable authors believe that ... [Jews] cultivate [communists] in larger quantities than others," he wrote in *L'Action nationale* under his pseudonym Jacques Brassier, "and this gives us sufficient grounds for wariness."[6]

Students, many of them Groulx's acolytes, took to the streets in protest against the Jews on a number of occasions in the thirties. In 1935 a nasty demonstration of students began following the mass of the Holy Ghost held to mark the opening of the school year at the Université de Montréal. In October 1936 students "staged another anti-Semitic riot" in Montreal. *The Varsity*, the student newspaper of the University of Toronto then and now, found it "strange" that a minority always carping about "unfair treatment" would show injustice to a minority in their own province. The editorial claimed that the excuse offered was that the rioters were "just a 'noisy' and uninfluential 'group,'" but, said *The Varsity*, they come from "the foremost university of French Canada" and will become leaders of "federal and provincial councils." The editorial went on to say that it was French Canadians themselves who were the real exploiters of French Canada – meaning, almost certainly, the Roman Catholic Church.[7] A week later the paper reported another riot of Université de Montréal students, this time aimed at the McGill Union, which had hosted a Spanish Loyalist, who had appeared at the University of Toronto without incident.[8] On other occasions, students "paraded through Montreal's main streets chanting, 'A bas, à bas ... les Communistes. A bas les Juifs.'"[9]

The most memorable anti-Jewish demonstration of the thirties in Montreal occurred in 1934. That summer, twelve French Canadian interns at the Hôpital Notre-Dame, a teaching hospital connected with the Université de Montréal, declared a strike when Samuel Rabinovitch, a French-speaking Jew, joined their ranks. Within three days, the strike had spread to other French Canadian hospitals, and Rabinovitch was forced to withdraw. Interpretations of the event differed at the time and still do. Coming when it did, however, in the thirties, it shocked Jews and reinforced their feelings of victimization by French Canadians in particular.[10]

Lita-Rose Betcherman's *The Swastika and the Maple Leaf: Fascist Movements in the Thirties* surveys the extent of fascist sentiment in Canada in the decade of the Great Depression, as well as sympathy for Germany and Italy. She notes the popularity of fascist ideas among both English and French Canadians, but especially among the latter. The universities were not strangers to such sentiments.

THE RESPONSE FROM ACADEMIA

In 1933 and 1934, the new president of the University of Toronto, H.J. Cody, a canon in the Anglican Church, was "openly enthusiastic about some aspects of Italian fascism."[11] (In 1936 he also spoke out against universal suffrage.)[12] In a 1935 talk to the Montreal branch of the Canadian Engineering Institute, E.W.R. Staecie, who would head the National Research Council from 1952 to 1962 but at the time was an assistant professor of physical chemistry at McGill, claimed that during his recent extended stay in Germany, he had seen "no sort of fights, riots, or general disturbances." He went on to say that Goebbels was preferable as a censor to the "advertising manager of a big store" and that the "discrimination against" Jews in Germany "was justified" because they had been "the large mortgage holders and ... had gone to extremes in evictions." In an article in the *Montreal Gazette*, Staecie argued that concern for German democracy was misplaced, since 80 to 90 percent of Germans thought Hitler was "the best thing" for their country.[13]

Much student opinion tended to be rather more nuanced than Staecie's. In the fall of 1933 David Tough, who had earned an MA at McGill and spent the previous year on a Moyer Traveling Scholarship at the University of Munich, conceded that National Socialism was "not ... entirely an evil for the German nation." But he recognized that "their methods of asserting ... authority in university life" would "eventually prove disastrous for the intellectual life of the German people." Tough suggested that any "Canadian politician who tries to get the government to interfere with ... teaching should be given a free ticket to Germany to see what has happened there."[14] On the other hand, a second-year student at Trinity College, which was affiliated with the University of Toronto, hiding behind anonymity wrote to *The Varsity* ecstatically in 1935 about the high morale, prosperity, and freedom of speech in Nazi Germany. He (or she) acknowledged that "the lot of the Jew is hard." Sounding like Staecie, he went on to say that when "one hears the Germans' side of the case, the sympathy that has been built up by blood-curdling reports in the American and Canadian press wanes."[15]

In some respects, the universities in the 1930s offer an example of Canadian racism writ large. James Parkes, a distinguished scholar of Judaism – who was an Anglican clergyman who lived in England and a militant and outspoken opponent of antisemitism worldwide – told an audience at Hart House at the University of Toronto in 1933 that in Europe, antisemitism was centred in the universities. He seemed to imply that this was also the case in North America.[16] Already in the 1920s some Canadian universities, like those in the United States, had devised ways of limiting the number of Jewish students. In all of them, it was difficult, if not impossible, for even the most qualified Jews to be appointed to the faculty, and it was unthinkable to hire administrators who were Jewish.

In a move characteristic of the subsequent decades, the University of Toronto in 1911 chose the rather undistinguished historian, Gilbert Jackson, over the soon to be world famous Lewis Bernstein Namier. In 1935 the university turned down the refugee scholar Gerhard Herzberg, a future Nobel Prize winner, who was not Jewish although his wife was. Herzberg taught at the University of Saskatchewan and then the University of Chicago, and was appointed Distinguished Research Scientist at the National Research Council of Canada. Later he served a term as chancellor of Carleton University.[17] The universities' unwillingness to hire refugee scholars from Europe had much to do with the attitudes that kept qualified Canadian Jews from being appointed to faculty positions. It is also the case, however, that university income plummeted during the Depression, from a cumulative $22 million in 1930 to $15.4 million in 1935. By 1940, although enrolment figures were up, there had been only a very partial recovery of income to $17.5 million.[18] As a result, even kindly disposed administrators were reluctant to consider adding staff, especially Jewish foreigners. Of all this, more later.

Michiel Horn's *Academic Freedom in Canada* offers keen insights into events on campus during the years in question. Horn's focus on the right of professors to speak out on public issues – or rather, the often assumed lack of such a right in the 1930s and earlier – is related to the issue of Jews and antisemitism. At the least, it provides a background for the relative silence of faculty members, very few of whom had a personal connection to the issues, on questions such as quotas, refugees, and fascism, and their leaving it to students to voice dissent. One result was that public meetings called to pressure governments in Canada or abroad seldom had professors among their leadership, at least not until the end of the decade. Only then was the concept of academic freedom broadening to include activities outside the classroom, something long accepted in Britain and the United States.[19] (Christian clergymen, who were undoubtedly viewed as influential and uncontroversial, were almost always on the podium.)

In a 1933 editorial, *The Varsity* put its finger on the problem, stating that professors were reluctant to speak out on "delicate [or] controversial" subjects for fear of being accused in the press of "instilling atheism, high treason and revolt into the gullible minds of immature students." But the paper insisted that they needed to speak up and to relate the past to the present if they wanted their teaching to be useful. The next day, President Cody replied, claiming that if professors were silent, it was because they chose not to speak out. He declined comment on the question of whether some professors held their tongues because they feared for their jobs, which at a time when salaries were being cut and faculties downsized was a reasonable fear. An otherwise unidentified Professor Morgan averred that professors were too busy to comment on issues of the day. If they spoke out, moreover, they might be thought to be representing their department or the university. Free speech, he said, has limits, and professors, like ministers and judges, ought not to speak out on political issues.[20]

There were, of course, some outspoken professors. Three of the best known, all of them thorns in the flesh of administrators and boards of governors, were Frank Underhill, a prickly and provocative historian at the University of Toronto, Eugene Forsey, who lectured in economics and political science at McGill, and F.R. Scott, a poet and constitutional expert, who taught law at McGill. All three had been converted to socialism as students at Oxford, although not at the same time, and all three joined both the left-leaning League for Social Reconstruction and the Co-operative Commonwealth Federation (CCF) when they returned to Canada. Interestingly, all moved to the political centre during and after the Second World War. Forsey served as chancellor of Trent University from 1973 to 1977 and was named to the Senate, and Scott was dean of the Faculty of Law at McGill from 1961 to 1964. But in the 1930s, they and other faculty members who spoke publicly on issues of politics or social policy or on public events came in for considerable criticism from the press, from politicians, from university governors and administrators, and from the general public, especially if their views appeared at all left-leaning.[21]

Sir Edward Wentworth Beatty, the president of the Canadian Pacific Railway, who was also the chancellor and chair of the board of governors of McGill, is a case in point. Beatty believed that "socialist ideas permeated" the universities of Canada.[22] In a 1937 letter to Principal A.E. Morgan, he unambiguously stated the argument for limiting freedom of speech: "[Socialists and communists] are preaching a Holy War and ... are thus in a vastly different class to the Liberals and Conservatives, imperialists and nationalists, who never pretend that their doctrines have any inspired sanctity ... Thus it is vitally important that a university should submit the work of professed socialists and communists among its professors to a special form of scrutiny." Beatty went on to say that while Professor Scott should not be disciplined for his pronouncements and leftist associations, "we need to realize the fact that he is definitely a socialist propagandist and not a mere dispassionate examiner of political and economic principles."[23] Earlier, Beatty had written to Morgan that Dr Cody in Toronto considered Underhill "a thoroughly dishonest-minded individual and cleverly misleading in most of his contributions to public discussions on economic or political matters."[24]

While Underhill, Forsey, and Scott regularly denounced fascism in the thirties, only Scott showed particular interest in the Jews and antisemitism. Underhill underestimated Germany's strength, opposed Canada's participation in the war, and at that time had little or nothing to say about Jews.[25] His 1933 essay on Goldwyn Smith, one of Canada's best-known public intellectuals and a University of Toronto professor, makes no mention of Smith's well-publicized (by Smith himself) and rather crude antisemitic views.[26] Forsey was a CCF candidate for alderman in 1940 in a Montreal ward very heavily populated with Jews. Although he apparently understood Yiddish, his memoirs are all but silent on Jewish matters, except for some comments on the Jewish concept of time, which he thought amusing, and a riposte to a racial slur shouted by some French Canadian youngsters. Forsey silenced the miscreants by reminding them that the Holy Family and the apostles had all been Jews.[27]

F.R. Scott, on the other hand, was A.M. Klein's friend and fellow Montrealer, fellow CCFer, fellow lawyer, and fellow poet, and Klein was an ardent Zionist steeped in Jewish learning with hyperconsciousness of the impending catastrophe in Europe. Scott's book,

Labour Conditions in the Men's Clothing Industry (1935), written with University of Toronto Professor H.M. Cassidy, focuses on a Canadian industry in which many of the workers were immigrant Jews. (Many of the owners were also Jews, but they were not the interest of the authors.) The book highlights the economic insecurity, low wages, and poor working conditions in the Depression years and calls for government regulation of the industry. In 1936 Scott spoke out publicly against the antisemitism of Abbé Groulx and his followers in the French Canadian nationalist movement who, he charged, wished to establish an independent "anti-semitic state" where "local pogroms" might be the order of the day.[28] In the 1940s Scott lent his name to the Canadian Palestine Committee, which lobbied the public and the government in support of the establishment of a Jewish state.[29]

That Jews were often connected in the mind of the public with socialism and communism[30] would not have deterred Forsey and Underhill, socialists themselves, from speaking out on their behalf, although it might have flashed a yellow light for other, less courageous faculty members or those with other political loyalties. Knowing that they worked in faculties that were all but *judenrein*, however, may have undermined any moral reservations they might have had on the Jewish question.

In the 1930s, most university presidents defended academic freedom in public, but not wholeheartedly. All were anxious about funding; most were sympathetic to the general nervousness about socialism and especially communism; and most were queasy regarding adverse publicity in the press. But all this does not fully explain their stance on issues related to Jews and antisemitism. Two outstanding exceptions were Carleton Stanley, president of Dalhousie University from 1931 to 1945, and Arthur Eustace Morgan, principal of McGill from 1935 to 1937. Both did speak out on these issues – and also on academic freedom – and under both, their universities pursued relatively liberal policies towards Jewish students and refugee scholars.

Stanley was a political radical who had been a classmate of Underhill at the University of Toronto and had also spent time at Oxford.[31] At Dalhousie, he did his best to radicalize students in the cause of freedom. Early in his presidency, he spoke out against fascism, in favour of the Republicans in Spain, and in defence of academic freedom, and he condemned the harsh sentences that had been meted out to communists in Toronto. From 1933, he repeatedly denounced the destruction of academic life and freedom in Germany and insisted that universities everywhere must be bastions of genuine freedom. In 1937 Stanley tried to organize a session at the National Conference of Canadian Universities on the topic "In Light of Recent Events in Europe, Academic Freedom Is Nothing but the Instinct for Self-Preservation." No other speakers could be found for such a panel.[32] In the last of his sessional addresses at Dalhousie in 1944, Stanley issued a lightly veiled comparison of Canada with Nazi Germany: "It became plain in 1933 that education and life were perishing in Germany, not because ignorant murderers had armed power, but because learning had folded its hands ... At that time also, it was plain to any educated man that such an attitude could not be confined to Germany, and that everything worth living for was threatened, at least, in all parts of the world."[33] Soon afterwards, he was fired.

Morgan, as well, paid a price for his defence of academic freedom and his liberalism. In early 1936 the McGill principal addressed a Montreal lodge of B'nai Brith, the Jewish fraternal and social service organization. The lodge had been a regular contributor of scholarships to McGill for some years, and most of its members were acculturated Jews. Morgan had been in office less than a year, and this was the first time he had spoken to a Jewish audience outside the university. It may have been the first time any Canadian university president had addressed such an audience in person, though in 1934 President Cody in Toronto had responded favourably to requests from the *Canadian Jewish Review* for High Holy Day greetings to the Jewish community. In his reply, he noted that the "recent months" had been a "time of strain and suffering in many places for members of your race," but he expected that Jews surprised and shocked by Hitler would find "comfort in the fact that at the University [of Toronto], Jewish students win their share of academic distinctions and take part in the various student activities of the institution."[34]

At the 1936 B'nai Brith meeting, Principal Morgan spoke more sensitively and meaningfully about liberty and freedom. According to the account in the *Canadian Jewish Chronicle*, Morgan emphasized "the ideals of liberty and the part that has been played by the British people in the fight for freedom." The weekly found Morgan's words "a breath of fresh air ... in contradistinction to the noxious propaganda emanating from university life in Europe." There, the editorial continued, "academics have been relegated to a position of inferiority, and the university has become a laboratory for the dissemination of vicious propaganda. The principal of McGill decried that brand of patriotism." Morgan went on to tell his eager audience that the "amount of freedom in any country is determined by the tolerance that is shown for other people's viewpoints, especially minorities." The group found that the "comforting" message offered "hope for the ultimate triumph of tolerance and freedom over the chauvinistic claptrap of nationalist dementia."[35]

In general, Morgan, who had close Jewish friends in England,[36] was fair and apparently unbiased in his dealings with Jews during his short tenure at McGill, of which more below. His views on academic freedom and the role of the university were markedly different from those of his chancellor, Sir Edward Beatty, as noted above. This difference and perhaps, too, his consideration for Jewish concerns led to his forced resignation just two years after he had come to McGill from England.

As is clear from the words of Stanley and Morgan, anti-Jewish attitudes were by no means universal in Canada – at least, not in English Canada – even among the social and intellectual elite. On campus and off, there were many who were untainted by racism and some who directed their racist sentiments towards groups other than the Jews: Blacks and women, for example. A few, like Professor Charles Alexander Brodie Brockwell, who taught Hebrew and Semitic languages at McGill from 1906 to 1937, were outspokenly philosemitic. Brockwell, many of whose students were Jews, was an Anglican priest and an ardent supporter of Zionism. He often spoke to Jewish groups in Hebrew, which few if any in the audience understood.[37]

Others were equivocal. In the fall of 1933, Principal Currie of McGill received a letter from L.W. Bick of Asheville, North Carolina, representing the Silver Shirts of America. Bick claimed to have met Currie ten years earlier and now sought his support for the American Nazi movement. The letter included "proof" of the truth of *The Protocols of the Elders of Zion*, the notorious antisemitic polemic which had been forged by the czarist secret police. In his response, Currie admitted to sharing his interlocutor's distaste for Jews: "One thing I know ... [from] my experience at this University, is the aggressiveness and other peculiarities of the ... Jewish race." Still, he added, "I am not very much in sympathy with Hitlerism."[38] On all sides of the "Jewish question" in Canada, racist thinking and terminology underlay the public and private discourse of the day.

QUOTAS, FACULTY HIRING RESTRICTIONS, AND MORE

The pervasive antisemitism notwithstanding, Jews were making steady progress in Canada in the thirties, acquiring citizenship, becoming educated, finding success in a variety of endeavours. In Toronto during the decade, J.J. Glass, Nathan Phillips, and J.B. Salsberg, the last a Communist, were elected to the city council, and Ida Siegel was elected a school trustee. (In 1943, Salsberg was elected to the provincial legislature.) As students, Jews entered the universities in numbers well out of proportion to their percentage of the Canadian population, and they took an active part in campus life, as the columns of *The Varsity* and *McGill Daily* testify. As noted earlier, appointments to the staff were, however, almost never forthcoming. Still, the exclusion, discrimination, and contempt Jews encountered in Canadian universities, while unquestionably painful, seemed relatively mild compared with the antisemitism of Europe. In Germany from 1933, Jews were being deprived of basic civil rights; Jewish university students were expelled, and Jewish faculty members dismissed. In Poland in the same years, a government boycott of businesses owned by Jews led to the impoverishment of the Jewish community; in Polish universities, there was a *numerus clausus*, and Jewish students were required to sit on segregated "Jew benches." Later in the decade, Jewish professors were dismissed from Italian universities, and Jews were no longer permitted to enrol in graduate studies. To some Canadian Jews, their situation appeared better even than that of their co-religionists in the United States. In 1926 a writer in a Toronto Yiddish-language newspaper suggested that Americans having difficulty gaining admission to university should come to Canada, where they would be received with open arms. This was the same year that Dean Ira MacKay proposed the institution of quotas for Jews at McGill. A clipping from a Seattle Jewish paper with an English translation of the Toronto journalist's advice was sent to the McGill principal by the advertising manager of the Toronto paper.[39] One can only speculate about Currie's reaction.

One of the early developments that divide the 1930s from earlier years with regard to the relationship of Jews to Canadian universities is the imposition in many universities of a *numerus clausus*, a quota designed to limit the number of Jewish students. Concern about "the disproportionate and top heavy registration of Jews in the colleges, and more particularly in the schools of medicine, law and dentistry," was widespread.[40] In fact, the movement towards quotas began even earlier, as it did in American universities.[41] As noted above, in 1926 the dean of Arts and Sciences at McGill, Ira MacKay, wrote to Principal Currie about the necessity, as he saw it, of reducing the Jewish population of the university. Figures differ, but according to the most authoritative account, Jews constituted just under a quarter of the students in the Faculty of Arts and Sciences in the 1924–25 session, 15 percent of the Faculty of Medicine, and 40 percent of the Faculty of Law.[42] The high figures were not surprising considering that Montreal's Jewish community was the largest in Canada by far.

MacKay argued that in the economic conditions of the time, "the Jew is the least desirable immigrant." Jews tend to leave Canada for greener pastures, presumably to the United States, he claimed; they become money lenders, merchants, doctors, and lawyers, of which Canada did "not need any more"; and they are "a danger to the University." As the American experience demonstrates, MacKay averred, when the Jews move in, the gentiles move out, not because of anti-semitism, but for "purely personal reasons." In other words, Jews were unlikable. According to the charter of the university, the dean insisted, Christian money should not be spent on Jews, who give "almost nothing to the maintenance" of McGill. On the other hand, the university should not seek contributions from Jews, because then they will demand the admission of more Jewish students. The dean suggested that the maximum number of Jewish students be set at 20 percent, this figure to be achieved by requiring that Jewish students be born in Canada or on British soil and earn a grade of at least 70 percent on the matriculation examination, which they would have to write in English or French. For these regulations, MacKay wanted formal approval from the board of governors to provide protection from having "a mandamus served on me personally by some local court at the instance of some Jewish lawyer."[43]

By the 1932–33 school year, Jews made up only 15 percent of McGill's student body in the Faculty of Arts and Sciences, just over 11 percent in the Faculty of Medicine, and just under 20 percent in the Faculty of Law.[44] Six years later, only 12 percent of the students in Arts and Sciences were Jewish, under 13 percent in Medicine, and 15 percent in Law.[45] The reduction had been accomplished by requiring Jewish applicants to score 750 on their Senior Matriculation Examination, while gentiles were required to score only 600. The then dean of arts and sciences, C.W. Hendel, noted that "we do not apply the Jewish rule to students related to ... McGill graduates – a very doubtful principle – but we considered that these were good representatives of the Jewish Community."[46]

In the 1930s, McGill administrators had no problem in denying the existence of quotas to outsiders, frequently telling rather less than the truth. In 1937 a request from the editor of the Boston *Jewish Advocate* for a statement on "What a College or University May Expect of the Jewish Student and Alumnus," as part of a series, made its way to Sir Edward Beatty, who forwarded it to Dr W.H. Brittain, the acting principal. As he often did, Beatty told Brittain what to say, and Brittain, perhaps with Morgan's fate in mind, promptly complied. He wrote that McGill "expects from a Jewish undergraduate or alumnus exactly the same as from any other student or alumnus."[47]

The next year Dr Lewis W. Douglas, the new principal, received a complaint from a Jewish applicant in Detroit who claimed that no American Jews were ever admitted to McGill's medical faculty. Douglas was an American, who had worked in big business as a vice-president of American Cyanamid and in the U.S. government as director of the Office of the Budget in the early days of Roosevelt's presidency. New to McGill, Douglas inquired about its admissions practices before answering the letter. He was told by the associate dean of medicine, J.C. Simpson, that there were in fact three, possibly four, American Jewish medical students currently enrolled. Only eight spaces per year were reserved for Jews, however, and qualified Canadians had priority. Simpson went on to say that the quota had been set "after consulting with Jewish students and graduates and several prominent Jewish citizens of Montreal," who thought the quota "generous," keeping in mind "the difficulty that Jews have in securing hospital internships." Simpson said the decision was "purely administrative" and had never been brought to the Faculty or the Senate. He added that "the only discrimination that ... worried" him was "the higher fee for American students." Douglas's response to the disgruntled Detroiter talked about the limited number of spaces available, the large number of applicants, the priority given to Canadians, and the presence of a few American

Jews. Americans, he said, "are chosen upon their high qualifications to enter upon the course and on that basis alone"[48] – a half-truth, at best.

At the University of Toronto in the 1920s, "the central administration kept a running tally of the number of Jews at the University. In a "private letter," President Cody said the reason was that "'a small group of the Hebrew race' were entering university without funds rather than staying out, as he put it, 'until [they] ... can earn money sufficient to pay [their] ... way ... This has always been the way ... people of our stock have acted in the past,' he added."[49] In the thirties, Jewish women in physiotherapy at the University of Toronto were not allowed to do regular clinical training at Toronto General Hospital, a teaching hospital of the university, and "Jewish doctors were mistrusted and frequently excluded from University professional circles."[50] At the beginning of the thirties, only 7.2 percent of Toronto students were Jews, a much smaller percentage than at Dalhousie (11.3), Manitoba (11.4), or, of course, McGill, despite Toronto's large Jewish population.[51]

Perhaps some of the explanation for the low numbers can be found in a draft paper that Claris Silcox of the Institute of Social and Religious Research in New York sent to Cody in January 1934 for vetting. It is an argument for quotas in Canada's public universities, with which he believed Cody would agree and which he hoped would not "create any undesirable embarrassment for the University." The paper reads like a list of standard antisemitic canards and is worth citing at length, because of Silcox's later involvement with Jewish refugees from Nazi Germany and his ongoing connection with Jewish-Christian dialogue. In fact, he is generally regarded as a champion of both causes and "a friend of the Jews."

The paper is entitled "Canadian Universities and the Jews," though a more apt title would have been "101 Excuses for Intolerance toward Jews and the Institution of Quotas." In the paper, Silcox observed that quotas in American universities had led many Jewish students to look to Canada. In the past, some would have gone to Germany, but now that road was blocked. He felt that the "high percentage of [Jews in] the entering class in medicine" at the University of Toronto posed a danger "to the province, to the medical profession, to the Jewish students, ... [and] to the university." He asked "upon whom, in the light of present attitudes," would Jewish doctors practice? There followed complaint after complaint, ending with the standard Christian supercessionist view of Judaism: "The Jew is essentially an urbanite" who "doesn't take" to engineering and agriculture. In Quebec, Protestants drop out of school, "while the Jews go marching on." "The very itinerary of the 'wandering Jew' has given him a world outlook and mental acumen which few other races approximate." Most fraternities don't accept Jews, so Jews establish their own fraternities where they snub other Jews. Jews in university are not active in athletics. Some American colleges "have had to reorganize their dramatic clubs to prevent them from being entirely dominated by Jews." When the University of Chicago debates Northwestern, each side is represented by three Jews. Jewish journalists have "a certain lack of sensitivity." Jews "capture more than their share of scholarships." During the First World War before conscription, university "professors lectured mostly to women and Jews." "Much in Judaism is dry and arid and unbalanced, unless it is reinforced by the very Hellenism which Judaism rejected and which Christianity accepted."

Cody's response is not in the file, but he must have approved, since a version of the essay was published in the *Canadian Student* in January 1934. Amazingly, what is in the file is a letter from Silcox to Cody dated the next month. It is a proposal for a seminar on Jewish-Gentile relations in Canada, which Silcox planned to chair with Rabbi Maurice Eisendrath of Toronto's Holy Blossom Temple, which they wished to hold at the University of Toronto. Almost two years later, Silcox was still complaining about the disproportionate share of scholarships won by Jewish students.[52]

At other universities in English Canada, quotas were also instituted in the late 1920s and early 1930s. When Ernest Sirluck, the future president of the University of Manitoba, arrived at that university as a young student in 1935, he found antisemitism institutionalized in "an increasingly strict hidden quota for Jewish students, interns, and residents."[53] The percentage of Jews in Manitoba's Faculty of Medicine declined over time from twenty-eight to only nine in 1944, as "a result of systematic discrimination," which affected other ethnic minorities and women, as well. Only Anglo-Saxons, French Canadians, and Icelanders were on the "preferred list" there. In 1944 the discriminatory admissions policies at the University of Manitoba were given wide publicity by the Avukah Society, a Jewish student discussion and social club. The publicity eventually led to legislation by the Province of Manitoba barring such practices.[54]

At the Université de Montréal, the percentage of Jewish students never rose above five in the 1930s, and quotas were not deemed necessary. For a variety of reasons, Jews were reluctant to enrol in francophone universities. In part, as Pierre Anctil notes, the religious nature of the universities and the doubts of many churchmen about the appropriateness of admitting non-Catholics made Jews (and other non-Catholics) uncomfortable. Also, Anctil claims that many Jews did not know French well, although in fact more Jews spoke both French and English than did members of other minority ethnic groups in Quebec. English, however, was most certainly the more preferred of Canada's official languages by Quebec Jews.[55] Most importantly, the ultranationalist atmosphere, especially at the Université de Montréal among student and faculty followers of Abbé Groulx, made the atmosphere appear threatening. Already in 1915, Groulx had warned French Canadian professors and students that in their "daily contact with men of other faiths or of no faith at all, who do not recognize the supremacy of our biblical, Christian morality," they would be "deeply troubled by the daily compromising or indeed negation of truth."[56] As a result, the number of Jewish students at the Université de Montréal grew modestly, even as quotas at McGill reduced the number of Jewish students there rather dramatically. In the 1920–21 academic year, sixteen Jewish students were enrolled at the Université de Montréal (1.2 percent of the student body); by the 1935–36 academic year, the number had grown to sixty-nine (4.4 percent of the student body). Most of the Jewish students were enrolled in law, medicine, and pharmacy.[57]

Those Jews who were admitted to universities in these years had additional hurdles to jump. Most fraternities and sororities did not admit Jews, who founded their own Greek-letter societies, beginning with a chapter of Zeta Beta Tau, the American fraternity, at McGill in 1913. Interest clubs and campus newspapers were more open, and both *The Varsity* and the *McGill Daily* almost always had Jews on their editorial and reporting staff in the 1930s. In addition, Avukah and the Menorah Society, which catered to Jewish intellectuals, were established at a number of Canadian universities, and McGill had its Maccabean Circle. In 1923 the Hillel Foundation for the fostering of Jewish social, religious, and intellectual life on campus was founded at the University of Illinois, and by 1939 it boasted twelve chapters at universities in the United States, where it came under the sponsorship of B'nai Brith. In 1939, Hillel made application to

McGill to establish a chapter there. Considerable discussion ensued at the administrative and student levels. Principal Douglas, either misinformed or disingenuous, claimed that McGill had "never given official permission to the establishment of any sectarian organization among the students." This, despite the existence at that time of the Maccabean Circle for Jews, the Newman Club for Catholics, and the Student Christian Movement for Protestants. In the end, the Students' Executive Council turned down the request at the behest of the Maccabean Circle, probably eager to protect its turf.[58]

One additional aspect of restrictions on Jews and Jewish life at Canadian campuses requires some discussion: the hiring of Jewish faculty members and administrators. As mentioned earlier, it appears that no Jews were employed as administrators at Canadian universities in these years, and Jewish faculty members were few and far between. In the mid-nineteenth century, Rabbi Abraham DeSola of Montreal had served as professor of Hebrew and Oriental literature at McGill, and in 1858 the university had conferred upon him the first honorary doctorate awarded to a Jew in the English-speaking world. After DeSola's death in 1882, however, professing Jews were hardly ever found on Canadian campuses. In 1933, McGill claimed to have ten "Hebrews" on its "permanent staff" and eleven more on its "temporary staff." Of the twenty-one, ten were in the Faculty of Arts and Sciences, ten in the Faculty of Medicine, and one in the Faculty of Dentistry. Unfortunately, the list does not define "staff" or provide names and positions, but it is reasonably safe to assume that many of these were low-level positions, except perhaps for those in medicine.[59]

If quotas were one of the principal hallmarks of Jewish life on campus in the 1930s, another was university relationships with Germany and German culture. The issues include refugee students and professors, as noted earlier, exchange programs with German universities, participation in German university festivals and conferences, and the study of German culture and language. Although the picture is mixed, it has more positive aspects than the question of quotas.

One of the first challenges to Canadian complacency was the Nazi boycott of Jewish businesses and professionals on 1 April 1933, some two months after Hitler had come to power. The boycott shocked many into realizing how great a menace Nazism was to cherished principles of civilized society. This was not "polite" or disguised "harmless" prejudice directed at a marginal group, but a brutal threat, potentially at least, to all of Western society. In many locations in North America and Europe, including Montreal and Toronto, mass protest meetings were organized in the days following the boycott. In Montreal, Rabbi Herman Abramowitz of the patrician Shaar Hashomayim synagogue personally asked Principal Currie to attend the planned meeting there.

Currie told the rabbi that he felt "strongly indignant at such practices as reported" in the press, "namely the interference by German authorities with the preparation of food for the use of Jews ... Furthermore," he asserted, "I cannot and do not sympathize with the exclusion of all Jews from positions in the scientific and educational world." (That was a rather hollow statement, given the difficulty Jews had in gaining a position in the Canadian scientific and educational world. The irony would seem all the greater in the coming months and years.) In any case, Currie refused to attend the protest. He claimed that "leaders of Jewish thought in Germany have within the last few days requested that the Jews in other points of the world should not interfere in this matter." (The American Jewish Committee had warned weeks before of a backlash to overreaction to the Nazis.) Currie distrusted reports from France and Belgium, "enemies of Germany," he explained, and his presence at the meeting "would be open to grave misinterpretation" because in Germany he was known as "the former leader of the Canadian forces in the late War." Germany was in "a very disturbed and dangerous condition at present," he stated, and "it would be extremely unwise for anyone in my position to take public issue ... with the existing ... Government."

What Currie did not tell Rabbi Abramowitz was that advisers from outside the university feared that his presence at the rally might "seriously embarrass the British government."[60] On the other hand, the Anglican bishop of Montreal, the city's mayor Fernand Rinfret, Honoré Mercier, the provincial minister of land and forests and son of a former Quebec premier, and Senator Raoul Dandurand, a close friend and adviser of Prime Minister Mackenzie King, all attended the protest, apparently without fear of embarrassing the British. At the Toronto rally in Massey Hall, Ontario Premier George S. Henry spoke.[61]

It is not unreasonable to suspect that rather than discretion or pressure, a lack of sympathy was what kept Currie away from the protest. A few months later, a McGill student, William Hasler, invited Currie to attend a meeting of the new McGill chapter of the International Student Service and to meet privately with James Parkes, the distinguished scholar and minister who led the organization's efforts to assist students expelled from German universities. Again Currie refused. He professed "sympathy for the ... students who have been driven out of Germany by the actions of Mr. Hitler." But he said somewhat unfeelingly, "I frankly confess that I have more sympathy for the students ... driven out of McGill because they lack financial resources to see them through ... I believe many students in Germany have suffered persecution. I would throw no cold water on efforts to help them ... but were I able to contribute more than I do now, I should give my support here."[62]

The major issue for Canadian universities arising from the Nazi takeover in Germany was that of refugee students and especially scholars. Protests were one-time, symbolic events and required little commitment. Bringing refugees to Canada, however, especially Jewish refugees, required a major commitment of energy, time, and money and a willingness to stand up to the discreet but very real antisemitism of Canadian campuses and the implacable antisemitism of the immigration authorities, unhindered by their political masters. The issue arose already in early 1933.

Soon after Hitler became chancellor, German universities began dismissing faculty members of Jewish origin or those holding views of which the Nazis disapproved. Some fled the country in fear, and organizations sprang up, chiefly in Britain and the United States, seeking to find positions for those displaced. One of these was the Institute for International Education in New York City, which in March 1933 invited Principal Currie to serve on its committee. Currie replied to the assistant director of the institute, Edward R. Murrow – who would become one of the most highly regarded radio journalists in North America during the Second World War – with his accustomed reluctance and dose of "cold water." He could not, he said, "imagine the plan will receive cordial or unanimous support, [although] there can be no doubt that there are men among those displaced who, as scholars and research workers, have a contribution to make." He did not think that "there should be an effort to bring these men to this continent in any wholesale numbers." But if they were "carefully selected" and there was "no doubt of the men's scholarship and intellectual integrity," the plan would be "worthy of a trial."

Currie agreed to serve on the institute's committee, despite Dean MacKay's advice to "reject appeals for the admission to the faculty of 'displaced German scholars.'" MacKay told Currie, "There are

very few questions upon which I am defiant, but this is one of them."
Currie died later that year before he could take any active role in the
work of the institute.[63]

Subsequent appeals to aid the desperate and often very highly
regarded displaced scholars (Albert Einstein was one of them) came
regularly and frequently to Canadian universities from individual
academics and organizations, most notably the Academic Assistance
Council, founded in Britain in 1933 (which later became the Society
for the Protection of Science and Learning), the Emergency Committee in Aid of Displaced German Scholars, and the Carnegie Foundation. The first functioned largely as a clearing house. The Carnegie
Foundation offered a stipend for the Europeans for the first two
years of their employment at an American or Canadian university.
The stipend was available, however, only if the host institution indicated that there was a possibility of the scholar's receiving a regular
appointment afterwards. A guaranty was not required.

In the United States, there was more openness to refugee scholars
than in Canada, although there too it was a hard sell. The shortage
of funds was a contributing factor in both countries. In both, there
was a reluctance to hire even native-born Jews, though less in the
United States than in Canada. In the United States, some members of
the Jewish elite, most notably Albert Lasker in Chicago, feared that
the presence of Jewish refugees on campus would serve to increase
antisemitism, and not only on campus.[64] Still, even accounting for
the disparity in the size of the two countries and the small number of universities in Canada, the response to the refugee scholars
in the United States was much more open. The University in Exile
at New York City's New School for Social Research was staffed
entirely by refugee scholars, almost as many as the number in all
Canadian universities combined (sixteen to twenty, according to
Martin Friedland).[65] Dalhousie, under President Stanley, had opened
its doors already in 1934 to Lothar Richter and Martin Silverberg.
Richter became the university's first professor of German and then
the director of its new Institute of International Affairs.[66] Other universities, however, were reluctant to follow suit.

Appeals to self-interest were no more effective than pleas for compassion. On 4 July 1938, Terence W.L. MacDermot, the principal of
Upper Canada College in Toronto, a private school for the upper
crust of Ontario society, and a former assistant professor of history at McGill, went to Montreal to see Principal Douglas, who

was away from the office, probably celebrating American Independence Day. According to an unsigned memo to Douglas, most likely from Registrar T.H. Matthews, MacDermot argued for hiring refugee scholars to invigorate the "woefully weak" McGill Arts Faculty which, in MacDermot's experience, had only "one man ... actually working and interested in his work." The University of Toronto, he claimed, had "nine German-Austrian Jews, all brilliant men, including Einstein's former second in command," who were "just about reviving the place." McGill, on the other hand, was "steadily losing ground." Upper Canada College "had imported one of these German Jews" in music, and "the effect on the whole school was simply remarkable." There is no record of any response.[67] (Altogether, the University of Toronto took on ten refugee scholars, of whom half were Jews.)[68]

In 1939 the presidents of twelve American universities, among them Harvard, Yale, Columbia, and Princeton, circulated a "Declaration of Principles" which Nicholas Murray Butler, the president of Columbia and a rather recent convert to the cause of refugee Jewish professors, asked Principal Douglas of McGill to endorse.[69] The manifesto declared the "responsibility of all universities throughout the world to protect the solidarity of the international community of scholars and to further that ancient university tradition which recognizes no racial or national barriers to free inquiry or the promotion of sound learning." Regarding faculty appointments, the manifesto declared that "merit alone should be considered." The intent was to encourage the hiring of refugee scholars through emergency "asylum fellowships of $1,500 to $2,500 annually," a salary commensurate with that of regular faculty. Funds were to come from new sources. At first, Douglas was inclined to sign on and forwarded the "Declaration" to Monsigneur Olivier Maurault, rector of the Université de Montréal. Maurault declared his appreciation of "the generous gesture" of the Americans but said Montréal could not participate in the program "for lack of funds." In the end, Douglas also demurred, and in view of the "difficulties in the way of the program for action" raised by Canadian universities, the Americans "thought it best not to include" them.[70]

Refugee students were no more welcome in Canadian universities than their professors. In early 1939, Registrar Matthews, hoping "to see the Canadian universities making a really Good Samaritan gesture across the Atlantic," proposed to Principal Douglas a general policy for McGill, which the deans might formulate and which all Canadian universities, through the Canadian Universities Conference, might adopt. He included in his memo information about a number of students then applying to McGill, including one "threatened with arrest" in Germany and another whose father, "a very well known Berlin publisher, Mr. Springer, is now in a concentration camp." Douglas thought the whole subject a "controversial, even dangerous" one, "on which much embarrassment might develop from public discussion." Internally, he thought each case should be handled individually and quietly in discussion with the relevant dean. On "second and more mature thought," Matthews, who tended to be open and sympathetic to Jewish concerns, ate crow, claiming that he had written "after midnight, when my brain was even less stable than usual."[71] Douglas need not have been overly concerned. Some months before, students at Mount Allison University had urged "a relaxation in immigration laws to permit controlled entry ... of refugees from Germany," and they had voted to raise funds to support several refugee students, but their petition to the government went unheeded.[72]

If practical steps to alleviate the suffering of German Jews encountered almost insurmountable difficulties in Canada, programmatic and symbolic actions were having more success as the decade progressed. Of particular significance was limiting the scope of student and faculty exchanges between Canada and Germany. In this area, interestingly enough, Canadians did a rather better job than Americans.

On American campuses in the 1930s, exchange students from Germany and Italy served as conduits for the dissemination of Nazi and fascist propaganda, as did American students who spent time in Germany on the exchange programs that flourished throughout that decade. The Europeans were usually chosen because they were sympathetic to their country's regime, which paid for their stay in North America. The Americans, some of them innocents abroad, were often carefully sheltered from the ugly aspects of life in Germany and Italy and more often were "educated" in the virtues of fascism and Nazism. Departments of German and Italian also frequently promoted the prevailing ideology of their home countries in their teaching and even more so in extracurricular activities. This happened in Canada as well, but to a lesser degree. At Manitoba, Ernest Sirluck found himself confronting one of his German teachers, Herr Bürzle, whom he suspected of Nazi tendencies because of the way the man bullied one of the female Jewish students who spoke German with a Yiddish inflection. With the outbreak of war, the teacher, a German national and a suspected Nazi, was interned; after the war he continued his teaching career in North America. Such occurrences seem to have been uncommon in Canada, though much less so in the United States.[73]

An examination of the University of Toronto student newspaper, *The Varsity*, is instructive. In September 1933, a student recently returned from Germany told the paper she had met "nothing but politeness and consideration" during her stay.[74] In October of that year, the paper ran a series of articles by Italian students entitled "Roman Triumph Revived Again under Fascists."[75] In October 1935, Gerhard Leuschow, "a German storm trooper" and student from Kiel University doing graduate work in economics at the University of Toronto, assured readers that "Germans love England" and that "Germany will not go to war as an aggressor."[76] Such pieces were more than balanced, however, by others, such as "Politics Spoiling Academia in Germany," in which a Davis Exchange student at the Goethe University in Frankurt-am-Main reported that Jewish students in Germany had fewer privileges than gentile students and Jewish professors had been fired.[77] A 1935 editorial titled "Nazi Regime Facing Revolt?" summarized the findings of students, "educated men" who had visited Europe during the summer, whom the writer identified – erroneously, as it turned out – as the most "capable" observers. There was also an earlier piece, "Germany Believes Hitler Saviour," which conceded that Germany's ideals might be "admirable," though its methods were "loathsome and unfair."[78] In October 1935, *The Varsity* featured an account by Rabbi Maurice Eisendrath about a recent trip to Berlin, Rome, and Jerusalem. The rabbi told of being "heartsick with ... the martial atmosphere of Rome and the racial madness of Berlin." By contrast, in Jerusalem, "each can live for all and all for each," he asserted, and "justice, brotherhood, righteousness and peace reign supreme."[79] (Since Eisendrath was regarded in the Jewish community as singularly opposed to Zionism, this was an extraordinary statement.)

Aware of the pitfalls in exchanges with Germany, Principal Morgan refused German overtures regarding a student exchange with McGill. An "exchange between students of this University and a German university ... in present circumstances ... would be contrary to our policy," he told the Students' Executive Council in 1937.[80] The previous year, the Vereinigung Carl Schurz had offered a free "ten days' tour" in Germany to American students to promote "better understanding between our two countries." The organization tried to interest McGill in such a program but received no encouragement.[81] All through the thirties, most American universities, including the most prestigious, continued to facilitate the participation of their students in German exchange programs.[82] At the University of Toronto in early 1936, the university librarian cancelled subscriptions to most German journals. The "periodicals," he said, "are 'padded' with worthless material, and their value has decreased since the Nazis have forced so many of the leading scientists out of the country." The high prices were little more than a "racket" engaged in by rapacious German publishers, he added.[83]

One of the least expected milestones of the Canadian-German academic relationship in the 1930s, although one that was highly symbolic, was the flap over the 550th anniversary celebrations of the University of Heidelberg in 1936. When universities celebrated period anniversaries, the usual custom then, and even now, was to hold a special convocation to which representatives of other universities were invited. Usually, the celebrations consisted of pomp and perhaps some academic talks and cultural events. They were in no way political. But in Nazi Germany, every aspect of life had been politicized. By the mid-thirties, the universities had rid themselves of their Jewish students and professors as well as political opponents of the regime and had drastically reduced the number of women students. In most cases, the dismissed professors had been replaced by politically reliable people of questionable academic standing. Non-academic activities, such as ideological and para-military training and "volunteer" agricultural work had replaced more standard degree requirements. German universities became bastions of intolerance, where ideology trumped scholarship, and freedom of speech was a thing of the past.

In Heidelberg there had been a book burning in 1933, like that in Berlin, and the rector, Wilhelm Groh, always appeared on campus in a Nazi uniform.[84] The anniversary celebrations were graced by parades of students and professors in uniform and other demonstrations of fealty to the Nazi Party, and by the presence of Minister of Propaganda Joseph Goebbels. Anticipating that this would happen, many foreign universities hesitated about attending the festivities although Heidelberg was one of the oldest universities in the world and had been one of the most prestigious.

Not everyone outside Germany was fully aware of developments there or understood their significance, and of those who were well informed, not everyone disapproved. In the United States, Ivy League administrators and professors, backed by student newspapers such as the Harvard *Crimson* (although not the Columbia *Spectator*) eagerly accepted the invitation, rationalizing their action with talk of loyalty to the worldwide community of learning. In some cases, there was heavy pressure from Jewish students and organizations and from others against attending; at Columbia, there were violent demonstrations.[85] Almost all British universities declined to participate. Aware of the different reactions to the event in Britain and the United States, Canadians found themselves uncertain about what to do. At several institutions a vigorous debate took place.

At the University of Toronto, President Cody's first inclination was to accept the invitation. But he began to waver, perhaps because of the publicity *The Varsity* gave to the British refusal, or perhaps because of the rumour that the Germans had cancelled all invitations to universities in the British Empire as a result of the stand of universities in the mother country. In early March, Cody told *The Varsity* that "should the question of a matter of policy arise in connection with the invitation from the Nazi institution, the matter will be submitted to the Board of Governors." That he used the word "Nazi" and not "German" indicates that he understood the problem with attendance. In any case, he promised that only someone already in Europe would represent the university. No money would be spent on sending a representative. Cody admitted that the "officials here had not considered the problem in the light of policy" but had seen it simply as "a formal invitation from another educational institution, which invitations are usually accepted." He did not think the invitation should be refused because of the Nazis' "oppression of minorities and their oppressive educational policy." After all, he asserted, "Heidelberg's great work in the past is enough to honour her."[86] On 12 March, Cody wrote to Heidelberg thanking them for the invitation, commending them for "the great service which ... [Heidelberg] has rendered in the past to the cause of learning and freedom in the academic world," and wishing them "future prosperity," but declining the invitation. "It is not possible for this University to send a delegate," he wrote, in words laden with ambiguity.[87]

Not surprisingly, Dalhousie President Carleton Stanley's refusal was stronger and more explicit than Cody's, and he had consulted "the Senate of Professors" before answering. Stanley acknowledged "the great and glorious history of Heidelberg," which "in ordinary circumstances" would have made him "pleased to participate in your celebrations." He continued in language that was both complimentary and critical:

> Canadian universities are most desirous of promoting friendly relations with the academic life of other countries – relations in which the last war made so sad a break. Up till 1933 many Dalhousie professors visited Germany to their own great profit. In the most favourable times, it is a struggle for universities to maintain academic freedom – *Lehrfreiheit* – to use the excellent German word. And we are aware that the struggle has [gap in the text] however, that it is impossible for us to participate in any university celebrations in Germany under the present regime.[88]

For McGill's Principal Morgan the decision came easily, but afterwards he seemed unsure that it had been the right decision. He regularly refused invitations to German events, such as a reception in Toronto given by the German State Railways, and he opposed student exchanges, as noted above. And in this case, as well, he said, "No!" Not only did he not attend the Heidelberg ceremony, but he refused even to attend a conference hosted by an old friend from Britain to be held in Heidelberg before the anniversary celebration. "I regret," wrote Morgan to Professor R.C. McLean at University College in Cardiff, "that I feel unable to accept any invitation at the moment to attend a meeting to be held in a German university." On 11 April 1936, Morgan spoke at Princeton and discussed the issue with President Harold Dodds. (Princeton had not been invited to Heidelberg because it had given high-profile sanctuary to Albert Einstein.) When he returned to Montreal, Morgan sent Dodds copies of letters on the question that had appeared in the London *Times* and again sought Dodds's opinion regarding his decision. Dodds agreed with those who refused to go to Heidelberg.[89] Only two Canadians attended the Heidelberg ceremony. One was Francis Owen, a professor of German from the University of Alberta. "Having studied at German universities," he "strongly disapprove[d] of the action of some universities in mixing politics with matters of this kind."

He assured the Heïdelberg rector that all of his "colleagues who have studied in Germany feel the same." It was the only unequivocal endorsement to come from a Canadian university.[90]

A year later Göttingen University celebrated an anniversary. This time even Harvard and Yale refused the invitation, although two British universities did send delegates. At McGill, "the Senate decided to decline, practically without discussion and ... with unanimity."[91]

A NEW DIRECTION?

By the end of 1938, many Canadians were feeling the urgency of the situation in Germany and guilt about what had not been done in their own country to help. A new organization for refugee advocacy emerged in which professors took an active part, although its concern was not primarily professors and students or freedom of inquiry. A month after Kristallnacht, the November 1938 pogroms in Germany and Austria, the Canadian League of Nations Society convened a conference of national organizations, all but one of them non-Jewish, to discuss the refugee question. (Jews deliberately kept a low profile in order not to to be seen as tainting the organization.) The group morphed into the Canadian National Committee on Refugees and Victims of Political Persecution (CNCR) under the leadership of Senator Cairine Wilson.[92] Patrons of the committee included Sir Robert Falconer, the president of the University of Toronto before Cody, and Sir Frederick Banting, the co-discoverer of insulin and perhaps Canada's most famous scientist of the day. Banting had once said, "If I'd known so many Jews had diabetes, I don't think I'd ever have gone into it." By the mid-thirties as events in Germany unfolded, however, he had apparently mellowed, and he recruited two refugee Jewish scientists for his laboratory. For one, Hermann Fischer, an organic chemist who was the son of a Nobel Prize recipient, President Cody raised private funds for ten years.[93]

The CNCR campaign committee included Mrs George M. Wrong, wife of the distinguished Toronto emeritus professor of history. Academics and their spouses were now joining other community leaders in activities designed to ameliorate the lot of Jews in Germany, a sign that such public activities were now more acceptable than in the past and perhaps also an indication of the rising stature of academics. But it was very late in the day. In March 1939, Claris Silcox, then a leader of the efforts to bring refugees – especially refugee scholars

– to Canada, had apparently changed his mind and renounced the very negative notions about Jews he had been espousing just five years earlier as an advocate of quotas to restrict the number of Jews at Canadian universities. In an address at the University of Toronto under the auspices of the CNCR, entitled "A Post Mortem on Refugees," Silcox warned the audience that after the dismemberment of Czechoslovakia, refusing to open Canada's doors would result in many suicides.[94]

Students also were mobilizing. A group of Canadians studying in England from universities across the country (British Columbia, Manitoba, Bishop's, Ottawa, McMaster, and Toronto) wrote to *The Varsity* reminding fellow students that countries with an "absorptive capacity infinitely smaller than that of Canada" had done far more to alleviate the "indescribable suffering of the hapless thousands" in Europe. The call to action was signed by Ellsworth Flavelle and others, and was also printed as a broadside dated 3 March 1939.

In June 1939, another public protest over the response of Canada to the fate of Europe's Jews was mounted, this time in the form of an outcry over the MS *St Louis* crisis. Refused entry into Cuba, its original destination, the *St Louis* sailed north along the eastern seaboard of North America while American Jews and non-Jews negotiated in vain with their government to relax immigration regulations and allow the hapless passengers at least temporary asylum. As the ship sailed slowly up the coast, Canadians swung into action; church people and academics were among the leaders of a crusade to persuade the government to open Canada's doors to the refugees. Influential Canadians, including Principal Douglas, were invited to a CNCR meeting "to develop a public opinion which will make possible a more generous interpretation of our immigration laws." Douglas refused the invitation. Perhaps as an American, he felt he could not become involved in Canadian politics; perhaps he was already preparing to return to the United States and disengaging from Canadian issues; or perhaps he just did not care.[95] A petition to Prime Minister Mackenzie King spearheaded by the CNCR and signed by Sir Robert Falconer, Principal Malcolm Wallace of the University of Toronto's University College, Professor George Wrong, and many others urged that the country's doors be opened a crack and the refugees not be returned to Europe.[96] But the doors remained shut. The *St Louis* returned to Europe. More than 250 of its passengers would perish in the Holocaust.[97]

This last public protest of the 1930s on an issue of concern primarily to Jews, although now clearly a matter of life and death, proved as ineffectual as the first in 1933. One cannot say, however, that nothing had happened in the intervening years. In 1933, academics had been reluctant to lend their name to a cause involving Jews, and in any case, the stature of academics among the public was not sufficiently important to make much difference. Furthermore, many inside the academy and out felt that academics had no right to be involved with public affairs. By the end of the decade, some Canadian academics beyond the usual outspoken few were awakening to action. Although their voices did not yet matter much, their advocacy for a "Jewish cause" signalled the coming change of atmosphere on campus and in the country as a whole, although it was still many years off. Quotas were still in place for Jewish students, and the numbers of Jewish faculty members were still negligible, although a few fairly high-profile refugees had been added to their ranks. For the Jewish people of Europe, the worst was yet to come. For Canadian Jews, however, better times on and off campus lay not far in the future, partly because of the shame later felt by many Canadians over their country's behaviour during the 1930s, not the least that of its university administrators and faculty.

NOTES

The author wishes to thank the staff of the McGill University Archives, the University of Toronto Archives, the Canadian Jewish Congress National Archives in Montreal, the Jewish Public Library in Montreal, and the Ontario Jewish Archives, all of whom were most helpful in directing me to appropriate files and other material. Thanks as well to my former student Alexander Regel, who unearthed some very interesting material in the archive of the University of Heidelberg.

1 Molson to Currie, 17 October 1933; Currie to Molson, copy, 19 October 1933. Both letters in McGill University Archives (MGA), RG2, file C46, 445. Currie's count of Jews in the incoming law class is probably exaggeratedly low. See the discussion of quotas below.

2 Unsigned copy of letter to Currie, 21 July 1933 in MGA, RG2, file C46, 443. One can assume that MacKay was the author of the letter, since

the language is very similar to a signed memo of his to Currie from several years earlier. In *Making a Middle Class: Student Life in English Canada during the Thirties*, 33, Paul Axelrod also attributes the letter to MacKay.

3 Trofimenkoff, *Abbé Groulx: Variations on a Nationalist Theme*, 10.

4 Cook, "The Remembrance of All Things Past," 13. Cook is one of Canada's most distinguished historians and has written extensively about French Canadian nationalism.

5 Tulchinsky, *Branching Out: The Transformation of the Canadian Jewish Community*, 141, 180.

6 *L'Action nationale*, June 1933, quoted in Delisle, *The Traitor and the Jew*, 155.

7 "Riots and Rights," editorial, *The Varsity*, 19 October 1936. Martin Loeb, the editor in chief that year, was the only Jew on the editorial board.

8 "Montreal Students Riot," *The Varsity*, 26 October 1936.

9 Tulchinsky, *Branching Out*, 141.

10 See Anctil, "Interlude of Hostility: Judaeo-Christian Relations in Quebec in the Interwar Period, 1919–1939," 147–8, and many other sources.

11 Horn, *Academic Freedom in Canada: A History*, 94.

12 "Dr. Cody Criticizes Universal Suffrage," *The Varsity*, 12 February 1936.

13 Quoted in "Staecie Discusses German Situation," *McGill Daily*, 3 December 1935, and in Horn, *Academic Freedom*, 136–7.

14 Quoted in "Academic Life under Hitler Loses Freedom," *The Varsity*, 28 September 1933.

15 "Another Viewpoint on German Situation," letter to *The Varsity*, 25 October 1935.

16 "Anti-Semitism Seen as Centred in Universities," *The Varsity*, 31 October 1933.

17 Horn, *Academic Freedom*, 35; Friedland, *The University of Toronto: A History*, 343.

18 Ibid., 20.

19 See Underhill, "The Liberal Arts and Public Affairs."

20 "Our Silent Staff," editorial, *The Varsity*, 25 October 1933; "Faculty Reply to Criticism with Alacrity," *Varsity*, 26 October 1933.

21 One typical newspaper attack on Scott is "One of Our Teachers," an editorial in the Montreal *Gazette*, 15 August 1938.

22 "Beatty Says Socialist Ideas Permeate our Universities," *McGill Daily*, 28 October 1935. The article is an account of a recent speech by Beatty at the University of Western Ontario, where he had received an honorary LLD.

23 "Personal" letter, from Beatty to Morgan, 5 January 1937, in MGA, RG2, file C54, 729. See also "Beatty Says Socialist Ideas Permeate our Universities," *McGill Daily*, 28 October 1935, and many other sources.

24 Beatty to Morgan, 12 November 1935, MGA, RG2, file C54, 729. Among many other sources on the relationship of Underhill and Cody, see the letter of Dr W.R. Tutt, Sarnia, to Cody, 15 December 1932, and Cody's reply, 20 December 1932, in which he states that Underhill "has already been warned on account of certain actions in the past and will be dealt with in the future" (University of Toronto Archives [UTA], Cody Papers, box 005).

25 See Francis, *Frank H. Underhill: Intellectual Provocateur*.

26 "Goldwyn Smith," *University of Toronto Quarterly*, April 1933, in Underhill, *In Search of Canadian Liberalism*, 85–103. On Smith's antisemitism, see Brown, *Jew or Juif? Jews, French Canadians, and Anglo-Canadians, 1759–1914*, esp. 235–7, and the sources cited there.

27 Forsey, *A Life on the Fringe: The Memoirs of Eugene Forsey*, 62–63.

28 Frank R. Scott, "French Canadian Nationalism," *Canadian Forum*, March 1936, 12–13, and May 1936, 12–14, reprinted in his *New Endeavour: Selected Political Essays, Letters, and Addresses*, 27–36. See esp. 29.

29 Kay, *Canada and Palestine: The Politics of Non-Commitment*, 199; Bercuson, *Canada and the Birth of Israel: A Study in Canadian Foreign Policy*, 27.

30 Among a myriad of sources, see the anonymous letter to the Toronto *Evening Telegram*, 25 March 1933, that identified the leftist student "orators and strife fomenters" at the University of Toronto as the sons of Jewish immigrants who showed "their ingratitude" for "the equality of opportunity" shown them in "this new British land." The letter is quoted in Levitt and Shaffir, *The Riot at Christie Pits*, 252. See also, Tulchinsky, *Branching Out*, 141.

31 On Stanley, see Cahill, "The Higher Educator as 'Intellocrat': The Odyssey of Carleton Stanley"; and Horn, *Academic Freedom*, passim.

32 Horn, *Academic Freedom*, 3.

33 Quoted in Cahill, "The Higher Educator," 90.

34 Undated response of Cody to letter of Geo. W. Cohen, managing editor, *Canadian Jewish Review*, Toronto, 8 August 1934, in UTA, Cody Papers, box 013, Caput file. See also Cody's undated response to a similar undated letter from Cohen the previous year, in UTA, Cody Papers, box 006, Geo. W. Cohen file. Undated briefing notes (MGA, RG2, file C46, 446) for a talk to the Maccabean Circle, the Jewish student group at McGill, probably written by Registrar T.H. Matthews for Principal Morgan, could be for a talk that preceded Morgan's address to the B'nai Brith.

35 "Principal Morgan and Liberty," editorial, *Canadian Jewish Chronicle*, 20
    March 1936.

36 Letters from Morgan to B. Pearlman, Hull, England, 21 April 1936, and
    from Pearlman to Morgan, 1 May 1936, and letter from Morgan to Dr L.
    Eidlinger, Montreal, 11 May 1936, all in MGA, RG2, file C46, 446.

37 On Brockwell, see among other sources, Robinson, "The Canadian Years
    of Yehuda Kaufman (Even Shmuel): Educator, Journalist, and Intellectual."

38 Bick to Currie, undated, and Currie to Bick, 25 September 1933, both
    in Canadian Jewish Congress Charities Committee National Archives
    (CJCCNA), McGill University, Currie Papers, RG HD1, Jewish Students at
    McGill file.

39 *Jewish Transcript* (Seattle), 20 August 1926, quoting an editorial in the
    Yidisher zhurnal/Daily Hebrew Journal (Toronto). The article cites eight
    English and French universities in Canada with ostensibly open doors,
    including Toronto, McGill, Dalhousie, Manitoba, and Western Ontario.
    The Seattle clipping was sent by the advertising manager of the *Hebrew
    Journal* "To the principal of McGill for his information" on 27 August
    1926, MGA, RG2, file C46, 445.

40 Letter of Claris E. Silcox, 15 September 1933 (then working for the Insti-
    tute of Social and Religious Research in New York "under the aegis of
    Mr. John D. Rockefeller, jr.") to Principal Currie. A United Church clergy-
    man, Silcox fought antisemitism in the later thirties and advocated for
    German Jewish refugees, but he also believed in Jewish quotas at universi-
    ties (see below). The letter describes a research project he was conducting
    in twemty North American cities, including Toronto and Montreal (MGA,
    RG2, file C46, 445).

41 On two elite American universities, see Oren, *Joining the Club: A History
    of Jews and Yale*, and Rosovsky, *The Jewish Experience at Harvard and
    Radcliffe*.

42 Axelrod, *Making a Middle Class*, 30–2. In "Interlude of Hostility," 143,
    Anctil gives a figure of 32 percent for 1924–25 in Arts [and Sciences],
    25 percent in the Faculty of Medicine, and 41 percent in the Faculty of
    Law. Both Axelrod and Anctil rely on university documentation. On the
    assumption that advocates of quotas tended to inflate the number of Jews,
    I have chosen the lower figures as the more probable.

43 Letter, MacKay to Currie, 23 April 1926, MGA, RG2, file C46, 445.

44 "A Compilation Made by the Principal's Office Showing the Number of
    Protestants, Roman Catholics and Hebrews among the Members of our
    Staff and Student Body," 19 September 1933, CJCCNA, McGill University,
    Currie Papers, RG HD1, Jewish Students at McGill file.

45 Axelrod, *Making a Middle Class*, 33.

46 Memorandum from Dean C.W. Hendel, Arts and Sciences, to Principal L.W. Douglas, 11 October 1938, CJCCCNA, McGill University, Currie Papers, RG HD1, Jewish Students at McGill file.

47 Letters from Alexander Brin, Boston, to Sir Edward Beatty, 10 November 1937, Beatty to Brittain, 15 November 1937, and Brittain to Brin, 16 November 1937, MGA, RG2, file C46, 446.

48 Letters from Walter Menaker, Detroit, to Douglas, 10 January 1938, and Douglas to Menaker, 15 January 1938, and memo from J.C. Simpson to Douglas, 14 January 1938, CJCCCNA, Currie Papers, Jews-Matriculation file.

49 Friedland, *University of Toronto*, 324.

50 Axelrod, *Making a Middle Class*, 34, 71.

51 Ibid., 30–2.

52 Silcox, "Canadian Universities and the Jews," draft, and covering letter from Silcox to Cody, 8 January 1934; letter of Silcox, now with the title "director of the Study of Church Union in Canada," to Cody, 26 February 1934; all in UTA, Cody Papers, box 012; "Attitude of Jews Cited by Avukahs," *The Varsity*, 3 December 1935.

53 Sirluck, *First Generation: An Autobiography*, 32.

54 Axelrod, *Making a Middle Class*, 34.

55 Compare the figures in L. Rosenberg, *Canada's Jews: A Social and Economic Study of the Jews in Canada*, 258–9.

56 Groulx, "Le Devoir des universitaires," sermon at the mass of the Holy Ghost, held at the opening of the school year at the Université de Montréal, 6 October 1915, published in *Le Devoir*, 7 October 1915; translated in Cook, *French Canadian Nationalism*, 64–5.

57 Anctil, "Interlude of Hostility," 145–9.

58 Letters in MGA, RG2, file C49, 622, to and from a number of people. Especially relevant are the letters from Principal Douglas to Registrar T.H. Matthews, 22 March 1939, and from G.H. Fletcher, secretary-treasurer of the Students' Executive Council, to Rabbi Morris N. Kertzer, B'nai B'rith [sic] Hillel Foundation, University of Alabama, 29 April 1939.

59 "A Compilation Made by the Principal's Office Showing the Number of Protestants, Roman Catholics and Hebrews among the Members of our Staff and Student Body," 19 September 1933, CJCCCNA, McGill University, Currie Papers, RG HD1, Jewish Studies at McGill file.

60 Copy of "Private" letter, Currie to Abramowitz, 5 April 1933, and unsigned, undated memo to Currie from someone in his office reporting on a conversation with "Mr. Wright of the *Herald*," who "thought Jews

should be left strictly alone to handle it themselves" CJCCCNA, McGill University, Currie Papers, RG HD1, Jews, Education, and Germany file. On backlash and the American Jewish Committee, see "Beware Interference," editorial, *Canadian Jewish Chronicle*, 17 February 1933.

61 Betcherman, *The Swastika and the Maple Leaf: Fascist Movements in Canada in the Thirties*, 34–5; "Ontario Protests Persecution," *Jewish Standard*, 7 April 1933.

62 William Hasler to Currie, 31 October 1933, and Currie to Hasler, 1 November 1933, both in MGA, RG2, file C45, 365.

63 Currie to Murrow, 26 June 1933, in MGA, RG2, file C46, 443. MacKay quoted in Axelrod, *Making a Middle Class*, 33.

64 Norwood, *The Third Reich in the Ivory Tower*, 29–30.

65 Ibid., 30–1; Friedland, *University of Toronto*, 343. Zimmerman, in his essay "'Narrow-Minded People': Canadian Universities and the Academic Refugee Crisis, 1933–1941," 294, put the figure at 6 scholars placed in Canada by 1938, compared with 251 in Great Britain, 247 in the United States, and 7 in India.

66 Cahill, "The Higher Educator," 86–7.

67 Unsigned memo, 4 July 1938, MGA, RG2, file C46, 442.

68 Friedland, *University of Toronto*, 343–4.

69 On Butler and other American university faculty and administrators, see Norwood, *The Third Reich in the Ivory Tower*, passim.

70 The "Declaration of Principles" and letters of Douglas to Butler, 20 February, 1939; Maurault to Douglas, 8 February 1939; Douglas to Maurault, 20 February 1939; George H. Chase, Dean of the University, Harvard, to Douglas, 15 March 1939; and Douglas to Chase, 22 March 1939; all in MGA, RG2, file C46, 442.

71 Matthews to Douglas, 24 January 1939, 27 January [1939], and Douglas to Matthews, 26 January 1939, MGA, RG2, file C46, 442.

72 Abella and Troper, *None Is Too Many: Canada and the Jews of Europe, 1933–1948*, 60.

73 Sirluck, *First Generation*, 35–6. On the United States, see Norwood, *The Third Reich in the Ivory Tower*, passim.

74 "Falsely Reported Student Declares," *The Varsity*, 29 September 1933.

75 The first piece appeared on 6 October 1933.

76 Ross Munro, "Germany Unlikely to Support Italy," *The Varsity*, 4 October 1935.

77 *The Varsity*, 29 September 1933.

78 "Nazi Regime Facing Revolt," editorial, *The Varsity*, 16 October 1935; "Germany Believes Hitler Saviour," ibid., 6 October 1933.

79 "Eisendrath Finds Germans in Terror, *The Varsity*, 30 October 1935.

80 Letter, Morgan to G. Fletcher, Esq., secretary-treasurer of the McGill Students' Executive Council, 5 January 1937. The letter is the final answer to a request that originated with a "sales trainer" at the Bell Telephone Company, who had been at a youth conference in Germany the previous summer. See various letters to and from Morgan, Fletcher, T.H. Matthews, B.F. McNeish, Miss H. Gifford of the German Club, Mr. J.A. Nolan, president of the Students' Society, and E. de Haas of the Vereinigung Carl Schurz, "an organization [in Berlin] interested in improving the relationship between Germany and America," all in MGA, RG2, File C45, 365.

81 Letters to Morgan and/or Matthews from Dr. Droeger of the Vereinigung Carl Schurz in Berlin and Herr Adler of the Heidelberg University foreign department. Droeger was directed to McGill by the professor who headed the Deutsches Haus at Columbia in New York.

82 Norwood, *The Third Reich in the Ivory Tower*, passim.

83 "Subscriptions to German Cut as Periodicals Soar in Price," *The Varsity*, 21 October 1936.

84 Norwood, *The Third Reich in the Ivory Tower*, 61–2.

85 Ibid., 61–8.

86 "Heidelberg Invitation to Toronto Still Stands," *The Varsity*, 6 March 1936; "As Yet, No Official Decision on Heidelberg Invitation," *The Varsity*, 9 March 1936.

87 Cody to the Rector, Heidelberg, 12 March 1936, in University of Heidelberg Archives (UHA), file B–1812/26. The file also contains a letter from A.B. Fennel, the registrar of the University of Toronto, dated 31 January 1936. Fennel apparently understood his invitation as personal, and he answered simply that "it will not be possible for me to visit Germany during the coming summer."

88 UHA, file B–1812/26.

89 Morgan to McLean, 2 April 1936, MGA, RG2, file C42, 323; Morgan to Dodds, 11 April 1936, and Dodds to Morgan, 15 April 1936, MGA, RG2, file C46, 443.

90 Owen to Rector, Heidelberg, 15 April 1936, HUA, B–1812/26. From the lists in the Heidelberg Archives, it is not possible to determine who the other Canadian participant was.

91 Letters, T.F.S., vice-chancellor, University of Reading, to Morgan, 30 March 1937; Morgan to Sir Charles Grant Robertson, University of Birmingham, date lost, MGA, RG2, file C45, 365.

92 On the CNCR, see Abella and Troper, *None Is Too Many*, passim.

93 Friedland, *University of Toronto*, 344.

94 Silcox, "Canadian Post Mortem on Refugees: An Address."

95 Circular letter dated 5 June 1939, in MGA, RG2, file C46, 442.

96 Friedland, *University of Toronto*, 342; Abella and Troper, *None Is Too Many*, 64.

97 For a full account of the fate of the ship's passengers, see Miller and Ogilvie, *Refuge Denied*, 174–5.

6

The War and Before: Responses in Mainstream Canadian Literary Life

NORMAN RAVVIN

[S]o long as thousands of helpless men, women and children are suffering intolerable persecutions and abuse in Germany, or being herded like cattle from one already crowded European country to another, while we continue to slam our door and refuse them admission, there will be little reason for anyone to think better of us ... We merely exist, harming no one, and doing no one any good either.

Gwethalyn Graham, *Saturday Night*, 1938

It should come as no surprise to readers that in Canadian literature, between 1935 and 1945, there is almost no overt, sustained response to key phenomena such as fascism, German racist ideology, the Nazi conquest of Europe, and the mass deportations and annihilations that followed. A consideration of the literary and cultural atmosphere of the time demands careful examination in order to take account of what writers, publishers, reviewers, and readers thought and said about events in Europe and their relationship to Jews in Canada. The challenge is to recover a detailed and accurate sense of the mindset of writers and their audience during these years that is not swamped by our own perspectives and notions about what was at the forefront of daily and creative concerns.

This chapter will examine key novels and poetry, critical studies, and newspaper, magazine, and academic writing in order to recreate as clear a sense as possible of the tenor of the times. Aspects of this close reading will prove idiosyncratic – at times resembling a search for the proverbial needle in a haystack or, stranger still, a search for the absence of such needles in the haystack. This study will examine a range of counter-canonical developments, voices that were not necessarily central and are largely forgotten by contemporary and mainstream presentations of Canadian literary history. It will focus, though not exclusively, on non-Jewish English-language writers. It will not present an account of the earliest developments in what we now call Holocaust literature – such as A.M. Klein's 1951 novel *The Second Scroll*. Much of what comes to the fore in this essay reveals a lack of literary and intellectual attention to the depths of the catastrophe during the late thirties and early forties. By the time Klein was working on his novel in the late forties, postwar retrospection allowed writers to develop new historical and religious responses to recent events.

It is a coincidence, though an important one, that the late 1930s and 1940s were a time of transformation and self-definition in Canadian literary outlook and infrastructure. In this period of change and development, the relevance of the European Jewish catastrophe falls into particular relief, so the Canadian response is unlike anything found in more highly developed literary landscapes such as in England and the United States. Satisfyingly, for students of Canadian and Canadian Jewish cultural history, the Canadian story on this front is unique, with its own quirks and characteristic phenomena.

CANADA'S LITERARY LANDSCAPE

We gain a sense of the peculiarities of the Canadian creative and publishing scene by examining the Royal Commission on National Development in the Arts, Letters and Sciences that was undertaken in 1949 and published in 1951. Part of a much larger undertaking by the federal government to survey the country's nascent cultural nationalism, the commission's report on Canadian literary life is revealing. Its aims were both quantitative and qualitative. A call for briefs from interested organizations attracted contributions from such organizations as the Société des écrivains canadiens and eminent critics and publishers. In organizing their material, the report's authors asked such questions as "Is there a national literature?" They answered this through a summary of the report's contributing voices by confirming "that neither in French nor in English have we yet a truly national literature." The report includes a table comparing the number of English-language books published in Canada, the United States, and the United Kingdom in 1947, when the wartime lull in literary production had yet to be overcome. Canadian publishers brought out 34 books of fiction and 40 books of poetry. The British industry produced 1,723 and 352, respectively, while American production kept pace with 1,307 books of fiction and 463 volumes of poetry. The slightness of book publishing in Canada helps us recall the prewar and wartime contexts; consequently, the few books that did appear in these years are particularly precious objects of study.[1]

Just as the 1930s and 1940s can be characterized by the slightness of Canadian publishers' output, they are also recognizable for major shifts in creative focus in both English and French literature. A younger generation of writers, many of them poets from Montreal affiliated with McGill University, viewed themselves as part of a North American modernist vanguard in rebellion against what they perceived to be the Victorian stodginess of the previous generation's creative goals. The influence of American poet William Carlos Williams and European novelists such as James Joyce represented new creative possibilities that were seen to be linked to progressive political platforms. The assertion of a "new poetry" in Canada is made in a 1936 volume entitled *New Provinces: Poems of Several Authors*. With four of its five contributors representing a new generation of modernist poets, *New Provinces* represents a landmark that was far more meaningful than the hundred copies it reportedly sold in its first year of publication.[2]

The presence in this volume of A.M. Klein is a notable breakthrough, because Klein, a Jew, was the first non-Anglo, non-francophone ethnic voice to gain an important foothold in the Canadian canon. Born in Montreal, steeped in Jewish knowledge and language, but educated at his neighbourhood public school and McGill University, Klein straddled the Jewish and non-Jewish cultures of Montreal. The poetry included in *New Provinces* might give readers little excitement today, but when the volume is read in order to judge Klein's contribution, one recognizes an early intimation of what would come to be called multiculturalism in Canada. The two long poems by Klein are highly ironic dramatizations of Jewish themes. In "Out of the Pulver and the Polished Lens," he addresses Jewish tradition and rebellion through a loving depiction of Benedict Spinoza "plucking tulips / Within the garden of Mynherr, forgetting / Dutchmen and Rabbins."[3] In "Soirée of Velvel Kleinburger" he plays with Jewish types closer to home and sends up working-class card games in the "back-room dens of delicatessen stores"; but the point of the poem, which likely entertained his compatriots, is its intentional echoes of T.S. Eliot's "The Love Song of J. Alfred Prufrock," down to the pastiche of Eliot's habit of creating a collage of different voices.[4]

Klein's position as a vanguard figure in the mid-1930s was further established in a now little-read but once influential volume entitled *The White Savannahs*, by American-born W.E. Collin. Collin's 1936 collection of essays, some of which first appeared in the *University of Toronto Quarterly* and *Canadian Forum*, is arranged to present the story of Canadian literary history as Collin understood it. Beginning with an essay on Archibald Lampman, one of the Confederation Poets, followed by a study of Marie le Franc, who was French-born and sailed for Canada in 1906, Collin examines a major contemporary figure, Toronto's E.J. Pratt, before moving on to a quartet of young voices: Dorothy Livesay, F.R. Scott, Leo Kennedy, and Klein. It is Collin's positioning of Klein as a kind of consummate figure, more than his understanding of the creative sources of the poet's oeuvre, which interests us here. Collin takes the antiquated approach – signalled by his decision to title Klein's chapter "The Spirits of Palestine" – of highlighting Klein's links with autochthonous elements of Jewish culture rather than examining his roots in the contemporary Canadian Jewish scene.[5] "Klein's soul," Collin tells us, "is an ardent symbol of the spiritual rebirth of the Jewish people; the resounding anger and the prophetic vision, the impassioned lyricism of his poetry witness to the depth and intensity of Israel's awakening to a realization of her ancient and splendid destiny."[6]

Although Klein's poems had been appearing for some time in a variety of journals, including the left-leaning, entirely secular, Toronto-based *Canadian Forum*, Collin reiterates his notion that Klein's poetry is propelled by a religious tradition of prophets and is motivated by such colourful cultural accoutrements as "phylacteries or many-branched candelabra or unleavened bread."[7] Collin correctly credits the inherent power of Klein's poetic language, but he has no critical resources for recognizing the immediate political and historical experience out of which Klein's personality and creative efforts grew. The Canadian Jew, even a poetically avant-garde one like Klein, must be understood as "an exile gazing out of ghetto-lanes towards orange-groves and distant Palestine skies embowering home and love."[8]

Not all critics viewed Klein through this particular prism. Alongside such publications as *New Provinces* and *The White Savannahs*, the late 1930s and wartime in Canada are marked by the rise of little magazine culture. Key Montreal-based magazines of the period included *Contemporary Verse*, founded in 1941, *Preview*, which ran between 1942 and 1945, and *First Statement*, whose active years matched those of *Preview*. Klein was sought after by the competing editors of *Preview* and *First Statement*, and the latter, co-edited after 1943 by Irving Layton and Louis Dudek, exemplified a new modernist approach. Looking back on *Preview*'s editorial values, its founder Patrick Anderson described the magazine as a "war-saturated, highly documentary and strongly socialist publication."[9] In 1944 the magazine printed a variety of Klein's poems depicting Montreal, in which Jewish motifs and themes are notably absent. Rather than highlighting Klein's Jewish commitments, these poems represent Klein's visionary effort to create a *"language bilingue,"* a poetic language blending French and English that might be appreciated by both sides of the Canadian language divide.[10]

The December 1944 issue of *Preview* included two remarkable early short stories by Mavis Gallant that portrayed Jewish refugees in wartime Montreal. Gallant left Canada for her life's work writing in Paris, but these two pieces – "Good Morning and Goodbye" and "Three Brick Walls" – are among the most direct examinations of the connection between European Jewry and mainstream Canada that one can find in wartime Canadian literature. With its portrait of a young refugee named Paul, "Good Morning and Goodbye" takes the Jewish outsider's point of view. Although Paul recognizes his own voicelessness in his new life, he wishes he could be heard:

In the beginning, Paul understood nothing. He could say yes and no, please and thank you. They talked to him and at him and about him, but all he could do for answer was smile. Twice, he had tried to speak of himself. The first time was the most important. He told them that he had changed his name. "Paul, now," he said. It had taken all his strength and courage. Then he had spoken once more because he wanted to share and explain a great burden which was so overwhelmingly his own. He showed them his passport. There was a large red "J" stamped on each page.[11]

Exactly what happened to Paul and his absent family in Europe remains a mystery, as if the writer herself did not know or could not bring herself to break the frame of her Canadian stories with European settings and languages she was unfamiliar with. In "Three Brick Walls" Gallant tries out Paul's voice as a new Canadian. Awkwardly, he miscommunicates what he would like to order in a "lunch room" near his rented room. But Gallant's point, ultimately, is the confirmation of Paul's escape from his unspoken past. "Whatever happens," he thinks to himself as he returns to his room, "I am still free."[12]

These stories appeared late in the war when many of the darkest events in Europe were known. *Preview* readers were a small, young, well-educated, and left-leaning group whose political views made them sympathetic to the circumstances of Jewish refugees. But one can imagine that Gallant undertook such themes, as any good writer would, with the broadest audience in mind. In this, she was in the literary vanguard, and her stories, combined with *Preview*'s editorial goals, reflect a courageous public stance. Gallant has written and said little of this stage of her career, but a recollection of Montreal in wartime appears in her story "Varieties of Exile," first published in January 1976. The story begins in an autobiographical vein: "In the third summer of the war I began to meet refugees ... each of them – Belgian, French, Catholic, German, Jewish German, Czech – was a book I tried to read from start to finish ... I tried to see Montreal as an Austrian might see it and to feel whatever he felt."[13]

CANADIAN LITERATURE IN WARTIME

In the foregoing I have outlined some of the key characteristics of prewar Canadian literary and cultural infrastructure: the slightness of publication; an ongoing shift in writerly influence and approach; the Anglo-French divide in output; and the new, one might say startling, centrality of A.M. Klein in these developments. A review of literary journals from the late 1930s and early 1940s turns up only a smattering of creative and historical treatments of the European scene, often with a noticeably distanced tone. Through the early 1940s contributors to the *University of Toronto Quarterly* undertook to comment on such events as the publication, in English, of Hitler's speeches, while the German émigré scholar F.W. Foerster, in an April 1942 article titled "Germany as She Really Is," asserted that the "younger generation of Germans ... are won over to Hitlerism" without exploring the issue of Nazi racial ideology and its repercussions for Jews.[14] Also in 1942 the *University of Toronto Quarterly* published a rather tame, wistful story titled "One Nazi Victory," which took as its focus the destruction of a Norwegian fishing town by German bombardment. Its author manages to convey no specifics regarding the victims or the perpetrators, aside from the fact that before the war German travellers had been welcome and numerous in the town. The story's placidness and predictable moral – "the German people who had received from Norway nothing but good had repaid that good with evil"[15] – make one wonder what could possibly be meant by the editorial note informing readers that the author as cited – Olav Norsman – "is, of course, a pseudonym," and that the "name of the author, which (for good reason) it conceals, would be a complete guarantee of the accuracy of all that is said in the article."[16]

The work of leading writers published at the time of the outbreak of war and after is revealing for what is said as well as for what is not said about world events. This latter issue – that of not saying – presents its own challenges. Without detailed private letters or memoirs that discuss this subject, it is impossible to recover what a writer thought about the major issues that he or she did not address in published work. This conundrum relates, I would argue, to the challenge raised at the outset of this essay: the difficulty of separating our own assumptions about the salient developments of a past era from the contemporary views of those who lived at that time.[17]

Canadian writers presented with the challenge of addressing events unfolding in Europe before and during the war express, in their tentativeness and rhetorical positions, both diffidence and distress, but not necessarily great awareness. An unusual early poetic response to Jewish endangerment in Poland is Earle Birney's 1939 poem "Hands," which was collected in his 1945 Governor General's Award-winning volume *Now is Time*. Linking a peaceful canoe ride in early Vancouver light with European events, Birney begins this way:

In the amber morning by the inlet's high shore
my canoe drifts and the slim trees come bending
arching the palms of their green hands
juggling the shimmer of ripples.
                        Too bewildering

even in the dead days of peace was this manumission,
the leaves' illogical loveliness. Now am I frustrate,
alien. Here is the battle steeped in silence,
the fallen have use and fragrantly nourish the quick.
My species would wither, away from the radio's barkings,
the headline beating its chimpanzee breast, the nimble
young digits at levers and triggers. Lithe are these balsam
fingers, gaunt as a Jew's in Poland ... [18]

"We are gloved with steel," Birney writes at the poem's conclusion, "and a magnet set us in Europe."[19]

Birney is unusual among his poetic compatriots for his willingness to refer to the war, not through more stereotypic motifs but by jarring reference to the German persecution of Jews. *David and other Poems*, his 1942 Governor General's Award-winning collection, concludes with an antiwar poem whose first stanza ends with the lines: "And war, it's true, fouls both the flesh / Victorious and the flesh it slays."[20] The dustcover flap of the first edition of *David and other Poems* includes the detail that the volume was published while Birney was on "active service with the Canadian Army." The intimacy of his knowledge of wartime Europe may have accounted for his decision to include in his volume's final poem an image, however convolutedly presented, of Jewish suffering:

>   My mother will be kept
> From stumbling down a prairie road
> Illumed by burning barns and snowed
> By patterned death.
> >   Is it so rash
> To seek to rank with men who saved
> Your English father from a lash
> In London streets, and bent head shaved
> Because his mother was a Jew
> Who starved last year in Lodz?[21]

Wartime anthologies of Canadian writing typically reveal little acknowledgment of European Jewish experience or its repercussions on North American shores. This can in part be explained by the fact that some anthologized material was written before the war, and if we consider the time it can take to bring an anthology from conception to publication, the collections were likely envisioned in the prewar period and published later. Because so few anthologies devoted to Canadian literature appeared between 1935 and 1945, it is easy to gain a clear impression of what editors at the time felt was worthy of publication. One collection, *Voices of Victory: Representative Poetry in Wartime*, resulted from a call for poems whose publication would raise proceeds for "organizations active in aiding the Empire's war effort."[22] The judging of submissions was overseen by the Canadian Authors' Association, relying on editorial advice from Earle Birney, E.J. Pratt, and other leading writers and academics of the day.[23] The idea that the Canadian war effort was bound to "Empire" is strong in this collection, with the poem chosen to receive a first prize extolling the "glory" of England's "greatest hour."[24] One poem in the collection, bearing the rather abstract title "For This Freedom Too," acknowledges the Jewish experience in Europe. Its head note, quoting the Premier of Holland from a BBC broadcast, notes, "A professor of the University of Leyden has been sent to a concentration camp for protesting the dismissal of a Jewish colleague."[25] It becomes clear upon reading the poem that the "freedom" mentioned in its title is that of a non-Jew to speak for a Jew. Something notably shallower is on offer here than in Gallant's efforts to imagine her way into a German Jewish refugee's emotional life. Freedom in the abstract – the ability to do what one's conscience demands – is celebrated, rather than the specific nature of the collapse of Jewish freedom in Europe. This approach is reminiscent of W.E. Collin's way of acknowledging Klein – not for his specific personal and creative qualities, but for how his poetry might be linked to something universal, such as the narrative tableaux of the Bible.

More interesting and reflective of both a new Canadian critical consensus and growing international interest in Canadian literature is the 1944 volume *Canadian Accent: A Collection of Stories and Poems by Contemporary Writers from Canada*. Its editor, Quebec-born poet Ralph Gustafson, was based in New York City in 1943 when he signed his anthology's foreword. The standout piece in *Canadian Accent* is A.M. Klein's "A Psalm of Abraham, Concerning that Which He Beheld Upon the Heavenly Scarp."[26] In five traditionally rhymed stanzas, Klein links the tradition of Hebrew religious poetry and Jewish belief with the events of the war:

And on that day, upon the heavenly scarp,
The hosannas ceased, the hallelujahs died,
And music trembled on the silenced harp.
An angel, doffing his seraphic pride,
Wept; and his tears so bitter were, and sharp,
That when they fell, the blossoms shrivelled and died.

> . . .

The Lord looked down, and saw the cattle-cars;
Men ululating to a frozen land.
He saw a man tear at his flogged scars,
And saw a babe look for its blown-off hand.
Scholars he saw, sniffing their bottled wars,
And doctors who had geniuses unmanned.[27]

Klein's creative output is given pride of place in an even more canonical context – that of A.J.M. Smith's *The Book of Canadian Poetry: A Critical and Historical Anthology*. Published in 1943 with the imprimatur of the University of Chicago Press and edited by Smith, a leading poet, critic, and anthologist of his era, the collection highlights a better-known poetic response by Klein to Jewish catastrophe, "*In re* Solomon Warshawer."[28] Smith's introductory note to Klein's poems reflects both the esteem with which Klein was held in the 1930s and early 1940s, while repeating some of the stereotypical representations of Jewish culture that we find in Collin's treatment of Canada's first major Jewish English-language poet. "It is a somewhat paradoxical fact," Smith tells his readers, "that the greatest poet living today in Canada whose work is a conscious and inspired expression of nationalism is not concerned with Canadian nationalism but with an alien, proud, and ancient nationalism – that of Judea."[29]

This backhanded compliment is wrong-headed in at least two ways: Klein, by the 1940s, was deeply interested in the possibility of poetry written in a "*langage bilingue*," as mentioned above, a bicultural idea inspired by daily life in Montreal;[30] and his diaspora-bound conscience proved to be an early and ongoing source of guilt regarding his unwillingness to uproot himself and his family to pursue the Zionist dream. Similarly ironic and misleading is Smith's characterization of "*In re* Solomon Warshawer" as "one of the greatest, though most specialized 'war poems' to have come out of Canada during the second [sic] World War."[31] To be both great and specialized seems a rather peculiar condition, and undoubtedly it is the poem's theme of Jewish persecution that must lend it its "specialized" status. Smith would have prepared the introductory material for his volume in 1942 or 1943 – contemporary with the Nazis' years of killing at sites such as Belzec and Treblinka. But he could not be expected to know how central Klein would become to our understanding of the war's darkest years.

THREE NOVELISTS OF THE WARTIME ERA

The 1930s and early 1940s offer the reader no major Jewish Canadian English-language literary career through which to view the home front or the war. Klein's reputation was growing, yet he was still a young and in some ways idiosyncratic presence. Mainstream Canadian literature itself was short on major careers. Many of the early stars of modern Canadian literature are unread today outside the university classroom, which adds to the difficulty of recovering a sense of how Canadian literary culture responded to world events between 1935 and 1945. Of the three novelists I will examine here, Ralph Allen is entirely forgotten, Hugh Garner is in general eclipse, while the reputation of Gwethalyn Graham has enjoyed a recovery, in part through the efforts of Toronto-based Cormorant Books to bring her novels back into print. All three were important figures in the 1940s. Graham's career was secured with the 1938 publication of her first novel, *Swiss Sonata*, which, set in a Swiss girls' school and touching on Europe's refugee crisis, won the Governor General's Award. Allen distinguished himself as a journalist during the war and, like Garner, fought in the Canadian armed forces. These three authors' first novels offer insight into contemporary Canadian views of the Jewish catastrophe, while the novels' reception helps us gauge their Canadian audience.

Gwethalyn Graham's *Earth and High Heaven*, published in 1944, addresses Jewish themes in a more complete and direct way than its counterparts. Graham's own youthful experience in a Swiss boarding school, her work with European refugees before the war, and her journalistic forays, informed by left-leaning reformist goals in Canada, influenced her two novels' focus on the European crisis and the Canadian resistance to rescuing refugees. In late 1938 she wrote about these issues in *Saturday Night* magazine, where she criticized mainstream Canadian claims that Jews were unassimilable.[32] When

Earth and High Heaven appeared, its great success was mitigated to an extent by the belief that Graham's fiction was in the service of her political ideals. The novel addresses Canadian antisemitism through a story of unrequited love between Marc Reiser, a young assimilated Ontario-born Jewish lawyer and Erica Drake, the daughter of an elite non-Jewish Westmount family. Graham leaves no doubt that while the Canadian armed forces pursued a Nazi defeat, long-standing notions of a racial divide at home went unchallenged. Erica's break with her father – whom she loves and admires – follows her recognition of his view of Marc as a

> nightmare figure, a crazy conglomerate of a shyster lawyer, quick, insinuating and tricky; a fat clothing merchant with a cigar in his mouth, employing sweated labor with one hand and contriving to outsmart both his competitors and the Government with the other; a loud-voiced, flashy young man pushing his way up to the head of the queue; a skull-capped figure muttering incantations in a synagogue; a furtive, greasy individual setting fire to his own house or his own shop in order to collect the insurance ... all this not only combined in one individual, but an individual who was determined not to be assimilated but to remain an outsider, and who was perpetually turning up where he was not wanted, overrunning hotels, beaches, clubs.[33]

"I had illusions," Erica tells her father, "about practically everything. About you and Mother and this precious country of ours, and the kind of world we're supposed to be fighting for – I was so full of illusions that really, I must have been quite a spectacle."[34] Through her deeply felt affair with Marc, Erica comes to recognize what she calls the

> voices [that] were talking against a background of signs which she had seen in newspaper advertisements, on hotels, beaches, golf courses, apartment houses, clubs and the little restaurants for skiers in the Laurentians, an endless stream of signs which, apparently, might just as well have been written in another language, referring to human beings in another country, for until now she had never bothered to read them.[35]

As direct as it was in its treatment of antisemitism in Canada, *Earth and High Heaven* makes only a few comments regarding what the novel calls "war news."[36] The fact that members of Marc Reiser's family were "sent to Poland" and never heard from again receives passing mention. Toward the end of Graham's novel, in an editorializing mode that we encounter in other works of the time, Marc muses about his relationship to "the Jews of the world," including those in "barracks, concentration camps, prisons, torture chambers and pitiful, futile barricades."[37] This litany suggests to the reader that the character, as well as his author, is aware of European events even if the story he is engaged in does not touch on these things directly.

Graham was committed, in a variety of her writing projects, to offering Canadian readers an appreciation of the European Jewish disaster and its links to Canadian life. In 1938, in *Saturday Night*, she assailed Canadian inaction in the face of the refugee crisis:

> [S]o long as thousands of helpless men, women and children are suffering intolerable persecutions and abuse in Germany, or being herded like cattle from one already crowded European country to another, while we continue to slam our door and refuse them admission, there will be little reason for anyone to think better of us. Beyond certain material contributions, Canada has done little or nothing for humanity as a whole. We merely exist, harming no one, and doing no one any good either.[38]

In *Earth and High Heaven*, a link between the refugee crisis and Canadian responsibility arises only anecdotally, as when Marc Reiser is mentioned at the Drakes' home and Erica's mother remarks, "His name sounded foreign so I suppose he's a refugee."[39]

In the United States, *Earth and High Heaven* made its way into the hands of armed forces servicemen and women through a remarkable program begun in 1943, which produced Armed Services editions of novels, poetry, biography, and other genres in pocket-sized paperback formats. Overseen by a committee that included representatives from the US Army and Navy, publishers, librarians, and booksellers, the program released 1,322 titles, a total of 123 million books.[40] Of the one and a half million copies of *Earth and High Heaven* in print by the end of the war, 350,000 were released this way.[41] A substantially shortened version ran in *Collier's* magazine through late August and early September 1944.[42]

In Canada, the phenomenon of Graham's literary success bowled over critics and other writers. The fact of Samuel Goldwyn's payment of $100,000 to option the book's film rights is mentioned in review after review, suggesting a blend of awe and resentment over the book's status as a money maker on the scale of Hollywood blockbusters. Reviews of *Earth and High Heaven* are revealing historical documents. They appeared quickly and in large numbers in newspapers, magazines, and literary and academic journals. In newspapers, the provocative qualities of Graham's narrative were often raised without the journalist accounting for his or her position on the subject matter at hand. In an *Ottawa Citizen* review published in the fall of 1944, the author maintained that Graham was "[a]lready ... being charged with having written propaganda" of the kind found in Charles Dickens's efforts to reform child labour in *Hard Times. Collier*'s took "its life in its hands," the reviewer added, "when it published 'Earth and High Heaven.'"[43] The *Globe and Mail* pursued similar themes in its coverage of the book. In an article meant to address the novel's remarkable success rather than its literary strengths, the author suggested that its serialization in *Collier*'s "caused no end of controversy." Graham, she added, had "broken a lance for the Jews, demanding fair play for them." Here readers were offered a rare analogy to the *St Louis* in relation to the ongoing disaster in Europe: "Gwethalyn could not stop thinking of the boatload of refugees on the Danube who drifted up and down, and of that other boatload, who were turned back from this side of the Atlantic." Tantalizingly, the *Globe* piece noted that Graham's next novel (which never appeared) would focus on Montreal's distinctive triad of English Canadians, French Canadians and "Jewish people."[44]

More important for our purposes is the lengthy 1944 review by the *Globe*'s longtime literary editor, William Arthur Deacon, entitled "Canadian Novel Challenges Montreal's Race Prejudice." Like many other wartime accounts of Graham's novel, events related to the Holocaust go unmentioned. One wonders, as one encounters this effect again and again, if Canadian reviewers were being narrowly scrupulous in their attention to Graham's Canadian themes, whether the facts on the ground in Eastern Europe had not yet been fully acknowledged, or whether a general consensus reigned among journalists that these facts were not appropriate on the literary pages of a popular newspaper. Deacon opened by acknowledging that Canada was "in the greatest of our wars against unscientific German conceptions of race."[45] But his full attention was directed at what he saw as Graham's role as an "example of the kind of moral leadership Canadian authors can give; and which, in the past, with a few exceptions, they have failed to give."[46] For Deacon, Graham's "crusading spirit" reflected a new willingness among writers to be in "touch ... with the main body of Canadian opinion ... making Canadian books immediately vital."[47]

Judging from the range of response to Graham in literary and academic journals, Deacon's idealistic expectations were not universally shared. The general unwillingness to link accounts of Graham's work with contemporary European events seems misguided, even perverse. But here we encounter the problem raised at the outset of this essay – of appreciating views that are wholly unlike and uninformed in relation to our own. Starting with the most prestigious venue, the *University of Toronto Quarterly*, we find J.R. MacGillivray writing in 1944 that the

> principal sensation of our literary season was the lavish *début* of Gwethalyn Graham's *Earth and High Heaven*, an event that for a day or two actually raised a Canadian novel to front-page notice in our newspapers, and evoked from even the most unbookish among the author's fellow-citizens a solid respect and enthusiasm for a native writer.[48]

Without directly referring to events befalling Jews in Europe, the review points to the book's focus:

> The general problem is anti-Semitism, not the vulgar type, cultivated by the illiberal and the vicious for their own evil motives, but the more respectable and subtle variety which can influence our most ordinary social behaviour, and which commonly decent and reasonable people can carry in their minds without moral disquiet or any fear of harbouring the germs of the loathsome Nazi plague.[49]

In the *Canadian Historical Review*, Gwethalyn Graham, alongside Hugh MacLennan, was appreciated as a young novelist willing to "face frankly and fearlessly the problems of our Canadian society."[50] In its "awareness of Canada," *Earth and High Heaven* was said to stand out among other novels as one of the "first to be frankly and unselfconsciously Canadian."[51] This is high praise – an acknowledgment of the novel's ability to shift popular views – yet the article itself hesitates to link Canadian views regarding

"Frenchmen, Catholics, Jews and 'Bohunks'" with events touching these people in Europe.[52]

The *Dalhousie Review*'s substantial essay on *Earth and High Heaven* appeared in the summer of 1945. It made no mention of Europe as it might relate to Graham's themes, but it was anxious to remind readers "that the book is published not in Canada but in New York" and that "overwhelming success of a popular kind is not always a good thing for a young author."[53] The reviewer did recognize that Graham's portrait of Montreal focused on the city's "tri-racial, tri-religious" character.[54]

The review of *Earth and High Heaven* in *First Statement*'s spring 1945 number undermined the expectation that the "little magazines" were consistently open to new writers, new kinds of books, and the predicament of vulnerable minorities in wartime. The reviewer took no interest in these issues and perversely asserted that the "interest" of Graham's novel lay in "the striking way it points up that anomaly of fiction written by women – the symbolic castration of the hero."[55] The discussion supporting this is so irrelevant in its misdirection that it reflects the possibility of a review reflecting nothing beyond its author's personal obsessions – and maybe editorial laxity. (What, one wonders, were the editors thinking when they allowed this stuff through?)

Graham's 1944 novel is the most substantial response to anti-semitism by a Canadian English-language writer published in the decade after 1935. But two other novels deserve careful attention – Ralph Allen's *Home Made Banners* and Hugh Garner's *Storm Below*. Allen's novel grew out of his wartime experience and was published by a major publisher to reasonable acclaim in 1946. It reflected its author's youthful years in Saskatchewan, his duty in the Canadian D-day landing in Normandy, and the army's drive across France, Belgium, and Germany that followed it. *Home Made Banners* is entirely forgotten today. It has developed no critical consensus, and Allen is remembered not for his fiction but for his role as the longtime editor at *Maclean's* magazine. A combination of issues likely account for his slide into obscurity: although he published five novels, his influential career as a journalist overshadowed his fiction writing; and he died relatively young, at fifty-three, in 1966.

Home Made Banners is not inferior, in literary terms, to any number of Canadian novels from its era that have remained in print; and its subject matter is, arguably, more pressing and relevant today. The novel follows Michael Tully, a prairie kid who finds himself in Toronto in wartime. There, he acquires an education about himself, his country during war, and, ultimately, the European battlefield. Although antisemitism is only a sub-theme in *Home Made Banners*, Allen is direct in his effort to link it and Canadian ideals. In the early stages of the narrative, Tully is instructed by the man who will become his father-in-law regarding the ideological underpinnings of contemporary social and political ills. Tully's Pop is an astute if somewhat didactic anti-fascist, capable of offhandedly noting, "We're still selling scrap iron to the Japs. Arcand can get a police escort in Montreal."[56] He becomes a strong influence on Tully, who "began to read newspapers" to learn about "rearmament, the Nazis, the Fascists, unemployment and a little about the wars in Spain and China."[57]

Tully's education on the prairies prepares him for big city experience, which includes his friendship with an American named Nolan, who has enlisted in the Canadian Army ahead of his own country's entrance into the war. Nolan, known as "the Yank," is presented as the paradigmatic straight shooter, who "came up to win the war personally because that's what his country would have to do sooner or later anyway."[58] It is late 1941 when Tully and Dolan get to know each other in their Toronto training barracks, and Dolan – in contrast with the euphemism we encounter in other fictional and critical works – recognizes the crucial connection between the war and the Jewish catastrophe:

> Me, I always come back to thinking about the Jews. No matter what they say about Chamberlain and Hoare and Baldwin, and all of it might be right for what I know, I keep coming back to that poor old kike running down the street somewhere with a mob throwing rocks at him and his house burning down behind him and not a friend in the world but a few other poor old kikes. And I know the Germans are bad, and since I haven't got anything better to do anyway, I'm willing to fight them.[59]

This is remarkable material for its time – remarkable for the earliness in the war that Allen places it, for its outspokenness and apparent heartfelt quality, for the unselfconscious use of the word "kike" in this context, and for the narrative decision, on Allen's part, to put these words in the mouth of an American who must instruct his Canadian buddy (and, by analogy, the novel's Canadian readers) on what was at stake in the war they had thrown themselves into.

Such ideological and ethical discussions are otherwise largely absent from the main narrative of *Home Made Banners*, for it turns into a familiar battle narrative, with the now archetypal scene of men entering the water and breaking for the beach in Normandy – an account heightened by Allen's personal experiences of D-day and its aftermath. In his depiction of the Canadian Army's progress through Belgium into Germany, Allen depicts the soldiers' view that Canada was "not sending enough reinforcements overseas" in support of its battling troops.[60] When Tully is chosen to accompany a war correspondent farther into occupied Germany, he becomes the inquiring eye through which Allen's readers learn about the German concentration camp system. As they approach a camp for women, the correspondent describes the inmates as "bobby-sox girls" who fought "the Germans all last winter ... Now, far ahead, the black blob of a tower rose on spindly wooden legs from the waste, and as the jeep bounced on, Mike picked out a cluster of dark unpainted shacks lying beneath a tower, and later a tall wire fence around the shacks."[61] The place is overseen by a raffish Polish resistance figure named Sergeant Major Wanda Maczek, who reminds Tully of the film star Hedy Lamarr ("Here comes Wanda ... She's class. Her old man was a count.")[62] This tendency to glamorize wartime experience evaporates as Tully is driven farther across the "plains of Northern Germany ... to reach the concentration camp at Buchenwald."[63]

Allen's portrayal of one of the first-established German concentration camps is revealing in a number of ways. He relies on narrative strategies and motifs that would gain a stereotypic presence in Holocaust fiction, film, and reportage. Tully arrives at Buchenwald "late on a sunny afternoon," juxtaposing normalcy with camp chaos. But intimations of pleasant weather on the German landscape are poisoned by the familiar irony of the slogan placed at the camp's gate, which Allen renders in English as "To each man his desserts."[64] The German inscription at Buchenwald, less famous but as grim in its irony as that at Auschwitz, was "Jedem das Sein," or "To each his own." A "guide" who presents himself once they are inside the gates turns out to be a Flemish schoolteacher who had been imprisoned for his resistance activities. This man's way of presenting his surroundings is an unsettling mixture of the professional and the grotesque. "This is how they put the bodies in," he says before the crematoria. "Once they made me help."[65] As Tully surveys the camp, images of what historians now call the atrocity story appear as "insubstantial sallow figures shuffled across the square" and "a small pile of corpses glinted whitely in the sunlight."[66] Tully and his journalist companion say little as they visit the camp, possibly over-whelmed by what their guide has to show them.

Allen's decision to convey the German concentration camp sys-tem as a universal catastrophe, disconnected from the specific story of Jewish victimization, has historical weight – the earliest camp inmates were enemies of the Nazi state, and Buchenwald held large numbers of Soviet prisoners-of-war, Poles, and Romany – but Jews were a large and constant part of the camp population. One wonders what led Allen to remain silent on the impact on Jews of German genocidal ideology. One wonders, too, what Allen's readers made of the weirdly dramatic way that Tully's guide presents what he calls "our most famous thing of all. This is the lamp shade that was made for the wife of the commandant from the skin of a prisoner."[67] This final anecdote, intimately connected in our minds with Holocaust atrocity, is presented by Allen without any context for understand-ing where it fits in the larger German war effort. Historical evidence for such artifacts remains lacking, as in the case of reports of Ger-man production of soap from human fat.

Such limitations in Allen's willingness to confront Jewish vic-timization may be explained by the particular events the author experienced as a soldier and as a war correspondent for the *Globe and Mail*. Reporting in the newspaper in the summer of 1944, he reveals an early understanding of German methods in their con-centration camp system without linking these to their efforts to murder Jews. Following an encounter with Russian women made to do slave labour repairing railroads, he writes: "As the military situation became more urgent, working conditions for the Russian women became progressively worse. Near the end they worked four-teen hours a day, seven days a week. Their German 'overseers' car-ried clubs and beat the women, frequently without provocation."[68] A novel such as *Home Made Banners*, with its moments of clarity regarding prewar and wartime events, alongside its inability to con-vey the specific character and scope of German actions and Jewish catastrophe, is a telling document of its time.

Hugh Garner's *Storm Below* was published after the war, in 1949, though its author began to sketch his wartime experiences as fiction almost immediately after his discharge from the Royal Canadian

Navy in the summer of 1945.[69] Garner enlisted in the navy in 1940 and spent the better part of three years aboard corvettes, escorting merchant convoys and sounding for submarines.[70] Just as Allen offered his readers an early portrait of army enlistment training and extreme experiences in Europe, Garner's debut novel was an early effort to explain Canada's naval efforts in the Atlantic. Garner's *Storm Below* is lively and readable, but it is the strangest of the three wartime novels under consideration. All three are first novels, and only Garner went on to become a major postwar figure in Canadian fiction.

In letters to writer Marian Engel, Garner dismissed *Earth and High Heaven* as a book that "won't last." The *Collier*'s serialization "made it," he claimed, and the "Jewish community got behind it from the start."[71] Regardless of these musings, Garner's first novel traces some of the same social and religious fault lines that made Graham's novel a North American success.

The surprise in *Storm Below* is its Jewish subplot – as Garner begins his narrative with a portrait of a Jewish officer aboard a Canadian corvette in wartime. The HMCS *Riverford* is captained by a stolid Montrealer. Its crew is largely made up of central Canadians, with a few token westerners, a Quebecer nicknamed Frenchy, and the oddly named Lieutenant Winfield Harris, who is the son of a Jewish delicatessen owner from Winnipeg. Garner does not convey Harris's inner world, but around the *Riverford*'s lone Jew swirl arguments about different Jewish types, their proper social place, and in a few stunning cases, the meaning of Hitler's efforts to murder the Jews of occupied Europe. Harris's antagonist aboard ship is a haughty officer named Peter Smith-Rawleigh, whose ideas about Jews are expressed both inwardly and to his shipmates: "Even in the Navy," he thinks, "their Jewishness made them scheme and study to get ahead. Not that Harris was the worst type of Jew, but still it was a bit thick having to acknowledge him as a superior."[72] The presence of a Jewish officer is also contemplated by the *Riverford*'s captain: "Inscrutable like all Jews. Could not seem to get behind his façade somehow. Wonder what he was in private life? Lawyer perhaps, or in business. Hard to tell what sort of business a Jew was in these days. Used to be old clothes and pawn shops, but now it could be anything."[73]

Here Garner is surely on Graham's turf, whether he is aware of it or not, as he considers the social shifts taking place in wartime, which asserted themselves after the end of the war and resulted in substantial new social, educational, and professional freedoms for Jews. It is the Jew of "old clothes" and peddling who appeared first in Canadian folklore and literature – a kind of stock figure reminiscent of trolls and mysterious travellers, dressed in strange garb, appearing and disappearing without warning, an itinerant and marginal economic figure with no foothold in mainstream Canadian society.[74] Harris's confrontations with Smith-Rawleigh ripple out into discussions among the *Riverford*'s men, leading to a climactic scene that presents a kind of wartime Canadian court of opinion regarding Jews. One argues that "any Jew who joins up and fights is a white Jew," while another seaman insists, "As far as I'm concerned a Jew's a Jew no matter if he joined up in the Commandos on September the third, nineteen-thirty-nine ... I agree with Hitler, they should be wiped off the face of the earth."[75]

The fate of Lieutenant Harris aboard the *Riverford* is of interest to his creator as a measure against which to test the wartime ideas and events haunting *Storm Below*. The novel opens with a prologue that offers a catalogue of ways "to die" in the spring of 1943: "In the gas chambers of Oswiecim, on the spittle-caking roads of North Africa, in a birth-bed in the Queen Mary maternity Hospital in Sheffield, before a Ustachi firing squad outside Sarajevo."[76] Jarring today in its Polish form, the town the Germans called Auschwitz does not figure in *Storm Below*. It will not be mentioned again, and one wonders if its mention in the prologue was motivated by editorial afterthought, aimed at connecting the narrative more directly to world events. The climactic discussion on the *Riverford* regarding Jews is a bizarre, almost hysterical speech by Winfield Harris in which he criticizes his own identity: "I wish that I were the same as you fellows are ... I'm sorry that I'm a Jew ... I'm ashamed of being a Jew. Do you know what I'd like to be for a while? I'll tell you, I'd like to be a God-damn, white, Gentile, Anglo-Saxon. You fellows don't know how much you are the envy of every Yid and Wop and Nigger in this world ... That's why a Jew is – is so – Jewish, because he's eaten up with envy of you."[77] Once he has hurried away, Harris's shipmates discover that cut into the linen "of the table-cloth in front of Harris's place ... as though with a razor blade, was a swastika that Harris had made with his knife."[78]

This scene defies interpretation. Its unlikely wildness, Harris's lack of composure in contrast with his earlier near-aristocratic bearing, and the weird tattooing of the tablecloth all suggest Garner's inability to control his material. Whether the author witnessed such scenes in the navy is immaterial; exactly what he would have his reader learn from them is impossible to say. Not unlike the captain's recognition early in the novel of the unpredictable new status of Jews in the Canadian navy, Garner, and even Harris himself, appear to be unsure about where Jews fit in Canada, as well as in Europe, where Canada was at war with a regime founded on Jew hatred.

In his memoiristic writings, Garner describes his work on *Storm Below*, including his efforts to sell the manuscript and the book's success. As he records in his 1973 memoir *One Damn Thing after Another*, the novel was first serialized in the *Montreal Standard*, the *Newark Evening News*, and the *Chicago Sun-Times*, and it received "feature book reviews and generous critical acclaim from coast to coast ... [I]t was the first Canadian novel ever about the Canadian navy."[79] But Garner says not a word in retrospect about the character of Winfield Harris in the shadow of Hitler's war on the Jews. Garner's biographer, Paul Stuewe, takes the same approach in *The Storms Below: The Turbulent Lives of Hugh Garner* (1988). Stuewe tells us that *Storm Below* earned Garner a $500 advance, a third of which he spent on the Underwood typewriter he relied on for the rest of his career,[80] but nothing is said about the role of Jews, Hitler, or Oswiecim in Garner's debut work. These latter silences seem like a failure of nerve on the part of author and biographer. *Storm Below* is not, I think, open to serious criticism on this issue: Garner's debut novel offers an example of a young writer's choice of difficult material, with which he is unable to contend at a time when the themes that would become central to Holocaust literature were not yet part of the English-language literary tradition. But by the 1970s, when Garner looked back at his early years, and in the late 1980s, when his biographer detailed the development of Garner's oeuvre, consideration of the role of the Jew in *Storm Below* was overdue.

THE VIEW FROM QUEBEC

The foregoing discussion of the English-language literary context during the 1930s and 1940s tells us little about the specifics of French Canadian writers' responses to the war and the years leading up to it. The divide between the two cultures – "two solitudes," as Hugh MacLennan's 1945 novel put it – was solid. For those who address this divide by way of English-language texts, what is known about the French side of the wartime literary scene is coloured to a remarkable degree by the work of Mordecai Richler. Although Richler did not begin publishing until the 1950s, many of his novels drew on his experiences in Montreal during the war. For the most part, his novels portray Montreal without French speakers, with the notable exception of the girl Friday who becomes Duddy's girlfriend and business assistant in *The Apprenticeship of Duddy Kravitz*. Richler's views on wartime antisemitism and post–Quiet Revolution Quebec became front-page news with the publication of his controversial article "Inside/Outside" in the 23 September 1991 issue of the *New Yorker* and of the book that followed, *Oh Canada! Oh Quebec! Requiem for a Divided Country*. Richler's view of what it was like to grow up Jewish in wartime Montreal has become a dominant Canadian coming-of-age narrative, similar to Philip Roth's depiction of postwar Newark and John Updike's version of the Pennsylvania of his youth. Richler introduced these themes in a humorous vein in his 1971 novel *St. Urbain's Horseman*, and they are a driving theme in *Oh Canada! Oh Quebec!*:

I was brought up in a Quebec that was reactionary, church-ridden, and notoriously corrupt – a stagnant backwater – its *chef* for most of that time, Premier Maurice Duplessis, a political thug – and even its intellectuals sickeningly anti-Semitic for the most part. However, when I was first registered for school (at the age of six in 1937), within the sheltering confines of a largely self-contained working-class Jewish community, I was of course unaware that *Le Devoir* had advocated that Jews be denied civil rights or that one Anatole Vanier had already written in the influential *L'Action nationale*, "By their dispersion and their persistent habit of elbowing others out of the way, [Jews] are the authors of their own misfortune ... What is happening in the new Germany is germinating everywhere where Jews are considered as intruders. And where, one may well ask, are they considered otherwise?"[81]

Richler's highly critical attack on the reputation of Abbé Lionel Groulx, an early Catholic nationalist leader whose name is attached to a central Montreal metro station, contributed to the fervour with which French Quebecers responded to Richler's book. "From the beginning," Richler writes,

> French Canadian nationalism has been badly tainted by racism. The patron saint of the *indépendantistes*, the Abbé Lionel Groulx, was not only a virulent anti-Semite but also a nascent fascist, an unabashed admirer in the thirties of Mussolini, Dollfuss, and Salazar. In 1935 Groulx wrote that he longed for the appearance of *un chef* who would lead Quebec into "the new order which is evolving, in which the theories by which we live today appear perhaps to have expired."[82]

A favoured piece of evidence in Richler's arsenal against Groulx is the 1922 novel *L'Appel de la race*, which Groulx published pseudonymously. There, Richler finds a manifesto for racial purity, cultural exclusiveness, and religious supremacist views that he links with the rise of fascist and racist national ideologies in Europe in the 1920s and 1930s.[83] Staged as a narrative of recovery of ancestral roots, Groulx's protagonist, who has strayed from his cultural roots to become a successful lawyer in Ottawa, is put through a process of re-education by his priest. After a visit to his native village of Saint-Michel and much reading, the lawyer's moment of self-recognition is epiphanic:

> Thanks to you, Father Fabien, the great masters of French thought had gradually attuned my thinking; the countryside of Saint-Michel, the people, the things, the horizon, the memories of the home in which I was born have attuned my feelings. On the graves of the Lantagnacs I attuned myself to my ancestors and my people ...
>
> I want to add that the Christian future of my children concerns me more than anything else. My recent studies have showed me above all the deep-rooted affinities between the French race and Catholicism. No doubt that is why the French race is so often termed universal ... So I have decided: my children shall be diverted from their first education. If they are willing, I shall restore them to the tradition of their forebears.[84]

As Groulx was sketching his cultural ideal for Quebec in fiction, the province was undergoing substantial social and economic change, driven by industrialization and the movement of large numbers of people from the rural, church-dominated countryside to manufacturing centres such as Montreal. At the same time, a major influx of Eastern European Jews transformed the face of street life in Montreal. According to Edmund Wilson, a new literary tradition took shape to mark some of these shifts: the French novel of the "urban lower classes," whose major contributors included Roger Lemelin, with his 1944 *Au pied de la pente douce*, and Gabrielle Roy's *Bonheur d'occasion*.[85] One sees in this trend the French-language counterpart of the appearance of novels in the 1940s by Gwethalyn Graham, Ralph Allen, and Hugh Garner. On both sides of the language divide, a youthful generation, formed in prewar Canada and remade by the experiences of a country at war, developed a new literary voice.

Roy stands out among her compatriots for her attentiveness to the position of ethnic and religious minorities in Canada. Working as an itinerant journalist, she visited far-flung communities, often publishing her reports in less than prominent venues, such as the Montreal-based *Bulletin des agriculteurs*. It was in this journal, in 1943, that Roy published a remarkable essay portraying her visit to the Jewish farming colony of Edenbridge in northern Saskatchewan. She was met there by Mike Usishkin, whose own arrival at Edenbridge in 1910 she likens to the narrative of "many pioneers, Quebecers, Finns, Doukhobors, Mennonites."[86] The settlement's forty families have barley, oats, and rye under cultivation, but Roy reflects, too, on the surprising fact that she "saw books in all the houses at Edenbridge."[87] Like much of the wartime writing under discussion here, the developing catastrophe in Europe is not mentioned in the essay. Rather, Jewish life, as part of Prairie culture, is Roy's focus, while in conclusion she allows herself a touch of philosophizing regarding what Edenbridge tells her about Jewish life in the early 1940s: "Had I been wandering toward the past or the future of the Jew? I couldn't say, but I knew that somewhere on the road I had met them in their essential dignity."[88]

Roy reworked this material in her 1951 novel *La petite poule d'eau*, which takes place in the rural ethnic communities of northern Manitoba. Her portrait of a French Canadian matriarch named Luzina includes her country travels with a cart driver – "a Jewish merchant from Dauphin ... with an eye to a deal in muskrat skins" – who was like a character out of Sholom Aleichem:

> Abe Zlutkin took advantage of an interval when the road was
> a trifle less slippery to show her a photo of his wife. It por-
> trayed a plump young Jewish woman of dark complexion. Abe
> bethought himself that he loved her dearly ... [T]ravelling in
> itself had taught her lessons of an unexpected sort: it had shown
> her that human nature everywhere is excellent. The Jews were
> about the only folk she had had no opportunity to study; yet,
> deciding on the basis of her fur merchant that they were rather
> on the likable side, she let herself drift into a feeling of vague
> benevolence.[89]

This is a poignant scene on its own terms, but it also serves as a
marker of the ongoing shift toward a new literary focus in prewar
and wartime Quebec. Abe Zlutkin, like the "old clothes" Jew haunting the *Riverford* captain in *Storm Below*, is a thing of the past, part
of a prewar Jewish economy and society, which is still, for Roy, in
some ways iconic, but now exotic. The fact that a novel published in
1951 must go to the far rural West to find such a figure is reflective
of the near complete transformation of Jewish city life by the end of
the Second World War.

Beyond a voice like Roy's, beyond the ideological monotony of
Groulx and the insistent quality of Richler's childhood memories,
how can we acquire a sense of the French Canadian view of Jews
in the crucial years before and during the Second World War? The
work of English-language Jewish writers of those years – most notably, A.M. Klein and Irving Layton – is generally not viewed as an
avenue to understanding their French-speaking compatriots. But one
finds evidence and suggestions in unexpected corners. In his densely
argued 1972 study *The Shouting Signpainters: A Literary and Political Account of Quebec Revolutionary Nationalism*, Malcolm Reid
provides a detailed report of his encounter with Paul Chamberland,
a writer who staked out his Québécois nationalist position in the
early 1960s. To characterize Chamberland's upbringing in prewar
Quebec, Reid tells us he

> was born into a conventional, Catholic French-Canadian family
> of the Second World War, a period in which urbanization, the
> accession to a certain amount of comfort, to work and lodging
> less harsh than the manual labor and slum tenement of the newly
> urbanized rural Québécois, had not changed the basic reflexes:

signs in a male child of a contemplative, interiorized character were the makings of a priest; the only expression for other-
worldliness was the cassock and the breviary.[90]

It is out of Groulx's milieu and into that of the "young intellectuals
of Quebec" that Chamberland moved.[91] And what of the Jews –
what was their role and their influence – as Quebecers skirted this
fault line, which was both a generational divide and a true cultural
revolution? A fine answer to this is provided by a lengthy passage
in Reid's book, which stands as a historical document, an artifact
of forgotten worlds and the lines of influence that ran between
two communities that are often characterized as separate solitudes.
Though it begins with a discussion of 1960s Quebec, Chamberland works his way to a detailed reminiscence – set some fifteen
years earlier – of the period when Klein, Layton, and Richler were
young:

> "Who's important in young English-Canadian literature"
> Chamberland once asked me. "Some of us have had a few con-
> tacts – I once went to a party where I met Leonard Cohen. But
> the contacts can only go so deep. Our situation is so different –
> the national isolation, the defensive and revolutionary postures
> we feel driven to take don't seem to make any sense to them … "
> "There is also his Jewishness," I suggested. There is a
> Montreal-Jewish pre-eminence in Anglo-Canadian letters. The
> young poet Leonard Cohen, the novelist Mordecai Richler,
> the older poet Irving Layton – they summarize the past three
> generations of Canadian writing … The tradition of the Mont-
> real Jews is particularly suited to representing us: they are
> English-speaking, close to the Anglo-American mainstream, yet
> they are close, too, to our problem group in Canada, have lived
> alongside the French since childhood …
> They summarize us, the Montreal Jewish writers. Canadian,
> yes, a little uneasy about our French-speaking colony, but
> mostly anxious to shake off dull Canadianness and flee to
> universality … Leonard Cohen lived in Montreal, knew the
> city's colonialist section, English-speaking and (even for Jews)
> Protestant-school-attending, Greenwich-Village-style-coffee-
> house-supporting. Knew, too, that there was a colonized section,
> to the east, even if he didn't know it by that name. There had

been a time – Richler writes of it, Layton drew his early socialism from it – when the Jews lived in a poor area downtown, hard by the French-Canadian slums. No more.[92]

Chamberland and Reid debate but largely agree on the position of the Jews in relation to Montreal's cultural and economic divides, its ethnic rivalries and challenges associated with translating one community's experience into the language of another's. But aspects of their discussion are, to my mind, visionary. The two men understand the importance of history in the formation of identity; they highlight the generational shifts in French and Jewish identity; they recognize economic and geographic links, shared ideals and shared territory, and they organize all this under the rubric of missed opportunities. Their discussion points to generational shifts in French Canadian and Jewish identity, as well as to shared economic and geographical experiences. Reid's conversations with Chamberland, meant to explicate the relationship between the 1960s and the wartime era of Richler's and Layton's youth, offer an antidote to Groulx's elite exclusiveness and Richler's novelistic tendency to let his own memories of St Urbain Street overwhelm his sense of the relationship between Jews and others in Montreal.

WHAT THE LITERATURE REVEALS

Prewar and wartime writing in Canada offers its share of treasures and surprises. Some of what we learn from this literature is hidden in the absences, in off-hand remarks, and in the littleness of what is found in a poetry collection, a book review, or an influential critical study. Newspaper writers had their own way of acknowledging (often by evading) the particular awfulness of the European disaster and Canada's response to it. In the Jewish press things were notably different.[93] There, the events of the times were addressed early and often in a tone of heightened anxiety, and the details associated with Nazi war efforts and atrocities against Jews were well accounted for.

In Vancouver's *Jewish Western Bulletin*, for example, the European refugee crisis and details of Nazi atrocity were extensively covered as they occurred. A browse through wartime issues uncovers a wealth of material. A remarkable early example, in the 24 November 1939 issue, is the headline "Hitler Plans Ghetto State for Jews in Poland: Three Million Jews Face Misery and Starvation," which introduces the following London wire service article:

> Indications that Hitler's plans for a Jewish "reservation" in the Lublin area of Nazi Poland are being pushed by the Gestapo so that all Jews living in countries under Nazi domination may be removed into the ghetto-state by the end of March, 1940, are evident in the establishment of a special agency attached to the Gestapo headquarters at ... Maehrisch-Ostrau, which lies on the border between Czechia and Nazi Poland, is the transfer point from which thousands of Jews who lived in Austria, Czecho-Slovakia, Nazi-dominated Poland, Germany and from the provinces of Posen and Silesia, will be sent into the ghetto-state.
>
> At least 5,000 Jews were rounded up by the Gestapo in Germany and transported to Maehrisch-Ostrau, according to reliable information ...
>
> Meanwhile thousands of Jews have been uprooted from their homes in Austria, crowded into cattle cars and brought to the frontier town of Maehrisch-Ostrau where they wait an unknown fate. They are not allowed to leave the trains and Jews living in the town are not permitted to bring either food or clothing to the unfortunate refugees.[94]

Cultural events in Vancouver often reflected an effort to link European events with local concerns. In 1944, when the Yiddish writer Peretz Hirshbein lectured at the Vancouver Jewish Community Centre, his talk was titled "The Prophets in the Light of World Occurrences Today."[95]

In Montreal, as editor of the *Canadian Jewish Chronicle*, A.M. Klein revealed in his reviews an appreciation of the challenges that arose as writers struggled to meet European events with an appropriate literary response. In late 1941, he used a review of "Dunkirk," a book-length poem by E.J. Pratt, to suggest that the "great conflict which at this writing has embraced practically the entire world has not ... produced as yet, any great war poetry ... [I]n the literary production of the last two years, no work ... rose to the demands of the swelling theme."[96] Klein's understanding of this lack includes an answer to questions asked early in this chapter about why writers of the time neglected key wartime themes:

[E]vents have moved with such speed that many of the poets –
who, alas, are not political animals – have been unable to keep
pace with them. The third decade of this century was one which
was characterized in its literature by a too often indiscriminate worshipping of letters "of social significance" ... The war
and the alignment of war has wrought havoc with the cut-and-
dried intellectual compartments of the red robins, piping social
significance.[97]

Tentatively positioned among English-language Canadian writers,
Jewish writers were diffident about developing provocative themes
and motifs to examine the war and its victims. In a 1945 review of
Irving Layton's first collection of poems, *Here and Now*, Klein suggested that it was "regrettable" that although the author was a Jew,
"this particular aspect of Layton's heritage is the theme of only two
poems in this volume."[98] In normal times of peace and ease, this type
of reviewer's rebuke would seem parochial, an example of a reader's
recognition of what's not in a book rather than an appreciation of
what is. But a 1945 review by Canada's pre-eminent Jewish writer of
a poet in line to become his protégé is significant. In wartime, who
could write directly and with comprehension of the Jewish disaster in Europe if not a figure such as Layton? Klein does not explore
this absence in Layton's first book in any further detail. Rather, he
acknowledges indirectly what I have argued in this essay – that Jewishness, in mainstream Canadian literary culture, was still a mere
shadow by the end of the Second World War.

In an earlier piece published in the *Canadian Jewish Chronicle*,
Klein acknowledged the absence of appropriate voices to address the
war. Here, in the summer of 1942, he reflects on Chaim Nachman
Bialik's "The City of Slaughter," an anguished poem the author
composed in Hebrew and translated into Yiddish, in response to
the 1903 Kishinev pogrom. The poem quickly came to represent
an archetypal response to a modern Jewish massacre. The choice
of Bialik at a time when, as Klein puts it, the Jewish "cause is the
victim of so many reverses," reflects his sense of his audience and
its literary touchstones drawn from the context of Jewish history,
within which he interprets the German devastation.[99] The terms of
reference in "Bialik Thou Shouldst Be Living at This Hour" exclude
mainstream non-Jewish readers entirely. They are, Klein knows,
beyond his reach. As he writes, in 1942, the victims of Belzec and
Treblinka haunt his words, yet they are not named.

NOTES

1   www.collectionscanada.gc.ca/massey.
2   Keith, "How New Was *New Provinces*?"
3   Klein, "Out of the Pulver and the Polished Lens," 33–4.
4   Klein, "Soirée of Velvel Kleinburger," 35.
5   This approach is familiar in Canadian letters from the work of poets such as Duncan Campbell Scott, in their effort to describe encounters with native Canadians. Most famous is Scott's 1894 sonnet "The Onondaga Madonna," in which a native child is described as having a "primal warrior gleaming from his eyes."
6   Collin, *The White Savannahs*, 208.
7   Ibid., 219.
8   Ibid., 221.
9   Anderson, "Introduction to the Kraus Reprint Edition," iv.
10 Klein, *Huit Poemes Canadiens*, 14.
11 Gallant, "Good Morning and Goodbye," 1.
12 Gallant, "Three Brick Walls," 6.
13 Gallant, "Varieties of Exile," 149.
14 Foerster, "Germany as She Really Is," 250.
15 Norsman, "One Nazi Victory," 285–6.
16 Ibid., 248.
17 A recent consideration of the work of John Updike notes the absence in his youthful correspondence of any sustained discussion of key contemporary events, such as the Korean War or McCarthyism (Tanenhaus, "Write, Rewrite, Publish [Tweak]: A Record of John Updike at Work").
18 Birney, "Hands," *Now is Time*, 13.
19 Ibid., 14.
20 Birney, "On Going to the Wars," 38.
21 Ibid., 39.
22 King, *Voices of Victory: Representative Poetry of Canada in Wartime*, v.
23 Ibid., v–vi.
24 Ibid., 1.
25 Ibid., 50.
26 This poem appeared first in the Chicago-based journal *Poetry* in August 1942.
27 Klein, "A Psalm of Abraham, Concerning that Which He Beheld Upon the Heavenly Scarp," 97.
28 This poem appeared first in the *Canadian Jewish Chronicle* in April 1940, followed by the American *Menorah Journal* in the summer of that year.

29 Smith, *The Book of Canadian Poetry: A Critical and Historical Anthology*,
    1:390.

30 Klein, *Huit Poemes*, 14.

31 Smith, *The Book of Canadian Poetry*, 391.

32 Graham, "Economics of Refugees," 8.

33 Graham, *Earth and High Heaven*, 149–50.

34 Ibid., 232.

35 Ibid., 31–2.

36 Ibid., 126.

37 Ibid., 255.

38 Graham, "Economics," 8.

39 Graham, *Earth*, 21.

40 www.armedserviceseditions.com (accessed 21 July 2010).

41 Cameron, "The Wrong Time and the Wrong Place: Gwethalyn Graham,
    1913–1965," 156.

42 In the 2 September 1944 instalment of *Earth and High Heaven*, *Collier*'s
    ran a lengthy editorial note that began: "In serializing Gwethalyn
    Graham's novel, Earth and High Heaven, Collier's feels that it is per-
    forming a public service. The novel is not only a poignant love story, but
    also an outspoken and unbiased discussion of the 'Jewish problem,' so
    called, as it affects many intelligent Jews and Gentiles in both Canada and
    the United States today ... Jews and Gentiles alike, we think, can profit
    from a reading of Earth and High Heaven. We believe this book will make
    a solid and valuable contribution to the cause of informed and enlight-
    ened tolerance in a war-wracked world ... This belief of ours is backed up
    by many leaders in this and related fields of thought and controversy to
    whom we showed the manuscript before publication began."

43 W.J. Hurlow, review of *Earth and High Heaven*, *Ottawa Citizen*, 21 Octo-
    ber 1944, 13.

44 Dorothy Bromley, "Fair Play for Jews Demanded," *Globe and Mail*, 3
    October 1944, 13.

45 W.A. Deacon, "Canadian Novel Challenges Montreal's Race Prejudice,"
    Globe and Mail, 7 October 1944, 10.

46 Ibid.

47 Ibid.

48 MacGillivray, "Letters in Canada: 1944. Fiction," 267.

49 Ibid., 267–8.

50 Lower, review of *Earth and High Heaven*, 326.

51 Ibid., 328.

52 Ibid.

53   Stanley, "Voices in the Wilderness," 173.
54   Ibid., 175.
55   Glassco, review of *Earth and High Heaven*, 33.
56   R. Allen, *Home Made Banners*, 14.
57   Ibid., 12–13.
58   Ibid., 39.
59   Ibid., 46–7.
60   Ibid., 192–3.
61   Ibid.
62   Ibid., 194.
63   Ibid., 198.
64   Ibid., 199.
65   Ibid., 201.
66   Ibid., 200, 203.
67   Ibid., 202.
68   R. Allen, *The Man from Oxbow: The Best of Ralph Allen*, 55.
69   Stuewe, *The Storms Below: The Turbulent Life and Times of Hugh Garner*, 80.
70   Ibid., 76, 80.
71   Verduyn, *Dear Marian, Dear Hugh: The MacLennan-Engel Correspondence*, 48.
72   Garner, *Storm Below*, 111.
73   Ibid., 26–7.
74   This figure makes a conspicuous appearance in Lucy Maud Montgomery's 1908 novel *Anne of Green Gables*, where he appears with a "big box of interesting things" from which he sells Anne hair dye "warranted" to turn her red hair "a beautiful raven black." Instead, it turns her hair green, resulting in a "clipped head" (174–6).
75   Garner, *Storm Below*, 131–2.
76   Ibid., vii.
77   Ibid., 136.
78   Ibid., 137.
79   Garner, *One Damn Thing after Another*, 81–90.
80   Stuewe, *The Storms*, 90.
81   Richler, *Oh Canada! Oh Quebec! Requiem for a Divided Country*, 78.
82   Ibid., 81.
83   This aspect of Quebec history remains contested terrain, with Richler's view providing the most sustained criticism of the role of antisemitism in the prewar and wartime culture and political life of the province. A telling contrast is revealed by three related essays: John Hellman's "Monasteries,

Miliciens, War Criminals: Vichy France/Quebec, 1940–50," Chris Lyons'
"'Children who read good books usually behave better, and have good
manners': The Founding of the Notre Dame de Grace Library for Boys
and Girls, Montreal, 1943," and Josef Schmidt's "Lionel Groulx's *L'Appel
de la race* Revisited." The articles' approach to wartime history is notably divergent, in particular in Schmidt's argument – contrary to Richler's
– that Groulx's use of the word "race" should not lead us to link his book
with other fascist manifestos of its time: "[C]ontrary to the modern understanding, Groulx's novel is not about race but about culture, and a very
specific culture … and in this novel there is no anti-Semitic slant" (152).
Schmidt, notably, makes the latter claim without any direct reference
to passages in the book. Lyons's piece on libraries in wartime Montreal
reflects the peculiar lack of English-language libraries in the city and the
hostility, at the time, of clergy toward the dissemination of information
outside its control. In the French context, parish and church-run libraries
were predominately filled with religious material. This depiction of wartime culture complements Richler's views. The most disturbing of the three
essays is Hellman's study of the relationship of Quebec elites to those of
Vichy France. Published after Richler's work on Quebec history in 1997,
it could easily buttress his beliefs regarding the power structure in Quebec
leading up to and during the Second World War. Hellman focuses on the
strenuous efforts made by church, business, and political elites to protect
French pro-Nazi rightists, some of whom had pursued, tortured, and exe-
cuted French resistance fighters (543). Having been hidden in monasteries in France, these figures found haven in the same institutions in Quebec.
These three essays, admittedly, circle the issues at stake in this study, yet
they provide key elements of context and outlook from the times, which
help us read Richler's non-fiction and his novels dealing with such themes.

84   Groulx, *The Iron Wedge/L'Appel de la race*, 15–17.
85   Wilson, "A Reporter at Large: O Canada. An American's Notes on Can-
     adian Culture," 2:116.
86   Roy, "Palestine Avenue," 55.
87   Ibid., 55, 58.
88   Ibid., 63.
89   Roy, *Where Nests the Water Hen*, 24.
90   Reid, *The Shouting Signpainters: A Literary and Political Account of Que-
     bec Revolutionary Nationalism*, 110.
91   Ibid., 103.
92   Ibid., 129–31.
93   See chapter 4, by Rebecca Margolis, in this volume.

94 "Hitler Plans Ghetto State for Jews in Poland: Three Million Jews Face
     Misery and Starvation," *Jewish Western Bulletin*, 24 November 1939, 1.
95 "Peretz Hirshbein Famous Jew. Author to Lecture," *Jewish Western Bul-
     letin*, 9 June 1944, 1.
96 Klein, "The Decencies Had Perished with the Stukas," review of *Dunkirk*
     by E.J. Pratt, 206.
97 Ibid.
98 Klein, "New Writers Series No. 1," review of *Here and Now* by Irving
     Layton, 215.
99 Klein, "Bialik Thou Shouldst Be Living at This Hour," 35.

7

Claiming Equality for Canadian Jewry: The Struggle for Inclusion, 1930–1945

JAMES WALKER

After waiting for almost two hours, the girl in charge told me very politely that I am Jewish and only Gentile girls were needed. I consider that a very great injustice ... Jewish boys are giving their lives in the war just as the Gentiles.

Affidavit of Norma Sherman, applicant for a job in the war effort

The quest for equal rights could be considered an abiding theme in Canadian Jewish history, one that acquired a particular urgency against the backdrop of the years under review in this volume. The obstacle to equality was antisemitism, variously rationalized and expressed but with one common feature: exclusion. In the period under study, exclusion did not just relate to keeping out Jewish refugees from Europe. In Canada itself, Jews were excluded from or restricted within certain occupations, university programs, summer resorts, beaches and hotels, residential districts, and social and recreational clubs. While occupational and residential discrimination may have had the most intimate impact on Jewish lives, none of the manifestations of antisemitism can be considered trivial. Denial of access to a beach or tennis club violated the principle of equality; it demonstrated and reinforced, in the minds of non-Jews, that Jews belonged apart, that they were not equal to other Canadian citizens. It was the principle of equality that was assaulted by antisemitism, and all its symptoms participated in that assault. The fundamental "cause" of this phenomenon was believed to be ignorance, and efforts to overcome it therefore focused on dispelling the ignorance by providing corrective information and insisting that Canadian Jews did in fact belong, that they deserved to be considered equal.

The Jewish community of Canada is justifiably celebrated for leading the movement for racial equality in the postwar era. Yet many of the tactics employed after 1945 were pioneered between 1930 and 1945; that they were more successful in the later period is testimony to the effect of changing context rather than any sudden revolution in Jewish concerns and methods. Perhaps because of the postwar successes, the earlier activities have suffered in comparison. The prevailing image in the published literature is of a non-assertive, even submissive community, practising at best a "quiet diplomacy."[1]

Closer examination, however, reveals many parallels between the two eras. The research presented in this chapter does not show that previous interpretations were wrong, only that they are incomplete. It is true that Canadian Jews were generally polite, respectful, and diplomatic when confronting the barriers to their equality, but there were also recurring examples of legislative initiatives, legal challenges, public campaigns, direct conflict, and coalitions with allies.

There is a perceptible consistency in the objectives of Canadian Jewry throughout this history. The means evolved according to experience and to suit the circumstances, but the most dramatic change after the Second World War was how their claim to equality was articulated and especially how it was received by the mainstream. In the era being examined here, the claim was based on British justice and fair play, which if implemented according to their underlying principles would result in equality for all citizens. This was a sincere expectation of Canadian Jews, for at that time "to be British" meant to participate in an empire made up of subjects representing all "races" and creeds, united in their relationship with the Crown. Only "aliens," who did not share in that mystical relationship, could legitimately be excluded from any privilege normally enjoyed by a British subject. Or so went the rhetoric. At the same time, British tradition protected certain rights – freedom of association and freedom of expression, for example – that would permit one category of British subject to disassociate itself from another category, to malign it in speech or print, and to exclude it from participation in any activity, location, or occupation without restrictions imposed by government or public morality. It is in the conflict between these two "British" traditions – of fair play on the one hand

and freedom from interference on the other – that the battle between Canadian antisemitism and the Jewish claim for equality was contended between 1930 and 1945.

This chapter seeks to illustrate how Canadian Jews addressed the antisemitic restrictions they faced in their daily lives and how they grounded their claim to equality on principles then current in Canadian discourse. In the early 1930s they were "warming up," in the sense that a structure had not yet been organized to conduct a focused campaign. Individuals launched pioneering attempts to stifle the sources of their oppression, with limited success, revealing the potential benefits of cooperation and unity. The resurrection of the Canadian Jewish Congress in 1934 was the result, offering an opportunity for a more concerted "taking aim" at the problem of antisemitism. In the context of the Great Depression, of Hitler's adoption in 1933 of antisemitism as German state policy, of German-sponsored antisemitic organizations in Canada, and of the very contradictions inherent in the British traditions to which Canadian Jews could appeal, the efforts of the mid-1930s can be seen as remarkable. With the coming of war in 1939, the scene shifted again, introducing another distinct phase in the struggle for equality by and for the Jews of Canada, in which "scoring points" occurred to a newly significant degree. But while organized Nazi and fascist parties were driven underground and a new moral currency could be derived from a war against an antisemitic enemy, new rationalizations for Jewish exclusion had to be confronted. The story ends in 1945, not with victory over antisemitism but with a firm foundation laid for the systematic campiagn led by Canadian Jews against racial inequality in all its forms in the postwar decades.

WARMING UP, 1930–1934

The year 1930 was by no means the beginning of antisemitism in Canada, but it was the beginning of a cycle of events of increasing turbulence, which arose first in Quebec. The intrusion of industrialization and urbanization into a traditionally rural culture gave French Canadians the sense that their equilibrium was being upset by forces from outside their own community, provoking a resurgence of nationalism and resentment against "foreigners." Jews became a target of a more generalized xenophobia, for they were the largest non-British or non-French minority in Montreal. With their Yiddish background and their orientation toward the anglophone sectors of the economy and community, Jews were portrayed as representative of the threat to Quebec's integrity.[2] Unlike the rest of Canada, in Quebec the church often promoted the sense that Jews did not belong. The nationalist spirit was epitomized in the teachings of the priest and historian Lionel Groulx, who presented Canadian history as a contest between "races": on one side, "a stock that is more princely than any on earth" and on the other, "barbarians," aliens, the forces of cosmopolitanism. Groulx was a leading contributor to the journal *L'Action nationale* in 1933, in which there were calls to deprive Jewish Canadians of their civil and political rights, including the franchise, and to stifle any further Jewish immigration.[3]

A precipitating event launching intensified antisemitism in Quebec was provided by a 1930 controversy over the education of Jewish children, when the provincial government introduced a bill to permit Jews to establish their own school commission. Although the bill was passed, it was rescinded in the face of vehement public protest and because a divided Jewish community could not agree on its terms.[4] The issue seemed to demonstrate that Jews were attempting to upset the historical balance between Catholics and Protestants, French and English, and were demanding privileges to which they had no legitimate claim. The negativity generated in the schools debate reverberated throughout the decade, fuelling resentment against Jews that affected Quebec attitudes toward Jewish immigration in the later 1930s.[5] The schools dispute offered antisemite Adrien Arcand "a departure point for an assault on the legal status of Canadian Jews." Through a series of weekly newspapers, *Le Goglu*, *Le Miroir*, and *Le Chameau*, Arcand and his colleague Joseph Ménard issued a torrent of fascist and antisemitic venom, insisting among other things that Jews should be denied citizenship rights and ultimately expelled from Canada.[6]

It was in response to Arcand's racist diatribes that a Jewish member of the Quebec assembly, Peter Bercovitch, introduced a bill to enable individual members of a maligned group to obtain an injunction to halt publication of libellous material, even if that individual was not specifically mentioned in the publication. In introducing his bill in February 1932, Bercovitch explained that not only Jews but any nationality or religion could benefit from this restriction and that no financial damages or other punishments were allowed under his proposal; it would merely give a judge "the power to issue an injunction to restrain the repeated publication of libel against any nationality or race." His seconder, Joseph Cohen, evoked Quebec's long history of toleration toward minorities, and toward Jews in particular, for it was in Lower Canada in 1832 that Jews were the first in the British Empire to gain civil equality. But coming upon the heels of the schools controversy, the bill could be interpreted as yet another move by the Jews of Quebec to gain "special privileges," and the provincial press declared this to be tantamount to censorship. In any case, the opponents argued, existing law already protected Jews and other minorities, so the new bill was unnecessary. Rationalizing that if Arcand were ignored he would simply disappear, Premier Taschereau had a government member move to refer the Bercovitch bill to a special committee. It was still there when the legislative session ended, so the bill died with no further discussion.[7]

The Jews of Quebec had in effect been challenged to test existing law, having been told that they were already fully protected without special legislation. Cohen rose to the challenge, acting as attorney for the Lachine fruit merchant Erucham Abugov in the summer of 1932. He charged that Arcand and Ménard had damaged Abugov's business by publishing appeals to Quebec shoppers not to buy from Jewish stores, claiming they were inevitably dirty and ridden with disease. The judge denounced the malicious publications, pointing out that by challenging minority rights Arcand and his associates were undermining the very system that protected French Canada. But he declared that he was compelled to follow the policy implicit in the legislature's rejection of the Bercovitch bill. "It is now for the Legislature to find the remedy which at present is not available," he concluded.[8] The problem remained unsolved.

The legislative route to overcome the impact of antisemitism was at the same time being considered in Ontario. The target, interestingly, was discriminatory practices in the insurance industry. One might not think of insurance as a first priority for legislative protection when Jews faced so many barriers in employment and housing, but without insurance it was difficult to purchase a home and impossible to run a business or professional office. Some companies charged higher premiums for Jews, up to ten times the normal rate, and some refused to cover Jews at all. The alleged justification was that Jews presented a greater risk than non-Jewish clients. In 1932 E. Frederick Singer, the first Jewish member of the Ontario legislature, successfully introduced an amendment to the Insurance Act stating, "Any licensed insurer which discriminates unfairly between risks within Ontario because of the race or religion of the insured shall be guilty of an offence."[9] No penalties were prescribed in the new Insurance Act, and the burden of proof rested on the complainant; still, the "Singer amendment" was significant. It established the principle that since the companies required a licence from the public to operate their business, the public could set conditions on how the licencees should behave. Furthermore, the concept of "fairness" was included in the amendment, and discrimination on grounds of "race" or religion was declared to be an offence.

Later that summer of 1932, Toronto Jewish Alderman J.J. Glass applied the same principle to restrict the "Gentiles Only" or similar signs that began to appear on Toronto Island's beaches. Island land was owned by the city, and as chair of the Toronto Parks Commission, Glass inserted a clause in leases to city-owned property prohibiting discriminatory notices without the commission's approval.[10] But this promising momentum was not maintained. In the 1933 legislative session, Tory backbencher Argue Martin, a non-Jewish member from Hamilton, introduced a bill to outlaw public advertisements and signs that announced discrimination on the basis of "race" or religion, with penalties of up to $500 for offenders. His bill did not interfere with private communications announcing discriminatory practices; it simply prevented "gratuitous insults" in public. The bill made it to second reading, but the Legal Bills committee then dropped it, on the grounds that legislation was not the appropriate cure for discrimination, and merely recommended a resolution condemning the posting of discriminatory signs in public. Signs that had already been taken down at the urging of Toronto City Council then appeared again "with an even greater brazenness," the *Yidisher zhurnal* reported. "The rejection of the Martin bill ... gave the antisemities a kind of unofficial license." As with the failure of the Bercovitch bill, the fate of Martin's attempted bill could be read as "a stamp of approval" for continued defamation of Jews.[11]

All this was happening at the same time Hitler's Nazis were forming a government in Germany. As noted earlier in this volume, Canadians were kept informed of German events – the April laws, the persecution of Jewish citizens, the boycott of Jewish businesses, and public violence – through the *Toronto Star*'s Berlin correspondent Pierre van Paassen and stories picked up by other Canadian newspapers. Immediately, a series of protest rallies erupted across Canada, from Halifax to Vancouver, with thousands of participants and speeches from prominent Canadian Jews, but also from mayors, government ministers, Christian clergy, and labour leaders. On Sunday, 2 April, a provincial day of protest in Ontario endorsed by the premier, many churches included special prayers for the Jews of Germany in their regular services; public meetings, with ten thousand people at the 6 April Montreal meeting alone, passed resolutions demanding that the government make urgent diplomatic representations to Germany, and as the gathering in Halifax put it, "voice our protest to the German Hitlerites against the [anti-Jewish] atrocities."[12]

This gesture of support was, however, ominously overshadowed by a counter-demonstration held in Montreal denouncing the anti-German rallies and the participation of Christians in a Jewish-sponsored event. At the counter-rally, organized by the newly formed nationalist youth movement, Jeune-Canada, Jews were vilified as unassimilable, communist sympathizers, fomenters of social revolution, and useless parasites. Allegations of Jewish power, financial control, and plans to dominate the world were trotted out to convince the crowd that German atrocities were grossly exaggerated and, to the extent that they were true, were justified by the bad behaviour of German Jews.[13] There was already in place in Quebec a program of economic nationalism known as "Achat chez nous." Ostensibly meant to encourage French Canadians to patronize French Canadian business, the movement became an anti-Jewish boycott after 1933, endorsed by leading newspapers, the St-Jean-Baptiste Society, and many clergy. The influential Abbé Groulx urged Quebecers, to "Do as everyone else does, do as every ethnic group does: *Buy at home!*' and in six months, a year, the Jewish problem would be solved."[14]

Events in Toronto supplied further evidence of the threat faced by Canadian Jewry and of the readiness of its members to respond in self-defence. In the city's eastern Beaches district, a Swastika Club was formed to "keep the Beaches clean" from "obnoxious" behaviour. Club members patrolled the district, intending to intimidate lewd and inconsiderate bathers who changed their clothes in cars or even on the beach, made disturbing noise throughout their visit, and then left their mess behind them. Although some club members claimed that they were looking for any offenders, the Swastika emblem was a clue to their actual intent, and there were slogans and songs making their anti-Jewish purpose explicit.[15] Young Toronto

Jews, their sensitivity brought to the boiling point by images of German hordes hailing the Swastika, took matters into their own hands. They tore the Swastika badges from the shirts and bathing suits of club members, and several violent clashes occurred. At a more diplomatic level, the mayor called together senior members of the League for the Defence of Jewish Rights and Swastika Club leaders, in an attempt to end the disturbances.

Despite the mayor's efforts, an even greater conflagration occurred less than a week after the meeting, when a gang of non-Jewish youths unfurled a homemade Swastika flag at a baseball game between a Jewish team and a non-Jewish team held at Christie Pits Park. Jewish fans, their ranks swelled by recruitment of Jewish men in the neighbourhood who were prepared to join a fight, attacked the flagbearers and their supporters. As many as ten thousand people reportedly participated in the melee, many wielding lead pipes, baseball bats, and broom handles as weapons. Known as "the riot at Christie Pits," this night of violence is often portrayed as a mob attack on Jews. From contemporary newspapers and subsequent scholarship, however, it seems that Jews were responding to provocation and rather than being victims of an attack, were the initiators of much of the violence in an effort to silence and punish their tormentors. As one Jewish participant told a *Toronto Star* reporter, "Rather than submit to the outrages that have been perpetrated against our race, we would die on the streets. This is the feeling amongst the younger element of our people ... These boys are all British. They have been brought up in Canadian schools, and have learned something of the British bulldog idea never to give up without a fight. The teaching of passive resistance no longer carries any weight with them." Mayor Stewart issued a statement declaring that the Swastika emblem "is provocative and tends to incite riotous conduct and a disturbance of the peace," and he threatened to prosecute "to the full extent of the law" anyone who displayed the Swastika in Toronto thereafter.[16]

The young men and women of the Swastika Club were not of course genuine Nazis, but neither was the choice of that emblem coincidental. They were, in the language of the time, "Jew-baiters," antisemites intent on excluding Jews from city parks and beaches. The League for the Defence of Jewish Rights was correct to recognize something deeper in these juvenile antics: "While we know the incident was trivial," it announced in a formal statement, "Toronto cannot afford to act in the spirit which is contrary to the spirit and traditions of Great Britain. Hitlerism is subversive of Canadian ideals." Civic officials and leading clergy, as cited in the Toronto newspapers, had no sympathy for the pseudo-Nazis, calling them un-British, un-Christian, and un-Canadian.[17] Meanwhile, there were organized, politically motivated fascists and Nazis in Canada, importing and distributing Nazi propaganda.[18] In Winnipeg in September 1933, William Whittaker, formerly an organizer for the Ku Klux Klan, founded a fascist monthly periodical, the *Canadian Nationalist*, along with a group, modelled on the German Nazis, which marched through the North End of the city in brown-shirted uniforms. In Quebec, Arcand held the first meeting of his Parti national social chrétien in February 1934, with Swastika flags and blue-shirted followers performing the Heil Hitler salute.[19]

In the face of this domestic onslaught, and against the backdrop of spiralling Nazi persecutions abroad, there arose "a definite resurgence of Jewish feeling, and a greater Jewish consciousness, with a corresponding manifestation of greater interest and participation in Jewish communal and organizational life."[20] A hitherto highly fragmented Jewish community recognized a need for unity and coordinated action. Within a week of the 6 April mass meeting in Montreal, the committee that had organized the protest began discussing a proposal to convene a nationwide Canadian Jewish Congress (CJC), a plan that coalesced in succeeding months as Montreal Jewry united for this purpose. In May 1933, the Western Canadian Jewish Congress Committee was formed in Winnipeg, voting to re-establish a national congress. A month later the League for the Defence of Jewish Rights in Toronto hosted a national meeting where the foundation was laid for the revival of the CJC, which had not met since 1919.[21] The individual efforts by Bercovitch, Cohen and Abugov, Singer, Glass, and Martin had not been effective in confronting Canadian antisemitism or stemming the defamatory flood that kept it afloat.

TAKING AIM, 1934–1939

Delegates gathered in Toronto in January 1934 to mobilize their resources for self-defence.[22] Discussion topics revealed the community's urgent needs: countering German propaganda, seeking admission to Canada (and to Palestine) for Jewish refugees, combatting anti-Jewish prejudice by educating the Canadian public, gathering statistics to illustrate the Jewish contributions to Canada, taking legal action against antisemites and seeking protective legislation, and fostering Jewish culture and education. The revived CJC recognized three relatively autonomous regions, centred in Montreal, Toronto, and Winnipeg. Montreal MP Sam Jacobs was elected president, and Labour Zionist H.M. Caiserman was appointed general secretary. The battle was engaged.[23]

In 1934 the underlying problem of antisemitism seemed to be ignorance about Jews on the part of their fellow Canadians. An attack on the ignorance would undermine prejudice and discrimination caused by misunderstanding, since it was thought that discrimination meant "putting down what you're not up on." An early strategic decision was to form an alliance with sympathetic Christians to undertake this aspect of the program. Rabbi Maurice N. Eisendrath of Toronto's Holy Blossom Temple took this initiative in partnership with Dr Claris E. Silcox of the United Church of Canada.[24] The two men organized a seminar on Jewish-Gentile Relations, which was held over two days in Toronto in April 1934. The announced purpose of the meeting was the "elimination of imagined differences" in order to produce "a finer appreciation of each other and a deeper sense of brotherhood" between the two groups. The crowning event was a speech by the lieutenant-governor of Ontario, Herbert A. Bruce, entitled "Our Heritage of Tolerance," which Ben Kayfetz later called "one of the landmarks of positive public relations during the painful decade." Bruce reflected on the suffering of the Jews over the centuries, on the contributions of Jews to art and learning, and he reminded his audience of the "priceless heritage of tolerance, the precious gift of freedom which this city and this Dominion, as a part of a great Empire, hold in trust for this and future generations."[25]

Out of the seminar came the Committee on Jewish-Gentile Relationships, with Eisendrath and Silcox as co-chairs and an administrative committee of five Jews and five gentiles, to undertake the assault on ignorance and prejudice. Until its reorganization in 1940, this committee carried a major share of counter-propaganda conducted by and on behalf of Canadian Jewry. One of its chief activities was publishing and distributing pamphlets, such as "Facts and Fables about the Jews" by English Anglican theologian James Parkes, which directly confronted the most prevalent stereotypes. The pamphlet ended with a statement in bold print:

The British Empire and British democracy are based upon the principle of justice and toleration for all races and creeds. This is a principle to be cherished and preserved against the falsehoods disseminated by propagandists endeavouring to disunite Canada, and using anti-Semitism as a smoke screen behind which they mask their real objectives. Be Guided By Facts – Not Fables!

Committee publications insisted that Jews were not all communists, not international financiers, and not responsible for the death of Jesus. Over 100,000 copies of these various publications were distributed.[26] The committee also arranged pulpit exchanges between Jewish rabbis and Protestant ministers, "fellowship breakfasts" in churches and synagogues, and extensive speaking tours around Ontario and beyond for the co-chairs, who also spoke on regional and national radio, gave interviews to the press, and replied to negative newspaper articles and editorials. Parkes came from England to lecture across Canada, and Silcox criticized Christian clergy who were found to be making antisemitic statements in their sermons. Letters sent to the committee were answered personally by Eisendrath or Silcox, addressing questions (usually from non-Jews) about Jews and Judaism.[27]

The counter-propaganda effort, though vigorously performed, was not particularly aggressive or confrontational. It fitted generally with the "polite" image of the prewar struggle against antisemitism. There was, however, another campaign extending throughout this period that contradicts any notion of passivity or isolation: the boycott of German products that lasted from 1933 to 1939. This campaign incorporated a range of tactics – lobbying the powerful, legislative attempts, mass publicity, private pressure, research, and alliances with non-Jewish supporters – tactics similar to those used after the war. The boycott was "concrete action" and "our only effective weapon of defence," a CJC bulletin declared. "Mere protests against Nazi barbarism are a waste of effort! Economic strangulation is the only civilized method to combat the Nazi pest." J.J. Glass, chair of the Toronto Boycott Committee, claimed that since "the Nazi regime is deaf to the protests of world public opinion, the only means of diminishing the danger of the Hitlerite threat is through the economic boycott." Germany was perceived not only as the cause of suffering for the Jews of Europe but the main source of antisemitic propaganda in Canada and therefore at the root of the issues that most concerned Canadian Jewry. Until September 1939, the boycott was "the moral substitute for war," and a movement was conducted to recruit every Jew and every other Canadian to the battle.[28]

Even before the CJC plenary of January 1934, each of the three geographical regions had established committees to organize boycotts of German goods and services. The first meeting of the Dominion Executive Committee of the CJC, in November 1933, had formed a coordinating committee to manage the boycott nationally. The detail and precision were worthy of a military campaign. Under the main Boycott Committee there was a Vigilance Committee to monitor cooperation with the boycott, a Publicity Committee to enlist merchants and citizens into the boycott action, a Speakers' Committee to address trade meetings and community organizations, a Research Bureau to discover and suggest alternate sources of supplies for both manufacturers and consumers, and a host of industry-specific committees ranging from silk producers to medical suppliers.

First, a general letter was sent out to importers and merchants who were dealing with German material. The letter had two versions. The one sent to Jewish companies exclaimed, "It seems inconceivable that any Jewish firm or individual would willingly and knowingly lend encouragement and support to [the Nazi] regime"; the gentile letter made the appeal "in the name of humanity and righteousness" and reminded recipients of the "monstrous persecution of innocent men and women on the sole ground of race, religion or political conviction." Both letters offered assistance in finding replacements for any German goods or services the company might require. If the boycott invitation was ignored, a follow-up letter was sent to the company, followed if possible by a personal visit by members of the appropriate industry committee. Recalcitrant Jewish merchants could be called before the committee to explain themselves. For consumers, there was a pledge card with a commitment to "boycott Nazi goods and services as long as the present persecution continues." Pamphlets and mimeographed circulars warned the public that the money they spent on German goods would be returned to them in the form of Nazi propaganda and eventually as weapons of war. And because German materials were not always easy to identify, the CJC lobbied for effective "marking laws" so that consumers could be confident of the origin of their purchases.[29]

The targeted products were numerous, and success varied from one to the other. For example, the federal government agreed to adopt a marking law for gloves but not for velvet; use of German velvet was halted by the refusal of Jewish garment workers to cut material of doubtful origin. The largest and most intricate campaign was conducted in the coal industry. In its quest for foreign exchange, Germany "dumped" coal into the international market at a reduced price, making it attractive to Canadian importers. As the boycott gained publicity, certain dealers mixed German with Welsh coal and sold the combination as if it were Welsh. The Boycott Committee contacted all the leading coal dealers and asked them to sign a pledge that they would not use German coal. To ensure compliance, the CJC insisted on access to company records, which were audited by a chartered accountant, and an experienced coal inspector was hired to examine stocks to see that they were uncontaminated with German product. The names of cooperating firms were then publicized in a series of pamphlets, in the tens of thousands, alerting consumers to the issue and urging them to buy from the "clean" cooperating companies. Coal dealers not listed evidently suffered, for there were several appeals by unlisted companies asking the CJC to permit them to join the boycott. At the urging of Toronto CJC leaders, the city council passed a by-law requiring bills of sale for coal sold in the city to be identified by country of origin. Montreal had a similar by-law under discussion when the outbreak of war in 1939 ended the boycott. The committee claimed that its activities had cost the Germans "at least 20,000 tons" in lost sales.[30]

Undoubtedly, the effectiveness of the boycott was restricted by the fact that the Canadian government throughout this period was actively promoting trade with Germany. One company encouraged by the CJC to join the boycott replied, "Why should we even discuss this matter with you when the government of our country is making every effort to further trade with Germany?" The city council of Kitchener, Ontario, passed a resolution opposing the boycott, and a federal cabinet minister publicly deplored the efforts of "certain groups" to boycott Germany and urged Canadians to purchase more German merchandise. Besides an apparent reduction in coal, the imports of furs from Germany dropped from approximately $300,000 in 1933 to around $15,000 in 1938 (perhaps explained by the dominance of Jewish members in the Furriers' Union).

Success with Jewish unions prompted a move to extend the boycott to non-Jewish labour. A sequence of Trades and Labor Congress annual conventions passed resolutions "not to purchase German-made goods or services so long as the German workers remain under the heel of the present dictator." Similar resolutions were passed at local Trades and Labor Councils, and the CJC conducted a campaign to have union locals form their own boycott committees, supplying them with draft resolutions and printed material for distribution. Pamphlets with titles such as *Fight Hitlerism, Destroyer of Organized Labor* emphasized that the trade union movement had been outlawed in Germany and that the use of slave labour enabled the Germans to undercut the prices of union-made exports internationally. The results are impossible to measure, but it is surely significant that 25,000 copies of *Fight Hitlerism* alone were distributed to Canadian workers, along with many similar publications and stickers bearing boycott slogans.[31]

Jewish leaders also sought to have legislation passed to outlaw group libel. An attempt to initiate an amendment to the federal Criminal Code in 1934 came to nothing,[32] but there was a more positive result in Manitoba. The inflammatory content of Whittaker's *Canadian Nationalist* prompted Jewish MLA Marcus Hyman to introduce a bill permitting action against group libel, which he modelled on the Bercovitch bill in Quebec. With government support, his bill was passed unanimously in March 1934 as the Manitoba Defamation Act. Almost immediately, the new law was tested in court by William V. Tobias, seeking an injunction against Whittaker for statements claiming that Jews regularly practised ritual murder. In February 1935, Justice Percival Montague granted the injunction and forbade Whittaker from publishing "any similar libels injuriously affecting those belonging to the Jewish race ... or faith."[33]

"Quiet diplomacy" was one other arm of the Jewish attack in the 1930s. In December 1933, Caiserman informed the chief commissioner of the RCMP of German hate literature being imported into Canada, explaining that he was doing so "because we are Canadian citizens, who wish to see harmony and good feeling prevail in our country, and that the fair name of Canada, which is the free home of many races should not be besmirched." The appeal worked, at least to some extent, for the commissioner of customs replied to Caiserman asking for assistance in identifying "the channels used for smuggling the matter in question into Canada" so that he could take action to suppress it.[34] Jews across the country were asked to keep clippings from local newspapers or any other community information that might indicate antisemitic tendencies.[35] An appeal to Anglo-Canadian democratic tradition had a positive effect on the

Canadian Radio Broadcasting Commission in April 1934, when a candidate for municipal office in Montreal used the radio to broadcast antisemitic election advertisements. Such public utterances were characterized by the CJC as "seditious" and a threat to "the tranquillity of the State." Within two hours of receiving a protesting telegram from Caiserman, the head of the radio commission had the offending messages withdrawn.[36]

Directing quiet protests to authorities was a tactic used frequently in Quebec toward the Roman Catholic hierarchy, for church publications and even parish pulpits were often used to disseminate antisemitism.[37] With church officials, understandably, it was Christian principles that were held to be violated by antisemitism; with political leaders, the appeal was more likely to be to "the principle of justice and toleration to all, irrespective of race or creed," which was the foundation of "British democracy." In Quebec, the appeal could be articulated "in the name of our fair province and the great French-Canadian race which inhabits it [and] in the name of British Justice and civilization." Often, connections were made by elected Jewish politicians whose own influence or relationships could provide an opportunity to protest against an offending sign, speech, or publication.[38] While success in these "quiet diplomacy" endeavours was limited, they do reveal the variety of specifically tailored arguments designed to evoke "fair play" from different elements in Canadian society.

An excellent insight into the thinking of the Jewish leadership in the mid-1930s is offered by a speech delivered by Rabbi Eisendrath to the CJC General Session in May 1936, entitled "How can we combat the forces which assail us?" He agreed that "the Jew alone cannot solve nor end this problem" but insisted that "he can do much to attenuate" the situation. First, he said, "we must solidify our ranks" through adherence to the CJC. To prevent a repeat of what was happening in Germany, Jews must mount a united and proactive counterattack, not just to challenge the slanders but to prevent the defamation from arising at all. Anglo-Saxon ideals are "among the noblest political aspirations that have ever been devised by man," he said, but it would be a mistake to rely on those ideals to overcome the "vitriolic canards" aimed at Jewish Canadians. He suggested that the name of the "anti-defamation committee" be changed to the "public relations committee," and he urged the CJC to press for more legislation like Manitoba's and to enrich it with programs to "educate, educate, educate." Ignorance could be confronted with "indisputable fact." The writings of Parkes and Silcox, for example, should be put in the hands of every minister and teacher in Canada so that Christian teachings about Jews could be "rewritten in the light of modern scientific research, fair play and historic justice." To inform the population of "the true status and character of the Jew," said Eisendrath, the CJC should establish chairs of Jewish studies at Canadian universities, sponsor nationwide "good-will tours" and other initiatives such as those being undertaken by the Committee on Jewish-Gentile Relationships. And Jewish conduct should not itself provide "legitimate causes of friction or antagonism." As he later added, "general exclusion of any people ... is certainly unBritish and the very antithesis of the genuine Christian spirit. But ... it behoves each one of us to remove any slightest provocation to such unBritish and unChristian conduct." In these and other speeches, Eisendrath asked Jews to demonstrate their loyalty by flying the Union Jack "on every possible occasion," show more sensitivity to the Christian Sabbath, and become more modest in behaviour and attire. In effect, he was arguing that Jews must overtly contradict the "alien" charge that apparently justified so much of the exclusion and discrimination they experienced.[39]

The sense of urgency was very real, and contemporary Jewish leaders perceived an increase in antisemitic activity as the 1930s progressed. In 1937 the CJC reported, "During the past four years we have witnessed an amazing growth of anti-Semitism. Manifestations of an intensified anti-Jewish sentiment have been springing up everywhere." This was, the report noted, "an entirely new type of antisemitism ... a transition from the sporadic and unorganized type of anti-Jewishness to national organizations directed by professional agents."[40] The Social Credit Party had gained power in Alberta in 1935, bringing into the mainstream of Canadian politics a doctrine that included an alleged international Jewish conspiracy to control the world through financial dominance.[41] A year later, the Union Nationale formed the government in Quebec, a party associated with Arcand's fascist movement and with an antisemitic secret society known as the Order of Jacques Cartier. The new premier, Maurice Duplessis, "espoused anti-Semitism as a political device," warning Quebec voters of a plot to settle 100,000 Jewish refugees in the province and accusing Jewish leaders such as Peter Bercovitch of communist sympathies.[42] And there was the preaching of Arcand himself, with a national convention in Toronto in July 1938, where blue-shirted troopers gave the Heil Hitler salute before an estimated audience of 2,500.[43]

The CJC sent out a series of letters to Jewish individuals and organizations warning them of the dire situation they faced: "Are we to make the same fatal mistake that the German Jews have made? What is your answer?" A professional-looking pamphlet was used in a membership drive in 1938 with photographs of Canadian fascists performing the infamous salute and warning, "It may happen here" and "Fascist legions are preparing to march in the streets of Montreal." Arcand had 15,000 members already, the pamphlet claimed, and his ranks were growing. Across the top of the pamphlet was the banner "The CJC is a bulwark against anti-semitism," and across the bottom, "As a Jew you must support the Congress."[44] The genuine fear felt by the leaders produced not only anxious letters but a determination to create a more effective program to defeat the forces ranged against Canadian Jews.

B'nai Brith had been active in Canada since 1875, and anti-defamation was very much a part of the organization's concern. About the time of the founding of the CJC, the Canadian Conference of B'nai Brith began making plans to establish an office of the Anti-Defamation League in Canada to intensify this aspect of its activity. The seriousness of the situation by the mid-1930s encouraged B'nai Brith and the CJC to explore the possibility of a common front, and an agreement was reached in February 1938 to create the Joint Public Relations Committee (JPRC) of the Canadian Jewish Congress and B'nai Brith. Even though the twenty-member National Council would have equal representation from each partner and there would be three regional committees similarly constituted, Item 12 in the agreement stated, "The CJC shall be the medium through which public statements will be made when necessary," thus making the congress the public face of the new committee.[45]

The newly minted JPRC launched an immediate and enhanced program of what was tellingly known as "public relations." This was to be proactive activity to eliminate the ignorance and misunderstanding which, according to the current problem definition, lay behind every disadvantage faced by Canadian Jews. Operating in tandem with the Committee on Jewish-Gentile Relationships, whose directors included the leaders of the Toronto-based Central Division JPRC, "corrective" literature was distributed; in its first year alone, 10,000 copies of 52 titles were sent to schools, libraries, churches, influential Canadian figures, and citizens included on a developing mailing list. A booth set up by the League of Nations Society handed out JPRC literature at the Canadian National Exhibition in August 1939. Church, youth, and labour conventions were supplied with anti-defamation material. The JPRC Central Division established a Legal Committee to study the possibility of instituting court action against the purveyors of antisemitism, and sent samples of antisemitic slander to federal, provincial, and civic authorities, followed by personal interviews with senior officials, to promote legislation that would provide the legal basis for court challenges. These were activities that were already underway, by the CJC, the Jewish-Gentile Committee, or B'nai Brith; what the JPRC did was to coordinate and amplify the program, with an injection of funds and professional expertise.[46]

Two very interesting statements appeared in 1939, offering a description of the kind of activity being undertaken at this time and the principles upon which the claim to equality was based. First to appear was a booklet entitled *Jewish Occupational Difficulties*, prepared by the CJC's Committee on Economic Problems. This committee was created in early 1939 to take practical measures to overcome the employment barriers faced by Canadian Jews.[47] The committee observed that "occupational concentration" characterized Jewish employment patterns. Concentration sets up a vicious circle: because of exclusion from certain fields, Jews create careers for themselves in a narrow range of opportunities, for example, self-employed professional occupations; this concentration then perpetuates stereotypes and furthers the growth of antisemitism and more exclusion. One activity for the committee was therefore "vocational guidance" to prepare young Jews for a more varied range of employment. This involved not only advice but actual training, with experienced workers enlisted to help train others.

The committee then approached employers to seek their cooperation. Its presentation emphasized the democratic principles of equality of opportunity, the ideals of humanitarianism and fair play: "The cloak of justice covers all Canadians," and "it cannot be torn along any line without being eventually torn in all directions until at last all our liberties and safeguards are destroyed." The employer would be asked to adopt a fair employment policy "under which merit is the determinant as to who shall be engaged," indicating the benefits to the company that would result. The committee was also concerned for the Jews who were denied employment. The rejected Jewish applicant could develop "personality problems" and diminished self-respect. Participating in an effort to combat discrimination, on the other hand, would counteract the feeling of inferiority occasioned by experiences of discrimination and give Jewish youths the feeling that they were defending their rights and would thus bolster their self-respect.[48]

Fairness, decency, democracy, the tradition of justice, and benefits to the individual and to society – these same principles were stressed in the second publication, *The Challenge of Anti-Semitism to Democracy*, by Claris Silcox. The pamphlet was the amalgamated message from the author's speeches during a tour of western Canada in 1939. He approached his subject "first as a Britisher who believes in fair play." He also spoke as a Canadian, concerned for national unity, which would be threatened if any minority group were to lose its equality rights. Then he was a clergyman, conscious of Christianity's debt to Judaism and ashamed of the treatment of Jews by the church. Finally, he spoke as a gentile, knowing that "the unhappy and pathological condition of the Jews in many lands is not the result of any inherent, inalienable racial characteristic" but the product of discrimination by gentiles: "The Jewish problem is therefore essentially not a Jewish problem at all – it is a Gentile problem, created by Gentiles and to be solved only by Gentile action." Ultimately, the solution was democracy, which was "more than a form of government": it demanded respect for each human individual, "endowed with certain inalienable rights." Silcox was not the last Canadian to indicate that the "real test of any nation's democracy is the way in which it treats its minorities." The well-being and continued freedoms of all Canadians were threatened by antisemitism, which he called "the spear-head of the totalitarian attack on democracy." "If it succeeds," he said, "democracy will fail."[49]

SCORING POINTS, 1939–1945

In a report in May 1940, the JPRC stated that the outbreak of war completely changed many of its functions. In a war ostensibly in support of freedom and equality the committee expected that discrimination would cease, but "Anti-Semitic sentiment, far from diminishing, increased spectacularly shortly after the declaration of war with Germany, and the PRC was faced with problems of vast and tragic proportions."[50] Nazi propaganda from Germany was interrupted by the war, and many of the leading pro-Nazi Canadians were interned and their organizations banned. To this extent, some of the chief problems identified by Canadian Jews in the preceding several years were greatly reduced. But new problems immediately emerged. The perception arose that this was a "Jewish war," ignited in order to punish Germany and relieve the persecuted Jews of Europe. Furthermore, this perception was attached to a widespread assumption that Jews were shirking their responsibilities and not volunteering for the Canadian forces. One popular joke asked, "What is the Jews' favourite song?" The answer: "Onward Christian Soldiers." At a Lake Erie beach in August 1942, a crowd attacked two Jews wearing civilian clothes, crying, "There goes a couple of Jews. Why don't you so-and-so Jews enlist and fight for your country? You're all yellow." One of the men attacked was actually a sergeant in the RCAF. In another case, a high-ranking officer stated in an interview that Jews were not supplying their fair share of recruits. Asked how many Jews he thought there were in Canada, he replied "two million." (This was at a time when the census showed little more than 170,000.) Anti-conscription riots in Quebec, particularly at the time of the plebiscite held on the issue, often targeted Jews and Jewish property; at least once, this also happened in Ontario, in Hawkesbury in April 1942.[51]

Obviously, there was a demand for new tactics, along with an intensification of some of the older tactics. The impressions about military service had to be exposed as falsehoods; the need for a broader program of "mutual understanding" was apparent, given the currency of the negative stereotypes; and there was increasing interest in a political offensive through passage of protective legislation. An early prong in the counterattack was to identify antisemitism with the enemy and to label local antisemites as a fifth column for Germany and the Nazis. By repudiating "the democratic principles of our Dominion," people who repeated antisemitic slurs were "subversive elements." Only Hitler could benefit from a campaign to divide Canadians along lines of "race" or creed, and any antisemitic activity was playing into his hands.[52] Caiserman managed an information system from CJC headquarters in Montreal, gathering material on organized antisemitism and feeding it to the authorities. In early 1940, for example, he discovered that Arcand, though outlawed, had revived his National Unity Party and was continuing to distribute literature with titles such as *Les Juifs et la guerre*; a CJC "mole" was planted in Arcand's organization, who supplied names and addresses of party members that were then passed on to the RCMP. The Civilian Morale Committee in Ottawa was sent copies of antisemitic publications, warning that interracial strife would damage the morale of the population and impede the war effort; and three antisemitic newspapers in Quebec were suppressed as "subversive" after a complaint from Caiserman.[53]

Much of the public education aspect of "public relations" continued to be conducted in cooperation with the Committee on Jewish-Gentile Relationships, which was reconstituted in 1940 as the Canadian Conference of Christians and Jews (CCCJ).[54] The CCCJ, with a paid staff, a Toronto office, and a board of fifty prominent Canadians, was designed to combat the "new kind of antisemitism." Unlike the earlier committee, the CCCJ would be membership-based, with a fee of one dollar per year. Rabbi Eisendrath then presented the CCCJ's "ambitious program" to the JPRC and negotiated an annual subsidy of about $4,000, consisting of $3,000 in salaries and the rest in office expenses. Silcox became the salaried half-time director, and his place as co-chair was taken by the Rev. E. Crossley Hunter. Rabbi Eisendrath remained as the other co-chair.[55]

Like its predecessor, the CCCJ issued numerous pamphlets dismissing common stereotypes about Jews with "factual" information: *Facts and Fables about Jews* (now approaching a circulation of 100,000) was issued in a new edition; *What They Say about Jews*, *Father Coughlin – His "Facts" and Arguments*, *Jewish Communism Is a Lie*, and many others were sent by the thousand to Canadian editors, ministers, teachers, libraries, and universities. The most ambitious publishing project was a monthly journal, *Fellowship*, edited by Silcox. Eight thousand copies of volume 1, number 1 were distributed across the country in June 1940. The various issues addressed themes similar in vein to the pamphlets, with articles such as "Fight Hitlerism in Canada," "The Jews and Arson," "The Foundations of Anti-Semitism," "Why We Continue to Fight Anti-Semitism in Wartime," "Fifth Columnists and Trojan Horses," and "The Jewish War Effort."[56] Silcox targeted special audiences, such as schoolteachers and labour leaders, attacking not only antisemitism but the very idea of "race." In addition, the CCCJ established a network of local round tables, usually in association with Protestant churches, "designed to sensitize the group as to the main problems in Jewish-Christian relationships," and for this purpose provided pamphlets, further-reading lists, discussion topics, ideas for social events, and suggested speakers.[57]

Immediately after war was declared, Samuel Bronfman, CJC president since January 1939, called together a special meeting in Montreal, where plans were formulated for a War Efforts Committee. The committee members were concerned to counteract the myth about Jewish "shirking," and thus it was considered essential to record and publicize Jewish enlistment numbers and accomplishments. The committee set up recruiting centres in Montreal and Toronto, and mounted a campaign to encourage every young Jewish man to enlist. A glossy four-page pamphlet was published in 1940 with photographs of Jewish men in uniform, both for public relations and as a recruitment device. The committee could report late in the war that more than 15,000 Jews had signed up, a figure representing an enlistment ratio higher than the national average. Numbers were constantly released to the press, along with stories of heroism and casualties in the field and of decorations earned. National publicity emphasizing Jewish patriotism was generated by a series of "Rededication" rallies held across Canada in October 1942, with addresses from Jewish and non-Jewish leaders exhorting Canadians to give their utmost support to the war.

Beginning in February 1944, the committee issued a monthly journal, *Jews in Uniform*, "the first Jewish military newspaper ever published," with accounts of Jewish participation in the war. In the same interest, the committee produced a series of children's comic books with Jewish heroes. "Comfort boxes" containing such items as razor blades, cigarettes, socks, and chocolate bars were sent to servicemen overseas. At home, the committee created sixteen Servicemen's Centres, equipped with lounge furniture and recreational equipment and staffed by several thousand Jewish volunteer women, where servicemen and servicewomen could relax when on leave. In a ten-month period in 1944, these centres received approximately 300,000 visitors, sometimes on a drop-in basis and sometimes for organized programs of games, dances, or concerts. Various subcommittees conducted a War Savings Campaign, a Victory Loan Drive, salvage campaigns, blood donor clinics, a Next-of-Kin League to bolster community morale, and letter writing to soldiers overseas and to families at home. It was an ambitious and extensive program, projecting a Jewish contribution to service personnel and the general public.[58]

The Jewish Labour Committee of Canada (JLC) conducted its own war efforts campaign through its base in the Jewish-dominated "needle trades" unions. The JLC sent relief to European refugees, including money, clothing, blankets, and medical supplies. JLC funds were used to establish soup kitchens and tea halls in Polish towns, and to support the anti-Nazi underground forces there. Its wartime publication, *Underground and On the Ground*, reported on convention resolutions and donations sent abroad. The December 1944 issue revealed that "the chief feature of our [JLC] work for the past three years consisted of aid to the Underground Movement in Europe," for which $100,000 had been contributed through the affiliated unions. In early 1945, the JLC commissioned an Ottawa research institute to write three articles on the Nazi extermination camps, which were sent to about four hundred daily and weekly newspapers in Canada to make ordinary Canadians aware of the danger posed by antisemitism.[59]

Another CJC endeavour illustrates the range of tactics adopted to produce equality rights. The campaign against employment discrimination in war industries involved research, lobbying, publicity, public protest, and alliances with like-minded groups. For years, private companies had been refusing to hire Jews, and help-wanted advertisements regularly specified "No Jews" or "Gentiles only." When this practice was carried into the war industries, complaints to Ottawa exploded. In response, the minister of labour issued a statement in March 1941 declaring, "For the final outcome of the war ... we require the help of the various nationalities represented in our population regardless of creed or racial origin"; therefore "unjust discrimination should be avoided." One year later, the federal government established the National Selective Service (NSS) to assign available Canadian workers to employment that would most effectively contribute to the national war effort. Since this was now a government-sanctioned employment bureau, Jewish and other Canadians anticipated that they would be treated equally, but again they were disappointed. After further protest from the CJC, the NSS commissioner affirmed a policy of non-discrimination.[60]

Bureaucratic assurances notwithstanding, there was no obvious reduction in discrimination. CJC divisional offices were receiving reports of discriminatory treatment, and Montreal headquarters documented these cases and presented them to federal officials. "Not receiving the cooperation for which we asked," the JPRC mounted a systematic campaign to gather evidence through announcements placed in Jewish newspapers, inviting individuals to visit a CJC office, where they could make a sworn affidavit describing their experience.[61] And the evidence flowed in, overwhelmingly, as people related their heart-breaking encounters. Although the NSS admitted that it was short of qualified personnel to assign to war plants, Jews were rejected or could be fired if they were discovered to be Jews after beginning employment.

Norman Eckler, seventeen years old, was told he could not be hired because he was Jewish. He exclaimed to a CJC worker, "Now my dad pays his taxes like any other citizen and I don't think that [John Inglis Company] was at all fair to me, or other of my Jewish friends who have applied there. Haven't we the right to apply for a job just the same as any other true Canadian?" Norma Sherman raised the same argument following a visit to the NSS: "After waiting for almost two hours, the girl in charge told me very politely that I am Jewish and only Gentile girls were needed. I consider that a very great injustice, as my father is paying taxes as every other citizen and we believe that our race should have the same privileges or we should not be paying the taxes we do ... Jewish boys are giving their lives in the war just as the Gentiles." Indignation resonates through the affidavits: "I am a Canadian born British subject," stated Adeline Natanson, "and have always felt very patriotic towards my country. Particularly now, during this war crisis, when the word 'democracy' has so much significance and liberty-loving people are fighting to keep and protect all the decent ideals of civilization, it seems a shame that racial-discrimination should be so prevalent ... I believe we are fighting a war at present to erase and prevent just such Nazi-ideas from becoming dominant in this country." Similarly, Rose Margolese, whose husband was on active service, wrote, "I am a Canadian citizen, born and raised ... [I]f such conditions exist today when there is such a shortage of help, what have our soldier husbands to look forward to after the war?"

When Jews applied to technical schools for training to make themselves more qualified for war-related work, they were told that they required a "sponsor" who would guarantee them a job upon completion of their course. Because it was so difficult to place Jews, the schools did not want to fill a place and provide training that would be wasted. Sarah Green was advised by a friendly interviewer that she should use an alias. She complied and successfully completed the course, but when she went to find employment her Jewish identity was discovered and she remained unemployed. Faced with a demand to find a sponsor for admission to a class in industrial chemistry, Betty Stoffman asked if this policy also applied to Germans. No, she was told, only to Jews and Italians.[62]

The JPRC accumulated these and dozens of similar statements in preparation for the annual meeting of the CJC Central Division in October 1942. At the meeting, division president A.B. Bennet and Ontario politician J.J. Glass openly accused the NSS of fostering discrimination against Jews and demanded action to correct it. The assembly passed a resolution claiming that "such practices are a negation of the aims for which the United Nations are fighting," and it lodged "a protest in sharp and unequivocal terms" to the minister of labour and the director of the NSS. The very next day, NSS director Elliott M. Little issued a denial and demanded proof of the accusation. The sworn affidavits were thereupon collected into a thick brief for submission to Ottawa. The introduction declared that employment practices "constituted a denial of the rights of citizenship to the Jews of Canada." The expected abatement of antisemitism at the commencement of the war, stated the brief, had been doomed to disappointment; instead, the situation had been aggravated by the fact that the war industries and trade schools consistently excluded Jews. This had caused personal loss to the Jewish individuals, but especially had injured the war effort. In August 1942, the NSS director had said, "Voluntary unemployment in the present crisis is a luxury the country cannot afford." The brief commented, "If voluntary unemployment is a luxury, then enforced unemployment brought about by discriminatory practices ... can only be characterized as deliberate sabotage." There followed the sworn statements from Jewish applicants and also from employers who had actually been invited by the NSS to exclude Jews.[63]

The brief was carried to Ottawa by Saul Hayes, executive director of the CJC, and Professor Jacob Finkelman of the University of Toronto. Discussion with director Little and his senior officials produced a new policy statement that was sent to all NSS managers in offices across the country. Circular 81, dated 7 November 1942, declared that "discrimination impairs the war effort by preventing the most effective use of our total labour supply and tends, by developing well-founded resentment and suspicion, to defeat the democratic objectives for which we are fighting." NSS personnel were forbidden to do anything that might "encourage or facilitate" discrimination; forms requiring applicants to identify their "race" or creed were to be withdrawn; and advertisements specifying the "race" or creed of eligible candidates would no longer be approved. Employers were told to hire more women, older workers, the physically handicapped, and persons of nationalities, creeds, and colours who might previously have been excluded. Employers who persisted in discriminating could be denied further permits to offer employment to any applicants. The CJC issued a press release stating, "As a direct result of the representation of the Canadian Jewish Congress, the Canadian government has made illegal the discrimination in employment against Jews and against any other group on the basis of creed, colour or racial origin."[64]

Hayes wrote to Little expressing the "grateful thanks" of the CJC for the "alacrity" with which he had acted upon their presentation.[65] But celebrations were premature. Within days of the November 1942 circular, renewed reports of NSS discrimination were reaching the CJC. Caiserman, Hayes, and their colleagues resumed their complaints to Little and his successor Allan M. Mitchell; a delegation from the CJC met with deputy ministers and eventually with the cabinet ministers concerned with wartime employment issues, all with little or no result. Eventually, it was discovered that a subsequent order, circular 81A, had been sent in confidence to NSS managers telling them to use "good sense" and not to take the non-discriminatory policy "literally" by sending applicants to jobs "where it may not be practical to employ certain types." It was, in effect, permission to perpetuate discriminatory practices. This hypocrisy of the NSS and collaboration at the most senior levels was disillusioning. "Political offensive" became more and more appealing after about a decade of reliance on other tactics. Caiserman wrote in March 1943 that current methods of persuasion were not working, but "a bill is being introduced by the Ontario Legislature which we hope will be accepted."[66]

In this public phase of the protest, Jews were joined by African Canadians who were also facing discrimination from the NSS and had sent complaints to the government in the fall of 1942. Black community organizations and church groups in Windsor, Toronto, and Montreal passed their own resolutions, demanding "equality of opportunity to all people regardless of race or nationality" and asking for anti-discrimination legislation at both the provincial and the federal level. This was an early Canadian example of an alliance among the victims of discrimination in their common interest.[67] The resulting order of the NSS and its accompanying publicity had at least a moral impact, for it explicitly linked the war effort and Canada's war aims with the anti-discrimination drive. Insofar as the Canadian people were concerned, the Government of Canada had taken a stand in favour of equality. The *Congress Bulletin* later reported, with some validity, that circular 81 had "exercised a profound influence upon the legislative philosophy of the nation."[68] The benefits were by no means immediate, but a direction can be discerned.

The Ontario bill referred to in the Caiserman letter was introduced in March 1943 by the stalwart J.J. Glass. With advice from the Legal Committee of the JPRC and coaching from Silcox of the CCCJ, Glass produced a bill to outlaw exclusionary practices based on "race" or creed in employment, accommodation, signs, and notices that indicated an intention to discriminate, with fines up to $500 for violations. This bill went far beyond anything that had been proposed hitherto, though in the end it did not pass. But the proposed Discrimination Prevention Act is interesting for other reasons. First, there were public meetings declaring support for the bill, with participants from the mainstream and several minority populations, organized by the JPRC and also by African Canadian churches in Toronto. Second, Glass's introductory speech and accompanying memos set out a full rationalization for a legal assault on discrimination. He emphasized the inconsistency of fighting a racist enemy abroad while allowing racist practices at home and when thousands of Jewish and other minority soldiers were engaged in fighting the war. Canada as a leading member of the allied United Nations should respect the Atlantic Charter and its adoption of equality as a war aim, asserted Glass. Discrimination was incompatible with British fair play, and the future integrity of the British Empire would depend on a workable system of justice and fairness for all. There were, insisted Glass, inherent rights belonging to citizens of a democracy that could be undermined by the unchecked freedom of speech and association; to protect democracy it was necessary to restrain expressions and practices that are not only offensive to their target groups but stimulate latent prejudices and counter-democratic divisiveness. He admitted that education must take a share in addressing the issue of discrimination, but its failure in the past to effect any real change meant that something more must be done. Discrimination, he told the assembly, "is *your* problem and your shame."[69]

Just months later, an Ontario election brought the Conservative Party under Premier George Drew to office, with a minority government dependent on support from other parties, including the Labour-Progressive (Communist) Party, one of whose two elected members was Joseph B. Salsberg, a prominent member of the JPRC. Before the next legislative session, the new premier consulted opposition parties to determine which measures they would put as priorities, and Salsberg indicated that an anti-discrimination act was his price for supporting the government. Silcox meanwhile warned Drew that if the government did not introduce such a bill, the Co-operative Commonwealth Federation (CCF) opposition surely would do so, and then the government would be in the "morally indefensible position" of voting against the measure, or of supporting an opposition motion that was guaranteed to be popular among church and labour circles. Accordingly, Drew asked Salsberg to put his case in writing. Replying that "such legislation is necessary not merely as a protection for the victims of intolerance but as a defence for our entire body politic," Salsberg argued that it would

> place the stamp of public disapproval on all acts of intolerance
> and discrimination. It would place beyond the pale of the law
> all those who perpetrate such uncivilized acts and thus would
> restrain any who now engage in these vicious practices. It would,
> further, cause many, otherwise honest and fair-minded citizens,
> to seriously re-examine their attitude towards people who may
> differ from them in origin, colour or speech ... Last but not least,
> such legislation would provide the legal authority to prevent the
> perpetrators of disunity and intolerance from continuing their
> harmful practices.[70]

When Drew responded positively, the JPRC moved into battle formation. Its members prepared drafts of a possible bill, interviewed cabinet ministers and other elected politicians from both the government and the opposition, sought cooperation from journalists, and encouraged the expression of public opinion, through letters and resolutions, to support the concept of a law against discrimination. When the bill was introduced on 3 March 1944, however, only the publication, broadcasting, or display of a sign or other representation indicating an intention to discriminate because of "race" or creed was to be punishable, with a fine up to $100 for a first offence. Salsberg's attempts to insert protection against actual acts of discrimination were not successful. The Ontario Racial Discrimination Act, 1944, was therefore not entirely a victory for the anti-discrimination forces, but once again it served as a powerful statement. Only one vote was cast against it, by a Conservative member. In the legislature, Premier Drew predicted that the new law would be acceptable to anyone who believed in the basic principles of British democracy:

> [I]f you discriminate against any person because of race or creed in respect of their ordinary rights as a citizen, you deny that equality which is part and parcel of the very freedom we are fighting to preserve. It seems to me that we have a very simple choice to make. When we say that Canada is a land of freedom and of equality, we either mean what we say or we do not. If we permit signs and notices to be put up in conspicuous places indicating that any particular group of people are denied the ordinary rights available to all other people, then those who should be most indignant are not the people against whom the signs and notices are directed, but those whose basic principles of freedom, justice, and equality have been insulted. Equality is the very foundation of our social structure.[71]

Even though its direct impact was limited, the act carried an extremely significant message both with respect to its content and to the tactics employed by its proponents in getting it through the legislature.

In his presidential address to the CJC in January 1945, Samuel Bronfman lamented that the war "by itself" had not eradicated the plague of antisemitism "as it should have." Nor had the war efforts of the JPRC, JLC, CCCJ, and other bodies, or even the war service of 15,000 or more Jewish soldiers. The JPRC was forced to admit that "rabid Jew-baiting," employment discrimination, and derogatory publications had not been eliminated during the war.[72] Appeals to British justice, fair play, economic self-interest, wartime national unity, Christian values, democratic traditions, and Western civilization had apparently not brought the results anticipated by Canadian Jews and their allies. This is not to say that there was no result at all: the Ontario legislation had passed with an overwhelming majority, the NSS had publicly declared its opposition to employment discrimination, and public opinion had begun to accept that anti-semitism and other prejudicial attitudes were "bad." A 1944 *Toronto Star* editorial entitled "A Matter of Personal Culture" expressed the emerging sentiment neatly: "Combatting racial discrimination is a personal responsibility, particularly for those who do not suffer from it ... A person of culture and refinement is considerate and sensitive about people's feelings and therefore incapable of insulting behaviour."[73] Anti-discrimination as a matter of "personal culture" had been established by 1944, and the door had been opened slightly to make it a matter of public policy.

But just about that time a new discourse was becoming available, a new idiom with which to present the long-standing claims to equality. The concept of "human rights" was not new, but in the late wartime period it had been taking on a new meaning, and it included state and international responsibility for ensuring the equality of peoples; anti-discrimination could be considered within the sphere of public policy as well as individual morality.[74] Canadian Jewry adopted the idiom of human rights with enthusiasm. A delegation from the CJC attended the San Francisco conference at which the United Nations Organization was founded in April 1945. In advance, the CJC submitted a brief to the federal government outlining its major concerns and objectives for the postwar world; foremost was an International Bill of Rights that would guarantee "human rights to Jewish people," "full and complete protection of life and liberty," "unequivocal equality of rights in law," and "the outlawing of anti-Semitism as an instrument of internal and international policy." "Basic human rights," the brief insisted, are not matters "solely of domestic concern"; state sovereignty must no longer serve as a cover for violations of "human rights." Never before had the CJC made such an appeal.[75]

The suddenness of the shift in language can be illustrated by two briefs calling for action against employment discrimination. In the 1942 brief, described above, the case was made on the standard grounds discussed throughout this chapter, and the object was to prevent the government from actively participating in discriminatory activity. In 1947 a comparable brief from the CJC demanded fair employment-practices legislation that would enforce equality throughout the economy, private as well as public, and that justified its demand by referring to the human rights provisions in the United Nations Charter.[76] Pivotal in this shift was a court case known as *Re: Drummond Wren*. Restrictive property covenants preventing rental or sale to Jews had long been a concern to the JPRC members, and in 1938 a CJC delegation had presented a brief to the Ontario government asking for these covenants' elimination by law. After the Ontario Racial Discrimination Act was passed in 1944, an attempt was made to claim that racially restrictive covenants constituted a notice indicating an intention to discriminate and therefore were illegal under the terms of the act. In March 1945, Justice Chevrier heard a case challenging a covenant, and although he lamented "the unchristian action of racial discrimination," extended sympathy to the suffering Jewish people, and denounced the persecution and murder of the Jews of Europe, he decided that the Ontario act was not applicable and consequently he had to uphold the covenant as legal.[77]

When a new opportunity presented itself less than two months later, the community was well prepared. A blue-ribbon JPRC legal team consisting of J.M. Bennett, Professor Jacob Finkelman, Bora Laskin, and Charles Dubin appeared before Justice Keiller Mackay on 1 May 1945. John Cartwright and Irving Himel represented the Workers' Educational Authority (WEA), a non-profit association that proposed to hold a fundraising raffle for a property restricted by a covenant preventing its sale to "Jews or persons of objectionable nationality"; the WEA was petitioning the court to have the covenant removed so that it could sell tickets indiscriminately. In his judgment, rendered on 31 October 1945, Justice Mackay declared that the covenant was contrary to public policy and therefore illegal, citing the Atlantic Charter and the United Nations Charter, wartime statements by Roosevelt, Churchill, and de Gaulle in support of equality rights, the general principles in the Ontario act rather than its precise wording, and other domestic and international agreements. Rabbi Abraham Feinberg concluded:

The judgment of Mr Justice Mackay thus establishes ground for legal exploration of crucial import, by utilizing as legal basis for local issues the moral and spiritual principles documented in the San Francisco Charter and other international techniques for

the implementation of basic human rights. It clothes in concrete
reality for specific cases, the universally-acclaimed principles
for which WWII was pursued to a victorious end by the United
Nations.

Drummond Wren, the director of the WEA, called the case that bore
his name "the first post-war skirmish in a long battle."[78] This was
very true.

CONCLUSIONS

Several lessons of potential historical import are discernible in this
narrative. First perhaps, it should help to dispel any notion that Canadian Jews from 1930 to 1945 were "passive" or "apologetic" in the
face of antisemitism. Jewish leaders used a variety of tactics throughout this period, when "quiet diplomacy" could co-exist with juridical
and legislative offensives and a very confrontational boycott. They
challenged false propaganda, explained Jewish culture and traditions to non-Jews, demonstrated good citizenship, even began to
redefine Canadian democracy as inclusive, distinguishing religious
conformity from loyalty as part of their attack on the "alien" image
that could excuse their exclusion from full participation in Canadian
life. It was not simply a case of their shaping their arguments to suit
the context of Canadian society in their time; they were *part* of that
context, and it shaped *them*. When Rabbi Eisendrath or J.J. Glass
urged Jews to proclaim their loyalty and to adopt respectable British manners, they were merely calling for the same kind of deport-
ment that the *Toronto Star* editorialists or Argue Martin demanded
of non-Jews. This was the way Canadians were supposed to behave.
The rabbi and the Jewish politician were not being "ingratiating";
like every other human being, they were creatures of their own time,
sharing its sensitivities.

Second, there is no evidence here that Canadian Jewry was pur-
suing an "incremental" policy development, from passivity to legislation and court action, or from self-interest to universalism.[79] As
has been demonstrated in this chapter, the era began with attempts
at legal reform, and thereafter came experiments with different tactics to suit changing circumstances. Jewish leaders embraced the
discourse of British justice as a tool for their own equality, and it
was virtually by definition a universalist kind of discourse, for the

arguments put by Canadian Jews for their own rights could apply to British subjects and Canadian citizens of any background. They were never operating in total isolation from other elements in the population, either ideologically or practically, as their alliances with labour and Protestant leaders clearly show.

Third, Jewish "submissiveness" and "isolation" cannot explain the persistence of antisemitism in mainstream Canada. Canadian Jews were living in a situation rife with contradictions. Even Abbé Groulx could condemn antisemitism while extolling attitudes and behaviour that were profoundly antisemitic.[80] Canada prided itself on being a liberal democracy, yet Canadians of Chinese, Indian, and Japanese origin, even those born in Canada, were denied the vote in British Columbia and consequently the federal franchise until after the Second World War. Recruitment policies by the armed services during the war discriminated against those of Asian or African origin. As NSS practices showed, it was not only Jews who were treated unfairly in seeking wartime employment. Restaurants, hotels, swimming pools, barbershops, and skating rinks, along with many private and public enterprises, routinely excluded citizens of a non-British or non-French background. This kind of overt racism was rationalized by a belief in the existence of discrete "races" into which humanity was divided, each with its own physical features and, more importantly, characterological features, including honesty, bravery, and suitability for participation in Anglo-Saxon political institutions, and it was legally and morally justified by the traditional British freedoms, especially of speech and association, that could be used to elevate base xenophobia to liberty and principle.

The target for the Jewish campaigners well into the war years was the perceived ignorance of their non-Jewish neighbours, a problem diagnosis shared by their allies and by most academic analysts of the time. Their solution was programs aimed at countering this ignorance by presenting the true facts. As the war progressed, and especially as a result of the Holocaust, the problem required a new definition. Simple ignorance could not explain the murder of six million Jews. There was something more pathological – more resistant to factual education or public awareness – that underlay the phenomenon of racism, and antisemitism was increasingly identified as an aspect of the more generalized problem of "race." As is nearly always the case, the new problem definition evoked a new solution, implemented in campaigns for the realization of human rights.

The emergence of human rights in postwar Canada had its roots firmly embedded in the preceding era. Here, as indeed in many other countries, the leadership in the human rights campaign was assumed by Jews,[81] very often the same people and organizations already engaged in the claim for equality. They grasped the new idiom and used it with astonishing success: within another decade and a half, fair practices and human rights were being legislated across Canada. The human rights idiom offered an effective arsenal of new ammunition in the battle for equality and against antisemitism, yet it was often ammunition for the same weapons and the same warriors who had been fighting since 1930.

NOTES

1 Even the venerable Ben Kayfetz said that in this period Jews "were willing to put up with the discrimination" (quoted in Rome, *Clouds in the Thirties: on Antisemitism in Canada, 1929–1939*, sec. 2, 31).

2 Anctil, "Interlude of Hostility: Judeo-Christian Relations in Quebec in the Interwar Period, 1919–1939," 135ff; Wade, *The French Canadians, 1760–1960*, 2:862ff; Hughes, *French Canada in Transition*, 219; Trofimenkoff, *Abbé Groulx: Variations on a Nationalist Theme*, 15; Ouellet, "The Historical Background of Separation in Quebec," 15; Oliver, *The Passionate Debate: The Social and Political Ideas of Quebec Nationalism, 1920–1945*.

3 For an especially lively account of this era in Quebec, see Delisle, *The Traitor and the Jew: Anti-Semitism and the Delirium of Extremist Right-wing Nationalism in French Canada from 1929 to 1939*.

4 For purposes of school attendance, Jews in Quebec were considered Protestants and paid their taxes to the Protestant board, but the Protestant school commissioners did not extend equal rights to Jewish students or teachers. Gerald Tulchinsky has a full discussion of the Montreal schools in *Branching Out: The Transformation of the Canadian Jewish Community*, chap. 3, 63 ff. See also Anctil, "Interlude," 149ff, and Rome, *On the Jewish School Question in Montreal, 1903–1931*. There is a huge cache of documentation in Library and Archives Canada (LAC), MG30, C119, Louis Rosenberg Fonds, vol. 27, file "Source Material for the Jewish School Problem in Quebec," consisting of several hundred pages of typescript, minutes of meetings, court cases, etc.

5   Rome, "The Political Consequences of the Jewish School Question, Mont-
    real, 1925–1933," 3–15.

6   Betcherman, *The Swastika and the Maple Leaf: Fascist Movements in
    Canada in the Thirties*, especially chap. 1. The quotation is at p. 8.

7   Betcherman, *Swastika*, 14–18; Robin, *Shades of Right: Nativist and Fas-
    cist Politics in Canada*, 1920–1940, 132; LAC, MG31, K9, Frank and Libbie
    Park Fonds, vol. 8, file 142, "Bill: An Act Respecting the Publication of
    Defamatory Libel"; Rome, *Clouds*, sec. 2, 41–52.

8   Betcherman, *Swastika*, 27–30; Rome, *Clouds*, sec. 2, 71ff; Kernaghan,
    "Freedom of Religion in the Province of Quebec, with Particular
    Reference to Jews, Jehovah's Witnesses, and Church-State Relations
    1930–1960," 99–102; Robin, *Shades of Right*, 136–7, 329–30.

9   *Statutes of Ontario*, 1932, c. 24, s. 4. Singer first raised this issue in
    the house in February 1931 and secured a commitment that provincial
    authorities would advise every company operating in the province that
    nationality and religion were not in themselves acceptable factors on
    which to assess risk. At the same time they were assured that "no com-
    pany should be required or compelled to provide insurance upon a risk
    which inquiry dictated to be unsatisfactory." In response, Singer's own
    insurance policy was cancelled without explanation, leading to his legisla-
    tive initiative in the next session; see Sohn, "Human Rights Legislation in
    Ontario: A study of Social Action," 41–4; Robin, *Shades of Right*, 320–1;
    Toronto *Globe*, 27 February 1931; *Toronto Star*, 21, 24, and 31 March
    1932; Toronto *Telegram*, 26 March 1932; Rome, *Clouds*, sec. 2, 52–4.

10 Sohn, "Human Rights Legislation," 44, citing John J. Glass, "Footnotes on
    Our Times," *Jewish Standard*, 15 January 1971, 5; Betcherman, *Swastika*,
    50; Lambertson, *Repression and Resistance: Canadian Human Rights
    Activists, 1930–1960*, 199–200; Rome, *Clouds*, sec. 2, 55. Speisman
    ("Antisemitism in Ontario: The Twentieth Century," 122) says that Glass
    "attempted" to insert such a clause, and certainly it is the case that dis-
    criminatory signs later reappeared on the Toronto Islands. It is pos-
    sible that the prohibition lasted only as long as Glass was chair of the
    commission.

11 *Yidisher zhurnal*, 28 June 1933, quoted in Levitt and Shaffir, *The Riot
    at Christie Pits*, 11–12; *Toronto Star*, 1 and 14 March 1933; *Mail and
    Empire*, 12 April 1933; Betcherman, *Swastika*, 51–2. The council resolu-
    tion referred to was passed in June 1931, concerning a prominent sign
    placed on a building on Lakeshore Road in Toronto. Although the sign
    was not on city property, the council pronounced it "offensive to Jewish

citizens particularly," recorded its "disapproval and condemnation of all racial and religious prejudice," and asked to have the sign removed (Rome, *Clouds*, sec. 2, 55–6, and sec. 7, 24–5).

12 Levitt and Shaffir, *Christie Pits*, 207ff; Rome, *Clouds*, sec. 4, 19–20, 35, and sec. 6, 48–9 (the Halifax resolution is at 48); Rome, *Our Archival Record of 1933, Hitler's Year*, 67–67a.

13 Rome, *Clouds*, sec. 4, 21–32; sec. 10, 388–90; Rome, *Our Archival Record of 1933*, 67; Tulchinsky, *Branching Out*, 177–8.

14 Tulchinsky, *Branching Out*, 174–5; Rome, *Clouds*, sec. 2, 12, 26–7; Anctil, *Le rendez-vous manqué. Les Juifs de Montréal face au Québec de l'entre-deux-guerres*, 34; M. Schreter, "French-Canadian Anti-Semitism," 74, 84–8; Hughes, *French Canada in Transition*, 135, 212–19; Robin, *Shades of Right*, 108–12, 320–1; Kernaghan, "Freedom of Religion," 83–7; Oliver, *The Passionate Debate*, 187; Trofimenkoff, *Action française: French Canadian Nationalism in the Twenties*; Delisle, *Traitor*, 111, 135, 138, 148, 166.

15 For example, on the evening of 1 August, about one hundred Swastika Club supporters marched along the boardwalk at the beaches singing to the tune of "Home on the Range":

> O give me a home, where the Gentiles may roam,
> Where the Jews are not rampant all day;
> Where seldom is heard a loud Yiddish word
> And the Gentiles are free all the day.

(*Toronto Telegram*, 2 August 1933, quoted in Levitt and Shaffir, *Christie Pits*, 82). Levitt and Shaffir offer a thorough examination of all these events in Toronto in the summer of 1933. For a concise summary by the same authors, see "The Swastika as Dramatic Symbol: A Case-Study of Ethnic Violence in Canada," 77–96.

16 Levitt and Shaffir, *Christie Pits*, passim. The mayor's statement is in appendix A:1, 289–90; Rome, *Clouds*. Sec. 7, 26–32.

17 *Toronto Star*, 2, 3, 8, 15, 17 August 1933; Levitt and Shaffir, *Christie Pits*, 93, 113, 166, 168; Betcherman, *Swastika*, 54–9.

18 Wagner, *Brothers Beyond the Sea: National Socialism in Canada*, "The Deutscher Bund Canada," 176–200, and "Nazi Party Membership in Canada: A Profile," 233–8.

19 Betcherman, *Swastika*, 38, 65–8; Anctil, "Interlude," 153–8; Robin, *Shades of Right*, chap. 5; Rome, *Clouds*, sec. 2, 86.

20 LAC, MG28, VI33, B'nai Brith Fonds, vol. 3, file 3. Report of the Secretary, Lawrence White, 1934.

21 Rome, *Our Archival Record of 1933*, 68–70, 75, 83, 86; Rome, *Clouds*, sec. 4, 32ff; Abella, *A Coat of Many Colours: Two Centuries of Jewish Life in Canada*, 188–90.

22 *Congress Bulletin*, October 1951, 7. The first congress was held in Montreal in March 1919, but afterwards it lay dormant until this second congress in 1934.

23 Rome, *Our Archival Record of 1933*, 76; Rome *The Congress Archival Record of 1934*, 4; Rome, *Clouds*, sec. 4, 53; Abella, *Coat of Many Colours*, 189–90; Canadian Jewish Congress Charities Committee National Archives (CJCCCNA), CJC collection, series BA, Dominion Executive 1933–1939, box 5, file 1, Dominion Executive Committee 1933, and file 2, Dominion Executive Committee 1934.

24 An American who came to Canada in 1929, Eisendrath had been a founder and president of the Fellowship of Reconciliation, an ardent proponent of civil liberties, and a charismatic speaker. His partner Silcox was Canadian-born but also had extensive American experience with the National Conference on Christians and Jews and other service organizations there. He returned to Canada in 1934 as general secretary for the Social Service Council of Canada, a body supported by the major Protestant churches. The Eisendrath Papers and the Silcox Papers have brief biographies of the two men. See Ben G. Kayfetz, "Rabbi Maurice Nathan Eisendrath, 1902–1973," typescript, CJCCCNA, file "Various," Maurice N. Eisendrath Papers; and Graham Rockingham, "Finding Aid," United Church of Canada Archives (UCCA), Claris Edwin Silcox Papers. There is a published biography of Eisendrath, which deals mostly with his American years: Schulman, *Like a Raging Fire*.

25 UCCA, Silcox Papers, box 8, file 2, "Program for Seminar on Jewish-Gentile Relations, April 23–24, 1934," Kayfetz quotation from his brief biography of Eisendrath. Bruce's speech was published and distributed as a pamphlet by the Committee on Jewish-Gentile Relationships and was included in Bruce, *Our Heritage and Other Addresses*, 219–25.

26 CJCCCNA, CJC collection, series DA1, H.M Caiserman Papers, box 2, file 21, "Extract from a Report Submitted at the Fourth National Assembly of the Canadian Jewish Congress in Toronto," January 1939; UCCA, Silcox Papers, box 9, "Articles, Unpublished," box 12, "Periodicals and Pamphlets."

27 CJCCCNA, Eisendrath Papers, file "Correspondence"; CJCCCNA, Dominion Executive, box 5, file 2, Dominion Executive Committee 1934; Ontario Jewish Archives (OJA), Joint Community Relations Committee Papers (JCRC), temporary box 1, file PR160, "Committee on Jewish-Gentile

Relations," and file PR131.5.23, "Rev. Burgess, Toronto"; CJCCCNA, CJC collection, series DA2, Louis Rosenberg Papers, box 9, file 13, "Committee on Jewish-Gentile Relationships."

28 CJCCCNA, Caiserman Papers, box 2, file 21, mimeographed circular, "Boycott Committee Bulletin," July 1939; J.J. Glass, quoted in Rome, *Clouds*, sec. 4, 61. The associated campaign to boycott the 1936 Berlin Olympics is discussed in chapter 2 in this volume.

29 CJCCCNA, Dominion Executive Committee Minutes; Caiserman Papers, box 2, files 19, 20, and 21, "Boycott Committee Minutes" and other documents, including "Report Submitted at the Fourth National Assembly of the Canadian Jewish Congress in Toronto," January 1939; LAC, MG28, V75, Jewish Labour Committee Fonds, vol. 19, file 20, "Minutes of Meetings: CJC Boycott Committee."

30 CJCCCNA, Caiserman Papers, box 2, files 19, 20, and 21; LAC, MG28, V75, Jewish Labour Committee Fonds, vol. 19, files 20 and 21; OJA, MG6 B, John J. Glass Papers, box 1, file 1; Rome, *Congress Archival Record of 1934*, 18, 19, 35, 43, and *Clouds*, sec. 4, 61.

31 CJCCCNA, Caiserman Papers, box 2, files 19, 20, 21, and 41; OJA, JCRC Papers, file "Trades and Labor Congress of Canada – Fascist Activities in Canada, 1938"; LAC, MG28, V75, Jewish Labour Committee Fonds, box 7, file 13.

32 The draft read: "201a. Everyone is guilty of an offense and liable on summary conviction to six months imprisonment, or to a fine not exceeding $200 or to both, who utters, writes, publishes, prints, displays, circulates or otherwise disseminates any matter, propaganda, caricatures, statements, articles, addresses or reports which subject or expose or are calculated, intended or likely to subject or expose any person or groups of persons to prejudice, shame, hatred, ridicule, injury, insult or obloquy by reason of the fact that such person or groups or persons belong to or purport to be of any particular race, color or religion" (LAC, MG31, K9, Park Fonds, vol. 8, file 142; CJCCCNA, Caiserman Papers, box 2, file 29; Rome, *Clouds*, sec. 2, 59ff, and *Congress Archival Record of 1934*, 18, 22, 35.

33 Under the act, an individual could sue for an injunction against the publisher or author of statements "likely to expose" that person's "race or religion to hatred, contempt or ridicule, and tend[ing] to raise unrest and disorder" (*Statutes of Manitoba*, 1934, c. 23, s. 13A); Trachtenberg, "The Winnipeg Jewish Community and Politics: The Inter-War Years, 1919–1939," 126–7, 131–2; Betcherman, *Swastika*, 65–71; Rome, *Clouds*, sec. 2, 50, 88–97. There is a transcript of the hearing in CJCCCNA, Caiserman Papers, box 2, file 42. This was the only prosecution under the Manitoba

act. Louis Rosenberg called the act "a dead letter" and the CJC Dominion Executive pronounced it "utterly ineffective" (CJCCCNA, Caiserman
Papers, box 2, file 22, Rosenberg to Caiserman, 16 February 1942, and
Dominion Executive Committee, box 5, file 9, Minutes of 12 December
1943).

34 CJCCCNA, Caiserman Papers, box 2, file 29, Caiserman to J.H. MacBrien,
3 December 1933, Commissioner of Customs to Caiserman, 18 December.

35 Ibid., box 2, file 29, and box 3, files 25 and 26. Over fifty community
committees were created to monitor Nazi and related materials, which
could then be consolidated in CJC headquarters.

36 CJCCCNA, Dominion Council, 1935–1948, box 5, file 2, Minutes of the
Dominion Executive, 3 May 1934; Rome, *Congress Archival Record of
1934*, 34.

37 CJCCCNA, Dominion Council, 1935–1948, box 5, file 2, Minutes of the
Dominion Executive, 3 May 1934, 6 December 1934; Rome, *Congress
Archival Record of 1934*, 12; *Clouds*, sec. 7, 6. Christian leaders in Quebec could themselves be enlisted to make public pronouncements condemning antisemitism, though it was usually Protestant rather than Catholic clergy who participated in this. One highly visible example was
Anglican Archdeacon F.G. Scott, who wrote in the Montreal *Gazette* that
antisemitism was "not only unchristian, but, and possibly this may seem
to some patriots even worse, un-British," and called upon the British tradition of tolerance as "the spirit which we wish to preserve in Canada" (2
May 1934, copied in CJCCCNA, Caiserman Papers, box 2, file 42).

38 OJA, JCRC Papers, file PR131.5.10, "Musselman's Lake, Ontario, 1938,"
Oscar Cohen to Morgan Baker, MPP, 6 July 1938, and to Reeve A.E.
Weldon, 18 July; file PR131.5.6, "Pine Grove Park, Port Credit, 1938–
1940," Cohen, memo, 19 July 1939; series 5, subseries 3, Antisemitism
Cases, temp box 1, file PR211, "Dr Sam Rabinovitch and the Internes of
Notre Dame Hospital," Bercovitch to Premier Taschereau, 19 June 1934;
CJCCCNA, Caiserman Papers, box 2, file 2, "Correspondence with Government Bodies, 1937–1945." Numerous similar examples are in Rome,
Clouds, e.g., sec. 2, 66, sec. 3, 11, sec. 5, 37, sec. 7, 7–12, 22, 32–4.

39 CJCCCNA, Eisendrath Papers, file "Addresses and Sermons, 1936–1941."
He was not alone in this latter sentiment. In "Message to the Jews of
Toronto" in 1937, J.J. Glass said Jews must "conduct ourselves in such a
way as to gain the respect of our neighbours. In these critical times, every
Jew must feel that he is responsible for the entire Jewish people, and his
conduct, therefore, must be of the highest type" (OJA, Glass Papers, box 1,
file 1).

40 Rome, *Clouds*, sec. 2, 19. A slightly different version of the same report is quoted in sec. 3, 6. Note that even within this quotation there are two different spellings: "anti-Semitism" in one paragraph and "antisemitism" in another.

41 Stingel, *Social Discredit: Anti-Semitism, Social Credit, and the Jewish Response*, gives a thorough examination of the Social Credit phenomenon and the alarm it raised in the Jewish community.

42 An interesting analysis of the Quebec situation can be found in Gordon, "The Cagoulards and Politicians Who Fish in Murky Waters: An Inside View of the Order of Jacques Cartier and the Antics of Mr Duplessis."

43 Betcherman, *Swastika*, 113–25.

44 CJCCCNA, Caiserman Papers, box 1, file 1, "Membership drive 1935–1936," file 3, "Membership drive 1938," file 6, "Membership campaign, 1936–1937," and file 7, "Membership campaign, 1938."

45 LAC, MG28, V133, B'nai Brith Fonds, vol. 3, files 3–7, "District Grand Lodge No. 1, Proceedings," 1934–1938; LAC, MG31, H156, Herbert S. Levy Fonds, vol. 4, file 28, "Partial Minutes on JCRC and ADL Subjects starting November 10, 1935," and "Canadian Jewish Congress and B'nai Brith"; CJCCCNA, Dominion Executive, box 5, file 2, minutes, 3 May 1934, file 6, minutes, 1 June 1936, file 7, "Conditions of Agreement Regarding the Conduct of Anti-Defamation Work in Canada between the CJC and the Canadian Conference of B'nai Brith," 20 February 1938.

46 LAC, MG28, V133, B'nai Brith Fonds, vol. 3, file 8, "Proceedings, 1939"; LAC, MG28, V75, Jewish Labour Committee Fonds, vol. 19, file 21, JPRC meeting of 15 August 1939, file 22, minutes of meetings, CJC Eastern Division, 13 July 1939.

47 Gurston S. Allen, "Jewish Occupational Difficulties," issued by the CJC, 1939. There is a copy in CJCCCNA, series G, filed with "Memorandum on Unequal Employment," 1947.

48 Ibid., especially 10–20.

49 "The Challenge of Anti-Semitism to Democracy." There is a typescript copy in OJA, JCRC Papers, file "Silcox Correspondence," and a copy of the published pamphlet (Toronto: Committee on Jewish-Gentile Relationships, 1939) in UCCA, Silcox Papers, box 12, file 25.

50 LAC, MG28, V133, B'nai Brith Fonds, vol. 3, file 9, "Proceedings, 1940," Report of the JPRC.

51 Ibid., Report of the Director of Anti-Defamation Activities; Mergler, "Issues of War and Peace Face Jewish Congress," CJCCCNA, Caiserman Papers, box 2, files 22 and 23; Abraham Feinberg, "Anti-Semitism: What Can We Do?" *Canadian Jewish Review*, 31 March 1944, 12; *Globe and*

Mail, 24 May 1943. A much cruder demonstration of this misperception is in a piece of doggerel found in LAC, MG31, K9, Park Fonds, vol. 8, file 142: "Don't sit too long to take a crap, for if you do, you help the Jap. / Don't stand too long to take a piss, for Hitler loves the hours you miss. / So shit in your pants and piss in your shoes and win this war for 'THE GOD DAMN JEWS.'"

52 LAC, MG31, K9, Park Fonds, vol. 8, file 142; Silcox and Eisendrath to editor, *Toronto Star*, 18 May 1940; Feinberg, "Anti-Semitism," 10; *TODAY*, November 1944, 6–7; *Saturday Night*, editorial, 21 September 1940.

53 CJCCCNA, Caiserman Papers, box 8, file 5, "Anti-Defamation materials, 1939–1942," box 2, file 22, "Anti-Defamation, Jan–Apr 1942," and file 23, "Anti-defamation, May–Aug 1942"; CJCCCNA, ZA 1943, box 3, file 26, interview, H.M. Caiserman with representative from the National Film Board, December 1942.

54 OJA, JCRC Papers, file PR210, "Canadian Conference of Christians and Jews."

55 Ibid., "[JPRC] Report of Activities," December 1940, "Report of the Director to the Administrative Board of the Canadian Conference of Christians and Jews," 25 November 1940, and file PR160, "Committee on Jewish-Gentile Relations (Canadian Conference of Christians and Jews), 1940"; CJCCCNA, Rosenberg Papers, box 9, file 13, "Committee on Jewish-Gentile Relationships, February 1st, 1940," minutes, and "Resolutions adopted by Joint Public Relations Committee in reference to the Canadian Conference of Christians and Jews," 7 April and 6 December 1940; UCCA, Silcox Papers, "Second Report of the Director," 29 December 1941. Among the board members were B.K. Sandwell, editor of *Saturday Night*, Senator Cairine Wilson, and the presidents or principals of University College, Toronto, Queen's University, the University of Western Ontario, and the University of Saskatchewan. Of the initial 134 "ordinary" members, twenty were Jews and a "large proportion" of the remainder were Protestant clergy. The CCCJ was reorganized again in December 1944, after Eisendrath returned to the United States and Hunter moved to Winnipeg. The Anglican Canon W.W. Judd and Rabbi Abraham Feinberg became co-chairs; Silcox remained as director. See *Fellowship* 5, nos. 3–4 (November–December 1944): 1.

56 There are scattered copies of *Fellowship*, but no complete run, in UCCA, Silcox Papers; OJA, JCRC Papers, file PR210, "Canadian Conference of Christians and Jews"; CJCCCNA, CJC collection, series CJC-ZS/JC-G, "Canadian Council of Christians and Jews," box 2; and LAC, MG28, I103,

Canadian Labour Congress Fonds, vol. 201, file 11. Pamphlet distribution is recorded in *Fellowship* and in the director's annual reports.

57   OJA, JCRC Papers, file "Dr C.E. Silcox – Correspondence," notes for a speech by Silcox entitled "Racial Tolerance," 31 March 1941, file PR210.5, "Canadian Conference of Christians and Jews – A Manual for Round-tables, 1941," and another copy in CJCCCNA, "Canadian Council of Christians and Jews," box 2; C.E. Silcox, "What We Owe to the Jews," *Teacher's Quarterly* 6, no. 3 (1943): 1–4, copy in UCCA, Silcox Papers.

58   "The War Efforts Committee of Canadian Jewish Congress," *Canadian Jewish Year Book*, 1941–1942, 67–76; CJCCCNA, Caiserman Papers, box 8, file 3, "Resume of War Efforts Activities," and "Summary of Activities of Canadian Jewish Congress Servicemen's Centres," 20 October 1944; LAC, MG28, 1103, Canadian Labour Congress Fonds, vol. 201, file 11, "General Correspondence. Anti-Semitism, 1940," vol. 206, files 14–19, "General Correspondence, Canadian Jewish Congress," 1943–1946; CJCCCNA, ZA 1943, box 3, file 26, interview, H.M. Caiserman with representative of the National Film Board, December 1942; Mergler, "Issues of War and Peace Face Jewish Congress"; *Congress Bulletin*, October 1951, 6–7. Abella, *Coat of Many Colours*, 178–9, has illustrations of the comic book covers. "Comfort" services were provided to all enlisted Canadians. For Jewish soldiers specifically, the Religious Welfare subcommittee sponsored chaplaincies, both overseas and at home, and published a "Handbook and Religious Calendar for Jewish Veterans and Servicemen and Women." An interesting debate took place in Montreal and Toronto on 4 and 5 September 1939, even before Canada had formally declared war, in which the creation of a separate Jewish battalion was discussed. The conclusion was that it was better for Canadian Jews to "enlist as British subjects and not as Jews" (LAC, MG28, V75, Jewish Labour Committee Fonds, vol. 19, file 21, "Minutes of Meetings, CJC Central Division, 1939," and "Confidential minutes of meeting of Inner Executive Committee, 5 September 1939."

59   LAC, MG28, V75, Jewish Labour Committee Fonds, vol. 7, files 9 and 10, "Correspondence. JLC and the War Effort," File 15, "Correspondence, Reports collected by the JLC relating to the War Effort, 1943–1944," file 19, *Underground and On the Ground* 1, no. 2 (1944); LAC, MG28, 1103, Canadian Labour Congress Fonds, box 206, file 18, "General Correspondence, Canadian Jewish Congress, part 2, 1944–1946"; CJCCCNA, Caiserman Papers, box 2, file 3, "Jewish Labour Committee, 1940–1945."

60   CJCCCNA, ZA 1943, box 3, file 26, Memorandum by H.M. Caiserman, "Employment Discrimination in Canadian War Industries," January 1944;

CJCCCNA, Caiserman Papers, box 2, file 23, "Anti-defamation, May–Aug 1942"; Order-in-Council PC2250, 21 March 1942.

61 CJCCCNA, Caiserman Papers, box 2, file 22, "Anti-Defamation, Jan–Apr 1942," and file 23, "Anti-defamation, May–Aug 1942"; CJCCCNA, ZA 1942, box 5, file 63, and ZA 1943, box 3, file 26.

62 "Brief Presented to the National Selective Service by the Canadian Jewish Congress in 1942," being appendix E to the "Memorandum on Unequal Opportunity in Employment in the Province of Ontario and the Need for Fair Employment Practices Legislation," February 1947. There are copies in CJCCCNA, ZA 1942, box 5, file 63, in series G, and in Archives of Ontario (AO), RG3–17, George Drew Papers, box 436, File, "Fair Employment Practices Act."

63 Ibid., introduction; CJCCCNA, ZA 1943, box 3, file 26, "Memorandum Re: Illegalization of Discrimination in Canada," 24 January 1944.

64 CJCCCNA, ZA 1942, box 5, file 63, NSS Circular 81, 7 November 1942, and press release, 17 November 1942.

65 CJCCCNA, ZA 1943, box 3, file 26, Hayes to Little, 16 November 1942.

66 Ibid., numerous letters dated from 18 November 1942 to 25 October 1944. The final quotation is from Caiserman to Mrs S. Levitt, 22 March 1943; NSS Confidential Circular 81A, 9 December 1943; CJCCCNA, Dominion Executive, box 5, file 9, Dominion Council Minutes, 6–7 February 1943; CJCCCNA, Caiserman Papers, box 8, file 17, "Summary Report on Public Relations Work 1942–1944," Caiserman to JPRC, Eastern Division, 6 March 1944.

67 LAC, MG31, K9, Park Fonds, vol. 8, file 147; Douglas MacLennan, "Racial Discrimination in Canada," *Canadian Forum*, October 1943, 164–5; *Globe and Mail*, 30 October 1943.

68 *Congress Bulletin*, October 1951, 8.

69 OJA, Glass Papers, box 2, file 12, "Speech Delivered in the Ontario Legislature on March 31st, 1943"; file 9, "Memorandum on Bill 24, An Act to Prevent Discrimination on the Ground of Race and Creed"; AO, Drew Papers, box 434, file 74–G, Discrimination Bill 46, Petitions Re: Silcox to Drew, 10 November 1943; *Fellowship*, February–March 1943; CJCCCNA, Dominion Executive, box 5, file 9, Minutes of Dominion Council, 6–7 February 1943; LAC, MG31, K9, Park Fonds, vol. 8, files 146 and 147.

70 AO, Drew Papers, box 434, file 74–G, Discrimination Bill 46, Petitions Re: Silcox to Drew, 10 November 1943; box 458, file 247–G, "Salsburg [sic], Mr. Jos. B.," Salsberg to Drew, 2 February 1944; personal interview with Mr J.B. Salsberg, 26 July 1989. The candidate whom Salsberg defeated

in the 1943 election was J.J. Glass. The CCF had already declared itself in favour of anti-discrimination legislation.

71 AO, Drew Papers, box 458, file 247–G, Drew to Salsberg, 3 February 1944; text of Drew's speech in the legislature is in box 434 in a file without title or number, adjacent to file 74–G; CJCCCNA, Caiserman Papers, box 8, file 17, "Summary Report on Public Relations Work, 1942–1944, Legislation"; interview with Mr Salsberg. The progress of the bill through the legislature is described in Sohn, "Human Rights Legislation," 50–8, and Bagnall, "The Ontario Conservatives and the Development of Anti-Discrimination Policy, 1944–1962," 18–65. The act itself is *Statutes of Ontario*, 1944, c. 51. While the Ontario act was under consideration in Toronto, CCF MP Angus MacInniis introduced a private member's bill in Ottawa seeking an amendment to the Criminal Code, section 318, "to prevent public utterances or the dissemination of material calculated or likely to cause discrimination or disharmony on account of race or religion" (*Hansard*, 20 March 1944, 1626). Of course, it did not pass. The JPRC had examined and commented upon the bill in advance (CJCCCNA, Caiserman Papers, box 8, file 17, "Summary Report on Public Relations Work, 1942–1944, Legislation"). These two bills coming together roused a storm of opposition from individuals and groups, public meetings, and editorialists anxious that freedom of speech and of religion were under attack (AO, Drew Papers, box 434, file 74–G, Discrimination Bill 46, Petitions Re:; LAC, MG31, K9, Park Fonds, box 8, files 145 and 146.

72 Text of presidential address, 14 January 1945, in LAC, MG28, 1103, Canadian Labour Congress Fonds, box 206, file 19, "General Correspondence, Canadian Jewish Congress, Part 3, 1944–1946"; JPRC statement in document filed with CJCCCNA, Caiserman Papers, box 8, file 17, "Summary Report on Public Relations Work, 1942–1944, Legislation."

73 26 April 1944.

74 For example, see Auerbach, "Human Rights at San Francisco"; Burgers, "The Road to San Francisco: The Revival of the Human Rights Idea in the Twentieth Century"; Lauren, "First Principles of Racial Equality: History and the Politics and Diplomacy of Human Rights Provisions in the UN Charter"; Mazower, "The Strange Triumph of Human Rights, 1933–1950."

75 *Congress Bulletin* 2, no. 10 (1945); CJCCCNA, series CA, box 89, file 1025, "Memoranda submitted by the Canadian Jewish Congress and the Zionist Organizations of Canada to the Canadian delegates to the United Nations Conference on International Organization at San Francisco," April 1945.

The delegates were Samuel Bronfman, Saul Hayes, A.B. Bennet, and
Samuel J. Zachs.

76 "Memorandum on Unequal Opportunity in Employment in the Province of Ontario and the Need for Fair Employment Practices Legislation,"
February 1947, appendix J, copies in CJCCCNA, ZA 1942, box 5, file 63, in
series G, and in AO, Drew Papers, box 436, file "Fair Employment Practices Act."

77 *Re: McDougall and Waddell*, [1945] 2 *Dominion Law Reports*, 244.

78 *Re: Drummond Wren*, [1945] 4 *Dominion Law Reports*, 674; OJA, JPRC
Correspondence, 1947, reel 2, "Transcript of Drummond Wren Hear-
ing," 1 May 1945. Much more consideration of restrictive property coven-
ants and *Drummond Wren* in particular is given in my book *"Race,"
Rights and the Law in the Supreme Court of Canada*, chap. 4, and in
Lambertson, *Repression and Resistance*, 209–14. Feinberg and Wren quo-
tations are from the booklet "A Victory for Democracy," published by the
CJC in 1946. A copy is in LAC, MG28, I103, Canadian Labour Congress
Fonds, vol. 355, file "Racial Discrimination, Part 2, 1945–1952."

79 Stuart Svonkin presents this incremental model for American Jewry in
Jews against Prejudice: American Jews and the Fight for Civil Liberties,
and his interpretation has sometimes been adopted by scholars of Canadian Jewry.

80 As cited in Tulchinsky, *Branching Out*, 174.

81 The postwar campaign in Canada is described in my article "The 'Jewish
Phase' in the Movement for Racial Equality in Canada."

Bibliography

ARCHIVES

Archives of Ontario, Toronto (AO)
Canadian Jewish Congress Charities Committee National Archives, Montreal (CJCCCNA)
Library and Archives Canada, Ottawa (LAC)
McGill University Archives, Montreal (MGA)
Ontario Jewish Archives, Toronto (OJA)
United Church of Canada Archives, Toronto (UCCA)
United States Holocaust Memorial Museum Archives, Washington (USHMM)
University of Heidelberg Archives, Heidelberg (UHA)
University of Toronto Archives, Toronto (UTA)

NEWSPAPERS

Calgary Daily Herald
Canadian Jewish Chronicle (Montreal)
Canadian Jewish Review (Montreal/Toronto)
Der keneder adler/Jewish Daily Eagle (Montreal)
Der yidisher zhurnal/Daily Hebrew Journal (Toronto)
Dos yidishe vort/Israelite Press (Winnipeg)
Evening Telegram (Toronto)
Forverts/Forward (New York)
Gazette (Montreal)
Globe (pre-1936, Toronto)
Globe and Mail (Toronto)

Jewish Post (Winnipeg)
Jewish Transcript (Seattle)
La Presse (Montreal)
L'Action nationale (Montreal)
Le Devoir (Montreal)
London Free Press
McGill Daily (Montreal)
Mail and Empire (Toronto)
Montreal Daily Star
New York Times
Ottawa Citizen
Times (London, UK)
Toronto Daily Star
Vancouver Sun
The Varsity (Toronto)
Winnipeg Free Press
Winnipeg Tribune

SECONDARY SOURCES

Abella, Irving. *A Coat of Many Colours: Two Centuries of Jewish Life in Canada.* Toronto: Lester & Orpen Dennys, 1990

Abella, Irving, and Frank Bialystok. "Canada." In *The World Reacts to the Holocaust,* edited by David S. Wyman, 749–81. Baltimore and London: Johns Hopkins University Press, 1996

Abella, Irving, and Harold Troper. "'The Line Must Be Drawn Somewhere': Canada and Jewish Refugees, 1933–9." *Canadian Historical Review* 40, no. 2 (1979)

– *None Is Too Many: Canada and the Jews of Europe, 1933–1948.* Toronto: Lester & Orpen Dennys, 1982

Allen, Ralph. *Home Made Banners.* Toronto: Longmans, Green, 1946

– *The Man from Oxbow: The Best of Ralph Allen.* Edited by C. McCall Newman. Toronto: McClelland & Stewart, 1967

Allen, William Sheridan. *The Nazi Seizure of Power.* Revd. edn. New York: Watts, 1984

Altshuler, Mordechai. "Jewish Warfare and the Participation of Jews in Combat in the Soviet Union as Reflected in Soviet and Western Historiography." In *Bitter Legacy: Confronting the Holocaust in the USSR,* edited by Zvi Gitelman, 151–66. Bloomington: Indiana University Press, 1997

Aly, Götz. *Hitler's Beneficiaries: Plunder, Racial War, and the Nazi Welfare State.* Translated by Jefferson Chase. New York: Metropolitan Books, 2006

Anctil, Pierre "Interlude of Hostility: Judaeo-Christian Relations in Quebec in the Interwar Period, 1919–1939." In *Antisemitism in Canada: History and Interpretation*, edited by Alan Davies. Waterloo, ON: Wilfrid Laurier University Press, 1992

– *Le Devoir, les Juifs et l'immigration.* Quebec: Institut québécois de recherche sur la culture, 1988

– *Le rendez-vous manqué. Les Juifs de Montréal face au Québec de l'entre-deux-guerres.* Quebec: Institut québécois de recherche sur la culture, 1988

Anderson, Patrick. "Introduction to the Kraus Reprint Edition." *Preview.* Millwood: Kraus, 1980

Angress, Werner T. "The German Army's 'Judenzählung' of 1916 – Genesis – Consequences – Significance." *Leo Baeck Institute Year Book* 23 (1978): 117–38

Aronson, Shlomo. *Hitler, the Allies, and the Jews.* New York: Cambridge University Press, 2004

Ascher, Carol. *Afterimages: A Family Memoir.* Teaneck, NJ: Holmes & Meier, 2008

Auerbach, Jerold. "Human Rights at San Francisco." *American Jewish Archives* 16 (1964): 51–70

Axelrod, Paul. *Making a Middle Class: Student Life in English Canada during the Thirties.* Montreal & Kingston: McGill-Queen's University Press, 1990

Bagnall, John C. "The Ontario Conservatives and the Development of Anti-Discrimination Policy, 1944–1962." PH D dissertation, Queen's University, 1984

Bajohr, Frank. *"Aryanisation" in Hamburg: The Economic Exclusion of the Jews and the Confiscation of Their Property in Nazi Germany.* Translated by George Wilkes, 28–34. New York: Berghahn, 2002

Baron, Lawrence. "The Holocaust and American Public Memory, 1945–1960." *Holocaust and Genocide Studies* 17, no. 1 (2003): 62–88

Bauer, Yehuda. *American Jewry and the Holocaust: The American Jewish Joint Distribution Committee, 1939–1945.* Detroit: Wayne State University Press, 1981

Beer, Max. "What Else Could We Have Done? The Montreal Jewish Community, the Canadian Jewish Congress, the Jewish Press, and the Holocaust." MA thesis, Concordia University, 2006

Bendersky, Joseph W. *The "Jewish Threat": Anti-Semitic Politics of the U.S. Army*. New York: Basic Books, 2000

Benz, Wolfgang, ed. *Die Juden in Deutschland 1933–1945. Leben unter nationalsozialistischer Herrschaft*. 3rd edn. Munich: C.H. Beck, 1993

Bercuson, David J. *Canada and the Birth of Israel: A Study in Canadian Foreign Policy*. Toronto: University of Toronto Press, 1985

Bergen, Doris L. *The Holocaust: A Concise History*. Lanham, MD: Rowman and Littlefield, 2009

– "Storm Troopers of Christ: The German Christian Movement and the Ecclesiastical Final Solution." In *Betrayal: German Churches and the Holocaust*, edited by Robert P. Ericksen and Susannah Heschel, 40–67. Minneapolis: Augsburg Fortress, 1999

– *Twisted Cross: The German Christian Movement in the Third Reich*. Chapel Hill: University of North Carolina Press, 1996

Bering, Dietz. *The Stigma of Names: Antisemitism in German Daily Life, 1812–1933*. Translated by Neville Plaice. Ann Arbor: University of Michigan Press, 1992

Berkowitz, Michael. *The Crime of My Very Existence: Nazism and the Myth of Jewish Criminality*. Berkeley: University of California Press, 2007

– *Western Jewry and the Zionist Project, 1914–1933*. Cambridge: Cambridge University Press, 2003

Betcherman, Lita-Rose. *The Swastika and the Maple Leaf: Fascist Movements in Canada in the Thirties*. Toronto: Fitzhenry & Whiteside, 1975

Bialystok, Franklin. *Delayed Impact: The Holocaust and the Canadian Jewish Community*. Montreal & Kingston: McGill-Queen's University Press, 2000

– "'Greener' and 'Gayle': Relations between Holocaust Survivors and Canadian Jews." In *Remembering for the Future: The Holocaust in an Age of Genocide*, vol. 3, edited by John K. Roth and Elisabeth Maxwell, 32–46. Basingstoke, UK: Palgrave Macmillan, 2001

Birney, Earle. "Hands." In *Now Is Time*, 13. Toronto: Ryerson, 1945

– "On Going to the Wars." In *David and Other Poems*, 38. Toronto: Ryerson, 1942

Bluman, Barbara Ruth. *I Have My Mother's Eyes: A Holocaust Memoir across Generations*. Vancouver: Ronsdale Press, 2009

Boehling, Rebecca, and Uta Larkey. *Life and Loss in the Shadow of the Holocaust: A Jewish Family's Untold Story*. New York: Cambridge University Press, 2011

Booth Jr., Norman Gordon. "The Holocaust: General Jewish and Christian Media Perspectives." D LITT thesis, Drew University, 2002

Botz, Gerhard. *Nationalsozialismus in Wien.* 3rd edn. Buchloe: Obermayer, 1988

– "Non-Jews and Jews in Austria before, during, and after the Holocaust." In *Humanity at the Limit: The Impact of the Holocaust Experience on Jews and Christians*, edited by Michael A. Signer, 264–79. Bloomington: Indiana University Press, 2000

Brown, Michael. *Jew or Juif? Jews, French Canadians, and Anglo-Canadians, 1759–1914.* Philadelphia: Jewish Publication Society, 1986

Bruce, Herbert A. *Our Heritage and Other Addresses.* Toronto: Macmillan, 1934

Bryant, Chad. *Prague in Black: Nazi Rule and Czech Nationalism.* Cambridge, MA: Harvard University Press, 2007

Budnitsky, Oleg. "The 'Jewish Battalions' in the Red Army." In *Revolution, Repression, and Revival: The Soviet Jewish Experience*, edited by Zvi Gitelman and Yaacov Ro'i, 15–36. Lanham, MD: Rowman and Littlefield, 2007

Bukey, Evan Burr. *Hitler's Austria: Popular Sentiment in the Nazi Era, 1938–1945.* Chapel Hill: University of North Carolina Press, 2000

Burgers, Jan. "The Road to San Francisco: The Revival of the Human Rights Idea in the Twentieth Century." *Human Rights Quarterly* 14 (1992): 447–77

Cahill, Barry. "The Higher Educator as 'Intellocrat': The Odyssey of Carleton Stanley." *Historical Studies in Education/Revue d'histoire de l'éducation* 14 (2002): 68–92

Cameron, Elspeth. "The Wrong Time and the Wrong Place: Gwethalyn Graham, 1913–1965." In *Great Dames*, edited by E. Cameron et al., 145–64. Toronto: University of Toronto Press, 1997

Camp, William D. "Religion and Horror: The American Religious Press Views Nazi Death Camps and Holocaust Survivors." DA thesis, Carnegie Mellon University, 1981

Collin, W.E. *The White Savannahs.* Toronto: Macmillan, 1936

Cook, Ramsay, ed. *French Canadian Nationalism.* Toronto: Macmillan, 1969

– *The Politics of John W. Dafoe and the Free Press.* Toronto: University of Toronto Press, 1963

– "The Remembrance of All Things Past." Introduction to Esther Delisle, *The Traitor and the Jew: Anti-Semitism and Extremist Right-Wing*

Nationalism in French Canada from 1929 to 1939. Montreal & Toronto: Robert Davies Publishing, 1993

Davies, Alan T., ed. *Antisemitism in Canada: History and Interpretation.* Wilfrid Laurier University Press, 1992

Dean, Martin. *Robbing the Jews: The Confiscation of Jewish Property in the Holocaust, 1933–1945.* New York: Cambridge University Press, 2008

Delisle, Esther. *Le traître et le Juif: Lionel Groulx, Le Devoir, et le délire du nationalisme d'extrême droite dans la province du Québec, 1929–1939.* Outremont: Etincelle, 1992. Translated as *The Traitor and the Jew: Anti-Semitism and Extremist Right-Wing Nationalism in Québec from 1929 to 1939.* Montreal & Toronto: Robert Davies Publishing, 1993

Diner, Hasia. "Post-World-War-II American Jewry and the Confrontation with Catastrophe." *American Jewish History* 91, no. 3–4 (2003): 439–67

– *We Remember with Reverence and Love: American Jews and the Myth of Silence after the Holocaust, 1945–1962.* New York: New York University Press, 2009

Donnelly, Murray S. *Dafoe of the Free Press.* Toronto: Macmillan, 1968

Drake, Robert G. "Manipulating the News: The U.S. Press and the Holocaust, 1933–1945." PH D dissertation, State University of New York, 2003

Draper, Paula, and Harold Troper, eds. *Canada.* Vol. 15 of *Archives of the Holocaust,* edited by Sybil Milton and Henry Friedlander

Dwork, Deborah, and Robert Jan van Pelt. *Flight from the Reich: Refugee Jews, 1933–1946.* New York: W.W. Norton, 2009

Ehrenreich, Eric. *The Nazi Ancestral Proof: Genealogy, Racial Science, and the Final Solution.* Bloomington, IN: Indiana University Press, 2007

Engelmann, Bernd. *Inside Hitler's Germany.* New York: Pantheon, 1985

Ericksen, Robert P. *Complicity in the Killing? German Churches, German Universities, and the Holocaust.* New York: Cambridge University Press. Forthcoming

Erwin, Norman. "Making Sense of Mass Murder: Toronto's Media Coverage of the Liberation of the Concentration Camps and Trials of War Criminals, 1944–1946." Unpublished paper, York University, 2007

Evans, Richard. *The Third Reich in Power, 1933–1939.* New York: Penguin, 2005

Falbaum, Berl, ed. *Shanghai Remembered: Stories from Jews Who Escaped to Shanghai from Nazi Europe.* Royal Oak, MI: Momentum Books, 2005

Fink, Carole. "The Murder of Walther Rathenau." *Judaism* (summer 1995): 259–70

Fischer, Klaus P. *Nazi Germany: A New History.* New York: Continuum, 1995

Fitzpatrick, Sheila, and Robert Gellately, eds. *Accusatory Practices: Denunciation in Modern European History, 1789–1989.* Chicago: University of Chicago Press, 1997

Foerster, F.W. "Germany as She Really Is." *University of Toronto Quarterly* 11 (April 1943): 250

Forsey, Eugene. *A Life on the Fringe: The Memoirs of Eugene Forsey.* Toronto: Oxford University Press, 1990

Francis, R. Douglas. *Frank H. Underhill: Intellectual Provocateur.* Toronto: University of Toronto Press, 1986

Frank, Anne. *The Diary of a Young Girl.* Edited by Otto H. Frank and Mirjam Pressler. Translated by Susan Massotty. New York: Anchor Books, 1996

Friedland, Martin L. *The University of Toronto: A History.* Toronto: University of Toronto Press, 2002

Friedlander, Henry. *The Origins of Nazi Genocide.* Chapel Hill: University of North Carolina Press, 1995

Friedländer, Saul. *Nazi Germany and the Jews, 1933–1945.* Abridged edn. New York: Harper, 2009

– *Nazi Germany and the Jews. Vol. 1: The Years of Persecution, 1933–1939.* New York: HarperCollins, 1997

– "Redemptive Antisemitism in Its Epoch." In Friedländer, *Nazi Germany and the Jews,* 1:75–114. New York: HarperCollins, 1997

Frisse, Ulrich. "The 'Bystanders' Perspective': The 'Toronto Daily Star' and Its Coverage of the Persecution of the Jews and the Holocaust in Canada, 1933–1945." *Yad Vashem Studies* 39, no. 1 (2011): 213–43

Fritzsche, Peter. *Life and Death in the Third Reich.* Cambridge, MA: Harvard University Press, 2008

Fuller, Ainsley. "The *Winnipeg Free Press,* the *Globe and Mail,* and the Jewish Refugee Crisis, 1933–1939." MA thesis, University of New Brunswick, 2006

Gallant, Mavis. "Good Morning and Goodbye." *Preview* 22 (1944): 1–3

– "Three Brick Walls." *Preview* 22 (1944): 4–6

– "Varieties of Exile." *Montreal Stories.* Toronto: McClelland & Stewart 2004

Garbarini, Alexandra. *Numbered Days: Diaries in the Holocaust.* New Haven, CT: Yale University Press, 2006

Garner, Hugh. *One Damn Thing after Another.* Toronto: McGraw-Hill Ryerson, 1973
– *Storm Below.* Toronto: Collins, 1949
Gay, Peter. *My German Question: Growing Up in Nazi Berlin.* New Haven, CT: Yale University Press, 1998
Gay, Ruth. *The Jews of Germany: A Historical Portrait.* New Haven, CT: Yale University Press, 1994
Gellately, Robert. *Backing Hitler: Consent and Coercion in Nazi Germany.* New York: Oxford University Press, 2001
Gellately, Robert, and Nathan Stoltzfus, eds. *Social Outsiders in Nazi Germany.* Princeton: Princeton University Press, 2001
Gilbert, Martin. *Kristallnacht: Prelude to Destruction.* New York: HarperCollins, 2006
Glassco, J.S. Review of *Earth and High Heaven.* In *First Statement*, April/May 1945, 33
Goeschel, Christian. *Suicide in Nazi Germany.* New York: Oxford University Press, 2009
Goldhagen, Daniel Jonah. *Hitler's Willing Executioners.* New York: Knopf, 1996
Goldstein, Susy, Gina Hamilton, and Wendy Share, *Ten Marks and a Train Ticket: Benno's Escape to Freedom.* Toronto: League for Human Rights of B'nai Brith Canada, 2008
Gordon, R.S. "The Cagoulards and Politicians Who Fish in Murky Waters: An Inside View of the Order of Jacques Cartier and the Antics of Mr Duplessis." TODAY. *An Anglo-Jewish Monthly*, November 1944, 3–4, 29–30
Goutor, David, "The Canadian Media and the 'Discovery' of the Holocaust, 1944–1945." *Canadian Jewish Studies* 4–5 (1996–97): 87–116
Graham, Gwethalyn. *Earth and High Heaven.* Toronto: Cormorant, 2003
– "Economics of Refugees." *Saturday Night*, 8 November 1938, 8
Graml, Hermann. *Antisemitism in the Third Reich.* Oxford: Blackwell, 1992
Granatstein, J.L. Review of *None Is Too Many* by Irving Abella and Harold Troper. *American Historical Review* 89 (June 1983): 886–7
Groulx, Lionel. *The Iron Wedge/L'Appel de la race.* Edited by M. Gaulin. Ottawa: Carleton University Press, 1986
Gruner, Wolf. "The German Council of Municipalities (Deutscher Gemeindetag) and the Coordination of Anti-Jewish Local Politics in the Nazi State." In *Holocaust and Genocide Studies* 13, no. 2 (1999): 171–99

Harkness, Ross. *J.E. Atkinson of the Star.* Toronto: University of Toronto Press, 1963

Hart-Davis, Duff. *Hitler's Games: The 1936 Olympics.* New York: Harper and Row, 1986

Heim, Susanne. "Reaktionen internationaler jüdischer Hilfsorganisationen auf die Situation der deutschen Juden." Paper presented at the workshop "Everyday History Approaches to the Persecution of Jews of Greater Germany and the 'Protectorate,' 1941–45." University of Toronto, Berlin, November 2010

Hellman, John. "Monasteries, *Miliciens*, War Criminals: Victory France/ Quebec 1940–50." *Journal of Contemporary History* 32, no. 4 (1997): 539–54

Herf, Jeffrey. *The Jewish Enemy: Nazi Propaganda during World War II and the Holocaust.* Cambridge, MA: Belknap Press, 2006

Heschel, Susannah. *The Aryan Jesus: Christian Theologians and the Bible in Nazi Germany.* Princeton, NJ: Princeton University Press, 2010

Hilberg, Raul. *The Destruction of the European Jews.* 3 vols. New Haven, CT: Yale University Press, 2003

Horn, Michiel. *Academic Freedom in Canada: A History.* Toronto: University of Toronto Press, 1998

Hughes, Everett C. *French Canada in Transition.* Chicago: University of Chicago Press, 1943

Iggers, Georg, and Wilma Iggers. *Two Lives in Uncertain Times: Facing the Challenges of the Twentieth Century as Scholars and Citizens.* New York: Berghahn Books, 2006

Iggers, Kelly. "Through the Trap Door: Czechoslovak Jewish Immigration to Canada, 1938–1945." Unpublished manuscript. Toronto, 2008

Iggers, Wilma A. "Refugee Women from Czechoslovakia in Canada: An Eyewitness Report." In *Between Sorrow and Strength: Women Refugees of the Nazi Period*, edited by Sybille Quack, 121–8. New York: Cambridge University Press, 1995

Jacobson, Arthur J., and Bernhard Schlink, eds. *Weimar: A Jurisprudence of Crisis.* Berkeley: University of California Press, 2002

Jelinek, Yeshayahu A. *The Carpathian Diaspora: The Jews of Subcarpathian Rus' and Mukachevo, 1848–1948.* Translated by Joel A. Linsider. New York: Columbia University Press, 2007

Jones, Faith. "Primary Source Analysis: Der Kanader Yid." Unpublished paper, University of British Columbia, 2010

Kaplan, Marion A. *Between Dignity and Despair: Jewish Life in Nazi Germany.* New York: Oxford University Press, 1998

– *Dominican Haven: The Jewish Refugee Settlement of Sosua,
1940–1945.* New York: Museum of Jewish Heritage, 2008
Kay, Zachariah. *Canada and Palestine: The Politics of Non-Commitment.*
Jerusalem: Israel Universities Press, 1978
Keith, W.J. "How New Was *New Provinces?*" www.uwo.ca/english/
canadianpoetry/cpjrn/vol104/keith (accessed 28 June 2010)
Kernaghan, W.D.K. "Freedom of Religion in the Province of Quebec, with
Particular Reference to Jews, Jehovah's Witnesses, and Church-State
Relations 1930–1960." PH D dissertation, Duke University, 1966
Kershaw, Ian. *Hitler.* Vol. 1, *1889–1936: Hubris.* New York: Norton,
1998
– *Hitler, the Germans, and the Final Solution.* New Haven, CT: Yale University Press, 2008
Kidd, Bruce. "Canadian Opposition to the 1936 Olympics in Germany."
Canadian Journal of History of Sport and Physical Education 9, no. 2
(1978): 20–40
– *The Struggle for Canadian Sport.* Toronto: University of Toronto Press,
1996
King, Amabel. *Voices of Victory: Representative Poetry of Canada in Wartime.* Toronto: Macmillan, 1942
Klein, A.M. "Bialik Thou Shouldst Be Living at This Hour." In *A.M. Klein:
Literary Essays and Reviews*, edited by U. Caplan and M.W. Steinberg,
35. Toronto: University of Toronto Press, 1987
– "The Decencies Had Perished with the Stukas." Review of *Dunkirk*
by E.J. Pratt. In *A.M. Klein: Literary Essays and Reviews*, edited by U.
Caplan and M.W. Steinberg, 205–9. Toronto: University of Toronto
Press, 1987
– *Huit Poemes Canadiens (en anglais).* Montreal: 1948
– "New Writers Series No. 1." Review of *Here and Now* by Irving
Layton. In *A.M. Klein: Literary Essays and Reviews*, edited by U.
Caplan and M.W. Steinberg, 215. Toronto: University of Toronto Press,
1987
– "Out of the Pulver and the Polished Lens." In *New Provinces: Poems of
Several Authors*, 29–34. Toronto: Macmillan, 1936
– "A Psalm of Abraham, Concerning that Which He Beheld upon the
Heavenly Scarp." In *Canadian Accent: A Collection of Stories and
Poems by Contemporary Writers from Canada*, edited by R. Gustafson,
97. New York: Penguin 1944
– "Soirée of Velvel Kleinburger." In *New Provinces: Poems of Several
Authors*, 35–8. Toronto: Macmillan, 1936

Klemperer, Victor. *I Will Bear Witness: A Diary of the Nazi Years, 1933–1941*. Translated by Martin Chalmers. New York: Random House, 1998

Krüger, Arnd. "Germany: The Propaganda Machine." In *The Nazi Olympics: Sport, Politics, and Appeasement in the 1930s*, edited by Arnd Krüger and William Murray, 17–43. Urbana, IL: University of Illinois Press, 2003

Kueter, Hubert C. *My Tainted Blood*. Solon, ME: Polar Bear, 2008

Lambertson, Ross. *Repression and Resistance: Canadian Human Rights Activists, 1930–1960*. Toronto: University of Toronto Press, 2005

Langlais, Jacques, and David Rome. *Jews and French Quebecers: Two Hundred Years of Shared History*. Waterloo, ON: Wilfrid Laurier University Press, 2001

Large, David Clay. *Nazi Games: The Olympics of 1936*. New York: Norton, 2007

Lauren, Paul Gordon. "First Principles of Racial Equality: History and the Politics and Diplomacy of Human Rights Provisions in the UN Charter." *Human Rights Quarterly* 5 (1983): 1–26

Leff, Laurel. *Buried by the Times: The Holocaust and America's Most Important Newspaper*. New York: Cambridge University Press, 2005

– "When the Facts Didn't Speak for Themselves: The Holocaust in the *New York Times*, 1939–1945." *Harvard International Journal of Press/Politics* 5, no. 2 (2000): 52–72

Levendel, Lewis. *A Century of the Canadian Jewish Press: 1880s–1980s*. Ottawa: Borealis Press, 1989

Levitt, Cyril, and William Shaffir. *The Riot at Christie Pits*. Toronto: Lester & Orpen Dennys, 1987

– "The Swastika as Dramatic Symbol: A Case-Study of Ethnic Violence in Canada." In *The Jews in Canada*, edited by Robert Brym, 77–96. Toronto: Oxford University Press, 1993

Levy, David. "The Canadian Jewish Review: An In-Depth Look on Its Coverage of the Holocaust." Unpublished paper, Hebrew University, 2003–04

Lindeman, Yehudi, ed. *Shards of Memory: Narratives of Holocaust Survival*. Westport, CT: Praeger, 2007

Lindemann, Albert, and Richard S. Levy, eds. *Antisemitism: A History*. New York: Oxford University Press, 2010

Lipstadt, Deborah E. *Beyond Belief: The American Press and the Coming of the Holocaust, 1933–1945*. New York: Free Press, 1986

– "The Holocaust." In *Forverts, a Living Lens: Photographs of Jewish Life from the Pages of the Forward*, edited by Alana Newhouse, 170–3. New York: Forward Books, 2007

London, Louise. *Whitehall and the Jews, 1933–1948: British Immigration Policy, Jewish Refugees, and the Holocaust*. New York: Cambridge University Press, 2000

Lower, A.R.M. Review of *Earth and High Heaven*. In *Canadian Historical Review* 26 (Sept. 1945): 326

Lyons, Chris. "'Children who read good books usually behave better and have good manners': The Founding of Notre Dame de Grace Library for Boys and Girls, Montreal, 1943." *Literary Trends* 55, no. 3 (2007): 597–608

MacGillivray, J.R. "Letters in Canada: 1944. Fiction." *University of Toronto Quarterly* 14 (April 1945): 267

McKenzie, Vernon. *Through Turbulent Years*. New York: Robert M. McBride, 1938

Mann, Fred. *A Drastic Turn of Destiny*. Toronto: Azrieli Foundation, 2009

Margolis, Rebecca. "The Yiddish Press in Montreal, 1905–1950." *Canadian Jewish Studies/Études juives canadiennes* 16–17 (2010): 3–26

Marrus, Michael R. *The Unwanted: European Refugees in the Twentieth Century*. New York: Oxford University Press, 1985

Mazower, Mark. "The Strange Triumph of Human Rights, 1933–1950." *Historical Journal* 47 (2004): 379–98

Medres, Israel. *Between Two World Wars: Canadian Jews in Transition*. Translated from the Yiddish by Vivian Felsen. Montreal: Véhicule Press, 2003

Mendelson, Alan. *Exiles from Nowhere: The Jews and the Canadian Elite*. Montreal: Robin Brass Studio, 2008

Mergler, Bernard. "Issues of War and Peace Face Jewish Congress." TODAY: *An Anglo-Jewish Monthly* 1, no. 1 (1944): 8–10

Meyer, Beate. "Between Self-Assertion and Forced Collaboration: The Reich Association of Jews in Germany, 1939–1945." In *Jewish Life in Nazi Germany: Dilemmas and Responses*, edited by Francis R. Nicosia and David Scrase, 149–69. New York: Berghahn Books, 2010

– "Der Traum von einer autonomen jüdischen Verwaltung – Die Reichsvereinigung der Juden in Deutschland, Auswanderer und Zurückbleibende in den Jahren 1938/39 bis 1941." In *Wer bleibt, opfert seine Jahre, vielleicht sein Leben. Deutsche Juden 1938–1941*, edited by Susanne Heim, Beate Meyer, and Francis R. Nicosia, 21–39. Göttingen: Wallstein, 2010

Meyer, Beate, Herman Simon, and Chana C. Schütz, eds. *Jews in Nazi Berlin: From Kristallnacht to Liberation*. Translated by Caroline Gay and Miranda Robbins. Chicago: University of Chicago Press, 2009

Miller, Scott, and Sarah A. Ogilvie. *Refuge Denied: The St. Louis Passengers and the Holocaust*. Madison: University of Wisconsin Press, 2006

Moeller, Susan. *Compassion Fatigue: How the Media Sell Disease, War, and Death*. New York: Routledge, 1999

Mosley, Paul. "'Frightful Crimes': British Press Responses to the Holocaust, 1944–45." MA thesis, University of Melbourne, 2002

Mosse, George L. *Confronting History: A Memoir*. Madison: University of Wisconsin Press, 2000

– *Germans and Jews: The Right, the Left, and the Search for a "Third Force" in Pre-Nazi Germany*. New York: Grosset & Dunlap, 1970

Mount, Graeme. *Canada's Enemies: Spies and Spying in the Peaceable Kingdom*. Toronto: Dundurn, 1993

Nicosia, Francis R. *Zionism and Anti-Semitism in Nazi Germany*. New York: Cambridge University Press, 2008

Noakes, Jeremy, and Geoffrey Pridham, eds. *Nazism 1919–1945*. Vol. 3: *Foreign Policy, War, and Racial Extermination: A Documentary Reader*. Chicago: University of Chicago Press, 2001

Norich, Anita. *Discovering Exile: Yiddish and Jewish American Culture during the Holocaust*. Stanford University Press, 2007

– "'*Harbe Sugyes*/Puzzling Questions': Yiddish and English Culture in America during the Holocaust." *Jewish Social Studies* 5, no. 1–2 (1998–99): 91–110

Norsman, Olav. "One Nazi Victory." *University of Toronto Quarterly* 11 (April 1943): 285–6

Norwood, Stephen H. *The Third Reich in the Ivory Tower: Complicity and Conflict on American Campuses*. Cambridge, UK: Cambridge University Press, 2009

Novick, Peter. *The Holocaust in American Life*. New York: Houghton Mifflin, 1999

Oliver, Michael. *The Passionate Debate: The Social and Political Ideas of Quebec Nationalism, 1920–1945*. Montreal: Véhicule Press, 1991

Oren, Dan A. *Joining the Club: A History of Jews and Yale*. New Haven, CT: Yale University Press, 1986

Ouellet, Fernand. "The Historical Background of Separation in Quebec." In *French Canadian Nationalism*, ed. Ramsay Cook. Toronto: Macmillan, 1969

Patterson, Orlando. *Slavery and Social Death: A Comparative Study.* Cambridge, MA: Harvard University Press, 1985

Pegelow Kaplan, Thomas. *The Language of Nazi Genocide: Linguistic Violence and the Struggle of Germans of Jewish Ancestry.* New York: Cambridge University Press, 2009

Quack, Sybille, ed. *Between Sorrow and Strength: Women Refugees of the Nazi Period.* New York: Cambridge University Press, 1995

Reed, Patrick. "A Foothold in the Whirlpool: Canada's Iberian Refugee Movement." MA thesis, Concordia University, 1996

Reid, Malcolm. *The Shouting Signpainters: A Literary and Political Account of Quebec Revolutionary Nationalism.* Toronto: McClelland & Stewart, 1972

Richler, Mordecai. *Oh Canada! Oh Quebec! Requiem for a Divided Country.* Toronto: Penguin, 1992

Rigg, Mark Bryan. *Hitler's Jewish Soldiers.* Lawrence: University Press of Kansas, 2002

Robin, Martin. *Shades of Right: Nativist and Fascist Politics in Canada, 1920–1940.* Toronto: University of Toronto Press, 1992

Robinson, Ira. "The Canadian Years of Yehuda Kaufman (Even Shmuel): Educator, Journalist, and Intellectual." *Canadian Jewish Studies/Études juives canadiennes* 15 (2007): 133

Rome, David. "Canada." In *The American Jewish Year Book 46* (1944–45), edited by Harry Schneiderman and American Jewish Committee, 196–204. Philadelphia: Jewish Publication Society of America, 1944

– *Clouds in the Thirties: On Antisemitism in Canada, 1929–1939: A Chapter on Canadian Jewish History.* 13 sections. Montreal: Canadian Jewish Congress National Archives, 1977–

– *The Congress Archival Record of 1934.* Montreal: Canadian Jewish Congress National Archives, 1976

– *On the Jewish School Question in Montreal, 1903–1931.* Canadian Jewish Archives, NS, no. 3. Montreal: Canadian Jewish Congress National Archives, 1975

– *Our Archival Record of 1933, Hitler's Year.* Montreal: Canadian Jewish Congress National Archives, 1976

– "The Political Consequences of the Jewish School Question, Montreal, 1925–1933." *Canadian Jewish Historical Society Journal* 1, no. 1 (1977): 3–15

Rosenberg, Danny. "The Canadian Jewish Congress and the 1936 Berlin Olympic Boycott Movement." In *Sport and Physical Education in*

Jewish History, edited by George Eisen, Haim Kaufman, and Manfred Lamner, 133–45. Jerusalem: Wingate Institute, 2003

Rosenberg, Louis. *Canada's Jews: A Social and Economic Study of the Jews in Canada*. Montreal: Canadian Jewish Congress, 1939. Reissued as Morton Weinfeld, ed. *Canada's Jews: A Social and Economic Study of the Jews in Canada in the 1930s*. Montreal & Kingston: McGill-Queen's University Press, 1993

– "Jewish Population Characteristics." *Montreal Congress Bulletin*, September 1956, 3

Rosenberg, Otto. *A Gypsy in Auschwitz*. London: London House, 1999

Rosovsky, Nitza. *The Jewish Experience at Harvard and Radcliffe*. Cambridge, MA: Harvard Semitic Museum, 1986

Ross, Robert W. *So It Was True: The American Protestant Press and the Nazi Persecution of the Jews*. Minneapolis: University of Minnesota Press, 1980

Roy, Gabrielle. "Palestine Avenue." In *The Fragile Lights of Earth: Articles and Memories, 1942–1970*, 55. Toronto: McClelland & Stewart, 1978

– *Where Nests the Water Hen*. Translation of *La petite poule d'eau*. Toronto: McClelland & Stewart, 1961

Safrian, Hans, and Hans Witek. *Und keiner war dabei. Dokumente des alltäglichen Antisemitismus in Wien 1938*. Vienna: Picus, 1988

Sbacchi, Alberto. *Legacy of Bitterness: Ethiopia and Fascist Italy, 1935–1941*. Lawrenceville, NJ: Red Sea Press, 1997

Schleunes, Karl. *The Twisted Road to Auschwitz: Nazi Policy toward German Jews, 1933–1939*. Urbana, IL: University of Illinois Press, 1970

Schmidt, Josef. "Lionel Groulx's *L'Appel de la race*. Revisited." *Literature & Theology* 16, no. 2 (2002): 148–59

Schneider, Gertrude. *Journey into Terror: Story of the Riga Ghetto*. New York: Ark House, 1979. New and expanded edition, Westport, CT: Praeger, 2001

Schreter, Sheldon M. "French-Canadian Anti-Semitism." *Strobe* 3 (1969): 74, 84–8

Schulman, Avi M. *Like a Raging Fire. A Biography of Maurice N. Eisendrath*. New York: UAHC Press, 1993

Scott, F.R. *Labour Conditions in the Men's Clothing Industry*. Toronto: Nelson, 1935

Sernoe, James Lawrence. "Press Coverage of the Holocaust, 1933–1945: A Comparison of Three Milwaukee Newspapers." MA thesis, University of Wisconsin-Madison, 1989

Shapiro, Robert Moses, ed. *Why Didn't the Press Shout? American and International Journalism during the Holocaust*. Newark: KTAV, Yeshiva University Press, 2003

Sharf, Andrew. *The British Press and Jews under Nazi Rule*. London, New York: Oxford University Press, 1964

Silcox, Claris Edwin. "Canadian Post Mortem on Refugees: An Address." Toronto: Canadian National Committee on Refugees, 1939

Sirluck, Ernest. *First Generation: An Autobiography*. Toronto: University of Toronto Press, 1996

Smith, A.J.M. *The Book of Canadian Poetry: A Critical and Historical Anthology*. 2 vols. Toronto: Oxford, 1982

Sohn, Herbert A. "Human Rights Legislation in Ontario: A Study of Social Action." Doctor of Social Work dissertation, University of Toronto, 1975

Speisman, Stephen. "Antisemitism in Ontario: The Twentieth Century." In *Antisemitism in Canada: History and Interpretation*, edited by Alan Davies, 113–33. Waterloo, ON: Wilfrid Laurier University Press, 1992

Stanley, Carleton. "Voices in the Wilderness." *Dalhousie Review*, July 1945, 173

Steinweis, Alan. *Kristallnacht 1938*. Cambridge, MA: Harvard University Press, 2009

Stephenson, Jill. *Hitler's Home Front: Württemberg under the Nazis*. New York: Hambledon Continuum, 2006

Stingel, Janine. *Social Discredit: Anti-Semitism, Social Credit, and the Jewish Response*. Montreal & Kingston: McGill-Queen's University Press, 2000

Stoltzfus, Nathan. *Resistance of the Heart: Intermarriage and the Rosenstrasse Protest in Nazi Germany*. New York: Norton, 1996

Stone, Daniel. "Coverage of the Holocaust in Winnipeg's Jewish and Polish Press." *Polin* 19 (2007): 183–203

Studniberg, Robin. "'One Shudders to Think What Might Happen': Vancouver Newspapers and the First Twelve Months of the Third Reich." Unpublished paper, 2010

Stuewe, Paul. *The Storms Below: The Turbulent Life and Times of Hugh Garner*. Toronto: James Lorimer, 1988

Svonkin, Stuart. *Jews against Prejudice: American Jews and the Fight for Civil Liberties*. New York: Columbia University Press, 1997

Szobar, Patricia A. "Telling Sexual Secrets in the Nazi Courts of Law: Race Defilement in Germany, 1933 to 1945." *Journal of the History of Sexuality* 11, nos. 1–2 (2002): 131–63

Tanenhaus, Sam. "Write, Rewrite, Publish (Tweak): A Record of John Updike at Work." *New York Times*, 21 June 2010

Thilo, Schulz. *Das Deutschlandbild der Irish Times, 1933–1945*. European University Studies, series 3, History and Allied Studies, vol. 838. Frankfurt am Main: P. Lang, 1999

Thomas, Gordon, and Max Morgan Witts. *Voyage of the Damned*. New York: Stein and Day, 1974

Tooze, Adam. *The Wages of Destruction: The Making and Breaking of the Nazi Economy*. New York: Penguin, 2007

Trachtenberg, Henry. "The Winnipeg Jewish Community and Politics: The Inter-War Years, 1919–1939." *Papers of the Historical and Scientific Society of Manitoba*, series 3, nos. 34 and 35 (1977–78/1978–79): 126–7, 131–2

Trofimenkoff, Susan Mann. *Action française: French Canadian Nationalism in the Twenties*. Toronto: University of Toronto Press, 1975

– ed. *Abbé Groulx: Variations on a Nationalist Theme*. Vancouver: Copp Clark, 1973

Tulchinsky, Gerald. *Branching Out: The Transformation of the Canadian Jewish Community*. Toronto: Stoddart, 1998

Underhill, Frank H. *In Search of Canadian Liberalism*. Toronto: Macmillan, 1960

– "The Liberal Arts and Public Affairs." Address at the University of Saskatchewan, Saskatoon, 16 January 1961, 12–13

van Pelt, Robert Jan. "Without a Right of Return a Refusal of Arrival: An Examination of the Architecture of a Paper Wall." In "Proceedings: The St. Louis Era: Looking Back, Moving Forward" (Toronto, June 2009). http://www.StLouis2009Conference.ca/pages/English/Sessions/Conference_Proceedings (accessed January 2011)

van Rahden, Till. *Jews and Other Germans: Civil Society, Religious Diversity, and Urban Politics in Breslau, 1860–1925*. Translated by Marcus Brainard. Madison: University of Wisconsin Press, 2008

Verduyn, Christl. *Dear Marian, Dear Hugh: The MacLennan-Engel Correspondence*. Ottawa: Ottawa University Press, 1995

Vincent, C. Paul. "The Voyage of the *St Louis* Revisited." *Holocaust and Genocide Studies* 25 (2011): 252–89

Voticky, Anka. *Knocking on Every Door*. Toronto: Azrieli Foundation, 2010

Wade, Mason. *The French Canadians, 1760–1960*. 2 vols. Revd. edn. Toronto: Macmillan, 1968

Wadia, Roy Vinci. "*The New York Times* Covers the Holocaust: All the News That's Fit to Print?" MA thesis, University of Georgia, 1989

Wagner, Jonathan. *Brothers Beyond the Sea: National Socialism in Canada*. Waterloo: Wilfrid Laurier University Press, 1981

– "The Deutscher Bund Canada." *Canadian Historical Review* 58, no. 2 (1977): 176–200

– "Nazi Party Membership in Canada: A Profile." *Social History/ Histoire social*, 14, No. 27 (May 1982), 233–8

Walk, Joseph, ed. *Das Sonderrecht für die Juden im NS-Staat*. Heidelberg & Karlsruhe: Müller Juristischer Verlag, 1981

Walker, James. "The 'Jewish Phase' in the Movement for Racial Equality in Canada." *Canadian Ethnic Studies* 34 (2002): 1–29

– *"Race," Rights, and the Law in the Supreme Court of Canada*. Toronto & Waterloo: Osgoode Society and Wilfrid Laurier University Press, 1997

Waterford, Helen H. *Commitment to the Dead: One Women's Journey toward Understanding*. Frederick, CO: Renaissance House, 1987

Weilbach, Susanne. *Singing from the Darktime: A Childhood Memoir in Poetry and Prose*. Montreal: McGill-Queen's University Press, 2011

Weinberg, Gerhard L. *Germany, Hitler, and World War II*. Cambridge: Cambridge University Press, 1995

– *Kristallnacht 1938 as Experienced Then and Understood Now*. Monna and Otto Weinmann Annual Lecture Washington, DC: United States Holocaust Memorial Museum, 2009

– *A World at Arms: A Global History of World War II*. 2nd edn. New York: Cambridge University Press, 2005

Wenn, Stephen R. "A Tale of Two Diplomats: George S. Messersmith and Charles H. Sherrill on Proposed American Participation in the 1936 Olympics." *Journal of Sports History* 16 (1989): 37

Wilkes, Helen Waldstein. *Letters from the Lost: A Memoir of Discovery*. Edmonton, AB: Athabasca University Press, 2010

Wilson, Edmund. "A Reporter at Large: O Canada. An American's Notes on Canadian Culture." Parts 1 and 2. *New Yorker*, 14 and 21 November 1964, 2 and 116

Wolf, Hubert. *Pope and Devil: The Vatican's Archives and the Third Reich*. Translated by Kenneth Kronenberg. Cambridge, MA: Belknap Press, 2010

Young, Robert J. "Hitler's Early Critics: Canadian Resistance at the *Winnipeg Free Press*." *Queen's Quarterly* 106 (Winter 1999): 578–87

Zimmerman, David. "'Narrow-Minded People': Canadian Universities and the Academic Refugee Crises, 1933–1941." *Canadian Historical Review* 88, no. 2 (2007): 291–315

Contributors

DORIS L. BERGEN holds the Chancellor Rose and Ray Wolfe Chair of Holocaust Studies at the University of Toronto. Her research focuses on issues of religion, gender, and ethnicity in the Holocaust and Second World War and comparatively in other cases of extreme violence. Bergen is a member of the Academic Advisory Committee of the Center for Advanced Holocaust Studies at the US Holocaust Memorial Museum in Washington, DC.

MICHAEL BROWN is professor emeritus of humanities and Hebrew at York University, Toronto, where he served as director of the Centre for Jewish Studies. He also holds rabbinic ordination from the Jewish Theological Seminary. His books include *Jew of Juif? Jews, French Canadians and Anglo-Canadians, 1759–1914*. His most recent is *Not Written in Stone: Jew, Constitutions and Constitutionalism in Canada* (2004), written and edited with Ira Robinson and the late Daniel Elazar.

AMANDA GRZYB is assistant professor in the Faculty of Information and Media Studies at Western University. Her teaching and research interests include genocide studies, media and the public interest, the representation of homelessness, and African American literature. She is the editor of *The World of Darfur: International Response to Crimes against Humanity in Western Sudan* (2009).

L. RUTH KLEIN is executive director of Canada's National Task Force on Holocaust Education, Remembrance and Research. She serves as national director of B'nai Brith Canada's League for Human Rights and Institute of International Affairs, roles in which she promotes research and education on the history and current manifestations of antisemitism.

REBECCA MARGOLIS is associate professor at the University of Ottawa's Vered Jewish Canadian Studies Program. Her research focuses on Yiddish culture in Canada and she is the author of *Jewish Roots, Canadian Soil: Yiddish Culture in Montreal, 1905–1945*. She was the recipient of the University of Ottawa's Young Researcher of the Year Award for 2011.

RICHARD MENKIS is associate professor of history at the University of British Columbia. He is founding editor of the journal *Canadian Jewish Studies* and divisional co-editor for the *Encyclopaedia Judaica*. His recent publications include a CD-ROM, *Canada Responds to the Holocaust*, which he co-authored with Ronnie Tessler.

NORMAN RAVVIN has been chair of the Institute for Canadian Jewish Studies at Concordia University since 1999. His books include *A House of Words: Jewish Writing, Identity and Memory*, *Hidden Canada: An Intimate Travelogue*, and the novel *The Joyful Child*. He is co-editor with Richard Menkis of *The Canadian Jewish Studies Reader*.

HAROLD TROPER is professor of history of immigration and ethnic relations in Canada in the Department of Theory and Policy Studies at the Ontario Institute of Studies in Education at the University of Toronto. He is recipient of the John Simon Guggenheim Memorial Fellowship, the American Jewish Book Award, a Canadian Historical Association Prize, and the Joseph Tanenbaum Book Award. His books include *None Is Too Many*, co-authored with Irving Abella.

JAMES WALKER is professor of history and associate chair (graduate studies) at the University of Waterloo, where he specializes in the history of human rights and race relations. In 2003–04, he was the Bora Laskin National Fellow in Human Rights Research. His publications include *"Race," Rights and the Law in the Supreme Court of Canada* (1997).

Index